SACRED SEA

A JOURNEY TO LAKE BAIKAL

SACRED SEA

A JOURNEY TO LAKE BAIKAL

PETER THOMSON

OXFORD
UNIVERSITY PRESS
2007

OXFORD
UNIVERSITY PRESS

Oxford University Press, Inc., publishes works that further
Oxford University's objective of excellence
in research, scholarship, and education.

Oxford New York
Auckland Cape Town Dar es Salaam Hong Kong Karachi
Kuala Lumpur Madrid Melbourne Mexico City Nairobi
New Delhi Shanghai Taipei Toronto

With offices in
Argentina Austria Brazil Chile Czech Republic France Greece
Guatemala Hungary Italy Japan Poland Portugal Singapore
South Korea Switzerland Thailand Turkey Ukraine Vietnam

Published by Oxford University Press, Inc.
198 Madison Avenue, New York, New York 10016

www.oup.com

Oxford is a registered trademark of Oxford University Press

Library of Congress Cataloging-in-Publication Data
Thomson, Peter.
Sacred sea : a journey to Lake Baikal / Peter Thomson.
p.   cm.
Includes bibliographical references.
ISBN 978-0-19-517051-1
1. Natural history—Russia (Federation)—Baikal, Lake.
2. Thomson, Peter—Travel—Russia (Federation)—Baikal, Lake.
3. Baikal, Lake (Russia)—Description and travel. I. Title.
QH161.T52 2007
508.47—dc22   2006039074

Please visit the companion Web site at
www.oup.com/us/sacredsea

1 3 5 7 9 8 6 4 2

Printed in the United States of America
on acid-free paper

For my father, Peter,
my mother, Anne,
and my brother, James,
without all of whom I would've just stayed home

A lake is the landscape's most beautiful and expressive feature. It is earth's eye; looking into which the beholder measures the depth of his own nature.

—Henry David Thoreau, *Walden, or Life in the Woods*

You ought to come to Siberia. Ask the authorities to exile you.

—Anton Chekhov, *Letter to his brother*

Author's Note

Sacred Sea is a work of nonfiction. That is, other than those sections in which something is clearly imagined, everything in this book actually happened. In fact, even some of the imagined parts actually happened, such as the underwater encounter with the Baikal seal, which is based on an actual encounter with a seal in the Pacific Ocean off California's Catalina Island.

This book is also a work of journalism. Quotes and dialogue are taken from recorded interviews, notes, or, very rarely, clear recollections. Assertions of fact are based on personal observation or research drawing from a wide array of sources, all of which are listed at the back of the book. And with the exception of my ex-wife and a very few other peripheral characters, the names and details of all people the reader will encounter are real.

But this is also a work of subjectivity, memory, and imagination, and as such, I have taken occasional liberties that diverge from a strict rendering of the "facts." In particular, I have taken a far more subjective approach in trying to capture the experience of traveling than would be appropriate in a more strictly journalistic work. And it is important to remind the reader that, when it comes to events and relationships prior to this journey but remembered along the way, in particular those passages referring to my ex-wife and our life together, what I have written is strictly my version of the past, no more or less true than hers.

Finally, what this is not is the work of an authority on Lake Baikal or Russia, or an exhaustive examination of the many environmental challenges facing the Baikal region. I have tried to engage questions of science, history, culture, and politics fairly, deeply, and with an open mind, but by necessity and choice, I have done so more from the perspective of an inquisitive and reasonably well-informed first-time visitor than as a journalist on assignment. When my brother and I set out from Boston, I had no intention of writing a book about our travels. When a book began to emerge, I set out to tell *my* story of Baikal, not *the* story. I hope that readers will feel they can trust my reporting and observations, but I also hope that they will to follow their own curiosity to other sources, or perhaps even to their own journeys to these places.

A note about measures and spelling:

As an American, I quantify the world using the arcane system of weights and measures known as the U.S. Customary System. I think in feet and miles, pounds, and Fahrenheit, units based on such beautiful but baffling increments as 12, 5,280, 16, and 32. Nearly all other humans, however, including Russians, use the supremely rational metric system. They think in meters and kilometers, liters, kilograms, and Celsius, units based on that most fundamentally human number, 10. Anyone traveling between the United States and the rest of the world has to reckon with this absurd divergence, and as much as I bemoan it, I have more or less maintained it in this book. When writing as my subjective American self, I have used the U.S. system. But when describing Russia and the rest of the world in a more objective manner, and particularly when delving into scientific matters, I have used the native tongue of these realms, the metric system. (Then there is the *verst*, an archaic Russian unit of distance that shows up once or twice in this book. A *verst* is equal to 3,500 feet, about two-thirds of a mile. Or, if you prefer, 1,066.8 meters—just a hair over a kilometer.)

As for the spelling of Russian words in English, there seems to be no standard system for transliteration between the two languages—writers of English are free to choose their favored approach, which seems to lead only to endless argument among scholars and confusion among readers. I have chosen to use the Library of Congress system for all Russian words in *Sacred Sea*, including names, but without diacritics (accent signs) or soft-signs; the endings -ий and -ый have been simplified to -y, and initial e, ё, ю, and я are rendered as *ye*, *yo*, *yu*, and *ya*. Familiar Western forms (Dostoyevsky, Nicholas II, etc.) have been retained.

CREDITS

I thank the following publishers for permission to reproduce the song lyrics and play excerpt found in the text:

"New England" by Jonathan Richman
© Rockin' Leprechaun (ASCAP) admin. by Wixen Music Publishing, Inc.
All Right Reserved. Used by Permission.

"Once in a Lifetime"
Words and Music by Brian Eno, David Byrne, Chris Frantz,
Jerry Harrison, and Tina Weymouth
© BMG Music Publishing Ltd. (PRS) / Warner Chappell Music Limited
All rights for the world on behalf of BMG Music Publishing Ltd. (PRS) /
administered by Careers-BMG Music Publishing (BMI)
© 1981 Index Music, Inc., Bleu Disque Music Co., Inc. and E.G. Music Ltd.
All rights for Index Music, Inc. and Bleu Disque Music Co., Inc.
Administered by WB Music Corp. All Rights Reserved. Used by Permission.

Contents

AUTHOR'S NOTE ix

PROLOGUE: *Blagopoluchnoe* 3

PART ONE: THE SACRED SEA

1 A Flash of Blue Light 9
2 Songs and Whispers 16
3 The Earth Splits, Water Rushes In 25
4 Into the Lake—Shallow 30
5 Into the Lake—Deep 40
6 Buryatia, in Black & White and Color 54
7 On the Trail with Pod Boy and Monkey Mind 68
8 Bad Roads Are Good for Baikal 76
9 Traveling and Staying Home 85

PART TWO: 180°

10 The Long Way Home 93
11 The Great Circle 107
12 Zigzag to Russia 118
13 Power in the East 128
14 Across the Sleeping Land 139
15 Angels and Ghosts in Irkutsk 153

PART THREE: BAIKAL, TOO, MUST WORK

16 One of the Best Enterprises in Russia 171
17 Righteousness, Uncertainty, and the Point of No Return 189
18 Connecting the Dots 199
19 Dr. Hope and Dr. Despair 219
20 Blind Love Is a Dangerous Thing 235
21 360° 252

EPILOGUE: The Great Baikal Chain 263

AFTERWORD 279
ACKNOWLEDGMENTS 281
ILLUSTRATION CREDITS 285
SOURCE NOTES AND FURTHER READING 288
INDEX 309

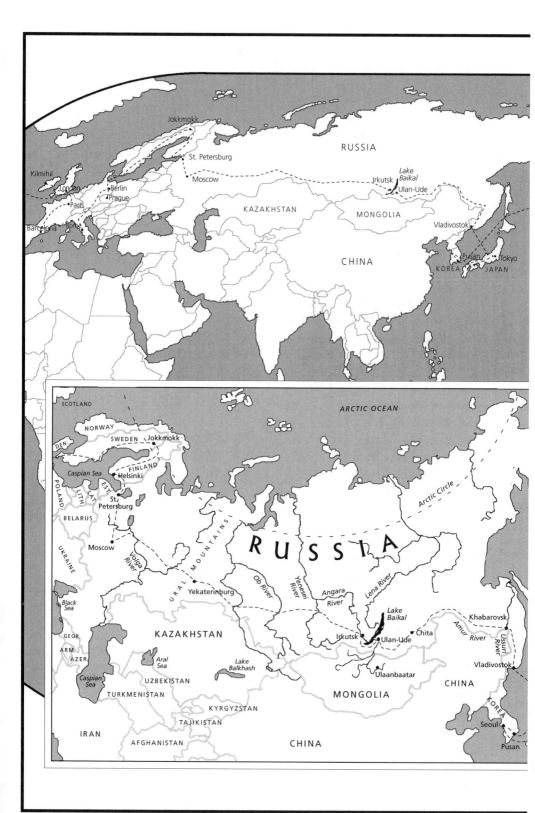

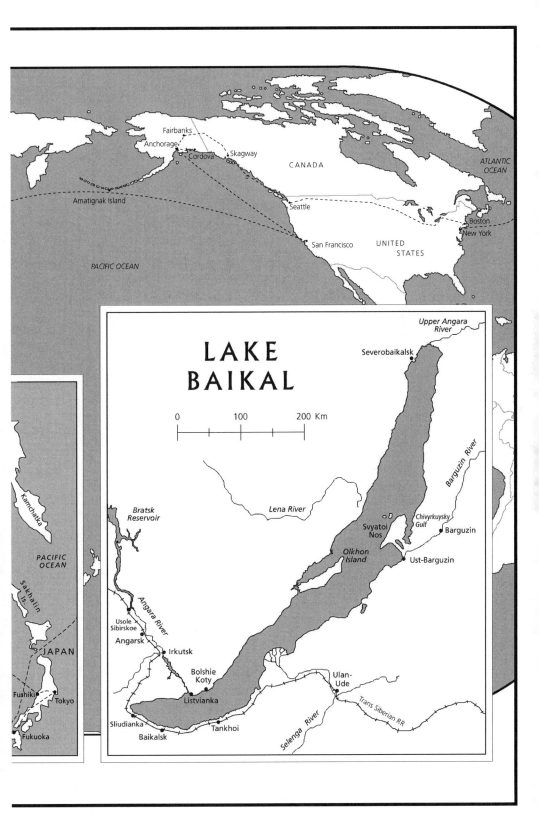

Fairbanks
Anchorage
Cordova
Skagway
CANADA
ATLANTIC
OCEAN
Amatignak Island
Seattle
Boston
New York
UNITED
STATES
San Francisco
PACIFIC OCEAN

Kamchatka

PACIFIC
OCEAN

Sakhalin Is.

JAPAN

Fushiki
Tokyo

Fukuoka

LAKE
BAIKAL

0   100   200 Km

Upper Angara
River

Severobaikalsk

Bratsk
Reservoir

Lena River

Barguzin River

Svyatoi
Nos

Chivyrkuysky
Gulf

Barguzin

Olkhon
Island

Ust-Barguzin

Usole
Sibirskoe

Angarsk

Angara River

Irkutsk

Bolshie
Koty

Ulan-
Ude

Trans Siberian RR

Listvianka

Sliudianka

Tankhoi

Selenga River

Baikalsk

SACRED SEA

A JOURNEY TO LAKE BAIKAL

Blagopoluchnoe

In which we learn about the perfection of Lake Baikal

On a set of wooden steps above a thin beach on a gray October afternoon, a man in a wool hat stands and calls out to his granddaughter down the shore.

"*Zdravstvui!*" "Hello!"

"I love her very much," the man says, gesturing toward the girl with a broad smile, "and I would like her to live forever. I want all of us to live forever here!" His breath hangs in the cold October air, his voice settles with the snowflakes onto the dark pines that rise above Lake Baikal.

The man's name is Slava Maksimov, Sr., and he turns his gaze from his granddaughter to his visitors.

"I am an aboriginal person here," Dr. Maksimov says. "There are no high mountains and no deep depths in Lake Baikal that I failed to visit. I am drinking Baikal water, eating Baikal fish, the air I breathe is Baikal air. So I can only benefit from telling the truth! The truth about the lake!"

One look at Slava Maksimov's animated eyes tells you that he is a man of strong convictions, and that you should expect to hear some of them soon. He is a scientist by training, a microbiologist who has worked in and around the lake for more than thirty years. But his manner is more that of a preacher spreading the Good News. We have just met, and he has already dispensed with the usual scientific caveats and gotten straight to the undeniable truth about the largest body of fresh water on earth.

The truth, the professor says, is that Lake Baikal is perfect.

"*Absoliutno blagopoluchnoe!*" he declares. "As a creature that lives within Lake Baikal, I can say it is in a perfect state!"

Dr. Maksimov chuckles, folds his arms, and leans back, giving us a moment to consider his message. *Blagopoluchnoe,* our translator Olga will tell us later, is a curious term to use in describing a lake. It means "happy, safe, stable, perfect" all in one, she says, and it's usually used to describe not nature but a family or a society, and implies an accumulated material history as well as a moral base. It has, Olga says, deep and complex meaning. But just to be sure we understand that he has chosen precisely the right word, Dr. Maksimov repeats himself.

"*Blagopoluchny Baikal!*" he says, with a sparkle in his eye.

"Baikal is in a perfect state," Dr. Maksimov continues, "because there are specific oligotrophic organisms in its waters, and they consume every molecule of any substance that comes to its waters...." The professor launches into a detailed and impassioned explanation of the lake's special properties, thick with references to obscure creatures and arcane processes. There are few simple explanations in science and, my brother James and I are learning, no simple explanations in Russia. But there are lots of good stories here. Dr. Maksimov's is engrossing, and it has a host of compelling characters, chief among them a nearly microscopic shrimp that's unique to Baikal, called *Epischura baicalensis.*

"These microorganisms are numerous," Dr. Maksimov declares, "and they are always hungry!" Together, we are told, the uncountable numbers of these creatures filter Baikal's water more efficiently than any human-designed machine ever could, removing nearly every scrap of organic matter and many of the pollutants that enter the lake. "These creatures will consume everything that is polluting the lake! They are the natural purifying system! And they will keep it pure for a long period of time...."

As Dr. Maksimov continues his tale, big snowflakes settle onto his hat and coat. Winter is bearing down on Baikal, and with his animated gestures and gleeful smile, it seems that he couldn't be happier. Cold is as elemental here as water and earth, and it too plays a vital role in Dr. Maksimov's story, helping to shape the ecosystem that allows the epischura and other life to prosper in even the deepest reaches of the world's deepest lake. And since there's life throughout the lake, Dr. Maksimov concludes, the self-cleansing process extends throughout the lake, as well. "The fact is that Baikal is controlled by the powers of cold," he says, with a nod at the descending snow. "Fortunately, cold has come already, this year!"

The harsh climate of Siberia and the rim of mountains on all sides of Baikal have isolated this place from most of the rest of the world for millennia. Humans are finally beginning to breach these barriers, but no matter, Dr. Maksimov says, the lake's exquisite ecosystem will continue to keep its water as pure as any on earth. This mighty lake can withstand every challenge, he says. Whatever harm humans do, Baikal has the power to heal itself.

"In the coming one thousand years," the Professor says with a wide grin, "Baikal is not threatened by anything! Ha ha!" All stories in Russia have a lesson, and as he finishes his story, Dr. Maksimov again makes sure we don't miss his lesson. "As long as it is cold at Lake Baikal, there is no need to be concerned about its future! It is perfect!" "*Absoliutno blagopoluchnoe ozero Baikal!*"

Like his granddaughter down the shore, Baikal will live forever.

PART ONE

THE SACRED SEA

October, 2000

*It is a most excellent job, this of being a man upon the
Earth; you see so much that is wondrous....*

—Maxim Gorky, *Birth of a Man*

I

A Flash of Blue Light

*In which the Trans-Siberian Railroad brings us
to the shore of Lake Baikal, we ponder
the lake's significance
and think about why we've come*

S ome places are just a place. Some places are a journey.

Three days out of Vladivostok, the westbound Number One train lumbers across the Siberian outback like a team of driven oxen. The train's nineteen hulking, crimson and blue cars creak and groan as they throw themselves forward at speeds not much different than when this track was hacked through half a continent of nearly impenetrable forest and bog in the days of the last tsars a hundred years ago. Three days aboard this beast-machine has gotten us deep into Russia, beyond a hundred ragged towns with names like Obluche, Zilovo, Spassk-Dalny, and Shimanovskaia, nearly every one of which, it seems, was established as a gateway to the mines and prisons of the tsars' exile system or of the Soviet Gulag, and which generations later still seem more outposts than towns. Clusters of log homes and cabbage patches line the tracks, ashen concrete apartment blocks rise beyond, and doleful bands of kerchiefed women at each station peddle *pirozhki* and salted fish, unshelled pine nuts in newspaper cones, and hard-boiled eggs cradled in baby carriages. All are thinly tethered to Mother Russia by the lace curtains and flowers in every window, the stubbornly proud train stations, and these two thin steel rails.

We're three days deep into Siberia and, it seems, no place at all. Brown fields spread from the outskirts of the settlements, blotted at random intervals by abandoned and half-collapsed factories, and through the emptiness between passes an almost unchanging plain coursed by wandering rivers and deep thickets of dark pine and fir, wispy white birches, and larches glowing a brazen yellow. Dawn this morning revealed the regional capital of Ulan-Ude, the latest in a string of sullen cities of cinder blocks and smokestacks. This afternoon will bring us to the tarnished old imperial city of Irkutsk, first settled in the seventeenth century and later the destination of some of the luckier of the tsars' exiles. We're 3,700 kilometers west of the Pacific, 5,500 kilometers east of Moscow, 250 kilometers north of Mongolia, and south of nowhere. And through our dirty windows, Siberia seems covered in a mist of contradictions. Forlorn and entrancing, monotonous and mysterious, a chilling and soothing universe of gray, black, deep green, and gold.

On board the train, rumpled passengers pad the hallway in slippers and robes, while others appear each morning dressed as if for the most formal and somber occasion. Young soldiers anxiously await the next chance to stock up on cigarettes and vodka. My brother James and I practice our Russian, make clumsy conversation with fellow travelers, read about the misadventures of Raskolnikov and Gorbachev. And beneath our feet, the relentless, metallic rumble and intermittent lurch and clatter alternately lull us to sleep and jar us awake. Sealed in our canister of steel and glass, we have all long since settled into the unchanging rhythms of life on board the Trans-Siberian.

But on this third day, the rhythm is suddenly broken. As the train sweeps around a great bend, a dim glint of silver-blue flashes through the yellow birch leaves, and within seconds the windows of the hallway are crowded with Russians, clutching cups of tea and glasses of vodka, singing an ode to their beloved Lake Baikal.

Baikal. The name hangs in the Russian ear like the first notes of a Tchaikovsky symphony—singular, unmistakable, its grandeur and drama known and understood by Russians almost innately.

Russia's massive girth touches three of the world's great oceans—the Pacific, the Arctic, and an arm of the Atlantic. It also borders the Caspian and Black seas, mythic crossing points of commerce and culture for millennia.

Yet with all these rivals, only Baikal, a narrow blue crescent in the country's great empty quarter, is called Russia's *Sacred Sea*.

For most of history, no one could plumb Baikal's depths, catalogue its qualities, or measure it against other lakes. But the prehistoric peoples who first settled the lake's shores and the Russians who eventually followed knew nonetheless that there was something about Baikal that set it apart from all other places. Its waters were deep beyond measure, as cold as ice, and nearly as clear as air. Its storms would stir from calm to calamitous almost without notice. Its depths were home to creatures found nowhere else. And there were places on its steep shores and in its waters that had a power that no one could either describe or deny.

Today, modern science has confirmed what local residents have known for centuries—that Baikal is one of nature's most remarkable creations. It is the deepest and oldest lake on earth, and it holds far more water than any other. Its waters are among the clearest and purest on earth; they're home to hundreds of unique and sometimes bizarre animals and plants, including the world's only distinct species of freshwater seal, and to a mysterious and seemingly resilient ecosystem that baffles even some of the best scientists. And the lake is also something that scientists can't even begin to quantify but that they can't avoid trying to describe anyway—a place of transcendent beauty and wonder.

The Russians swaying by the windows in the passageway of the Trans-Siberian almost certainly know these things about their lake, and the fact that such a place exists within their borders is a point of tremendous pride for them. But Baikal is also far more than a collection of mere facts and superlatives. It's a place of profound symbolism, a place that reflects in its mystical waters the Russian nation itself—immense, powerful, and resilient. More than Americans planning visits to the Grand Canyon or Yosemite, millions of Russians long to see this place before they die. For those relatively few who can make the trip, traveling to Baikal is an almost patriotic act, a nearly religious pilgrimage to a place that's as much a part of the Russian soul as the novels of Dostoyevsky, the spires of the Kremlin, and the palaces of St. Petersburg. Amid the sorrowful emotional landscape of much of Russian history, Baikal remains pure and invulnerable. In the psyche of a country that feels it's never quite been given its due by others, Baikal can't be argued with or diminished. In a place that has suffered more than its share of hardship and humiliation, Baikal remains sublime and unassailable, more in the realm of God than of man.

Baikal occupies a powerful place in the Russian imagination, and also in the imagination of a stranger. It took root in mine, and the idea of traveling there just grew, untended, for almost a decade, until it suddenly emerged almost fully formed.

I come from a family of explorers. Not on the grand scale of Magellan or Cook or Lewis and Clark, or even many of today's *Rough Guide*-ing backpackers, but on the somewhat more modest scale of people who read books, look at maps, wonder what life and the landscape are like in other places and decide to go and find out. Thomsons tend to wander. My sister Sandy one day boarded a plane for Thailand without so much as the name of a hostel to stay in at the other end of the flight, and ended up spending two years in the Far East. My uncle John Thomson bought a motorcycle in Fairbanks, Alaska, and rode it all the way to Costa Rica. My grandfather William Orville Thomson died in Luxor, Egypt, at 83, while on a solo circumnavigation of the Mediterranean. And old Origen Thomson, my grandfather's grandfather's brother, walked the Oregon Trail in 1852, stayed a few years on the West Coast, and then went back to Indiana. For recreation and diversion at the end of a long and difficult day on the trail, he'd take long walks, to explore his new surroundings.

A few of the Pearmains, my mother's family, were similarly inclined. Among other meanderings, in the early 1950s my grandfather Jack Pearmain spent six months traveling by foot and bicycle through Europe, researching the then very odd practice of organic farming. Perhaps it was in hopes of instilling this same spirit of adventure and inquiry that my mother and father first waved me out the door at four years old to walk to school alone through the back alleys up over Boston's Beacon Hill. Or that my father took me to Europe at seventeen, hauled me around from city to city for a month or so, and then left me to follow my own trail for a few weeks more while he flew home. Or maybe they needn't have bothered, maybe the gene would've begun expressing itself sooner or later anyway. But whether through genes or experience, the urge to see what's around the next corner or over the next hill took hold in me, too.

But if there was anything unusual about my family's somewhat vagabond ways, there was nothing at all unusual about the source of my interest in Lake Baikal. I first read about it in the *National Geographic*. The article ran in 1992, as the hard shell of Soviet Russia was cracking and peeling, exposing the full measure of life inside. Who knew that in the middle of Siberia, a place nearly synonymous in the Western mind with exile, deprivation, imprisonment, and death, was this piece of creation at its most fantastic? One of nature's jewels stuffed away in a dark corner of earth's basement? Certainly not me.

I remember being seduced not just by all the superlatives and the gorgeous photos in the *Geographic* story but also by the very remoteness of the place, isolated almost as much by politics as by geography. It was in the middle of the Evil Empire, the Anti-America, a place that was thoroughly distrusted by, and distrustful of, most of the rest of the world. I was fascinated, too, by a local culture that seemed to embrace not just the beauty but also the hardship of life there. I remember the photo of the young Russian couple standing on the frozen lake in midwinter, he in a suit, she in a wedding gown, beaming from ear to ear. It seemed an invitation to breach the distance in geography, culture, and politics and visit them and the place in which they clearly took so much pride. And, of course, there was a shadow, too, the legacy of damage from misguided Soviet development and the threat of something perhaps even worse in the coming era of economic openness.

But, of course, I knew there was no way I'd ever get there. I filed the thought away for another life. A life in which I'd be President, father Kim Basinger's kids, and go to Lake Baikal.

A few years later, a reporter pitched a story to me about the lake. I was editing NPR's *Living on Earth*, and I worked with her to bring it to air. As always happens with a good radio piece, hearing the sounds and voices of the place created a kind of intimate link that made it feel like part of me had already been there. It was like fertilizer for the seed that had been planted by the *Geographic* article. But still, Baikal seemed impossibly far away. When would I ever have the money or the time to get myself there? Who in the world would give me an assignment and pay my way? And if somehow I had the opportunity to go, would I have the mettle? Because I knew Russia could be a challenging place to travel, even for those who spoke the language and understood the culture, neither of which I did. And truth be told, despite the wandering gene, despite all the curiosity and taste for adventure, I'd never been a very bold or daring person. The peripatetic and inquisitive brain is locked in a lifelong wrestling match with a fearful and cautious soul. Traveling to Baikal remained as likely as living to see the Red Sox win the World Series.

But life isn't always predictable. Six or seven years later, the Sox were still finding new ways to break their fans' hearts, and Kim and the White House were still only the stuff of fitful dreams, but one day I found myself tapping out an email to a guy I'd never met, in a city I'd never heard of, who, I'd been told by another guy I'd never met, was the best guide on the eastern shore of Lake Baikal. Could he help me get out onto the lake, up into the woods, into the homes and lives of local residents?

"Thank you for your letter," he wrote back. "I'll be lucky to help you. Everything is possible."

I'd just gotten divorced. All my possessions were packed into a 6×8 storage locker in Berkeley, and I was back home in Boston, squatting at my father's house at 40, ambivalent about being back at the main office of *Living on Earth* in Cambridge after three years exploring California and the western United States as *LOE*'s western bureau chief. No spouse, no house, my life in a box, and a job

I wasn't sure I still wanted after nearly ten years. Even my cat was in foster care. My own private Year 2000 Bug had hit, knocking my whole life out of whack. And then, in a moment, I didn't even have a mother anymore. After a long and torturous slide into mental illness and dementia, she had died suddenly from a runaway infection, on the very day I sent my divorce papers back to California to be finalized. Just at the point at which I had expected to be finally settling into some kind of solidity after a circuitous path to full adulthood, my life had quickly become untethered. Loss and grief and anger and disappointment were washing over me in great swells, even as I pretended to remain as stoic and unshakable as all my stern Protestant forebears. What I did have was money in the bank and a vague feeling that my Prozac prescription wasn't quite the ticket I needed out of the big dark place I'd found myself in. I also had a younger brother who was about to graduate from college, and a nascent plan to go with him to Alaska in the summer. Someone put the thought into my head: Why not do some serious traveling?

It didn't take long for me to concoct a preposterous idea. I called my brother: What if we went to Alaska, and then just kept going? I'd always wanted to cross the Pacific by ship, travel the Trans-Siberian, and yes, visit Lake Baikal. Set out from Boston by train, put these all together, and you're already halfway around the world. Why not go all the way around, Boston to Boston, never leaving the ground? Why not do something in this life that I always figured would have to be left for another life?

On the idea for this circumnavigation, my brother James was, as always, circumspect. "Give me a couple of weeks to think about it," he'd said.

Oh yeah, and where's Lake Baikal?

There it is. A flash of blue light through the trees.

Three days into Russia and more than two months from home in Boston, I'm spellbound by my first fleeting glimpses of the place I've traveled halfway around the world to see. Like my fellow passengers at the windows down the hallway, I want to believe that everything I've heard about Baikal is true—that it's not only a place unparalleled in all its qualities, but also a place that somehow tells a different story from the ones I've grown so used to, and in many ways so weary of.

I've covered the environment for more than a dozen years as I stand here at this window, full time for the last decade at *Living on Earth*. The environment is not a beat with a lot of good news. Sure, there are the small success stories—the compromise that saves this part of a forest from the chain saws, the agreement to phase out that especially nasty chemical, the occasional new super-efficient somethingorother that promises to save the world. But for the most part, the environment beat is an endless recounting of the millions of large and small blows that humans inflict on our ecosystems every day, an ongoing chronicle of our often desperate attempts to come to grips with the unintended consequences of the stupid and ingenious things we do to carve out a life and make a living on planet Earth.

We've tarnished even the most remote frontiers of the globe. The breast milk of Eskimo mothers carries pesticides sprayed on crops thousands of miles away. Tiny island nations are disappearing under rising seas, caused by climate-warming gases produced to serve the appetites of people far over the horizon. But I want to believe that this remote place is different. I've been drawn here not only by all that I've heard about its beauty and its fantastic, almost preposterous qualities, but also by the possibility that having held out for so long, Baikal might somehow still manage to elude the corrosive influence of civilization. I want to believe that it's a place where I can trust not only in the power of nature but also in the power of humans to learn from our experience, and to make wise choices.

But hard as I try, the idealist that I want to be can't shake the cold-eyed realist that I've always been. I can't ignore the warnings. Look closely, I've been told: civilization is making up for lost time here. Waste from factories, farms, and human settlements is testing the limits of Baikal's delicate ecology. Newly minted capitalists are measuring its potential for development. A warming climate is threatening the future of a place defined by cold. And Russia and the world don't seem to be rising to the challenge.

In the most dire view, mighty Baikal may be on the brink of disaster, a fragile and irreplaceable treasure that could be knocked off balance and shattered before we even know what we've done. Potentially yet another epic tragedy of denial, hubris, and lessons not learned. But in the most optimistic view, disaster for Baikal is impossible. Like the soul of a person or a nation, this mighty lake can suffer endless indignities and still remain pure. It is eternal.

In the land of contradictions that our train is rumbling through, these two ways of seeing seem bound together. I've come to Baikal to try to take some kind of measure of the place, to find some kind of truth about it and lessons for other places, and for myself. But if a real picture of Baikal can be created, it may well be a tapestry woven of opposing truths, a portrait composed of stark contrasts and subtle distinctions, an icon of the imagination in which what people see is inseparable from what they want to see—whether they're scientists peering through the lens of a microscope, businessmen with visions of riches, or travelers standing at the dirty window of a train.

2

Songs and Whispers

In which we meet the lake and some of its inhabitants
for the first time
and peek under the rug of its history

A crumpled and broken strand of asphalt rises at the northern edge of
Ulan-Ude, wanders through the dark woods of the Khamar-Daban
Mountains, and finally settles into a band of fertile bottom land in a narrow
stretch of coastal plain approaching the eastern shore of Lake Baikal. A rattly
old Toyota van skitters along the road, passing lonely farms and tiny villages
that gather up out of nowhere and disappear just as quickly, domed churches
that seem miles from any worshipers, and an occasional solitary babushka
by the side of the road selling whatever she's been able to squeeze from the earth
or gather in the woods.

There are seven of us riding this highway on this raw morning in
October of 2000, crammed into the van and bobbing like buoys to its irregular
rhythms—James and me from Boston, our guide Andrei Suknev, his colleague
Igor and our driver Kim, all from the city of Ulan-Ude, and two young women
who have also signed on with Andrei for a few days—Elisa, from France, and
Chanda, from Canada. We're all eating pine nuts that we bought from one of
those women at a wide spot in the road—they're called *orekhi* here—and washing

them down with lemon soda from a huge plastic bottle. Andrei is showing us how to crack open the nuts' hard shells with our front teeth and excavate their soft and pungent meat with our tongues. At an austere restaurant in a tiny village that Andrei tells us is called "Noisy Place," we eat a lunch of rice and some sort of meat, dry bread, and a peculiar variation on *borshch*, and we pee in an outhouse across the road. We get back in the van and rumble on.

We're heading for a remote national park on Baikal's eastern shore, but at the moment I'm not quite sure where we're going. I'd asked Andrei to take us hiking and camping on the lakeshore, to introduce us to local residents, communities, and culture. He's promised to do that, but he hasn't provided much beyond the barest details, and none of us has been asking for more. Our small group of visitors seems to have been overtaken by a peculiar sort of lethargy, even Elisa, who is pretty well traveled here and speaks quite serviceable Russian. For our parts, James and I are still suffering from train-lag, culture shock, and the lingering effects of a bug that we both picked up somewhere between Tokyo and Irkutsk. But at least for me it's something else, as well. More than anywhere I've ever been in my life, I am a complete stranger here, utterly unlearned in the language or the landscape, and utterly dependent on our host. So, since hooking up with Andrei yesterday in Ulan-Ude, I've decided just to float along on his breeze. This is not my usual mode when traveling. My usual mode is to be the one leading the exploration, plotting the route, or at least asking the first and the most questions about *where what who how*—all those impatient and obnoxious journalist questions. I am usually obsessed with maps, place names, plans, landmarks, and routes, with getting myself oriented and being dependent on no one else to help me find my way in or out. But for the time being, at least, I'm trying to do exactly the opposite of my usual habit and just let myself be *guided*.

It's been four days since our first sighting of Baikal from the Trans-Siberian. I could tell you how, having caught that initial glimpse, James and I jumped off the train at the first opportunity and made a beeline across the narrow shoreline, threw ourselves into the cobalt water, and frolicked like seals, not even stopping to take off our clothes. I could tell you that, but that would be someone else's book. As Thomsons, James and I are genetically unable to frolic. And as New Englanders, we are well practiced in the art of delayed gratification. New Englanders dig rocks out of fields for generations before the land will give up its first decent harvest. We pledge undying loyalty to a baseball team that forever comes excruciatingly close, but never actually wins. We enjoy our nasty winters because they help us feel that we have earned spring. And so James and I dutifully watched Baikal rise up beyond the windows of the Trans-Siberian, flash us a long *come hither* glance, and then recede, as we rolled right on by. We had a plan, and we were sticking to it. Irkutsk, 120 rail kilometers beyond Baikal, would be base camp. We would get acclimated there for a few days and then double back to Ulan-Ude to hook up with Andrei, the first of our Sherpas. He would guide us to our summit. And so only today, days after our first sighting of the lake and four or five hours out of Ulan-Ude in our van, comes our first touch, our first direct encounter with Baikal. But not at a moment of great anticipation or drama, not at a moment or in a way that someone else would write it, but very much by accident.

The lake is running close out the left side, but our attention is largely on the road in front of and beneath the van, which has deteriorated from poorly maintained to barely passable. Kim's driving skills are being tested by ever-more formidable ruts, craters, and sand hazards when suddenly, after hitting a not-especially-bad pothole, an ominous growl begins to emanate from beneath the van. We grind to a halt, and within barely a minute, the three Russians have disappeared under the back end of the vehicle, assessing the damage from a snapped shock absorber mount, and the other four of us are on the beach.

There's a thin strip of sand, a sky like the underside of an old mattress, and a sea of choppy, slate blue water that stretches nearly to the horizon on three sides and pushes a thin band of white foam up onto the beach. There's an untethered boat the color of the sky and as empty as the sky, a set of footsteps from the waterline to the boat and above the boat the path of something dragged up the gray sand. And on the sand beyond the boat there's a chain of fifteen or so vertebrae—a spine, the color of the foam at the water's edge with no ribs attached, no pelvis, no skull, nothing but its soft, mammalian S-curve and the lake itself to suggest that it had once belonged to a nerpa, one of Baikal's unique and celebrated seals.

We scatter on the beach, and this time I really do make a beeline to the lake, kneel down, and splash my hands in the soft waves as they exhaust themselves at my feet. The water is as cold and clear as a glacial Alaskan stream. I splash around some more, still not quite believing that I'm actually here. But here's the thing: as I stand here with Lake Baikal water finally running through my fingers, recalling all the superlatives that I've heard about this place and how far I've traveled to see it, I'm surprised to find myself thinking not only about how extraordinary it is but also about how utterly ordinary it is. It's an unfathomable amount of water—the most fresh water in any single place on earth—but it's still only water. It's the same stuff that flows out of every tap and pump and spring in every corner of the world, that washes our clothes and irrigates our crops and carries our crap out of our houses and keeps our own bodies lubricated and is so ubiquitous and useful and vital for every link in the chain of life and civilization that every creature on the planet understands it instinctively, and every person. Hundreds of millions of us don't have enough of it even as hundreds of millions of others think nothing of wasting it shamelessly, but the bottom line is that if any one of the six or so billion people on earth suddenly landed here on this beach like we have, and knew nothing at all about Lake Baikal, she or he would instantly relate to what was before them in the most basic way.

And perhaps, ultimately, that's why there's such reverence for this place, why it really *is* so completely unlike anywhere else. If it were the world's largest volcano, a 300-mile-long, mile-deep pool of molten rock, people would no doubt be impressed by it. If it were the world's biggest and deepest canyon it would certainly be a wonder of nature. But no one would be concerned with whether or not it was perfect. But *the largest body of fresh water on earth!* Fresh water is life itself! It's always captured the imagination and comforted the soul like nothing else, and it always will. And to stand before a place with so much pure, fresh water is almost like standing on the threshold of God's own reservoir. Or even the home of God himself. How could it not be perfect?

Back up the beach, I see that while I've been thinking idle thoughts about the lake, my much more enterprising brother has used driftwood to rekindle some smoldering embers he's found into a full-fledged blaze, by which we warm ourselves in the damp October chill. We sit by the fire in silence and look out over all that water to the thin band of mountains on the far side. And after a while Andrei comes down to tell us that we're ready to roll again, that he and Igor and Kim were able to jack up the van and wrench off the broken shock absorber mount. We pile back in and drive on, minus one shock absorber but the ride not noticeably worse than before, and continue our journey north.

•

A small gray boat chugs along the shore of a peninsula jutting out from Baikal's eastern rim, its engine groaning and spitting. Across the broad bay, a rack of mountains tears at the low clouds, and on the near shore a beach comes into view, with a handful of weary skiffs hauled up on the sand and a small clutch of men smoking fish on metal tripods over fires on the beach. A cluster of timber houses just above the beach reveals this to be a village, a place called Katun.

The boat settles its steep bow onto the sand. A crude wooden ladder goes down, and sacks of fish and loaves of bread are handed up. Up the beach, a woman hobbles toward the boat, a thin song pushed before her by the breeze. Soon she's climbing aboard, still singing, a little unsteady. Her face is round and red, her black hair falls out from under a green kerchief. Like our driver Kim on our way up from Ulan-Ude, she's a Buryat, one of the indigenous peoples of this part of Asia, close siblings to the Mongolians just over the border to the south of here. Her name is Lula, and although it's still before noon, her unsteady gaze and gait suggest that she may already have had a taste of vodka. She greets us through an ambivalent, gap-toothed smile.

The boat slips back off the sand, and we head for open water. Even under the heavy overcast, the water below is eerily clear, as if illuminated by its own light source. People say the clarity of Baikal's water can give you vertigo, the dizziness that comes with great heights, from feeling that there's nothing below you holding you up. As we pull away from the steep shoreline, ripples of diffuse light mingle with waves of water down five meters, ten meters, who knows exactly how far. I don't doubt what I've heard, that Baikal's water is among the clearest and purest in the world. It feels like we're floating on liquid air.

We're traversing the shore of the Svyatoi Nos—the Holy Nose, a peninsula on Baikal's eastern rim shaped like a gargantuan, pointy schnozz. Our boat is what passes for a ferry here. For Lula and the few dozen other residents of the three tiny towns on this stretch of coastline, it's the local bus. For James and me and our traveling companions, it's the way into Zabaikalsky National Park, a wild area of more than 2,000 square kilometers along the steep and thickly wooded shores of the Holy Nose and beyond to the north. The settlements of Katun, Kurbulik, and Monakhovo shelter the peninsula's only human residents.

"People from different places come here," Lula chirps over the groan of the engine, with Andrei loosely translating. "We keep our door open. If we have a piece of bread, we share it with you," she says, looking with her half-smile more through us than at us. But then she becomes slightly more animated. "We share our vodka! If you have a headache, we give you vodka!" She lets out a hearty laugh. "We have lots of fish here. I would like to give you some." Her offer seems more a wish than an intention, as she appears to have none to give. But we've already received plenty of fish in our stop at the village a few minutes ago, half a dozen or so silvery shards of Baikal life.

Lula drifts in and out of conversation with us like a butterfly on the wind. Her spoken words mingle with her song, her song more a murmur than a tune. It's about a woman going to live on a collective farm, Andrei tells us, and falling in love with a man there. She's singing her own story, it seems, or a version of it. She says she came here as a young woman, from the Barguzin Valley, just over the mountains to the east. "I fell in love with a man from here," she says, "but it was not good.... He's not here anymore...." She trails off and casts her eyes across the water, to the mountains and brooding clouds beyond, with a wistful expression that seems to say, *At least I still love the lake....*

In a moment, Lula's back from wherever her thoughts have carried her. "We are living very good here," she tells us. "The air is fresh! People are very friendly!" But, she says, things are changing. "There are more and more people coming, lots of tourists. It's not good. . . . " She trails off again, and slips back into her song.

Four hundred years ago, before there were Russians here, there were Lula's people—the Buryats. And before them were the Evenki, and before them the Kurykany, and before that . . . well, it gets very hazy.

There's no record of the first person to stand on the narrow shores of Baikal, to squint up at its rim of snow-covered mountains and down into its dizzying waters, and to wonder how this place came to be. There are no words or images capturing the emotions of its first inhabitants as they discovered this enticing and terrifying place, where earthquakes shake the land and sudden storms whip up the sea. But along with hunger and fear and cold and thirst, these first people undoubtedly also understood beauty and drama and mystery, and knew that they had found a place like no other.

These first humans arrived sometime before the end of the last ice age, perhaps as much as 30,000 years ago. Even though Siberia was even colder then than it is now, Baikal was never permanently frozen over during the Pleistocene. Among these early residents were a people known today as the Kurykany. They carved images of the lake's other residents onto rocks—sturgeon, seals, and birds. They fashioned hooks of bone to catch fish from the lake and made razor-sharp arrowheads to hunt reindeer, bison, and hairy rhinoceros in the surrounding forests. They knew the art of pottery, kept calendars, and developed religious rites. They built both permanent and portable homes, and they laid their dead into round, yurtlike burial sites.

Over time, other humans found their way to the region—bands of Turkic-speaking peoples from the southwest called Yakuts and Evenki, and Mongols from the southeast. The Mongols were beginning to spread out of the great central Asian plateau in the first waves of expansion that would ultimately bring them an empire spanning the breadth of the continent, from the Pacific Ocean to Central Europe. These Mongol newcomers settled into the forest and plain of south-central Siberia and into hospitable corners of Baikal's shore, its tributaries, and its only outlet, the Angara River. They absorbed the Kurykany, came to dominate the Evenki, and over time became known as the Buryats. But their language and culture kept them closely linked to the Mongols. According to local legend, Genghis Khan himself, the greatest of all Mongol rulers, was born on the shores of Baikal, buried here, or maybe both, although the historical record suggests otherwise. It's said that the Great Khan showed his respect for the power of the lake by naming it the Great Forbiddance Zone, in which no settlements could be built.

Early Buryats practiced shamanism, then Buddhism, and sometimes a hybrid of the two. They forged metal and led a seminomadic life raising horses and herding cattle and sheep. They caught fish and seals in their massive lake and were wary of its depth and its sudden and violent storms. And from time to time, at least, they seem to have entertained visitors from distant lands. The first known reference to Baikal in any language is found in Chinese histories, in the year 110 B.C. The Chinese called it *Beihai*, for Northern Sea, and even for them, as the region would become more than a millennium and a half later for the Russians, it was a place of political exile. Arabs came, as well. A twelfth-century Arabian volume describes Baikal as "a sea of remarkably transparent and tasty water.... The Most High has made it in the form of two joined horns. It has sprung up from an underground crevice. And it has been and it will be moaning till the last Judgment. And the sea is always rough and enraging...."

The Buryats established religious sites around this rough and enraging sea and believed that the lake itself was sacred. And it's from them that the Russian explorers eventually took its name: They called it *Baigal*. But the Buryats themselves likely took the name from others, probably the Yakut. Today the Yakut, or Sakha, live hundreds of kilometers away, in the basin of the Lena River to the northeast. But it seems that they, too, once lived in the Baikal region and may have been driven off by the Buryats over the course of several centuries. The Yakut have one word for "sea," "ocean," "plenty," and "Lake Baikal" itself, and that is, in one of its various forms, *baigal*.

•

The first whisper any Russians heard of *Baigal* probably came from the lips of an Evenk, one of the region's nomadic reindeer herders. These Russians weren't searching for a place of awe and wonder to rest their eyes and contemplate the great mysteries of nature. They weren't even looking for new places to settle. What they were looking for was furry animals that they could slaughter and that would make them rich. And from the Evenk these Russian trappers, or *promyshlenniki*, heard of a creature with the most lustrous fur to be found anywhere: the Barguzin sable, a close cousin of weasels and minks that they were told lived deep in the taiga forests beyond a great lake behind a wall of mountains. On their way to find the sable, the Russians found Baikal.

It was the middle of the seventeenth century, and Russian explorers were swarming over Siberia. Russians had finally breached the Ural Mountains following the collapse of the Mongol Yoke that had hemmed them in for centuries, and spilled over into what seemed the great void of Siberia—the "Sleeping

Land"—beyond. Ostensibly in the service of the tsar and wealthy merchant families, these bands of Cossack mercenaries, ex-convicts, runaway serfs, and other adventurers turned Siberia into an orgy of unbridled human appetites, mayhem, and slaughter, propelled in large part by the fur trade.

Furs at the time were considered "soft gold"—not just a symbol but also a source of great wealth. They were a primary currency and a major source of imperial wealth. And as the fur trade would later propel French and English explorers across North America, so too it propelled Russian explorers across Siberia, although compared to the 200 years or so it took European settlers to cross North America, the conquest of Siberia unfolded at lightning speed. The Russians found an intricate network of rivers that they used as expressways to race across Siberia's more than 8,000 kilometers of forests, bogs, tundra, and permafrost in less than fifty years.

But Baikal, only about half the distance from the Urals to the Pacific Ocean as the crow flies, lay south of the easiest routes across the continent and remained undiscovered. It was only in 1643, four years after the Russian flag had been planted on the shores of the Pacific, that an expedition led by the Cossack Kurbat Ivanov sailed up the Lena River, scaled what would come to be called the Primorsky Mountains, and descended to the hidden lake below.

The pursuit of the Barguzin sable seems to have left little time for Ivanov's party or those that soon followed to record their thoughts about the vast lake that they'd found carved out of the taiga forest. But it wasn't long before Russians engaged in less material pursuits than tracking animals and staking out territory began to write about the extraordinary qualities of the place that would eventually become revered throughout the empire as the "Pearl of Siberia," and Russia's "Sacred Sea." In 1662, the renegade priest Avvakum sailed across the lake on his return from exile in eastern Siberia. "It was with great difficulty that we found a place on the shore away from the waves," Avvakum later wrote. "Near it the mountains are  high and rocky cliffs exceedingly high. I have trailed over twenty thousand versts and more, but nowhere have I seen the like. On their tops are canopies, gates and pillars, stone walls and courtyards, all the work of God...."

A little more than a decade later, in 1675, the Russian envoy Nikolai Spafary visited Baikal while on one of his country's first diplomatic missions to

China. Spafary's account makes it clear that the Russians, unlike their Chinese and Arabian neighbors, had been ignorant of the place. "The Baikal Sea was unknown both to old and present day describers of the earth," Spafary wrote, "because they have described other small lakes and bogs, but of Baikal, which is large and mighty deep, there is no mention at all...." Like Avvakum before him and thousands since, Spafary found the lake almost overwhelming:

> Baikal can be called a sea because... it is impossible to travel all around it... because its size in length, width and depth is very great. And it can be called a lake because its water is fresh, not salt, and those lakes in which, although great, the water is not salty, are not called seas by those who describe the earth....
>
> Its length can be covered in up to ten days or twelve or more in a large sailing vessel, depending on the weather, its width... cannot be crossed in less than twenty-four hours. Its depth is very great, since many a time have a hundred or more fathoms been measured but the bottom not found, and this is caused by there being very high mountains all around Baikal, on which sometimes the snow does not melt even in the summer.... And the water in the lake is so clean that the bottom is visible many fathoms down, and it is exceedingly good for drinking....

•

Fifteen minutes or so up the coast, Lula climbs off the boat at Kurbulik, the last settlement on this part of Baikal for the next eighty kilometers or so, her song still on the breeze. The boatman, a lonesome-looking young man with a wave of blond hair, a shy smile, and searing blue eyes, flips the engine into reverse. We pull up the ladder, ease back onto the lake, and continue our journey up the shore of the Holy Nose.

3

The Earth Splits, Water Rushes In

*In which we contemplate the creation of Lake Baikal
and its place among the planet's coolest places*

Siberia is huge, but it isn't greedy. Of all the colors in the universe's paint box, it asks for only a few shades of green to have its massive portrait painted. The picture starts with a ragged band of soft sage, the treeless tundra of the Arctic and subarctic. Through the middle, a thick swath of deep emerald, the taiga forest that stretches from the Pacific to the Urals and beyond to Scandinavia. Finally, in the far lower left corner, a wedge of soft yellowish green, Siberia's share of the fertile Eurasian steppe. From a distance, this rough canvas is a study in chlorophyll, with just a single, stark break in the color scheme—a thin blue crescent slicing through the lower middle of the emerald taiga. It's almost as if the same gigantic hand that wielded the paintbrush then picked up a monstrous stiletto and in an impulsive Dadaist gesture cut a gigantic gash into the taut canvas, which pulled open and filled up with cobalt paint. And I suppose if you believed in such things, you could say that's actually what's happened here, that the hand was God's and that after the earth was sliced open, the gash grew ever wider and filled up with more and more blue water. Earth's surface has been torn apart here, and water has been flowing into the gash for eons.

A lake is a simple thing, really—just a big hole in the ground filled with water. And our restless planet finds all kinds of ways to make them. The earth is constantly reshaping itself, through processes great and small—from the epochal smashing and tearing of crustal plates, to the periodic growth and recession of glaciers, to the daily flow of wind, water, and sediment. As long as water flows and the earth moves, lakes will continue to be born, grow, and die.

Lakes can be formed in the buckling and cracking seams between the earth's tectonic plates, as with the Great Lakes of East Africa. They can be formed in the wake of receding glaciers, which leave long grooves, moraines, and kettle holes. Both the North American Great Lakes and demure little Walden Pond were formed in such a process ten or twelve thousand years ago. Lakes can gather in hollows between mountains or hills, where tectonic uplift and glaciation have combined to form a rumpled landscape, as in the European Alps. They can be made when the sudden rush of water breaking through a natural dam gouges out the earth, like the Grand Coulee on the Columbia River, or in just the opposite way, when a landslide or lava flow creates a natural dam, as happened in the early twentieth century, when a landslide blocked a river in Tajikistan's Pamir Mountains and formed another of the world's deepest lakes, Sarezskoye. They can be formed in the calderas of volcanoes, like Oregon's Crater Lake, or in the craters of meteorites, like Canada's Chubb Crater in northern Quebec. They can even be made by beavers damming up a stream—and, of course, by humans doing the same.

The vast majority of these wet holes in the ground are ephemeral—geologically speaking, they don't last more than the blink of an eye. They fill up with sediment and put themselves out of business, turning first into a swamp or a bog, and then a meadow. Or they break through whatever barrier is constraining them, start to empty out, and turn into rivers, leaving behind wide swaths of fertile "bottomland." Perhaps the climate changes and not enough rain falls to replace the water draining out and evaporating. Some lakes exist for only a few hundred years. Many others hang around for tens or hundreds of thousands, and a very few make it to the geriatric age of a million or more years. But in any group there are outliers, and among lakes, Baikal is on the far end of the curve. It's at least 25 million years old—the oldest body of fresh water on the planet, more than a thousand times older than North America's Great Lakes. Before there was Russia or Russians, before there were people or even apes, there was Baikal.

Those twelfth-century Arab visitors were right—Baikal has sprung up from an underground crevice.

It started with a shudder in the earth's crust, a reverberation, probably, from the ongoing collision of India and Eurasia thousands of kilometers to the south. The earth shook, a crack opened in the ground, and it filled with water. It was nothing remarkable at the time, and if anyone had been around to notice it, they certainly wouldn't have imagined what this little ditch might some day become. But with that first shudder, the earth around Baikal began—ever so slowly—to tear itself apart. Today, that once-tiny ditch is seventy kilometers wide and more than 600 kilometers long—roughly the distance from San Francisco to Los Angeles—and scientists calculate that it continues to open up by nearly an inch a year.

Actually, Baikal has sprung up from several crevices. Geologists have found that its basin is part of a complex series of cracks and fissures that stretch for more than 1,000 kilometers across this part of Asia, and that here at Baikal the land between two of these faults has fallen to form a type of valley that they call a "graben," which makes Baikal a graben lake. In less scientific terms, Baikal occupies a great rift valley, the result of a process seen elsewhere on the planet where two or more plates are pulling apart from one another. Perhaps the most famous example of this is in East Africa, where a part of the continent called the Somali plate is splitting off from the rest like a thumb moving away from a hand, creating a chain of rift valleys that runs more than 3,000 kilometers from Malawi to Ethiopia and then beyond all the way to the Red and Dead seas. East Africa's rift valleys contain dozens of lakes, including one, Lake Tanganyika, that's a lot like Baikal in many ways—very long, very deep, and very old.

Lake Tanganyika is also very big. In fact, it's one of a handful of lakes that are bigger, on the surface, than Baikal—Superior, Michigan, and Huron among North America's Great Lakes, and Tanganyika and its neighbor Lake Victoria among Africa's Great Lakes, with Superior leading the pack, the largest lake on earth in terms of surface area. So if the Battle of the Lakes were to be judged by what you can see, then Baikal wouldn't even take a bronze. But if the contest is more than superficial, then Baikal blows these other lakes out of the water. Dig a hole big enough to dump Tanganyika and almost two Lake Victorias into. Or, if you prefer, pour in Superior, add Huron and Michigan, and then make enough room to add the other two North American Great Lakes, Erie and Ontario. Only then will you have a hole big enough to be compared to Baikal. On a planet on which fresh water is an increasingly scarce and contentious commodity, Baikal is a glutton—it hoards roughly a fifth of earth's liquid fresh water.

People who like to measure things have figured out that this translates into roughly *23,000 cubic kilometers* of water—which, of course, is a meaningless figure in any real sense, impossible to comprehend. So picture this: New Jersey flooded under a kilometer of water. Or think of it this way: all the world's rivers—the Nile, the Amazon, the Yangtze, the Mississippi, the Congo, the Mekong, the Niger, all the other huge ones plus every little stream and creek and irrigation ditch—all of them together would take nearly a year to fill up Baikal. On the other hand, if every stream and river that does run into Baikal were to suddenly dry up, it would take roughly 400 years for Baikal to empty out. Or try this on for size: the world's six billion-plus people could drink, bathe, wash their dishes and clothes, flush their toilets, irrigate their crops and lawns, water their livestock, run their factories, make coffee, and brush their teeth using only Baikal's water for more than six years. Or, if the entire current population of the planet decided to use water from other sources for all those other needs and merely to slake its thirst with Baikal water, we could stick a giant straw in the lake, suck out the necessary three liters per person per day and not hear that gurgle at the bottom of the glass for more than 3,000 years.

The reason for all this gluttony, of course, is Baikal's extraordinary depth. The early explorer Nikolai Spafary was the first to note the futile attempts to find its bottom after measuring out "a hundred fathoms and more," or more than 600 feet, in 1675. Nor was the bottom found any time soon thereafter; in fact, the search continued for nearly 300 years. What scientists finally determined to be the deepest point was located only in 1959, and it turned out to be nearly ten times as deep as what those early explorers had been able to measure—895 fathoms. Or, in terrestrial terms, 1,637 meters, or 5,371 feet—more than a mile deep. But even that number is a moving target—some more recent sources put the lake's depth at 1,741 meters. And in an earthquake in 1959, parts of the bottom fell another fifteen to twenty meters. Whatever number you pick, no other lake on the planet comes close to Baikal's depth. It's 200 meters deeper than Tanganyika, and four times deeper than Superior. If you emptied it out, you'd have a chasm to rival the Grand Canyon among the world's deepest gorges.

But for geologists, even getting to the bottom of Baikal isn't getting near to the bottom of the story. They've been probing and drilling and shooting sound waves through the lake's basin and have determined that over the eons, Baikal has accumulated somewhere between six and eight kilometers of sediment, a nearly five-mile thick record of the natural history of Central Asia. So from the surface of the lake to the bedrock below, the Baikal rift dives altogether as much as nine and a half kilometers, or nearly six miles, approaching the depth of the world's greatest abyss, the Mariana Trench under the western Pacific. The Baikal rift may reach farther below the earth's surface than the Himalayas rise above it.

And if no one could have imagined twenty-five million years ago what that little patch of blue would one day become, some people are imagining today what it might yet become. They see its shores spreading at roughly the same rate as those of the Atlantic and Pacific oceans; they sense magnetic peculiarities similar to those along the mid-Atlantic rift zone; they see the sibling East African rift zone opening that continent up like a zipper; and they think that Baikal has greater aspirations: not content to be the world's largest lake, Baikal wants to split Asia open and become an ocean.

Now there is one other body of water that some argue trumps Baikal on biglakeness—the Caspian Sea, in southwestern Asia. The Caspian is nowhere near as deep as Baikal, but its surface area is more than ten times as big, so altogether it holds more than three times as much water. The Caspian is immense, far and away the biggest continental water body. And it's not connected to any ocean, which is why some people consider it a lake. But the Romans knew what they were talking about: when they discovered the Caspian, they called it a *sea* because it was full of *salt water*. And as we've heard, Nikolai Spafary, upon encountering Baikal, said more or less the same thing, only inside out: *"Those lakes in which, although great, the water is not salty, are not called seas by those who describe the earth. . . ."* Since ancient times, this definition of sea versus lake hasn't changed: *salt = sea, fresh = lake*. Look at the map. The world over, freshwater bodies are called lakes, while landlocked bodies of salt water are called seas—the Dead Sea, the Aral Sea, the Caspian Sea, even California's man-made Salton Sea. Sure, there is that thing in Utah called the Great Salt Lake, but the legend of its discovery by the Mormon pioneers proves the point— they thought they'd found the ocean. And even when they realized they hadn't, they had to give it a name that reflected its anomalous status—they didn't call it Joseph Smith Lake or the Lake of the Golden Tablets; they called it the *Salt* Lake. They knew it was weird, that it didn't quite fit, that a lake isn't supposed to be salty.

So never mind the Caspian *Sea*.

4

Into the Lake—Shallow

In which we camp in a not-so-isolated cove,
drink of Baikal's waters, and get wet

The air smells of rain and autumn decay and sends cold, sharp fingers poking through our clothes as the Lonesome Boatman steers our little craft along the shore of the Holy Nose. Beyond the gunwales of the boat, spears of orange and emerald march up the steep hillside—the ubiquitous larch and birch, cedar and fir, muted under the thick sky. And behind this abrupt shoreline rises a dark mountain chain that extends fifty kilometers southwest along the length of the peninsula, mirroring the ridges of the Barguzin chain across the bay to the east and the unseen peaks of the Primorsky, Baikal, and Khamar Daban ranges hugging the lake's western and southern shores. This is the vertiginous lay of the land around nearly all of Baikal's shoreline. It's not just the clear and deep water that can make one's head spin. On all sides, mountains rear up five, six, and seven thousand feet above the lake, and then plunge past the surface and on toward the depths with barely a pause to acknowledge the change from air to water. Bobbing in a boat on its surface, you get the peculiar feeling that Baikal is itself contained by some larger vessel. One English word that I've heard used to describe the lake basin, in keeping with the notion of Baikal being a "sacred sea," is "chalice," like some kind of holy vessel cradling these mystical waters. You get the peculiar feeling, as well, that the world begins and ends here. There are no landmarks that are not part of the Baikal ecosystem, not a spot of earth on which a drop of falling rain doesn't flow into Baikal.

And despite the lake's magnitude, it's actually a very small world, at least the part that humans can occupy. Around most of the lake there's almost no "shore" to speak of, just a narrow margin at the base of the mountains here and there where humans can get a toehold at the edge of the abyss. Baikal's more than 2,000 kilometers of shoreline harbor barely 80,000 people in fewer than fifty settlements, some of barely a handful of houses, and most of these are covered in the shadows of the looming hills long after the sun has risen or before it sets.

Fifteen minutes after dropping Lula at the last village, we stand with Andrei at the bow of the creaky little ferry as the boatman points us into a narrow inlet between folds of the Holy Nose's hills. The water calms, and a small cove opens up. "*Bukhta Zmeevaia,*" Andrei tells us—"Snake Bay, the most beautiful place on this part of the lake." On the shore is a fingernail of flat land with a rough table and a fire pit, before a scruffy October forest climbing a steep slope. The boat nestles up onto the beach, we lower the ladder onto the sand and follow it down.

There are six of us now; Kim has taken his hobbled van back to Ulan-Ude. We haul our packs and tents and the bags of fresh bread and fish that we picked up down the shore onto the beach. What we're not carrying is water. No need, Andrei tells me, we can take it right from the lake. As soon as we hit the shore, he leans down, fills his bottle, and hands it to me. "Come on, no problem," he assures me, figuring that I'd never drink unfiltered water most anywhere else. Where there are people, you have to worry about *E. coli* bacteria, *Cryptosporidium*, or other pathogens, and maybe industrial and agricultural contaminants, as well. And where there aren't people, there's often *Giardia* bacteria from other mammals. But I remember what I've heard about Baikal's built-in filtration system, and I have to trust that Andrei has no interest in making his customers sick. I take a swig, and then another, and it seems that still today, more than 300 years after Nikolai Spafary's first account, Baikal's water remains exceedingly good for drinking. It tastes unlike any stuff you find elsewhere these days—not a hint of silt or organic matter or chlorine or copper pipes or polyethylene or healing minerals or raspberry essence. It tastes like nothing at all. It tastes like water—the Platonic form, as fine and pure as if God, or the cosmos, or whoever, had just invented it.

Thoughts of unblemished creation come easily here, even for one who doesn't believe in a creator. Early scouts like the priest Avvakum and the envoy Spafary are usually harbingers of the almost geologic force that is modern human civilization. Since the onset of the Industrial Age, humans have gained the power to remake the landscape and alter its ecosystems like nothing short of a volcano, a glacier, or a cataclysmic earthquake, and in the 300 years since Europeans discovered Baikal, human endeavor has utterly transformed the landscape of much of the rest of the world, even the seas and the skies. But Baikal has largely been spared this blitz. Here you can still sense the forces of nature left to their own devices—geology, climate, wind, water, self-replicating DNA—the very things that gave birth to us and sustain us, brewing and churning, doing their work. The mountains squeezed out of the earth by the pressure and heat and tension of the planet's fitful and fractured crust. The wind and storms caused by the mountains and the differences they create in pressure, temperature, and humidity. The trees specifically adapted to the harsh Siberian climate, yet doing the work of plants everywhere—sucking carbon dioxide out of the atmosphere, turning the carbon and hydrogen from water into wood through photosynthesis, and releasing the waste oxygen back into the atmosphere. The whipping up of the water by the wind coming down off the mountains, bringing a rich froth of oxygen into the lake. The animals brought to the lake by its tributaries and sustained by that dissolved oxygen in the water, proliferating, battling it out, feeding on each other, establishing cooperative and symbiotic relationships, changing and adapting through random mutation and natural selection. The emergence through these processes of new creatures, which in turn have their own effect on the ecosystem and on the water itself, creatures like the Baikal epischura, the tiny and ubiquitous filter-feeding shrimp that helps keep the lake's water so clean that I can reach down and take a drink from the lake without fear of any kind of contamination.

The boat eases off the beach, the engine groans, and the Lonesome Boatman heads back for the open water of the broader bay beyond—the Chivyrkuysky Gulf, between the peninsula and the gray-green Barguzin Mountains to the east. Igor kindles a fire, hauls a big pot of water from the lake, and hangs it on a hook suspended from an iron rod over the fire pit. He starts scaling the fish—*omul* and *sig*, both Siberian relatives of trout and salmon that are mainstays of the local diet, and the ubiquitous pike. James and I and Elisa and Chanda set to work gathering firewood and peeling potatoes and onions for our lunch of fish stew while Andrei heads off down the shore toward a small wooden shack with a tin chimney, jutting out over the cove. It's a *banya*, he tells us, a Russian sauna.

By the time he returns, steam is rising off the stew pot and there's smoke coming from the *banya*'s stovepipe. Andrei points to it. "An entrepreneur built this," he says, "he gets permission from the national park." Andrei tells me there's also a small hot spring just down the shore that someone has captured by lining two tiny pools with wood. And in the summers, he says, the fellow who built the *banya* has begun bringing in a barge with a little cabin on it, sort of a floating motel, which has only recently weighed anchor and headed home for the season. When Andrei tells me this, I wonder aloud about the waste from its guests. "They declare that they bring all sewage to town," Andrei says, "but sometimes, if no control, they pollute it directly to the bay. Some people, they not care about nature." I think about the drink I've just taken from the lake and wonder how long since the barge pulled up anchor. I wonder whether in a few hours I'll still think Baikal's water is as fine and pure as Spafary found it. And I wonder how many more of these loosely regulated businessmen are at work around the lake.

Andrei reassures me that the water here is still fine, but he says he fears that the little tourist barge and its possibly rogue sewage are a sign of things to come. The total number of tourists at Baikal is still tiny, but it is growing, and many of them are leaving their mark. "More and more people are coming.... It's not good," Lula had told us. And as Andrei suggests, many of those drawn here don't seem to get it. On a hike up the shore later in the afternoon, I find plastic bottles and paper trash. Among the artifacts, a faded label from a container of bottled water.

•

The *National Geographic* in which I first read about Baikal included an excellent map of the region. And the map has a lot of green on it. By 1992, when the article ran, more than fifty percent of the lake's shoreline and a good deal of its uplands were under strict government protection. Among these protected areas was the place where we are now, Zabaikalsky National Park, on the eastern shore; Pribaikalsky National Park, spanning much of the western shore; and three highly restricted nature preserves. Abutting much of this was a less-restrictive coastal protection zone extending in some areas more than fifty kilometers from the lake. Since that time, still more environmental controls have been adopted on an even broader swath of land under the special 1999 Law on Protecting Lake Baikal, known commonly as the Law of Baikal. That law was adopted as a condition of Baikal being named a World Heritage Site by UNESCO, the United Nations Educational, Scientific, and Cultural Organization, in 1996, a designation that recognized the lake and its watershed as an area of exceptional environmental value and concern to the entire world.

The need for an unusual level of protection in the region has been recognized by Russian leaders for almost a century, although occasionally under unusual circumstances and not always having much to do with concern about the lake itself. The Russian Empire was teetering on the verge of collapse in 1916 when Tsar Nicholas II decided that the time had finally come to protect the habitat of the Barguzin sable, the creature that had lured the first Russians to the lake and was once the source of such rich tribute to the throne, but which, by the early twentieth century, had been hunted nearly to extinction. Nicholas's legacy, the Barguzinsky Nature Reserve just north of here, was the first of what would become a network of *zapovedniki*, or strict nature reserves, across Russia and the Soviet Union. Five years later, after leading the revolution that toppled Nicholas and when Russia was still engulfed by postrevolutionary chaos and civil war, Lenin decided that not just the sable but all wildlife in the Barguzinsky reserve should be protected, a move that may have had less to do with a concern for nature than for Moscow's need to consolidate its tenuous hold on power in the Irkutsk and Transbaikal regions. Since then, successive Soviet and Russian governments have taken further steps to at least put themselves on record as being concerned about the lake and its watershed. Two more nature preserves and a national park were established in the years between Lenin and Mikhail Gorbachev. Gorbachev himself presided over the establishment of two more reserves, two national parks, including this one, and the coastal protection zone. And then came the Law of Baikal under Boris Yeltsin.

But, Andrei says, most of these measures remain merely pieces of paper. In general, he says, Russian governments have at best acted indifferently toward the country's environment, and the current one is no different. "In real life," he says with a shrug, "they care not a lot about nature."

Andrei's comments echo those of many critics of the Russian government and its Soviet predecessors. In their 1992 book, *Ecocide in the USSR*, Murray Feshbach and Alfred Friendly, Jr., place Soviet and Russian environmental laws and regulations squarely within "the old Russian practice of *pokazukha*, putting a false front over a grubby reality," as epitomized by the fake villages erected by Prince Potemkin to fool Catherine the Great into believing that all was well in Russia's new territories along the Dnieper River in the eighteenth century. Behind the modern Potemkin façade of protective laws, as Feshbach and Friendly and a host of others have chronicled, lies a continental swath of environmental havoc, from the destruction of the Aral Sea in Central Asia to the nuclear reactors lying at the bottom of the Arctic Ocean in scuttled Soviet submarines.

Here at Baikal, critics contend that the façade of laws and regulations largely obscures a long list of ongoing offenses, running from the egregious to the merely neglectful. Topping the list are the polluting heavy industries operating in the lake's watershed and "zone of atmospheric influence," or "airshed," and the increasing runoff into the lake and its tributaries of nutrients from farms, human settlements, and deforested areas. Nearer the bottom is the serious underfunding of national parks like this one. On the way here, we'd stopped at its headquarters in a dingy building in the unremarkable town of Ust-Barguzin and had spoken with its director, a weary-looking man named Vladimir Melnikov. He told us that the park's budget was less than a third of what's needed merely for basic infrastructure and maintenance, that the park had only sixty-two employees to look after an area the size of a small American state, and that it hardly mattered that hunting had been banned in the park, since most of its wildlife had been hunted out long ago.

Somewhere in the middle range of threats are such things as continued logging and gold mining within the lake's watershed and a plan to develop oil and gas deposits in the delta of the Selenga River, the largest river flowing into the lake and a particularly sensitive ecosystem. Andrei says the petroleum plan violates the Law of Baikal, but that the government of President Vladimir Putin has taken no steps to stop it. "They say, 'We take the gas and we keep Baikal well,'" Andrei tells me, "but I think they have no idea how to save Baikal. Because it's impossible to get gas and to save Baikal, by my opinion. Maybe they have another opinion."

•

Without the resources to carry out its most basic functions, new amenities are not among the highest priorities of national park administrators here. Which is why it was left to the local "entrepreneur" Andrei told us about to build the *banya* down the cove from our campsite. Of course, when first I saw it, I wondered how the park could let  someone build a *banya* in the middle of the wilderness at all. And then I remember, *This is Russia—how could they not?*

The *banya*—the Russian cousin of the Finnish sauna, the Turkish bath, and the Native American sweat lodge—is ubiquitous in rural Russia and far older than the country itself. The first known history of early Russia, *The Russian Primary Chronicle of* 1113, tells a tale, almost certainly apocryphal, of a journey by the apostle Andreas from the Holy Land to present-day Kiev in the first century A.D., during which he was said to have encountered this already well-established tradition. "Wondrous to relate," the *Chronicle* quotes Andreas as having written. "I was in the land of the Slavs, and while I was among them, I noticed their wooden bath-houses. They warm them to extreme heat, then undress, and after anointing themselves with tallow, take young reeds and lash their bodies.... Then they drench themselves with cold water, and thus are revived.... They make of the act not a mere washing but a veritable torment." Bathing in a *banya*, the *Chronicle* quotes Andreas as saying, was "voluntary torture."

Russians, of course, see it a bit differently. "The *banya*," Alexander Pushkin wrote, "is like [a] second mother." And for some, the relationship is still more primal. According to one old Slavic legend, God took a *banya*, dried himself off, and then created man out of his towel. *Banyas* aren't simply places to wash—they're sources of strength and rejuvenation, and symbols of the vigor and resilience on which they pride themselves as a nation. Russians believe that the traditional *banya* ritual, which includes punctuating the blistering heat of the room with dousings of frigid water and floggings with wet switches, have a host of health benefits. The claims range from strengthening the circulatory and immune systems, to purging toxins, to alleviating arthritis, to just providing an overall sense of well-being.

Modern science remains skeptical about many of these assertions, but it's starting to produce evidence in support of others. One study has suggested that a *banya* a couple of times a week can help you avoid colds, while another has found marked improvement in heart function among people with heart failure who use saunas regularly. And there's no question that since the heat of a *banya* relaxes the muscles, it can help relieve aches and pains. Sweating, meanwhile, helps expel dirt and contaminants from the pores and cleanse the skin, which was and remains a vital part of life in places where wood is plentiful but soap is not. Finally, there's the powerful symbolism in a cold climate of encounters with blistering heat alternated with frigid water, a ritual in which participants defy the elements in the most ostentatious way.

As dusk slips down over Snake Bay, Andrei emerges from the half-light hanging over the beach with an announcement: the *banya* is ready. We spent much of the afternoon gathering wood for its stove. Now, we grab our towels and head down the shore toward the thin trail of smoke rising from the cabin on the water's edge.

The shore is so steep by the *banya* that we have to enter from above, by means of a plank dug into the hillside on one side and nailed to the wall of the shack on the other. We stumble off the board onto a small platform over the water, then push open a creaky door to a small outer room, warm and musty, where we shed our clothes before ducking through a second door into the Venusian chamber beyond. The heat blanches our skin. The air is pungent, thick with an elixir of wood smells—the burning logs, the planks of the walls, the sweet birch switches that Igor has gathered for the flogging. We hunch on crude benches, stacked two high against the wall to reach the hotter heat toward the ceiling. After its initial recoil, our skin slackens. The heat is brutally seductive. We start to cook.

We have the hot stove in the small room. We have the birch switches. The only ingredient we don't have to fill out the traditional *banya* is a bucket of cold water. All we have is the lake itself. And after a few minutes, we're ready. One by one, we step back out onto the landing, into the dusk, and into the water. . . .

Imagine walls shut around you with a thousand tons of pressure. Imagine the oxygen in your lungs being compressed to a solid as the temperature plunges toward absolute zero. Imagine your circulatory system snapping into emergency shutoff, red lights flashing and alarms blaring. Except that the world is suddenly only black and silent, as black and silent as space, and you're floating weightlessly like in space too, which is really, really cool 'cause it's something you've wanted to experience ever since you were a kid and saw John Glenn up there in his space suit, except you don't have a suit on, in fact there's nothing at all between you and this hostile new environment that's going to kill you right quick if you don't get the hell out of there faster than humanly possible so before you've even had a chance to think or feel any of these things, before you've had a chance to wonder whether you've surprised a nearby Baikal seal or disturbed one of those weird perpendicular-swimming golomyanka oil fish or perhaps nearly touched the knobby back of a rare Baikal sturgeon with your toes, you shoot yourself back out of the bone-breaking cold like a sea-launched ICBM, grab hold of the landing like it's the last ship leaving for Earth and haul yourself out like a sea lion onto the rocks at mating time, all awkward and clumsy and with only the crudest dexterity in your already-numb limbs, and you sit there for half a second wondering what the hell just happened. And then you stand up, shake your body like a dog, scream like a howler monkey, and grin.

Back into the *banya*, back out into the lake. Back into the *banya*. . . . Local lore has it that every time you swim in Baikal you add an extra year to your life. If that's true, this evening has given each of us at least another five or six years before we get hit by a bus.

Inside between dives, Igor thrashes us with his wet birch branches. On flesh already stunned by the alternating extremes of temperature, it's like a soothing caress. The sounds caress us as well—the thwack of the switches, the hiss of the stove, Andrei's and Igor's hushed voices in the relaxed cadence of friends who have grown up together. We're intoxicated by sound, smell, and sensation. And through the lace curtain of the *banya*'s one window, above the craggy black peaks of the mountains across the water, a waxing crescent moon hangs in the purple sky.

•

The fire snaps and spits, a million tiny explosions turning fallen larch and cedar into heat, light, and a primeval comfort. Above, countless more explosions fill the night sky with more stars than it seems could possibly exist. A few feet away, a soft finger of Baikal caresses the shore. The air smells of smoke and autumn decay. Here on our tiny cove off a shallow gulf around the back of a mountainous peninsula jutting into the middle of the lake, we're at the tail end of a helix through which powerful Baikal is transformed into something deceptively, seductively serene. Baikal is known as a fierce and restless lake, where a storm can howl out of nowhere, churn up fifteen-foot waves, and swallow ships whole, but here, tonight, it couldn't seem more peaceful.

We're sharing Russian vodka and sweet Romanian wine after our *banya* and a dinner of cheese and sausage sandwiches and birch-fungus tea. Andrei and Igor are softly humming a tune as familiar and soothing as my own bed at home, but so out of place that I don't even recognize it at first. Then it comes to me—the Melodians' "Rivers of Babylon," from the Jamaican film *The Harder They Come*, which Andrei tells me was popular in the USSR in the 1970s, as it was back home in the U.S. The fingernail moon hangs over the highest, sharpest tip of the mountains of the Holy Nose looming to the west, then slips behind the peak, cut in two as if by a shark's tooth, then the trailing edge of light sits for a long moment perched on the precipice like just another star, like a single spark from our fire. Then just the faint glow remains, and the silhouette of the jagged peak against it, then just blackness, nothing at all. Except the stars, which are brilliant beyond belief.

When the fire dims and a deep chill sets in, we all bid each other good night and start to shuffle off toward our tents. Andrei asks me if I'll be warm enough. I assure him that I will be. He and Igor have been regaling us with stories of the Siberian winters of their childhood and of running miles through the subzero temperatures in their underwear while training in the Soviet army. Andrei looks like he could still do it, and I'm reluctant to come off like a thin-blooded American. "If you get cold," he tells me, "you can sleep in the *banya*." *Thanks*, I tell him again, *I'll be fine*. But of course I *am* a thin-blooded American, and my thin, three-season American sleeping bag just isn't up to the demands of early October in Siberia. I'm cold, even in sweaters and long johns, and I sleep badly. In the morning, when Andrei asks me how I slept, I tell him, "not so well," and confess that I was cold. When I ask him how he and Igor slept, he tells me, "We slept well. We slept in the *banya*."

5

Into the Lake—Deep

*In which, during a restless night after a swim in the lake,
we imagine a trip to the bottom of Baikal
and other preposterous things*

D*ress warmly, hold your breath, and take a dive . . .*

You pierce the surface of Baikal at a soft angle and slip like the low rays of the high-latitude sun into a prism of liquid glass.

The water molecules release their bonds with each other to embrace you. Sunlight follows you, wiggles, and scatters; the photons themselves become liquid. Sound becomes a liquid, too, thick and syrupy. Gravity loses its bearings and presses at you from all around. Normal reference points fall away—up and down, left and right—your sense of where you are comes only from subtle changes in light, temperature, and pressure.

This will take some getting used to.

But not to worry, here in the world's oldest lake, still in its youth at twenty-five million years, you've got nothing but time. And if you put on your special magnifying goggles, you'll see that you've got plenty of company, as well. You're surrounded by a haze of tiny creatures, each no longer than a millimeter and a half. They're *Epischura baicalensis*, those elfin shrimp that float through the lake, sucking massive Baikal through their little digestive tracts, feeding on algae and bacteria, pulling out impurities, and helping to keep the lake clean and clear.

Epischura baicalensis are members of a group of organisms known as zooplankton—tiny animals and larva that drift and swim through the water, buffeted about by waves and currents. The miniscule creatures that make up zooplankton live everywhere, in just about every body of water on earth, and like *Epischura baicalensis*, many of them are little shrimp, or copepods. But *Epischura baicalensis* live nowhere else, and apparently can't live anywhere else. It's said that they can't live even in a glass of Baikal water removed from the lake. Perhaps they die of homesickness.

The water surrounding you as you float in Baikal is about as close as you can get in nature to pure H_2O. It's what aquatic scientists call "oligotrophic"—there's very little in the way of nutrients and minerals running off into it from the surrounding landscape, and so a very limited supply of some of the basic building blocks of life. Baikal's epischura are exquisitely adapted to the unique chemistry of their home, and some scientists believe that makes them highly sensitive to subtle changes in the water, as well. Mess with it by adding even small amounts of contaminants, even natural substances like nitrogen and phosphorus, and you could make life very difficult for these little guys, which would in turn make it difficult for just about everything else that lives in the lake. The epischura are what scientists call a keystone species, one that plays a large role in an ecosystem compared to its relative biomass. Their filter feeding helps keep the water clean and clear for other creatures, and they're also a key link in the food chain. Baikal's zooplankton is a major source of food for fish and other higher animals, and the epischura constitute as much as ninety percent of the zooplankton.

Turn your goggles up to a higher power and you can see some of what the epischura graze on: phytoplankton—plants that are even more miniscule, mostly algae—and bacteria. Many of the algae species are diatoms, single-cell organisms with glass-like shells made of silicon dioxide that love cold water and come in crazy geometric shapes that look like they were dreamed up by a god on acid. There are more than 500 species of diatoms in Baikal, each with its own unique form. And like *Epischura baicalensis*, hundreds of them live only here. Diatoms and other algae are at the base of Baikal's food chain—they're what scientists call "primary producers." They turn the sun's energy into food energy, which feeds every other creature here, from epischura to humans.

Turn your head quickly—something's just flashed by out of the corner of your eye. It's a weird fish with a big bony head and no scales—a sculpin. By the latest count, there are thirty-one kinds of sculpins in Baikal, and all of them live only here. Like finches in the Galápagos Islands, sculpins have gone to town in Baikal, evolving over the ages from perhaps just a single species to the nearly three dozen that fill a host of ecological niches throughout the lake. Now, as you start to orient yourself and move around, you notice other glimmers of light all around you. There are more than fifty kinds of fish here. All of them are members of larger families that are common throughout the world, such as salmon and trout, grayling, perch, and burbot, but more than half of the species and subspecies here are unique to Baikal. There are three endemic subspecies of omul, that tasty Siberian relative of salmon and trout that are a mainstay of the local diet, served smoked and salted or boiled with onions and potatoes. There are ancient and massive sturgeons and a bizarre little variety of sculpin called the golomyanka. There's one now, hovering alone right in front of you, the wrong way up.

Golomyankas swim perpendicular to the surface of the water like a seahorse, their heads and tails pointing up and down rather than forward and back. And that's not all that makes these guys very weird creatures. Like their other sculpin cousins, they have no scales. But unlike those other fish, golomyankas are lustrous, as if generating their own soft glow. At times you can see right through parts of them. Like sharks, they're among the very few kinds of fish anywhere that give birth to live young, but unlike sharks, they spawn whole broods, as many as 3,000 at a time. And the largest golomyankas are roughly forty percent fat. It's said that if you caught one and pulled it out of the water, it would virtually dissolve into a gooey puddle. Their oil is high in vitamin A, and for centuries natives have rendered their fat and used it as a treatment for rheumatism and an ointment for stubborn gashes. Under the right conditions, they can even be dried and burned like a candle—hence their colloquial name, the candlefish. There are two species of golomyanka, known straightforwardly enough as the big and the little—although even the big one tops out at less than a foot long—and between them, there are about twice as many golomyankas by weight in Baikal as all other kinds of fish put together. By one estimate, there are almost as many golomyankas in the lake as there are people on earth. But no one has ever successfully harvested golomyankas commercially, because unlike many other fish, they're loners. They rarely swim together, and it's just not worth the trouble catching them one by one. Unless, of course, you're a seal. Baikal's seals, the nerpas, do catch golomyankas—lots of them. Nerpas gobble up as many as forty percent of the golomyanka, and they rely on the fatty fish for as much as eighty percent of their diet.

Like the Baikal epischura and many of the lake's other creatures, golomyankas have evolved to fit precisely into Baikal's unique conditions. In particular, these eccentric fish are very sensitive to temperature—they don't like water much warmer than Baikal's average of four degrees Celsius, and temperatures above ten or twelve degrees Celsius will kill them. That means they tend to avoid the shallow coastal areas and loll about instead in the deep open water. It also means that any significant change in the lake's temperature could cause serious trouble for the golomyanka and the web of creatures with which they interact. On the other hand, golomyanka have a peculiarity that allows them to migrate to the most inhospitable parts of the lake—they don't seem to care a whit about pressure. Most fish can't withstand pressures below more than a few hundred meters, while a very few are specifically adapted to high-pressure, deep-water conditions. But the golomyanka range throughout the water column, from the surface to its deepest reaches, where the pressure is so enormous that if you fired a cannon, the cannonball couldn't get out of the barrel. Golomyanka don't seem bothered at all by this extreme change in conditions.

A human, of course, would be crushed to death long before reaching such depths, if he or she hadn't already drowned or died from hypothermia. There are lots of ways for us unadapted humans to perish quickly in Baikal. And if you were to die here, chances are that your body would never be found. You'd be picked at by some of the 300 unique Baikal species of gammarid shrimp, the epischura's bigger cousins. Bacteria would go to work on you. All manner of other critters would join in the feast. Baikal is so devoid of organic matter and minerals that the creatures here ravenously consume nearly everything that finds its way into the lake. Researchers say it's rare to find so much as a fish skeleton or a stray clamshell on the bottom. It's said that the body of an unfortunate human would be gone within two days.

But that's not you. Along with your special goggles, you've been outfitted with a special suit. Temperature isn't a problem, pressure isn't a problem, little nibbling shrimp aren't a problem. You're heading to the bottom of the lake, alive and in one piece.

As you drift downward, the water occasionally sparkles and flashes as a glint of sunlight catches a copepod or a fish. Baikal's exceptional clarity allows abundant light to penetrate as far as forty meters, or more than 130 feet, depending on the time of year. By fifty meters down, the light has thinned considerably—only about five percent of the sun's energy can penetrate this deep. But these are the most energetic of the sun's visible rays, the ones that plants need to photosynthesize. So even here, algae can live, and life-sustaining oxygen is being produced. You're in the deep-water lake, what some scientists call the "true" Baikal.

The temperature changes as you descend, as well. You're taking your dive in the summer, so the temperature falls from the sun-warmed surface layers until you reach somewhere between 250 and 300 meters. If it were winter, the temperature below the frozen surface would rise until you reach about the same depth. The rest of the way down, regardless of the season, the water hovers around 3.9 degrees Celsius.

At 450 meters, parts of the lake bottom are covered with an eerie lattice of sinuous white fibers—a web of bacteria, perhaps sustained by methane seeping from below the lakeshore.

The light fades still further as you descend, the deepening water a giant dimmer switch on the sun. At 500 meters, the lake seems as black as crude oil, but even here a Soviet spacecraft orbiting above the lake was able to discern a few last vestiges of light, deeper than in nearly every other lake in the world. Other experiments with photographic plates have captured a rogue photon or two even deeper still—at 1,500 meters, almost at the bottom of the abyss. The place you're now approaching.

Nearing the lake's floor, you pass through a pocket of warmer water. The bottom of Baikal is rent with cracks and fissures, some of which spew superheated water from the earth's crust, the same stuff that blasts out of Yellowstone's geysers and seeps out in hot springs all over the planet. Researchers have only recently discovered these thermal vents and believe the conditions around them, including the presence of thermophilic bacteria, are similar to those along the spreading zones of the oceans—another reason some think that Baikal is really more an infant ocean than a lake.

Finally, you settle onto the bottom, startled, for a moment, by the feel of something solid beneath you. Solid, but soft—the muck of the millennia oozing through your toes, the accumulation of a slow-motion rain of the few nearly invisible bits of silt and dust and diatom shells that somehow manage to slip through Baikal's fine biological filter. Your feet settle into fresh lake bottom that's already ancient—the top couple of inches alone take you back to the days before Spafary and Avvakum, before Genghis Khan, before the first tsars. You're standing on the deepest spot on any of the world's landmasses, more than a kilometer and a half below the surface of the lake and almost 1,200 meters below sea level.

It's darker than space down here, and under a mile-thick blanket of water it's as still and silent as any place on the planet. Here at the bottom of Baikal, it's as if nothing ever existed or ever will. But it is alive. The muck. The water. The lake itself.

You feel it before you hear it—a dull shudder becomes an abyssal groan becomes an apocalyptic roar that barrels through the water and collapses your legs under you as the plates along the Baikal rift crack and shift like the vertebra of a continent-sized beast turning in its sleep. One of Baikal's frequent earthquakes is reconfiguring the lake's floor, as if the lake is determined to keep scientists busy, to keep its depth and breadth a moving target.

As the shudder finally recedes, you pick yourself up, switch on your headlamp, and find that you've got company in this place where it seems impossible that anything could live, where the pressure is unbearable and there has never been a ray of natural light. It seems impossible, but there it is: Hauling yourself through the gloom, you encounter globular gray flatworms and white gammarid shrimp, scouring the floor for tiny scraps of nutritive debris, completely blind but guided by highly developed senses of touch and smell. Perhaps you'll encounter a curious sculpin of the family *Abyssocottidae* that haunts the lake's deepest stretches and is among the most *abyssal* fish anywhere. You might even catch sight of a wandering golomyanka. Life is sparse down here, but a few hearty animals are able to scratch out a living, more than twice as far below the surface as in any other lake.

They may not be the most engaging company, but the creatures here more than 1,600 meters below Baikal's surface sure beat what you'll find in the depths of the world's next-deepest lakes. At the bottom of the only two other lakes more than 700 meters deep—Baikal's East African cousins Tanganyika and Malawi—your only company would be sulfur-emitting bacteria. Tanganyika is roughly 1,470 meters deep, and Malawi is roughly 705 meters, but animal life in both of these lakes is restricted to a surface layer of only about 250 meters, below which is nothing but a dead zone. Baikal's next closest peer with an abyss fit for habitation is the Great Slave Lake, in Canada's Northwest Territories, a mere 614 meters deep.

The difference between Baikal and its closest relatives isn't the water per se—it's the oxygen. As we've discovered, animals can adapt to live in a world without light, a world of crushing pressure. But what they can't adapt to is a world without oxygen. Free oxygen—O_2—is a highly reactive gas that helps animals break down other substances and use the energy embodied in them, and every creature on earth save a few kinds of bacteria needs it. As it happens, oxygen is the most abundant element on earth. Almost half of the planet's crust is made up of oxygen, in the form of mineral oxides—things we know mostly as rocks—while the water that covers most of its surface is roughly ninety percent oxygen by weight—two light hydrogen atoms bound to one heavy oxygen atom. But like the oxygen in rocks, the oxygen in water is useless to animals by itself because they can't separate it from the hydrogen; it's what scientists describe as "biologically unavailable" to animals. Water is indispensable to the workings of all known organisms as a solvent and as a fluid medium for transporting nutrients and other substances, but fish and clams and worms and every other kind of aquatic animal can actually live in water only if it contains something else: tiny bubbles of free oxygen gas—*dissolved* oxygen, squeezed in among the water molecules.

Much of this oxygen gets into water from the atmosphere, which is roughly twenty percent oxygen, when wind and waves mix up the air and the surface water like a big eggbeater. And some of it comes from algae and other aquatic plants, which use the biological alchemy of photosynthesis to break apart water molecules, combine their hydrogen with dissolved carbon dioxide to form the sugars that they use as food, and release O_2 as a waste product—dissolved oxygen, now biologically available.

With their vast surface area and global circulation currents, the world's oceans are full of dissolved oxygen, top to bottom. But the oxygen supply in the much smaller systems of lakes is much more limited, and it's often confined to the upper layers of the water column reached by the sun and mixed by the wind. Even many shallow lakes don't have any oxygen below a relatively thin surface layer, and hardly any deep lakes do.

But here you are, in the deepest of lakes, and there they are in front of you, those weird little colorless creatures scrounging around in the muck and breathing in tiny bubbles of oxygen, and even though they probably aren't concerned with how the stuff gets here, you're a human, a curious creature, and you have to ask, *How does that stuff get here?* And the best answer that scientists seem to have come up with is this: *We still don't really know.* And it's possible that you and I will be dead before they figure it out. The science of deep-water lakes in general still isn't very well understood, and as we know, our lake is particularly mysterious.

But you don't have to be a scientist to figure out that one key factor is temperature. All you have to do is take a look at the best-studied of the world's other super-deep lakes. The exact number is in dispute, but there are probably fewer than a dozen lakes more than 500 meters deep, and of those, scientists have taken a close look at only a half a dozen. Two of these—Tanganyika and Malawi—are equatorial, warm-water lakes, and they're dead not far below the surface. The rest—Canada's Great Slave Lake, Crater Lake in Oregon, Lake Tahoe on the California-Nevada border, and Baikal—are all cold-water lakes, and they all support life all the way to the bottom. Temperature clearly makes a crucial difference.

The reason for this is that water is not a uniform substance. Variations in its temperature affect its density, and its density can determine whether or not the water in a lake mixes substantially. Water is heaviest at 3.9 degrees Celsius, or about thirty-nine degrees Fahrenheit, what's known as its temperature of maximum density. In tropical regions like East Africa, the surface water of lakes generally stays well above this point. Their warm climate keeps these lakes stratified—warm, light, and oxygenated water above, and cold, heavy, and anoxic water below. But in cooler regions like northern Canada, the mountains of the western U.S., and Siberia, the density of water in a lake is more dynamic, as it warms and cools with the seasons. When it reaches that 3.9-degree threshold and gets a little nudge from the wind, heavy surface water starts to sink and becomes a liquid conveyor belt, carrying a cargo of dissolved gases, nutrients, and other resources into the depths. Here in Baikal, this happens every spring and fall—Siberia's seasonal temperature changes cause the lake's upper reaches to turn over twice a year, bringing life-giving dissolved oxygen into the deep water.

For years, many Baikal researchers believed that this was pretty much all there was to it—that changes in temperature and density explained the presence of dissolved oxygen all the way to the bottom of the lake. Some still believe this. But scientists studying the movement of water in the lake now believe that temperature alone doesn't solve the riddle. For one thing, they invoke a basic physical principle—that unless something else is going on, even the densest fresh water can sink only until it reaches a layer of water with the same density, which in Baikal is at most about 300 meters down. And these scientists haven't been able to find anything else going on that suggests that temperature drives mixing deeper in the lake. Researchers have also discovered that the water down here at the bottom of Baikal circulates not twice a year but roughly every ten years or so. Seasonal, temperature-driven mixing, these scientists have said, is out as the major conveyor of dissolved oxygen to the depths of the lake.

What's in, they say, is salinity. As we've heard, the water here in Baikal is extremely pure—its salt content is minute even compared to other freshwater systems. But a team of researchers has found that the water flowing into Baikal from the Selenga River and its other major tributaries is ever so slightly saltier than the water already in the lake. And as with temperature, the salinity of water affects its density—saltier water is heavier. The difference in salinity between Baikal's tributaries and the lake itself is tiny, these researchers say, but it's enough to make the river water ever so slightly heavier, as well, and when the saltier river water is also cold enough, its increased density causes it to sink beneath Baikal's main body of water, bringing oxygen from the surface with it. As with so much else about Baikal, the details of how this water then circulates through the lake remains obscure, but these scientists believe this is the overall process that makes these deepest reaches of the lake fit for habitation.

Case closed? Well, of course not. Other scientists have since discovered seasonal plumes of cold water flowing down here into some of the deepest reaches of the lake. And they've found that these "cold intrusions," as they call them, aren't significantly saltier than the rest of the lake, which, they say, means that they almost certainly don't come from Baikal's tributaries. Instead, these researchers attribute the jets of cold water to such well-known phenomena as *thermobaric instability* . . . *Ekman pumping* . . . and *coast-parallel cyclonic currents*.

Look them up, if you want. For myself, I'm content to stop there for the time being. Baikal guards its secrets tightly, and the scientific exploration and debate are certain to go on for years. But what is certain is this: Baikal is the only terrestrial body of water in which you can descend, as you've just done, to 1,000 meters, 1,500, and beyond, to the deepest, darkest place on the world's continents, and still find oxygen in the water, and things wiggling between your toes.

Oxygen sustains these and Baikal's other strange creatures, but it was evolution that created them. It's the source of Baikal's riches. Just as Baikal started as a far more ordinary body of water, a small depression that was merely part of a much larger ecosystem, the first animals and plants here were ordinary as well, indistinguishable from their nearby relatives. But as Baikal changed ever so slowly over the eons, so did its residents.

Every so often, something goes wrong in the copying of the DNA in reproductive cells. A tiny error is made, and this mistake is passed on to the next generation. This happens at a more or less regular rate, in all species, everywhere. Most of the time, these genetic changes are meaningless—they don't affect the ability of the organism to survive. Occasionally, they can be harmful, making an organism less able to survive. But every now and then, a mutation will make an organism more able to survive—it gains a new tool that allows it to exploit a new niche or make use of a new resource, and that gives it an edge over its neighbors. And at that point, natural selection kicks in, sorting out the creatures that adapt well to their changing environment from those that don't. Eventually, when a series of mutations and adaptations cause a creature to become so distinct from its relatives that it can't breed with them, you have a new species.

These kinds of changes generally take place over huge sweeps of time—hundreds of thousands, even millions of years. They generally require complex areas, in which organisms must respond to a range of conditions. And they're aided significantly by the emergence of natural barriers like a mountain range or an ocean. Baikal has each of these elements, in spades—a time frame of at least twenty-five million years, a large variety of conditions, and the high mountain ranges that have grown up around the basin, cutting it off from the surrounding landscape. Together, these have created what Grigory Galazy, perhaps the best known of all Baikal researchers, called "a gigantic natural laboratory and center of origin of species."

Galazy's allusion to Charles Darwin probably wasn't accidental. Darwin's discovery of a host of previously unknown creatures in the Galápagos Islands, including thirteen species of finches, helped give birth to his theory of evolution by natural selection, laid out for the first time in *On the Origin of Species*. Their isolation and diverse habitat niches made the Galápagos a natural laboratory, and the same forces at work there have achieved the same result here in Baikal, although on a far grander scale than what Darwin saw. If the *Beagle* had brought Darwin here to Siberia rather than to South America, Baikal would have become the archetypal evolutionary hothouse. Here in Baikal, random mutation + natural selection + a large number of diverse niches + isolation + time = not thirteen or even dozens but roughly 1,750 unique kinds of organisms.

But enough of this Dr. Science stuff. Back to our dive.

If you really had a special suit for swimming in this extraordinary menagerie, it might be made of this: a heavy layer of specially designed insulation surrounded by a tough, impermeable shell covered with a thick forest of heat-trapping fibers. And if you wore it, you might look like this:

For humans and most other warm-blooded animals, Baikal's frigid waters are utterly inhospitable. This is true even in the summertime, when surface temperatures in a few spots can peak in the twenties Celsius, or roughly seventy degrees Fahrenheit, but when capricious currents and winds can quickly disperse these pockets of warmth. Year-round, the surface temperature of the lake averages the same as in the deeper lake, about four degrees Celsius, or forty degrees Fahrenheit, cold enough to render an unprotected person unconscious in as little as fifteen minutes, and kill him or her in as little as thirty. For a human, an extended swim would be inadvisable. But if you had a special suit like this, that is, if you were a seal, there couldn't be a more fantastic place for swimming. Just ask them: of all the world's lakes, seals have chosen to take up residence in just one, and this is it.

The nerpa, the Baikal seal, is the world's only freshwater pinniped species. It's not that other seals can't live in fresh water. They often venture up rivers in search of food, and some populations are even stranded in lakes from time to time when sea levels fall, as happened in the Baltic region and northern Canada after the last ice age. But these small, isolated populations remain genetically indistinct from their ocean-going relatives. The ancestors of the nerpa, on the other hand, a few adventurous Arctic ringed seals, made their way to Baikal on their own, more than 3,000 river kilometers from the nearest sea, took up residence, and evolved over the ages into a distinct species, with their own unique morphology and habits. As far as we know, this is the only time such a thing has happened. Lakes that might be big enough to support viable populations of big predators like seals are nearly all blocked off to access from the sea by waterfalls and rapids. And as we've heard, few lakes last longer than 10,000 years or so, so most are just too ephemeral for big animals with long life cycles to get much of a foothold and start evolving before the lakes disappear. But Baikal seems to be uniquely suited for seals to visit and then to take up long-term residence. Before humans blocked off its outlet half a century ago, it was accessible to the sea; it's big; and it's been around for a long time.

No one's quite sure what route the nerpas' ancestors took here—it's possible that the lake's outflow has shifted over the ages—but the likeliest scenario is that a few Arctic ringed seals followed some fish up the Yenisei River from their home in the Arctic Ocean sometime between half a million and a million years ago, and just kept going. *Up the Yenisei, take a left at the Angara, the lake's dead ahead, about five hundred miles, can't miss it....* However it was that they got here, the seals found the lake's size, temperature, and depth to their liking and settled in, eventually adapting to Baikal's fresh water and becoming their own distinct species.

You might think of nerpas as "lake beagles," diminutive versions of the "sea dogs" found in oceans the world over. Nerpas are among the smallest of seals, less than a meter and half long when fully grown and weighing in at no more than seventy kilograms. But they tend to be long-lived—some graybeards have been known to surpass fifty years—perhaps because until humans came along, their only predators were brown bears that an unlucky seal would occasionally encounter along Baikal's shore or in an ice den, or birds that might prey on an exposed pup. Their longevity may in part be a result of good cardiovascular exercise, as well—nerpas love to swim. They dart through Baikal at speeds of up to twenty-five kilometers an hour, and plunge to depths of 300 meters. Their thick layers of fur and fat—that special suit—allow them to live most of their lives in the frigid water, and their high-capacity circulatory systems let them to dive for three-quarters of an hour at a time. And every fall they migrate not south but north, to the coldest stretches of the lake, where they scratch air holes in the ice with their sharp claws, make their dens, and bear their young in the snow on Baikal's frozen surface.

To see a one of them, let's go climb a mountain.

The deepest spot in Baikal, where you've been standing with your feet in the muck throughout this science lesson, is in the middle of its three basins. Not far to the north, the central basin ends at a steep underwater ridge, known as the Akademichesky Range. To the southwest, the ridge breaks through the surface entirely to form Olkhon Island, a fifty-kilometer-long ragged block of stone that many Buryats consider to be the most sacred part of Baikal. To the northeast, the ridge emerges again to form the small Ushkani Islands and the Holy Nose Peninsula. Between these, the Akademichesky Range rises at one point to just 260 meters below the surface. If we hike up there, we might catch site of a nerpa, gliding through the sea-sky.

Above the highest peak of these submerged mountains, a small pod of nerpas dart through the again-luminous water like fat swallows with their wings tucked. As you push off the ridge and rise toward the surface, one of them eyes you cautiously from a distance, and then, forgetting for a moment that its relatives have long been hunted by creatures like you, it tentatively approaches, its curiosity about this unfamiliar creature as strong as yours about it. Finally, it stops and hovers in the water, barely an arm's length away, its alert, intelligent dog's eyes fixated on yours, each of you testing the bounds of trust and fear to catch a glimpse of something familiar within the other. You hang there suspended in time and space, transfixed by this flash of recognition in something so unknown, until, in response to some cue undetectable by the human ear, the seal begins to edge away, stopping every few meters to look back, until it eventually rejoins the company of its own kind and you're left suspended, alone, in the liquid glow of the sunlight from the nearing surface.

To see creatures like this, to encounter them face to face, is to be reminded of the sublime power of nature, of the mysterious and wondrous process through which the blind biochemical processes of DNA replication, mutation, and evolution through natural selection conspire to produce things that seem to utterly transcend these mundane forces—curiosity, consciousness, beauty, complexity, the beauty *of* complexity, of the unexpected and unknowable, of seeming perfection amid constant change. You want to understand it all, and you're in love with the fact that you can't understand it all—that part of all this beauty is the very existence of mystery, of gaps recognized but unbridgeable. You understand why some people, grasping for an explanation, for the sense of meaning that defines us as humans, punt, and chalk it all up to

God. The existence of nerpas, of sea dogs in this far-inland freshwater sea, knocks the mind for a loop and leaves you laughing at the creativity and whimsy of nature. You're amazed by what nature is capable of, and you're reassured that there are still places where you can see evidence of this. What you don't want to think about is the fact that the nerpa population is shrinking. You don't want to think about this, but you have to, because not to think about it might mean one day only being able to imagine these creatures rather than to see them in the flesh and fur, being unable look into their eyes and recognize something at once unknowable and deeply familiar.

Humans and nerpas have lived more or less in equilibrium, if not harmony, for thousands of years. The Kurykany petroglyphs on Baikal's shores suggest that the seals have been an important part of human cultures as long as people have been here, contributing their meat, their fur, and their oil to the local human economy. But today, that relationship seems to be slipping out of balance. Hunting seems to be colliding with other unnatural forces to put the seals' future in jeopardy.

No one knows how many nerpas there are in Baikal these days. A government survey in 1994 estimated that there were roughly 100,000, but studies by others since have produced significantly lower estimates, ranging from 85,000 to as few as 55,000. Between an officially sanctioned hunt, illegal poaching, and unintended deaths in fishing equipment, more than 10,000 nerpas a year may have been directly killed by humans in the late 1990s, including an especially high proportion of soft-furred pups. The government recently lowered the legal hunt from 6,000 to 3,500, but little is done to enforce the limit, and in the current difficult economy, poaching is reportedly on the rise.

Meanwhile, under pressure from hunters in their traditional denning areas in the north of the lake, many nerpas have begun wintering farther south, where they're encountering another growing problem, also likely man-made—a warming climate. Spring has generally been coming earlier to Baikal in recent years as the global atmosphere warms under the influence of industrial emissions, and this can destroy nerpas' dens before the young are ready to emerge, leaving them vulnerable to predators and the elements. At the same time, on-shore habitat is being lost to development, with unknown impacts on the seals. And then there's pollution. Scientists have recently found high levels of industrial chemicals in nerpa blubber. Many observers believe the contamination may be causing chronic reproductive and other health problems in the seals, and that it has been responsible for the deaths of thousands of nerpas in three mass die-offs since the late 1980s.

As with their overall numbers, no one knows the threshold of concern, the number below which the nerpas' survival as a species might be in danger. Some fear it may have already been reached; others believe that there's still no cause for alarm. The question is whether, in a country largely unprepared to deal with such challenges, enough will be done to find out before it's too late.

The nerpas have slipped away, and you float farther upward, and toward the lake's shore. You pass through a school of omul, a silver cloud that moves through the water as if a single organism. As you approach the coastal shelf, you find yourself wandering in the canopy of a forest of bright green, cactus-like sponges and huge, colorful worms, coursed by underwater valleys and canyons inhabited by some of Baikal's more than 100 unique species of mollusks and 300 unique species of gammarid shrimp—one of the largest examples in the world of what evolutionary biologists call adaptive radiation. As you float over a patch of sponge forest, you catch sight of one of the gammarids hopping along the bottom like a slow-motion jack rabbit—*Acanthogammarus victorii*, one of the largest crustaceans in the lake, seven centimeters long, its arched body covered with spikes like some kind of medieval weapon. On another day you might be lucky enough to encounter an underwater behemoth, the endangered Baikal sturgeon, an ambling, armored giant that grew up to 125 kilograms before humans started to hunt it aggressively. Finally, you break the surface of the water and haul yourself out onto a thin gravel beach, back into contact with those nearly forgotten elements, earth and air. You shed your diving suit in the Siberian sun, gaze back out across the glimmering surface of the hidden world of Baikal, and make your way toward the campfire, where your companions have already prepared your morning cup of birch-fungus tea.

6

Buryatia, in Black & White and Color

*In which we recall our arrival in Ulan-Ude,
our trip up the Selenga River,
and our encounter with a community of* **Raskolniki**

The trail along the eastern shore of the Holy Nose south of our campsite is maybe a foot wide, just a narrow track of compacted leaves and dirt, a path that could just as easily have been made by centuries of hooves and paws as by shod human feet. And perhaps it was. I've walked such trails in the Arctic, etched into the tundra by caribou and wolves and musk oxen. It's a humbling and exhilarating experience, the trails a simple but stark reminder that you are in someone else's habitat and that humans are not the only species to have left their mark on the planet. This one weaves between thick-barked evergreens and leathery aspens, clinging precariously to a slope that could easily throw a clumsy hominid to the waves fifty or more feet below. Andrei is lost in the thickets ahead, charging on to the next clearing, at which he'll wait for us, again. James, Elisa, Chanda, and I keep to a more leisurely pace, in no more of a hurry to see the next sparkling facet of Baikal than this one, or to catch a toe on the next stone or gnarled root than the previous one. Igor stayed behind with our stuff at the campsite, to be picked up by the Lonesome Boatman. We'll rendezvous with them farther down the coast this afternoon.

Yesterday's ragged clouds blew out in the evening, and the sky over Baikal today has the clarity of vodka and carries a cool, yellowish luminescence, as if after their ninety-three million mile dash the sun's photons have slowed down to admire the little corner of the solar system that they've been lucky enough to have been sent to. There is no sign that any of the billions of humans who have ever lived have set foot in this place. We walk mostly in silence.

From high above the lake, the trail drops down to the water, the steep slope giving way ahead to a thin, gracefully arcing beach dividing the lake from a narrow stand of wispy wetland trees and a soft amber field beyond. On the hard trail behind us, we could only imagine what creatures may have traversed the same route before us, but here on the soft sand of the beach, local residents have left clear evidence of their presence, and perhaps a tale of a day's drama. A set of small, rounded hoof prints follows the waterline along the beach—the path of a small ungulate, maybe even a now-rare musk deer. Before long this trail is joined by another set of tracks, each print following just inches behind each hoof mark. With their four rounded pads and pointed tips from permanently extended claws, these are the unmistakable tracks of a canine. A few wolves still prowl Baikal's forests, and one of them seems to have recently paid a visit to this stretch of waterfront, quite possibly on the trail of the deer. As the two sets of tracks continue in lockstep down the beach, I imagine the wolf's nose and whiskers twitching as it scans the air for the scent of the deer, and perhaps a few hundred meters ahead the deer's ears doing the same as it picks up the almost imperceptible sound of its pursuer's soft paws on the sand. But before the story reaches a climax, the tracks veer up the beach and disappear into the woods, leaving us only to imagine the outcome.

Farther along, we find the tracks of a small cat, birds of various sizes, a brown bear. Here on this rare stretch of flat shoreline, we see the traces of a day's business at Baikal. Despite what Melnikov had told us back at the park headquarters about the paucity of wildlife here, some of its aboriginal residents clearly still reside in this part of the park, at least, and our beach seems a sort of marketplace for all manner of them, each coming to the lake in search of its daily supply of food, drink, perhaps even entertainment, some wary of being spotted in such a public place, others doing the watching, some sneaking in under cover of darkness, others brazenly showing themselves in full daylight, each an integral part of the natural economy of this place. And amid the animal tracks, I find the first evidence for miles of my own species, an artifact that would seem less randomly placed if it were a meteor fragment—two little red and white interlocking Lego bricks, washed ashore from who knows where. Severobaikalsk at the head of the lake? Ulan-Ude up the Selenga River? Little Ust-Barguzin, just down the coast? I pocket them to take home, a gift from a Siberian child to my Lego-obsessed ten-year-old friend Adam in Seattle.

A kilometer or so down the beach, a stream emerges from the trees and runs parallel to the shore for a while, then turns abruptly toward the lake and cuts the beach in two. Andrei waits at the breach for the rest of us to catch up. When we do, we sit for a bit, munch on our pine nuts, and listen to the little river meeting the big lake. After a few minutes, we all take off our boots and socks, roll up our pants, and ford the river, frigid and knee deep—all but Andrei, who, rather than rolling up his pants, sheds them altogether and wades across in his underwear. On the far side, he slips his pants back on and quickly is back out ahead of the group, perhaps challenging the rest of us to pick up the pace so we don't keep the boatman waiting. *He could just tell us*, I'm thinking, but this seems to be Andrei's way—not at all unfriendly but certainly taciturn, rarely initiating conversation, usually sharing information only when we ask him. But it's been no real surprise to find him this way in person—he's sometimes been frustratingly uncommunicative ever since our first contact several months ago, and I wasn't at all sure that our planned rendezvous would take place until we actually saw him in the half-light of the Ulan-Ude train station a couple of mornings ago.

•

"Everything is possible," Andrei had told me in that email a few months back, but since then we had corresponded only haltingly, and the human chain connecting us to him at times seemed awfully weak. The chain began with an environmental group called Baikal Watch, run out of David Brower's Earth Island Institute in San Francisco, which I'd found on the Internet when I first began thinking about this trip. A phone call to their offices revealed the group basically to be the work of a single tireless and generous guy named Gary Cook, who became a lynchpin of our entire endeavor. Gary gave me an email address for a man that he said was the best guide that he knew in the Baikal region, Andrei Suknev. Andrei lived in Ulan-Ude. "Ulan-Where? Baatar?" I had to get out my atlas. Ulaanbaatar is the capital of Mongolia. Ulan-Ude, I found out, is the capital of Russia's Buryat Republic, the semiautonomous region between Baikal and the Mongolian border. Further reading revealed the city to be the distinguished site of the largest Lenin head on the planet. I found it hard to believe that the Internet had reached this outpost, but of course it's reached nearly everywhere that has telephones, which is, well, nearly everywhere, even Ulan-Ude. I sent off a query and got a quick response, as if it had come from a cubicle down the hall: "I'll be lucky to help you."

But if the technology was dependable, I soon came to wonder about Andrei himself. His communications were somewhat cryptic, and he would disappear entirely for weeks at a time, leaving key questions unanswered and crucial details unconfirmed. It was nerve-wracking. But as we'd have to do throughout this journey, there was little James and I could do but take it on faith that Gary's recommendation would be borne out. It was either that or stay home. We were planning the trip in a hurry and had little time or opportunity for comparison shopping.

And, of course, the recommendation was borne out. There Andrei had been, as we stumbled down the metal steps of our overnight train from Irkutsk into the bitter predawn cold of Ulan-Ude's austere concrete station—fortyish and thin, with a woolen hat and squarish glasses straight out of 1975, holding a sign that read PETER TOMSON, just as he'd promised.

He greeted us with barely more than a "Hello, nice to meet you" and then motioned for us to follow him through the dark corridors of the station to the darker parking lot beyond. Under normal circumstances such an introduction to someone we were going to spend the better part of a week with might've been a little off-putting, but in this case James and I were too tired to be put off. Between the late departure the night before, the herky-jerky trip, and the predawn arrival, we'd barely slept on the overnight train from Irkutsk. The only good thing about it had been the beautiful and unusually gracious young *provodnitsa*, the female train attendant who had welcomed us onto the train, taken us to our compartment, turned down our bedding, and offered us tea before flashing an enchanting smile and bidding us *dobry vecher*—good night. But by morning—or should I say by our arrival in Ulan-Ude, because even though it was 6:45 A.M. it could by no rights be called morning—lovely Liudmila, or whatever her name was, had been replaced by a severe and scolding senior attendant, which I only found out when she pounded on the door of the bathroom to shoo me out shortly after I'd stumbled there half asleep to do my bleary-eyed morning business. The toilets on Russian trains dump directly onto the tracks, you see, and apparently we'd just entered the restricted "no-flush" zone outside the city.

At the station, Andrei ushered us into a white Toyota van and headed out into the gloomy Buryat dawn. As the light grew, it revealed a city that seemed to have been cast entirely out of the same drab concrete forms as the station. We didn't pass a single structure that looked as if it had been designed for human habitation.

I'd learned since gathering my initial intelligence about the Lenin head that Ulan-Ude has in fact had a long and somewhat celebrated history. It was established in the seventeenth century as *Verkhne-Udinsk*, which roughly translates as "Upper Uda Town," after the river that flows through the city. It originally served as a Cossack garrison and collection center for *yasak*, or fur tribute to the tsars from local Buryats and other natives, and soon grew into a trading center and meeting place for merchants from the Far East and European Russia.

Meanwhile, as the Buryats slowly relinquished their nomadic lifestyle under the influence of the Russians, the city became a focal point of Buryat culture and their adopted religion, Buddhism. With the arrival of the Trans-Siberian in the late nineteenth century, the city ballooned into a sprawling railroad town, and with the Soviets came a new name—Ulan-Ude, or "Red Ude"—and, apparently, a concerted effort to efface most of the city's previous identity. A few remnants of earlier times are said to remain, but we won't see them on this visit.

Fifteen or so minutes in Andrei's van had us out of the city and turning off a country road onto a long dirt driveway that ended at the steps to a low wooden building of distinctly Asian design, the first such structure we'd seen in Russia. Andrei had told us that we would spend our first night at what he said was a "traditional Tibetan health clinic," and apparently this was it. What he hadn't told us was why we were here now, just past sunrise, or what we'd be doing later in the day. In fact, he hadn't told us much at all. But our sense of disorientation and the same chronic, low-level unease that we'd been hauling across Russia was trumped by sleepiness—James and I were both still in too much of a stupor to ask or really even care what was going on. And then there was this: We were in Andrei's hands now. We'd given ourselves over to him and were just going to have to trust in his wisdom. This was my new mental bumper sticker: *Let Go and Let Guide . . .*

The lobby of the clinic was appointed with the kind of cheap wicker and vinyl furniture that you might find at an old New Hampshire cabin, and after a few minutes we were greeted by a short, stout Buryat woman in a white coat, who led us to our room. It was a tiny chamber with two narrow sagging beds with threadbare blankets, a window with a fraying curtain, and a couple of bath towels the size and texture of worn dishrags. Gary Cook had told me this place was an example of the resurgent interest in traditional Buryat medicine, similar in its teachings and methods to Tibetan medicine, and he'd said that this resurgence was due in part to the collapse of Russia's conventional medical system. I hoped not to see the inside of any Russian hospitals, but I found it hard to believe that they're more hard up than this sorry place. Cockroaches scurried everywhere. When I went to close the curtain, it tore off its rod. And later, when I turned on the shower, the pipes gave a tired shudder and the ceiling around the showerhead collapsed on me in a rain of plaster.

As we settled in, Andrei finally let us in on some of the day's plans, although in our still half-awake state only a few key words registered—"Sleep . . . breakfast . . . I return at noon."

A couple of hours later we were up, somewhat refreshed and staring down into bowls of two unfamiliar substances, one white and goopy, the other yellow and lumpy. Breakfast—and another leap of faith. The white stuff was thick and slightly sour, with a taste and texture somewhere between yogurt and ricotta cheese, which we took to be the famous Central Asian favorite *kumiss*, or fermented mare's milk. The yellow stuff, meanwhile, seemed a cross between grits and tapioca pudding—salty and sweet, smooth and grainy, a tasty porridge whose contents I still hope to discover someday. But there was no one who could tell us about either one. The staff was sort of like elves—we could see the results of their work, but other than the woman who welcomed us, we never actually saw them. Not that any of them were likely to have spoken any English even if we had seen them. We could've mustered *Pozhaluista, chto eto?*—"Please, what's this?"—but I'm pretty sure we wouldn't have been able to understand their response. And when Andrei returned at noon to gather us up for the first day of our exploration of Buryatia, he couldn't tell us what the porridge was, either. Nor could he tell us much about the kinds of illnesses treated here or the kinds of therapies used, or much else about the place.

We would return late that evening and leave again early the next morning, and that would be all we would see and learn about this traditional Buryat health clinic. I almost found myself wishing that the mystery breakfast would make me sick, so I could get a glimpse of some of their treatments. Almost.

•

Ulan-Ude fell away like crumbling gray chalk as we headed south along a narrow strip of pavement, the city replaced by the broad, nearly treeless plain between the Khamar-Daban Mountains and the Selenga River, and less than an hour after the yellow porridge James and I were standing before two bright yellow tigers perched on blue concrete blocks in front of a small white brick building with brilliant red, green, blue, and yellow trim and a sweeping, three-tiered golden roof. This was the main temple of the Ivolginsk Datsan, by local accounts the only center of Buddhist study and worship in all of Russia to have made it through the seventy-plus years of Soviet rule. The local story, confirmed to one degree or another by various guidebooks, is that after Stalin closed and bulldozed most of the country's other temples, he allowed this one to reopen as a symbol of the Soviet Union's embrace of cultural and religious diversity. Now, with the great changes of the last fifteen years, the complex of several dozen windswept buildings has become a center for the rebirth of Buddhism and Buryat culture.

Buddhism first descended to the plains of Buryatia from Tibet in the sixteenth century, and the nontheistic belief system, which holds that suffering can be transcended through right-thinking and the abandonment of desires, settled in relatively comfortably alongside the region's traditional Shamanist beliefs, in which enlightened shamans could harness and control the power of the spirits that live in all things. Within a century or so, Buddhism was a central part of Buryat identity, and neither the powerful agents of Russian Orthodox Christianity nor those of Soviet atheism were able to dislodge it. Again today, after decades of repression of their religion, most Buryats consider themselves Buddhists, and many who are able make pilgrimages to this place. The Dalai Lama, one of our guidebooks tells us, has visited five times.

We followed a trickle of visitors past the grinning concrete tigers and two fat, scowling dragons by the steps and up into the temple, and as we entered I was struck by the ways in which this place was at once completely different from and utterly the same as the Buddhist temples we'd seen a couple of weeks earlier in Japan, in the same way that, say, an Irish wolfhound and a toy Yorkshire terrier are completely different but utterly the same—the same basic design, springing from the same evolutionary origin, but adapted to reflect the specific values and resources of the local human culture, and so utterly distinct in their execution. The Japanese and Buryat versions are both boxy buildings with multiple, low-pitched roofs sweeping outward toward the corners like the wings of great birds, only many of the Japanese temples are massive, such as Todaiji in the ancient capital of Nara, said to be the largest wooden structure in the world, while this one was somewhat more modest at about the size of your average American three-car garage. Inside, the temples share roughly the same floor plan—one large room with a representation of the Buddha in the middle, around which visitors walk in a clockwise circle, with the outer reaches of the room crammed with other images of the Buddha and other figures, stylized flowers, candles, and lanterns. But while the items in the Japanese temples are all meticulously crafted of bronze, lacquer, and ebony and everything is placed with the most precise atten-tion to detail, here the images and artistry are cruder, the materials are mostly clay, paint, and paper, and the objects are spread almost haphazardly throughout the temple. And while the Japanese temples are dark and brooding, this one is bright and airy, with bold swatches of color and big, sunlit windows.

Outside the temple, we passed an occasional crimson-robed lama and his novice as we wandered along gravel paths between smaller temples painted green and red, a white octagonal library of sacred texts, strange, stubby white-plaster and gold obelisks, and a small greenhouse sheltering a tree that's said to have been grown from a cutting taken from the one under which the Buddha himself gained enlightenment. Scattered throughout were prayer wheels, large wooden polygonal barrels painted with intricate designs and Tibetan script, which, like the path through the main temple, Andrei told us, should be turned only clockwise. Next to each wheel, visitors had left offerings of coins, candy, stones, scraps of cloth, and prayers scribbled on pieces of paper. Nothing is too insignificant, Andrei told us, but everyone should make an offering of some kind. We left a few rubles. Behind the compound, a forest of saplings spread toward the hills, each little tree tied with dozens of scraps of white prayer cloth. Squinting my eyes in the sun, it looked like an Alabama cotton field ready for harvest.

As we walked through the Datsan complex, we were followed by an old woman supplicant, hunched and toothless, at once apologetic and insistent, communicating both her need and her shame in exaggerated hand and body gestures and a few barely audible words of Russian. Andrei gave her a few rubles and told us not to give her more, and tried politely but unsuccessfully to shoo her away.

We left the old woman, the tigers, the Buddha, the lamas, and the prayer wheels behind and headed on south through the Selenga Valley.

•

A leaf falls into the Tuul Gol River in Ulaanbaatar, high on the Mongolian Plateau, and a scrap of that leaf, a tiny speck of Mongolia, settles onto the shore of the Arctic Ocean, 4,000 kilometers to the north. The Tuul Gol becomes the Selenga River becomes Lake Baikal becomes the Angara River becomes the Yenisei River becomes the Kara Sea becomes the Arctic, and water dissolves the steppe into the ocean.

South of Ulan-Ude, the Selenga unfurls like an old strand of blue ribbon, crumpled and torn but still iridescent and perhaps more alluring than the brand new item because it's been somewhere, has done something, carries memories and knowledge in its tangles and kinks. The Selenga wanders broad and flat through a brown valley even more broad and only slightly less flat, beneath soft brown hills that roll back over the edge of the horizon and over the edge of time.

The river gathers on the Mongolian plateau out of lonesome threads that slowly find each other and weave together and in their strengthening fabric find purpose, definition, and direction. The river gives life to Ulaanbaatar and three-quarters of all Mongolians and then spills out of Mongolia and into Russia without knowing or caring that in so doing it rudely ignores all of the long fought-over distinctions between one human domain and the other.

It brings that place into this one, and this one into the next, and quietly proves that they are all part of the same place.

The Selenga also carries a memory of Ulaanbaatar and Mongolia with it as it crosses into Buryatia, a waterborne cargo of the used, recycled, worn away, and unwanted stuff of the life of the earth and humans—silt and organic matter, along with toxins and all manner of other waste from human settlements and worksites. Here in Buryatia, the river off-loads some of this cargo and picks up more—from streams running off the mountains and plains, from the cities of Ulan-Ude and Selenginsk. Then it continues its journey north and spills out onto the rim of Baikal, where it spreads out, slows down, and drops most of the rest of its cargo in a broad delta that fans out into the great lake, and then on into the depths of the lake itself, where a faint record of the debris of nature and man is stored in the historical filing cabinet of Baikal's millennia of sediments. A few remaining specks of Mongolia and Buryatia float on through Baikal, out into the Angara River, and on toward the sea.

We watched the Selenga from atop a massive pile of rocks and dirt on its shore, an outcropping that somehow the river has not yet washed away. From the south it braids around islands and weaves between hills and brightens in the sun. To the north it's a wide path the color of a Steller's jay that ducks through the mountains toward the Great Lake. There is not a building in sight. Nothing happened during our brief stop here. It may well be that nothing has ever happened here—except that the river flows by, and it's beautiful.

•

"Old Believers like color," Andrei said, as the chalk blue and green windows and shutters of the traditional Siberian timber farm houses were slowly joined by other hues splashed on fences, windows, gates, and barn doors—the bold yellows, reds, and greens of a kid's paint set. We were two hours and a hundred years from Ulan-Ude, heading into Old Believer territory.

It's hard to believe that in a country where the dominant Russian Orthodox Church seems to have barely made it out of the thirteenth century there is an even more conservative splinter group known as *Old* Believers. But there is. In the seventeenth century, the hierarchy of the Russian church made what some might consider to be modest changes to some of its liturgy and symbols, in an effort to make them more consistent with the traditions of their sister Greek Orthodox Church. But many of the faithful refused to accept the changes, and a schism erupted in the church. Many of the traditionalists set their churches ablaze, with themselves inside, rather than submit to the dictates from Moscow. And the church seems to have taken the matter equally seriously, torturing many of the heretics. Some were eventually allowed to maintain their old traditions, but only after Empress Catherine the Great banished many of them from Russia's European territories to Siberia. The renegade priest Avvakum, who wrote about Baikal while serving twenty years in exile, was an early leader of these schismatics, who were known at the time as the *Raskolniki* and more recently as the *Starovery*, or Old Believers. Over the generations, a few isolated pockets of the ancestors of these folks have survived, along with otherwise lost traditions in dress, folklore, music and, as we were learning as we drove through their communities, domestic color schemes.

We had long ago passed the last vestige of the twentieth century as we headed south, toward Mongolia, through the broad flood plain of the meandering Selenga, and then up out of the valley into the low hills to the east. Forest and field alternated haphazardly, cows munched on bronze grass and unharvested cabbage, families gathered hay with pitchforks, their dogs chasing each other between the haystacks. Half an hour or so from the river we passed the only building we'd seen since we left the city that looked like it had been built since the time of the Romanovs, a new church with fresh timbers and a shiny metal roof. On the steps were a dozen or so older men and women in jackets and overcoats, and as we passed by an eerie sound seeped through the closed windows of our van and over the growl of its engine—they were singing, to no one in particular, a sharp and dissonant and mournful chorus that wafted through the van like a breeze carrying the aroma of strange and acrid spices. It was instantly entrancing and suddenly I couldn't imagine that any unique seal or bizarre fish or perfect and eternal body of water that I might yet encounter elsewhere in these parts would capture my imagination more, or seem more worthy of preserving, than the culture that produced the harsh beauty of those voices.

The van rumbled on and the singers passed quickly out of earshot, but I remained so transfixed by this almost hallucinatory moment that I barely noticed when we turned off the road and passed through one of those paint-box gates, being opened by a robust old woman wearing a bright blue kerchief, a brown dress embroidered in gold thread, and a huge smile. The opening gate revealed two other old women, slighter, and dressed in even more colorful garb, all orange and green and pink and blue, and suddenly all three of them were singing too, a distilled and somehow even purer version of what we'd heard passing the church a moment before. They huddled around us as we spilled out of the van, still singing and thrusting a huge round loaf of bread toward us, from which we tore ragged pieces and stuffed them in our mouths.

The van had come to rest in a small yard enclosed by a small house, small barns, and small sheds, all bright blue, yellow, and green and filled with the women's cacophonous chorus, which started and stopped almost at random, like a needle being placed down and picked up on an old record player—a voice would drop out, then two, then all three would stop at once as they'd say hello and introduce themselves and say something else more complicated that Andrei didn't translate, and then the song would resume in mid-line.

Their names were Masha, Pana, and Lena, two sisters and a lifelong friend, and they told us that they had lived in this village for their entire lives, which stretched out well over seventy years, back to the time before these farms were collectivized by Stalin. Apparently the village itself doesn't even have a proper name, but in order to distinguish it from others in this part of Buryatia, the women told us that they call it "Kuitun," or Cold Place. "It is still a collective farm," Masha, the largest and roundest of the trio, told us, with Andrei translating. "When I was young we worked hard. Now we are retired people, but we're still working!" As she spoke, one of the sisters dashed out the back gate, a huge, serpentine-handled scythe in her hands, slashing away at the grass at the edge of a vast field. "This is how we had to do it during the war!" she shouted, in a voice as sharp as the tool itself. "It's how we still do it!" The other sister pantomimed milking a cow. As the women demonstrated their agricultural prowess, three young boys lurked on the periphery, almost certainly more intrigued by us than by the performance.

I call it a performance because none of us had any pretense that it was anything else. We were tourists, and they were putting on a show for us. Andrei was paying them for the encounter, and we were paying Andrei. But it was also clear that this was not just some kind of historical reenactment, a Siberian Plimoth Plantation from which these women would clock out at the end of the day, shed their costumes, and return to their real lives.

Lena led us through a low doorway into the house, through a darkened kitchen with an ancient soapstone sink, and into the front room, where a long table was set with the most opulent display of food this side of a Las Vegas buffet. Fish and onions, potatoes, meat, egg and ham salad, honey, jam, bread, pancakes, mushrooms, pickles, beets, tea, and of course, homemade vodka. The walls were painted in a thick, chalky blue, which we'd come to recognize as the national paint scheme in Russia, either the favorite color or the only one Soviet factories produced. Heavy tapestries hung from two walls, and against another stood a glass-covered cabinet displaying some of the family's few valued heirlooms—a few pieces of china, some framed photographs, and a small wooden chest holding who knows what. Several clocks hung on the walls, none of which displayed the correct time, which seemed entirely appropriate.

A man in a plaid shirt entered the room and was introduced as Anatoly, Lena's husband, but his appearance seemed purely ceremonial—it meant that the feast was about to begin. Anatoly poured the vodka and proposed a toast— "To the visitors!"—but this was the last we would hear from him. There was no question who the stars of this show were. Plates were passed, food was piled on—pancakes spread with honey next to pigs' knuckles and salty fish. More vodka was poured, more toasts proposed—"To the Motherland!" "Just a little more—*choot choot!*" "To safe travels!" "To visitors from far away!" Lena, Masha, and Pana talked just like you'd expect women who'd spent seventy years together to do—incessantly, and all at once. Andrei translated maybe a quarter of what they said, and James and I understood maybe half of that. Our heads were spinning, and it wasn't from the vodka, which we were trying discreetly not to drink very much of—we knew it was bad manners to refuse a drink offered by a Russian, especially in their home. But Anatoly was on to us. When I placed my still half-full glass on the table, he flashed a reproachful look, clearly not in jest.

Fragments of the women's lives started emerging through the clamor, among them the tale of their only trip outside of Siberia—to Germany in 1993, when they were invited on a singing tour. The money they raised on the tour paid not only for the trip but also for the new church we'd just passed down the road.

Somewhere between plates of fish and beets, Lena had slipped out of the room and now returned with an astounding new addition to her already kaleidoscopic outfit—a necklace of massive gobs of amber—four strands, each bearing at least a dozen luminous, honey-colored beads the size of walnuts. As she rolled them between her fingers, her voice became even more animated, and I asked Andrei to translate a little more closely than he had been. He said that Lena was telling the story of her ancestors bringing the necklace from Poland when they went into exile, and how when she wore it during her trip to Germany, one of her hosts offered her a car for it. She declined the offer when she realized that she wouldn't be able to get the car back to Siberia.

And then they sang. They started while still sitting at the table and soon rose with their voices and stood in the middle of the floor, swaying in their scarves and sneakers, their eerie intervals and odd harmonies reflecting the discordant beauty of their dresses. Their songs were like jangly, white-knuckle trips on precipitous mountain roads, all deep ruts and hairpin turns, following a route and a rhythm and cadence that took us to a place well back before the time of Bach's *Well-Tempered Clavier*. They seemed at times less like songs than interwoven wails, springing up from a deep well of sorrow and loss. But when our hosts stopped for long enough for us to ask what the songs were about, we were told, "Drinking. And asking our young people not to drink so much." And other mundane subjects of daily life. Then they raised their glasses, downed their vodka, and resumed their songs.

I recorded some of the songs and afterward played back part of the recording for each of them. They listed intently, with headphones over their scarves, a look of amazement and pride washing over their faces. Andrei said it was the first time they'd ever heard themselves sing. I promised to send them each copies of the recording. I felt that the recordings would be as rare and precious a collection of gems for me as Lena's amber necklace was for her.

"Singing is our life," Masha told us. "We couldn't survive without songs. When we sing, we become younger. I have seven children and seventeen grandchildren—we teach them too. At least we try to, but they prefer modern style! This is old style—it's difficult to understand."

Masha went on. "All of the changes here in Russia have not been good. It's difficult for all our officials, for Putin, to keep people in the same direction, because there is no discipline after Perestroika. We are concerned about our children, how they will live. Times are difficult economically, too.

"But our songs have helped us survive. They are our food, and our air."

The songs of the Old Believers continued as Lena, Masha, and Pana walked us out to the van, as we said goodbye and drove out of the yard, as they closed the painted gate behind us and we headed back out of Cold Place, weaving around cows loping back into the village. They sang until the cows came home. They're still singing.

As we returned to Ulan-Ude at dusk, monstrous smokestacks carried black ash over the flickering city and huge, smoldering heaps of I dare not think what sent flames and billowing clouds of smoke into the orange sky.

7

On the Trail with Pod Boy
and Monkey Mind

*In which we continue our hike, learn how these two brothers
ended up on the other side of the world together, and get a slightly
unsettling glimpse inside the narrator's mind*

We are stretched out along the Holy Nose trail, the five of us, clinging to
the steep hillside above Chivyrkuysky Gulf. The trail has narrowed even
further, and it struggles to get around big trees and through thick brush. Andrei
is ahead, as usual, but not as far as before and at a more relaxed pace. Elisa and
Chanda walk together, talking. James and I walk separately, not talking. Not *not
talking* as in *pissed off at each other* not talking, just *not talking* as in *keeping our
thoughts to ourselves and being alone here* not talking, which we both do a lot. Baikal
inspires many things in many people, but it has not yet inspired in either
of us the gift of gab. Halfway around the world, cut loose from everything
and everyone we've ever known, we're still the same old us—both reserved, con-
templative, a little anxious, and more than a little self-conscious. We both
have a hard time letting loose and opening up. We are eighteen years apart,

we're only half-brothers, but we're very much alike, in ways that I'm only now beginning to recognize.

In the early part of the trip, James played around with the recording equipment I'd brought, and when I listened back to his recordings later I was stunned to find that sometimes I couldn't tell who was talking—him or me. And I'm a radio journalist, a guy who listens to his own voice for a living. I should know who's me and who isn't. It was more than weird. James and I had different mothers and separate childhoods, but listening to these recordings, I realized that our voices have the same tone and cadence, that we use the same peculiar idioms and even stop and start our conversations in the same way. That we don't just talk alike but that in some basic ways we clearly even think alike. I still can't figure out how this happened, but it's probably why this joint venture is working so well. I would not have done this trip alone, and I don't think I could have done it with anyone other than James.

James and I have a strange sort of partnership on this journey. We've never really spoken about it, but it's absolutely fundamental to the enterprise. Essentially, the deal is this: we don't have to talk to each other much, we're each paying our own way, and we can wander off on our own when it suits us. But whenever it matters, we are absolutely in it together. We didn't settle on this with a handshake or over a beer—we just knew it to be true. There's never been any doubt.

James came along when I was almost out of high school, an unanticipated addition to a family that was already complicated and messy. My parents had gone through a difficult split when I was six, and the bitterness of the divorce stuck to me and my two older sisters like tar from the oil-and-gravel road in front of our new house in the country. Twelve years later, my relationship with my father was still strained, and I still thought of my stepmother as an interloper in the family. The idea that these two could produce a kid and foist this new sibling on the family made me squirm. I wasn't even sure I loved them—how could I love their kid? When I first went to see James I could barely look at him. *The Baby Who Fell to Earth*, I thought. *Pod Boy. Must flee.*

A year and a half later I was wandering aimlessly through the last of my teen years, hovering between high school and college as if between the poles of two magnets. After a disastrous experiment in apartment life had ended with everything of value that I owned being stolen, my father and stepmother offered me a room in their house. I was surprised at the offer, but I sheepishly accepted it, and then locked myself away in a top-floor room and did my best to pretend that I wasn't there. But then a strange thing happened. James didn't pretend that I wasn't there. He could barely talk, but he could walk, and he kept wandering into my room. He wanted to know what I was doing. He wanted to know who

I was. He was a gentle and curious kid, and he didn't give a hoot about whatever difficult relationships had come before. In his one-and-a-half-year-old way, he more or less demanded that I reckon with him and that we start with a clean slate. We quickly grew to enjoy each other's company. And before I knew what was happening, I had become very attached to him. Maybe I even grew to love him. I guess I realized this all one day when he got into my records—the things that I thought I loved more than anything in the world—and drew all over their covers with a blue magic marker, and all I could do was give him a mild talking-to, and secretly laugh.

After that six months living at my father's house, James and I rarely spent more than a few days together at a time, but we had developed a special bond, forged by an unspoken pact that we wouldn't let the tangle of difficult emotions in our family interfere in any way with our friendship, as much as such a thing is possible to express between a largely preverbal two-year-old and a largely inarticulate twenty-year-old. None of this was ever talked about—it just was. Which in itself was perhaps the very essence of the difference between our relationship and my relationship with everyone else in my family—I could take it for granted. Our affection for each other was utterly unconditional and uncomplicated. We had a kind of trust that I could never quite share with my two closest sisters, with whom intense sibling rivalry and the legacy of other fractured and volatile relationships were always lurking in the background. And we didn't have the sort of generation gap that I felt between myself and my much older half sister and brother, from my mother's first marriage. I was nearly old enough to be James's father, but it seemed like there were very few years between us. It was almost like we were growing up together. Which, of course, we were, as were my father and stepmother and I. James's appearance marked the beginning of a slow but profound shift in my relationship with both of them.

And as we grew up, we discovered that we shared a lot of interests. When James was seventeen, we ventured off alone together for the first time, taking a road trip from Boston to the Outer Banks, and learned that we could travel well together. A few years later, we drove with our father from Indiana to the Pacific Northwest along the Oregon Trail, following the route described in old Origen Thomson's journal. We pretended to fight as we reenacted the split in Origen's party in the harsh terrain west of the Continental Divide and as we bowled for the good bed at the motel in The Dalles, Oregon, with the loser getting the cot. But our mock battles were just a parody of the fights we never had. James is the only person in my family with whom I have never exchanged caustic words, or even thought bad thoughts about. He's also completely reliable, is about as patient and unflappable as Thomsons get, and has managed to strike a fine balance between caution and adventurousness.

He's definitely got the Wandering Gene—before he'd finished college he'd walked alone across much of England and spent three months kayaking, hiking, and sitting in the rain on a glacier in Patagonia. But he's careful about what he gets himself into, and responsible about how he conducts himself once he's gotten into it. I knew I could trust him. I knew that our temperaments, our taste for adventure, and our tolerance for risk and uncertainty were pretty similar. And—most important, I suppose—I knew that I really liked him. He was the only member of my family with whom I could take such a trip and not end up wanting to kill after a week or so, or have him end up wanting to kill me. He may have been the only such person on the planet. And then there's this: James's calm solidity may have been exactly what I needed after three years in a marriage in which I felt like I'd lassoed myself to the horns of a bull.

And like I said, I would not have done this trip alone. I'm just not that emotionally self-sufficient. After not too long away from home, I need contact with something, someone, familiar and reliable. I needed to get away, I'm always hungry to explore and engage with the world, but if I'm out for more than a few weeks, I need something strong tethering me to home. A lifeline. Here in Russia, James is my lifeline.

James, on the other hand, doesn't at all mind keeping his own company. Not long after the completion of this trip, for instance, he'll end up living on a mountaintop in New Hampshire, with only the company of crows, bears, and the occasional hypothermic hiker who stumbles into his Appalachian Mountain Club hut to escape the November White Mountains rain. But I don't think he would have done a trip like this without me. I provided the impetus, the focus, the rough itinerary. James provided enthusiasm, smarts, and a sane and steady, grounding presence.

Of course, James and I do have our disagreements. He owns Pink Floyd records, while I purged mine from my collection about the time he was born. I play basketball religiously, while James has no interest in games played indoors on hard surfaces. He wants to keep a detailed accounting of our expenses on this trip and make sure that we both pull our own weight down to the last penny, while I'm more willing to let a few hundred bucks slide one way or the other. Other differences are proving to be complementary, as we navigate new cities, new languages, and new cultures. James is more sociable than I am and so strikes up conversations with strangers more easily. He's also better with languages—he quickly picks up such vital niceties as "hello," "goodbye," "please," "thank you," "nice to meet you," and "delicious" and, unlike me, doesn't feel flustered or awkward when he needs to use them.

On the other hand, he's terrible at finding his way around, at least in the city. Let him loose in the deepest woods and he'll find his way back to civilization, but plant him on a street corner in Los Angeles and he'll never be seen again. I, meanwhile, can find my way anywhere. I think I first noticed this when I was ten or eleven and on my way with my mother to Washington, DC for an anti-Vietnam war rally. She was driving through the night and I was sleeping in the back seat, and at about two in the morning she woke me up to tell me we were lost somewhere in the middle of New Jersey. Of course, I had no idea where we were either, but I remember taking a quick look at the map, glancing around for some signs, and leading her back to the highway. In short order we were back underway and I was asleep again. Since then, I have never been lost. I've ended up places I didn't know I wanted to go, but I've never been lost.

So James's and my mix of strengths and weaknesses works well together on a venture like this. I can get us where we're going, and then, when we get there, James can pretty much do the talking. Along the way, sometimes we talk, sometimes we play cribbage and rummy and argue about the rules, and sometimes we just sit quietly and read or write or think, and know that the other one is there.

•

So here we are, on the shore of the world's most perfect lake, walking and not talking and I am alone in this place. I'm thinking about the nerpa, which we'd hoped to be able to catch a glimpse of. *Too late*, Andrei told us, *they've already gone north . . . .* I'm thinking about crossing the lake by boat, rather than just skimming along the shore. *Too late*, Andrei told us again, *it is dangerous after September . . . .* I'm thinking about the Old Believers, whom I am very grateful it was *not* too late to see, and about Snake Bay and the *banya* and swimming in the lake and the animal tracks on the beach . . . and now, out of nowhere, I'm suddenly thinking about the problem we have with our visas, how we've discovered that they're not properly registered but how nobody can tell exactly how to get them registered, and now I'm thinking about traveling without proper papers in this xenophobic country with laws that are so complex and unsettled that even its own well-educated citizens don't understand them and how crazy and anxious this makes me and how I really would like to be rid of this ridiculous cloud of anxiety, how I'd really just like to be out of here, to be home, except that now I'm remembering what a friend wrote in an email I got the other day in Irkutsk—*No need to rush back, it's the same as it ever was . . . .* And now the refrain from that Talking Heads song is rattling around in my brain—*Same as it ever was . . . Same as it ever was . . . Same as it ever was*—and now I'm no longer alone in this place because I'm no longer here at all—my mind has drifted far away, jumping from thought to thought, swinging from tree to tree.

Monkey Mind, roaming everywhere but here.... *Same as it ever was ... Same as it ever was.... Yeah, but I wouldn't mind that sameness right about now, all those same people and same places. I feel completely dis-placed here.... And how are we going to get back home, anyway? Another freighter? Everyone tells us not to try to cross the North Atlantic by ship after October—it's way too rough. But we can't fly. All the Way Around, On the Ground, that's the plan. Maybe a ship going from Spain to South America or something, maybe we could sign on as crew on a sailboat. Of course, I'm secretly hoping that the QE2 is sailing in December and that somehow I can stomach the fare. That's something else I've always wanted to do, too, cross the Atlantic on an ocean liner.... Of course, James might not even come home with me, he's talking about going on to South Africa. Too bad I can't go on with him, too bad I promised I'd be home by January to start set-tling Mom's estate. Jesus, what was I thinking when I offered to be her executor? I don't know the first thing about that shit. And I'm gonna have to sift through all those little shards of her fractured memory and find a way to divvy it up among her five kids without setting off a thousand emotional land mines. What the hell was I think-ing? Oh yeah—that I'd be good at it. That she knew she could trust me to make good decisions and maybe avoid triggering those explosions. That after all those years of playing the parent to her child this was one last thing I could do for her. And for myself. But it's all gonna be so damn sad, and that's one reason I had to get out of there for a good long while.... Mom ... why didn't I even cry when she died? Maybe Emma so thoroughly exhausted me that I've got nothing left for anything else—I've used up my lifetime supply of emotional energy. Maybe I'm just repressing all that grief. Maybe I'd already been grieving her loss for all those years when she was slipping away, and her death really was just a relief. Maybe I'm really just a coldhearted bastard.... Huh, just remembered a dream I had about her the other night. She was alive again, and she was her old self, before Jesus and Satan started fighting for her soul, before the voices and the visions, before her brain started to dissolve and even Jesus disappeared. It was so good to see her.... Had some dream about Dad, too. What was it about? I've got to get back and get to work with him on the farm project, too, that's what I went back to Boston to do, set up the conservation restriction, put his mind to rest about the future of the place. Shit, that's the last thing I want to do. Why did I let myself get sucked back into the family vortex? I didn't let myself get sucked in—I jumped. No one asked. What the hell was I think-ing when I left Berkeley? Here's what I was thinking: Mom's disappear-ing into a black hole, I want to spend time with Dad before that happens to him. And New England is home, it's where I belong. I don't want to become a Californian. Like the Jonathan Richman song....*

> *Y'know, Ladies and Gentlemen,*
> *I've already been to Paris, I already been to Rome*

De da da dum de dum de dum dum-de-dum day
and what did I do but miss my home?
Oh, New England . . .
I have been out west to Californ—
De da da dum de dum de dum dum-de-dum day
But I missed the land where I was born
Oh, New England
I can't Help it . . .
Dum de dum de dum dum-de-dum day
Oh, New England . . .

Of course Jonathan lives in California now. . . . Who am I fooling? I can't get over California. Emma. . . . Why do I miss something so badly that was so completely messed up? It's been a year, I still can't get her out of my head. I wish I'd never met her. No I don't, I'm glad I did it, no matter how badly it ended up. I loved her. I loved our house. I loved Berkeley. All she could do was complain about them. And now she's still there and I'm gone. What's that about? Put it out of your mind! That's over! I wish this was over. What the hell am I doing here? I feel like I'm on another planet where I can't breathe the air and I'm twice as heavy and ten times as stupid. What was I thinking? I don't have the stamina to travel in places like this. . . . Those goddamn visas. "They are not properly registered. You must get them properly registered." How the hell can we get them properly registered if no one even knows what that means? And when every-one tells you that the one place that does know the rules, that inter-nal security office, is the last place you should go because they'll take your passport and you'll be stuck in Irkutsk for a month or they'll demand a bribe and you're completely at their mercy but if you don't go there and work it out who knows what will happen if you get stopped later, or try to leave the country with bad visas. This is making me crazy. I want to get out of here. We've barely arrived and I'm already exhausted. Here's the dirty little secret that I can't even tell James: I hate Russia. How many days do we have left in this damn country, anyway? Why do I do this to myself? When I'm at home all I can think of is taking off and exploring, then I go off all I can think about is home. . . .

. . . Home . . . is where I want to be . . .
Pick me up and turn me round . . .

I feel numb...mmm...mmm...mmm...
...guess I must be having fun...

But where is home, anyway? Stuffed into a storage locker on San Pablo
Avenue.... I miss my cat. I miss my friends. Emma. What was I thinking?
That she was unlike anyone I'd ever met, made me feel like a different person,
more energetic and quick-witted and confident. Like the best drug ever invented,
and that I'd never forgive myself if I didn't take it as far as it could go, no matter
what kind of rehab it might land me in.... Fuck... I don't know whether Baikal
can fix itself, but I'm pretty damn sure it can't fix me.... Lake Fucking Baikal. I
still can't believe I'm here. It feels more like a dream than my dreams do. It's amaz-
ing. Look at those mountains! I love this place. I love the names of these places. Svyatoi
Nos. Barguzin. I love the sound of Russian. Zdravstvuite. Spasibo. Pozhaluista. Kartofel.
Golomyanka. I love all these new people we're meeting .... And those crazy Old Believers!
I can't believe it. I can't believe I'm here .... And here we are, at a flat spot by a little
swamp with a fire pit in a sun-drenched clearing, between the dazzling green of
the swamp and the brilliant blue of the lake. We strike up a small fire and fix
ourselves a late lunch—more cheese and sausage and hard bread and sardines
and pine nuts and birch fungus tea and wood smoke—and once again we don't
talk much, we just soak this place up, inhale it, imprint it.

This is the rendezvous spot—we got here in plenty of time, and after a
while there's the boat, and there's Igor and the Lonesome Boatman, and we're
hauling ourselves back on board and heading back south, toward the beach
where we first got on board. And along the way the Lonesome Boatman wants
his picture taken with us, especially with the winsome Elisa, whom you know
he's fallen in love with because she's young and French and has a quick smile
and also speaks Russian, and he imagines her taking him far beyond the rim of
mountains that surround us and his lake, where he's never been and may well
never go. And then we pull back up onto the beach in Katun, not for fish this
time but for some home-brewed vodka, which is delivered to the Lonesome
Boatman in a plastic soda bottle without a cap, and then he continues back
down the shore a ways and drops us on the beach where the van is waiting and
we say goodbye and clamber into the van and head back along the narrow finger
of sand that connects the Holy Nose to Ust-Barguzin and the mainland.

8

Bad Roads Are Good for Baikal

*In which we explore the benefits and challenges
of isolation and development
while following a river into the mountains*

The Barguzin River flows out of the Barguzin Mountains, through the town of Barguzin and then the coastal community of Ust-Barguzin before it finally loses itself in a broad cove of Baikal known as Barguzin Bay. The only way across the river for miles upstream from the lake is a ramshackle little wooden ferry with a tiny, corrugated steel shed with a wood stove in it and room on its deck for about half a dozen cars. The ferry slips noiselessly away from the end of the road on the south bank, and looking west toward the lake, two ghostly, rusting timber loading cranes loom on the horizon while the river spills over into a grassy marsh on its north bank. Turning back to the east, there's a small motorboat laboring to get upstream—laboring because it's attached to a tow rope, which is attached to the ferry. The ferry, it turns out, is just a hapless little barge, at the mercy of the river without the guidance of the motorboat pilot on the other end of the towline. Our crossing takes less than five minutes, and connected to it by nothing but that single strand, the pilot directs the barge into place perfectly on the far side. But the deckhand fails to secure it, the ferry swings wide in the current, spins ninety degrees, and slams butt-end into the dock. The pilot scowls as he turns the motorboat around and uses its blunt bow, covered in a tractor tire, to push the barge back into place, where the deckhand finally lashes it to the dock.

The Barguzin is Baikal's third largest tributary, after the Selenga to the south of here and the Upper Angara to the north. It carries about six percent of the water flowing into the lake, along with migratory fish like omul and sturgeon, born in the shallow gravel beds upriver before wandering downstream to spend most of their lives in the lake. And even though it flows through only two towns between its headwaters and the lake, the Barguzin carries a significant pollution load into Baikal, as well, especially organic chemicals from timber operations. As with the Selenga and the shores around the Baikalsk Pulp and Paper Mill, the *National Geographic* map depicts the contamination at the mouth of the Barguzin as a purple smudge in the lake.

From the riverbank, our driver skirts the rim of the sandy Svyatoi Nos isthmus and plunges the car into the thick forest and cool, damp air of the narrow Barguzin Valley. James and Andrei and I are heading upriver to the town of Barguzin and the foothills of the Barguzin Mountains, leaving Elisa, Chanda, and Igor behind in the quiet town of Ust-Barguzin.

Of all the communities on Baikal's shores, the fates have dealt Ust-Barguzin perhaps the luckiest hand in terms of natural and recreational values. It's nestled between the deepest and broadest stretch of the lake on one side and the rugged Barguzin River on another. It's at the base of a towering coastal mountain range and close to a chain of small islands where nerpas often haul out. It's the entry point to the deep forests where Russians first hunted the Barguzin sable and where Nicholas II created the country's first nature preserve. It has access to fishing, rafting, boating, hiking, sightseeing, and rich local history. And it's the gateway to Zabaikalsky National Park and some of the wildest and most beautiful territory in the Baikal basin. But for all these attributes, Ust-Barguzin remains just another modest Siberian town—somber timber houses with filigreed molding behind blue or green painted fences, set side by side along wide, sandy streets. If there's anything in particular to do or see or buy in Ust-Barguzin, or anything of any interest that was ever said to have happened or even be possible in the town, there's certainly no effort to draw anyone's attention to it.

In the U.S., a place like Ust-Barguzin would in all likelihood have long since become what's known as a "gateway community"—a town like Gatlinburg, Tennessee or West Yellowstone, Montana where civilization has heaved a landslide of commercial rubble up against the boundaries of national parks in hopes that distracted visitors will stumble over a piece of debris and spill the contents of their pockets on their way into or out of paradise. To the extent that such towns once had any charm or significance of their own, these qualities have generally been buried under expanses of asphalt, concrete, and billboards extolling their "historic" and "scenic" qualities.

Ust-Barguzin can only dream of such glories, and it's probably wise that, so far, anyway, no one seems to have tried to turn that dream into reality. When it comes to tourism in these parts, ambition is usually only a precursor to disappointment.

The landscape around Baikal is littered with melancholy monuments to failure. Along the lake's eastern shore on our way here, we passed decrepit little "resorts" and "spas," shabby clusters of buildings with big rusting metal signs out front, their light bulbs long ago burst, declaring the nothing of the places to the no one who passes by. On the lake's more accessible southwestern shore, as we'll later see, multistory buildings sit half-built on the bluffs above the lake in the town of Listvianka, hollow and abandoned. And elsewhere in the area, Andrei tells us, the grand plans of Russian and Japanese businessmen to transform parts of the region into the next Tahoe or Banff by building jetports and five-star hotels have foundered on the realities of life here.

A decade ago, when the Soviet Union was collapsing and Russians were starting to get their first whiffs of free enterprise, the landscape here held much more promise. Adventure travel to exotic locales around the globe was booming, and a whole new world of possibility was opening up within Russia. And in the grand geography of the earth, Baikal was more accessible than many places—there were reasonably modern airports in Irkutsk and Ulan-Ude, and the fabled Trans-Siberian Railroad, linking the eastern flank of Europe to the Pacific Ocean, came right to its shore. In a cash-starved economy, the tourism prospects of Baikal made many would-be developers salivate.

And they made environmentalists cringe. In recent decades, environmentalists had watched—often in despair—as huge numbers of people had begun flocking to previously remote places like Nepal, the Galapagos Islands, even Antarctica, leaving a trail of deforestation, degraded habitat, and junk in their wake. Unprecedented leaps in wealth, technology, communications, and just plain sheer numbers of people had changed the nature of travel—suddenly almost no place was too extreme or too difficult for lots of people to get to. The world's Last Best Places were now on the to-do lists of millions, and with each new visitor, each place qualified a little less for that distinction. Environmentalists feared that Baikal was about to be added to that list and that it was utterly unprepared to absorb the impact of the building wave of global tourism.

But so far, nothing close to either the dream or the nightmare of large-scale tourism has come to pass here. Certainly, people are starting to come, and their presence—our presence—is being felt. But the ripples—trash even in remote woods, untreated sewage, a growing number of visitors like James and me bringing a growing sense of unease to tiny villages like Lula's—haven't yet become a tsunami. Ambitions have been thwarted, and likely a surge of ill-advised development averted, by an array of obstacles. Before it could even get off the ground, Russia's new market economy tanked, and the recovery that's begun in the cities far to the west hasn't yet reached this far into Siberia. The country's legal and regulatory systems remain byzantine, corrupt, and unpredictable, and the Baikal region remains politically and economically isolated. Then there's the local infrastructure, which at the end of the twentieth century seems little advanced beyond the description of the nineteenth century Russian poet Prince Pyotr Viazemsky, who wrote, "pits and bumps, ruts and grooves—all that is called a road in Russia." It took us the better part of a day to travel just the 200 kilometers or so between Ulan-Ude and Zabaikalsky National Park, and even at that rate we were lucky to make it. As we sat on the beach after our run-in with the pothole, the old joke about advice to travelers in rural Down East Maine rattled around in my mind: "You can't get there from here." Andrei had primed me for this sort of delay, and the ambivalence he felt about it, the day before. "Bad roads," he'd said, "are good for Baikal."

But, of course, bad roads aren't good for local residents. The same divots and craters that help restrain an outbreak of thoughtless development in towns like Ust-Barguzin are also obstacles to food, consumer goods and building supplies, newspapers and books, emergency vehicles, health care workers, access to universities, good jobs, and everything else that local residents do want and need from the outside world. And that, in a nutshell, reflects the challenge here, as in so many other places: how to develop in a way that brings good jobs and access to the outside world without causing a landslide of civilization to smash up against towns like Ust-Barguzin, Baikal's national parks, and the lake itself.

•

The trail ascending through the woods above the town of Barguzin has turned from a rough old mushroom- and pine-nut-gathering road into a meandering streamside path into a narrow animal trail between spindly aspens and pines, and now it has disappeared completely and we are bushwhacking through steep underbrush, twigs and branches snapping beneath our feet, thorns and brambles snagging on our jeans, and finally Andrei has declared that the trail is "not convenient" and that we should probably turn back. Our quiet, lazy hike to nowhere through these steep hills has had an almost hypnotic effect on me, and I almost don't want to break the trance, but I'm also sweating in the cold from the climb and certainly wouldn't mind a bit of a rest and the cup of tea that Andrei has proposed, so we reverse course and head for a fire pit that we passed back down the hill. When we reach it, we gather up some dry wood, kindle a fire, and hang a pot of water over it.

"This is my favorite place in the world, Buryatia," Andrei says as we sit on a cushion of dry leaves, sniffing the cool air. To all appearances, Andrei is 100 percent ethnic Russian—pale skin, angular face, sandy brown hair—but it's clear that he considers himself a native Buryat, and ethnicity has nothing to do with it. He was born in Ulan-Ude and grew up exploring places like this, the thick forests, broad plains, and river valleys east of Lake Baikal. He says he's gotten to see much of the rest of his huge country and others, first in the Soviet army and more recently while traveling to meetings around the world, but that he's never wanted to live anywhere else. "Every time I go away, when I return I am so glad to be back. It is home."

Andrei and I are slowly starting to warm up to each other, and it's not just the fire that's now crackling in front of us. I'm realizing that he's less gruff and aloof than perhaps pensive and even a little shy, in a way that his line of work initially disguises, and that in that way, perhaps, he's even a little like me. I'm not sure what he's realizing about me, but it seems that he's starting to relax and open up a bit. And after several days together, we're finally sitting down for a real talk.

For much of the year, Andrei tells me, he teaches in the economics department at the Eastern Siberian Technological University in Ulan-Ude. But when the days lengthen and the air warms, he disappears for long stretches of time to places like this—the back country and small towns of Buryatia and the eastern shore of Baikal, with small groups of mostly American, European, and Japanese visitors. He began guiding foreigners through this territory back in the last days of the old Soviet Union, when the country was throwing off its veil and starting to ease travel restrictions. And in the years since, he says, his ability to help others see and learn about his small corner of the world has made him a rich man. "Not really in money," he says, "but communication. I like to communicate with different people. Not much people can say I know lots of people around the world, but I can say, and I like it."

Of course, the money isn't bad, either. James and I are paying Andrei seventy bucks a day each. That covers our transportation, food (and tea) on the trail, park entrance fees, room and board in the health clinic and private homes, and whatever Andrei is paying Igor, but even if he pockets only a quarter of his net, thirty-five bucks a day is what most people around here earn in a month. It's reasonable for us, and not at all bad for him. At least someone has figured out how to make money on tourism here.

But it seems that Andrei's communication with people from around the world has brought him more than just a decent income and a warm feeling of friendship. It becomes clear as we talk that it's helped transform him from just another guide into something of an evangelist for low-impact tourism.

Andrei's education on the subject began with some very simple lessons, he tells me as he sips brown tea sweetened with coarse sugar from a metal cup.

One of the most important came from an early visitor from California who'd been engaged in the challenge of developing low-impact tourism elsewhere. Andrei and his client had had lunch on a remote beach, he says, roasting fish over a fire, and when they were set to leave, Andrei stamped out the flames but left the fire pit and the smoldering logs within it. "The waves will come and put this out," he'd said to his companion, "no problem." But his American guest suggested that there might be a problem, unless they erased any evidence of their having been there. "He said it's OK if only a few people come," Andrei says, "but if hundreds come and do the same thing it will change this place. He say by our rules we should clean up everything, leave it way we found it." This practice of "leave no trace" camping is the standard for backcountry hiking in the U.S. but it was a revelation to a Russian. "I follow these rules now," Andrei says. "It's good rules."

Since those early days, Andrei has been drawn deep into a growing international community of activists and entrepreneurs, philanthropists, and even government agencies from within Russia and abroad, united by their interest in spurring the development of sustainable tourism. And he quickly learned the power of this global network. "We can study each other," he says. "We can teach each other." Among the things he's learned: that the beginnings of a new low-impact-tourism-based economy can be built on a foundation of what's already in place here, without waiting for the death spasms of the old order to cease or for outsiders to arrive with new investment. And that low-impact tourism initiatives can in turn help foster a range of social goals, from sustainable development, to environmental protection, even to democracy itself.

Among the resources already in place here are plenty of warm homes, comfortable beds, and basic Russian hospitality, and out of these Andrei has begun organizing an informal network of bed and breakfasts where travelers seeking both rugged landscapes and authentic experiences can find inexpensive accommodations, experience local food and culture, and provide a livelihood for local families, all without requiring a ruble of new investment or adding so much as a single new cement block to the landscape. Also in place are hundreds of local residents ready to work as guides, drivers, boat captains, and providers of other goods and services. Properly trained in the new "leave no trace" camping ethic, these folks can bring still more income directly into local communities without creating significant new environmental impacts.

But Andrei also hopes that this steady new stream of tourism income will have a more substantial conservation impact: it will help communities feel that they have an economic stake in preserving their local environment, and motivate them to act accordingly. "People should understand," he says, "that if they protect the land, they protect themselves."

Meanwhile, he sees the environmentally minded tourists who help create that stake as more than passive participants in the process, investing their dollars and just hoping local residents will do the right thing. Andrei says they can play a direct role in protecting Baikal, and help make up for the lack of governmental and nongovernmental resources here, by keeping watch for illegal or harmful activities, reporting on animal movements and populations, even helping to build and restore low-impact infrastructure like hiking trails. These kinds of unconventional tourist activities have taken root elsewhere, and Andrei says he knows they can work here because he's seen them in action. White water rafters have reported to him about an area of dirty water, which led to the discovery of an illegal gold mine. Other visitors have helped build trails and clean up degraded areas. "They paid for the trip," Andrei says, "but also they work as volunteers because they like this beautiful lake. They became patriot of this lake. And they should save it for future generations."

Ultimately, in Andrei's big picture, he believes that the process of developing a low-impact tourism economy here also will also help the region's political development. Charting a sustainable course for the local economy and environment—one that doesn't sacrifice the future to the needs of the present—means tackling an endless series of questions, challenges, and decisions. What kinds of development projects are appropriate? How many visitors is too many? Where is the right balance between protecting the environment and putting too tight a squeeze on what people can do? Who gets to decide? Andrei has little faith that the federal government in Moscow or the regional governments in Ulan-Ude or Irkutsk will be of much use in helping answer questions like these. "Presidents and governments, they come and they disappear," Andrei says with a dismissive shrug. "But people, they stay in the same place." Local people are the hosts of Baikal, he says, and they are largely responsible for its future. And acting on that responsibility means developing strong democratic processes and institutions.

"We should have decision-making groups who can decide what is best way," Andrei tells me, in a deadpan voice that betrays no suggestion that he thinks his friends and neighbors may not yet be quite up to the challenge after a thousand years of authoritarian rule. "They should represent different groups of people who live in area, some of them fishermen, some businessmen for tourism development, some of them staff of protected areas, some for agriculture. If they have problem with the land, they should just agree about this land, and then follow these rules, year by year, and see what happens. If something bad happens, they should change these rules. But if it's OK, they should follow rules that they developed. It's very basic, I think."

Basic, idealistic, and, I think, more than a little naive about the challenges of really making democracy work. Even in the U.S., with our supposedly deep democratic traditions, it's a very messy business, and dealing with local environmental challenges can be particularly excruciating, with neighbor often pitted against neighbor, opponents demonizing each other and clinging like baby monkeys to their own mutually exclusive truths. But Andrei's enthusiasm as a newly minted democrat, someone who hasn't yet become cynical about people claiming their own power and working together to solve problems, is refreshing, even a little inspiring—for me and, I imagine, for other Russians. Which I figure is exactly what it will take—a good deal of inspiration and idealism, along with equal measures of patience, an ability to compromise, and a willingness to gracefully accept losing—or winning—to start tackling the challenges inherent in Andrei's vision for the Baikal region. Or in anyone else's vision for the region, because Andrei certainly isn't the only person with designs on the future here. Change is inevitable—better roads will come to Baikal, carrying more people and a host of other new challenges with them. And those same basic questions—What's an appropriate development project? How much impact is too much? Where is the right balance between the environment and the economy? How much asphalt, concrete, and neon is appropriate for the gateway to paradise?—will be fought over again and again on Baikal's shorelines, in forests like this and in sleepy communities like Ust-Barguzin.

We've finished our tea and another fistful of pine nuts, doused the fire, and started back down the trail toward Barguzin. What we didn't do in this case was scatter the logs and break up the fire pit. This isn't wilderness. We're just a few kilometers above town, and these woods are used a lot by local residents. Better to have a few known spots for fires than have them be set at random spots along the trail.

Back down the drainage, the path broadens as it meets back up with the stream, and the canopy opens a bit above us. Through the yellowing larches and cone-laden pines we can see the jagged pinnacles of the forward column of the Barguzin Mountains thrusting themselves into the white sky. I'd like nothing more than to get farther up into these mountains and explore the truly wild territory to the north. Alas, we don't have the time. Besides, the few trails here are almost all like the one we were just on—"not convenient," as Andrei put it. Hiking trails as we know them in America are almost nonexistent in Russia. But Andrei's been to the U.S., he's seen trails in national parks and national forests, and he has an idea for this part of Russia: a network of hiking trails around the entire length and breadth of Baikal. A Circum-Baikal trail, maybe 2,000 kilometers long, modeled on trails like the Appalachian Trail in the U.S.. And local volunteers and visitors would help build it. Here again, Andrei says he knows it can happen because he's seen it work elsewhere—trails built and maintained by volunteer work crews. And he has a vision for the trail, inspired by something he brought home from America. "I show to my students a picture of President Clinton and Vice President Albert Gore," Andrei tells me, "and they are doing some work as volunteers on Appalachian Trail. It is first time President is coming to trail, and doing some job for it. And I would like for my President, President Putin, to come to Baikal trail, first national trail, and do something for this trail, for example, build a bridge. And my dream is to have such a photo. Our President, he's first in our nation, he should show good example."

The stream meets the woods road, and the woods road finally flattens out and drops us back at the foot of the hills, on the floor of the Barguzin Valley just outside of town. We head off toward Barguzin and the home of Sergei and Tania Filippov.

9

Traveling and Staying Home

In which we learn about the world
as seen from the town of Barguzin

"I have not tested this—it is secret recipe!" Sergei Filippov says, as he tends to a pot of what look like meatballs simmering on his small stove, and his kitchen fills with their aroma. "I don't know if it will be any good. If not, we will have fish!" There are seventeen kinds of fish in the Barguzin River, Sergei tells me, and he has three varieties on hand tonight, in case his secret beef recipe fails to please. "Omul, sig, and—how do you say in English?—carp? I cook often. My wife is a teacher, she works a lot. I like to cook, but not all the time!"

Sergei may well be the only person in his town who speaks more than a few words of English, and he didn't learn it in school. He's taught himself. "I began to learn English from an American friend of mine," Sergei says. "Patricia. She came to stay with us. She did not speak Russian. I did not speak English. We began writing to each other, in both languages, side by side, on one piece of paper."

Sergei's round face and wavy, dark hair carry hints of both Buryat and Russian, but mostly they carry a warm smile and a soft and welcoming demeanor not immediately found in many of his countrymen. He's the first Russian I've met whom I felt immediately drawn to. We've come fifty kilometers up the

Barguzin River from Baikal to stay with Sergei and his wife, Tania, here in the town of Barguzin. Through Andrei, we're paying them for dinner, breakfast, and a night's lodging in their small apartment. But I get the feeling that if he could afford it, Sergei might pay us for the visit.

Sergei's world barely even reaches Baikal, much less far beyond. But in this tiny town, he is a traveler. A few times a year, Andrei arrives with people like us, from America, Europe, Japan. And with each visit, Sergei's world expands as he learns a bit more about life beyond Barguzin, beyond Baikal, beyond Russia. He learns about the habits and interests of others, how they live, and the often surprising ways that the ordinariness of their daily life is similar to his, or not. Sergei is amazed to find that, like him, our father keeps bees. He tells us that he was equally amazed to find that another visitor, from Japan, had never peeled a potato. But whatever he learns, Sergei tries to keep in touch with his visitors after they leave. He corresponds in English with those who speak the world's lingua franca, and he's begun to teach himself Japanese by corresponding with visitors from Japan. "It is good to have friends around the world," he tells us, echoing his Russian friend Andrei.

Sergei did leave Barguzin once. After high school, he went to study physics across Lake Baikal in Irkutsk, a relatively worldly city with a rich history and cultural heritage. "But then," he says, "my older brothers said, you are youngest, you must come home and take care of our father. So I came back. I have been back eighteen years."

Sergei tries hard not to sound dissatisfied with his life here, but his praise of his hometown is faint. It has wonderful mountains, he says, lots of good forests and rivers and fish and gardens. "And mosquitoes! They say lots of mosquitoes means good nature!" And there is his family. His father is still living, and his daughter and six-year-old grandson are here as well. He speaks of his family with affection, but even this turns toward lament. "Maybe it is not so good, so many generations here. There are not many jobs here. Many young people leave."

Like others we've met and will yet meet on this journey, Sergei's wistfulness is almost too much to bear. His is a life not of lost opportunities or poor decisions but of few opportunities at all, and decisions made, or circumscribed, by people and forces at work far beyond his own close horizons. And even when he's had opportunities to travel, he hasn't been able to take advantage of them. His friend Patricia, from whom he began to learn English, invited Sergei and Tania to come visit her in Japan, where she lives. She even offered to pay their airfare. But Sergei says he still couldn't afford to go. "Japan is too expensive," he says, "and we haven't much money. Maybe after my daughter is finished with school. We have to pay for it all. My son and my older daughter, too, we had to pay for everything. Perestroika! I think Perestroika was not so good. You know,

I grew up in communist system. Our education was paid for, medicine, the government in Moscow built many schools and universities all over the country. Now, here in Buryatia, we haven't money to build anything. Now it is difficult. So maybe I go to Japan later on."

Perhaps it's just the slice of Russian life that we're encountering on this journey, people who take in visitors to supplement their meager salaries or to rebuild savings decimated by the collapse of the ruble, but many here clearly mourn the demise of the old cradle-to-grave communist system, however repressive and limiting it may have been. I'll find it from these isolated hamlets of Siberia to the farthest western reaches of European Russia. The New Russia, the Russia of freedom and opportunity, does not hold hope and promise for all.

But as they do everywhere, people here find things that sustain them.

As Sergei and I talk in the kitchen, Tania arrives, bearing a thin iron crescent, perhaps a yard long and an inch and a half wide. She holds it up for us, balancing it between her fingers. It's the blade of a saber, she says, just dug up at a local archaeological site. Then she pulls from her pocket two heavily tarnished coins that she says some local kids found and brought to her. She's seen coins like these before, she says. They're from the mid-nineteenth century. Tania will add all of the items to the collection of the local museum of Barguzin history and culture, of which she's the curator, a volunteer position that she squeezes in around her job as a teacher at the Barguzin school.

Unlike her husband's, Tania's initial bearing seems reserved, almost stern. But her brusque demeanor quickly melts, although her forcefulness does not. She demands that we come with her to see her school and her museum. We bundle up and head into the chill outside. Over the few blocks to the school, we pass along gravel streets under a sky of the same color, fronted by cold brick apartment blocks like Sergei and Tania's, brooding dark timber houses with their ornate blue windows and lace curtains, fences of chicken wire, white pickets, and ragged planks, one tagged with graffiti—"Scooter," written large and small, a hundred times in stylized English. The school, Barguzin's only one for its 2,000 or so students, was built in the 1970s, but its masonry and wood walls look much older. A caretaker leads us into the school's dark and cavernous halls, our footsteps clattering on the wooden floors and echoing off the blue plaster walls. Big posters commemorate the hundred-somethingth anniversary of the school, started by exiled Decembrists—plotters against Tsar Nicholas I in 1825 who were banished to Siberia.

Two flights up, Tania ushers us into a small classroom, where she teaches math to high schoolers. It's prim and tidy, the chairs neatly turned atop their desks, the shelves proudly displaying their meager collection of books, the blackboard wiped clean in front. And in back there's a doorway to an even smaller room—the school's computer lab. A dozen or so terminals line the walls,

1970s-vintage models with tiny black screens and green pixels that I think might be more appropriately placed in her museum, next to a quill pen and an abacus, perhaps. This is where Tania teaches basic programming, to help prepare students for life in twenty-first-century Russia. Two machines in the corner represent the state of the art for Barguzin's entire school-age population—PCs from the stone age of the early 1990s, running a primitive version of Windows and linked to the World Wide Web with a glacial Internet connection. Tania shows all of this off—the dank halls, the sparse classroom, the prehistoric computers—matter-of-factly, without any sense of irony or embarrassment. She's proud of her school and her students, proud that she's helping educate Russia's next generation of citizens, proud that they're able to make the most of such meager resources.

From her classroom, Tania leads us back downstairs and out across the schoolyard to an unassuming, one-story building—her museum. And as we approach, she suddenly becomes more animated. She's dedicated to her work back in the school, but this museum is clearly her passion. This is Barguzin's ark—the repository of its history and its culture. Over the next ten minutes, Tania whisks us through a time capsule of her community, containing everything from arrowheads to samovars to a stuffed moose. In this corner, a mastodon tusk and bones. Over there, a stuffed sable, the animal with the lustrous fur that drew the first Russians to the Baikal area. And in that cabinet, documents from the early history of the town, settled in 1646, just three years after those first Russian trappers arrived. The clutter and near-randomness of its organization recall the odd old museums that fascinated me as a kid, places like Harvard's dusky old Peabody Museum, a Victorian relic crammed with human and natural artifacts pilfered from the far corners of the world and presented in an incoherent jumble that stimulated abundant fascination with the world, even if it did little to actually elucidate the significance of the items. Except that this raucous assemblage is utterly sincere and specific, and it tells you more than you thought there could possibly be to know about this tiny spot on earth.

At one point, Tania opens a glass case, pulls out two stone arrowheads, and hands them to me and James. It was with objects like these, thrust and thrown with Koufax-like accuracy, that the first human inhabitants of Siberia, of Barguzin before it was Barguzin, likely cleared the forests of wooly rhinoceroses and mastodons. Their perfect shape and scalpel edges are testimony to the tremendous skill of these early craftsmen, and I'm amazed to be holding these ancient weapons in my hands. But I barely have time to marvel before Tania leads us on to the next item, and the next. And in the midst of the whirlwind tour, the lights suddenly go out, and, it now being well after sundown, the museum is thrust into total darkness. Tania instantly excuses herself, vanishes into the void, and returns thirty seconds later with two candles, resuming her tour without missing a beat. This is life in Siberia—you learn to adapt.

Almost as quickly, the lights are back on and we're in a corner looking at a large piece of paper covered with Hebrew letters. It's part of a small exhibit on the Jews of Barguzin. They were among the early settlers, Tania tells us, and were later involved in mining for gold and other minerals. Among the documents is a scrapbook chronicling the life of a Jewish resident who immigrated to Palestine and became one of the founders of the state of Israel. His son recently returned to Barguzin for a commemoration of the man's life. The exhibit is given no special prominence in the museum, but Tania seems as proud of it as of anything here.

As I survey her museum, I'm awestruck by Tania's labor of love for her place and community. Her husband's imagination wanders off far beyond Barguzin and Russia, but in this small building, Tania seems determined to prove that Barguzin is as worthy of interest and attention as anywhere on the planet.

At precisely 8:00 the door opens and I remember why Tania has been rushing us through her collection. It's Sergei, here to collect us for dinner in his rattletrap old Soviet jeep, just as he said he would.

Sergei's meatballs are good, as are his three kinds of fish, potatoes and beets with sour cream, the bread, honey, and jam, and the tea made with a local herb. And of course the vodka, which, having begun to develop a taste and a tolerance for, I drink more freely than I did at the Old Believers' home a few days ago. Over dinner, James and I present them with a few modest gifts that we've brought from home—a Red Sox hat, some postcards of famous Boston landmarks, some newly minted Massachusetts quarters, and a jug of maple syrup from a farm down the street from our family's farm in the Berkshire foothills. They're surprised at how old some of Boston's buildings are. They've never heard of maple syrup. They have heard of the luckless Red Sox.

After a while, and more vodka, Sergei brings out a guitar and starts singing—sweet, sorrowful ballads of the kind that manage to conjure up longing for a place and time and people completely unknown to you. But the songs are merely brief interludes. Sergei wants to know more about life in America, and grills James for information on how our father's beekeeping in America compares with the way he practices the same craft here. While they talk, Tania tells me that, like James, her twenty-three-year-old nephew has just earned his biology degree and that he wants to become a game manager but is now working as a commercial hunter of sable, deer, and squirrel. She asks me whether James likes to hunt or fish. I tell her no, and she replies, "then he'll be a good biologist." And as the evening wears on, another face appears in the small living room—a radiant young woman wearing an astonishing leopard-skin pillbox hat, like something right out of an Audrey Hepburn movie or the Bob Dylan song. She's introduced as Olga and has apparently come by to return a videotape, although I'll find out later that this was just a pretext to come meet the Americans. Olga knows some rudimentary English and stumbles through a halting conversation with far more grace and good humor than I'm able to muster in Russian. We're even able to talk a bit about work—she teaches ecology at the Barguzin school, and I'm able to convey that, back at home, I often write about ecology. As we talk, her face radiates a beguiling warmth and charm and engagement with life. I am totally smitten. And like Tania, I'm suddenly thinking that Barguzin might be as interesting as anywhere on earth. Fortunately, over the course of our conversation, I also learn that she's married. Barguzin will stay just a vivid memory.

Sergei, of course—the traveler—also wants to hear of our journey. How we got here to Barguzin.

PART TWO

180°

July-October, 2000

To believe in the journey is to have already arrived.

—Harvey Oxenhorn, *Tuning the Rig*

10

The Long Way Home

*In which we rewind to the very beginning of our journey,
start following the trail west, and realize that
if we get no farther we will have gone far enough*

A Friday in July . . .

Boston is a tangle of cranes and earthmovers, half-built flyovers and half-dug
trenches and a huge steel snake slithering along the narrowest of paths through
the chaos—Amtrak's *Lake Shore Limited*, weaving its way through the city's $15 bil-
lion highway construction project known as the Big Dig and heading westward
toward Albany, Cleveland, and Chicago. We've said our last goodbyes to the
family, hauled our backpacks into our two-person sleeping compartment, and
finally, after weeks of ever-more frantic preparation, begun to feel the rhythm
of the world rumbling slowly by beneath us, the rhythm of our lives for the next
six months.

    The train picks up headway as it groans past the hallowed green walls
of Fenway Park, home of the Boston Red Sox and the spiritual center of New

England, the dense triple-decker blocks of the inner suburbs and the verdant lawns and oak groves of the outer suburbs. James and I sit across from each other, grinning slightly, both a little intoxicated by a cocktail of excitement, relief, and anxiety. Family, friends, work, school, daily antagonisms, and well-worn rituals are all receding physically if not yet mentally. Over the horizon ahead loom Alaska, the Pacific, Japan, Vladivostok, Lake Baikal, and 25,000 miles or so of who knows what else. But it's no big deal, we tell ourselves. We're heading home, just taking the long way.

Just past dawn, west of Cleveland, we're running two and a half hours late. Our sleeping car attendant, Fred, tells us that we lost time overnight to track repairs, slow-loading mail shipments, and freight trains. Once you start to lose a little time on this run, he says, you quickly end up losing a lot, because the tracks are owned by the freight companies, and their trains have priority. If an Amtrak train slips off schedule, it starts the kind of chain reaction of delays that have earned this train the nickname the *Late Shore Limited*. I ask Fred if we're going to make our connection in Chicago. "Not if we keep stopping like this," he says. I ask him if it's hard working on a train that's always late, with anxious passengers always cranky at him about something that's never his fault. "You get used to it," he says, with a weak smile. Beyond the windows of our compartment, we're being passed by cars running along a 30 mile-an-hour zone of a two-lane rural road.

Fred confirms what a look around the train suggests—that most of the passengers on this run are people who aren't in a hurry to get where they're going. They're mostly elderly or retired, he says. And then there are the single mothers with kids, usually trying to leave something, or someone, behind. "Many of these folks just can't wait to unload their stories," Fred tells me. "They just want to talk to someone unconnected to their lives." These women are all sad and stressed out, he says, anxious about what they've left behind and what lies ahead. "But they all say that things could be worse," he says. "They say, 'At least we're not riding the bus!'"

When his shifts are done, Fred tells me, he flies from his base in Chicago back home to Cleveland. "It's just not worth wasting time on the train."

North of Milwaukee, the *Empire Builder* rolls across a Wisconsin that is flat, brilliant green and coursed with countless small rivers and lakes. The *Late Shore*

Limited limped into Chicago three and a half hours late, but they held the *Empire Builder* for the many passengers like us who were making the connection. This is a big and crowded train, jammed on this July weekend with vacationers heading for the upper Midwest, the northern Rockies, and the Pacific Northwest, even taking a 10,000-mile loop around the whole country. A Boy Scout troop from Ohio, with at least one girl member, is bound for Glacier National Park. A couple who may be the only Americans between the Hudson River and San Francisco Bay who don't own a car are heading home to Minneapolis. A marriage counselor is taking a long vacation from her home in Texas with her retired military husband. Over dinner in a dining car of clattering dishes and sloshing wine glasses, she tells us that the only thing she couldn't forgive our recently impeached president for would be if he really did have an affair with Paula Jones. "She's so ugly!" she says. "She had a face lift and she's *still* ugly!"

Sleeping in the seats, single moms with kids.

The setting prairie sun casts a deep amber glow over the heartland. I am loving America.

Stars and Stripes lamppost flags, the Golden Age Club, a Dry Goods and Mercantile store, a hot, bleaching sun, not a single person—the main street of Stanley, North Dakota, population 1,279, as observed on a July Sunday morning from the bathroom of the *Empire Builder*. This is one of my favorite things about this train—clear windows in the head, rather than opaque glass. You can watch the world roll by while sitting on the can. But apparently not everyone shares my enthusiasm for this amenity. Every time I come in I open the curtain, and every time I go back, it's always closed again. I guess most people just don't want to be seen sitting on the can, even if it's only by cows and jackrabbits.

Beyond Stanley, a blanket of wheat and soybean fields covers a soft, undulating plain. The thick green shimmers and swirls in the squalls barreling out of the west.

We meet the Missouri River at Williston, North Dakota. The great river loops toward and away from us like a big, soft coil, light coffee brown. Liquid soil, Montana flowing to the Gulf of Mexico.

Sandstone buttes and spires have started to appear to the south, cottonwood trees on the riverbanks. We're definitely in the West now.

In western Montana, the plain rises almost imperceptibly and slowly begins to crumple, and then, almost out of nowhere, the Rockies rear up and blot out the sun, like a monstrous rogue wave. At East Glacier Park station, passengers stream off the train and into a massive log lodge built by the Great

Northern Railway in 1913 out of the five-foot-thick, 600-year-old Douglas firs that used to carpet the Rocky Mountain Front.

Heading into the park, the orange sun still catches the bare, razor-sharp peaks beyond the muted greens of our dark valley. We cross the Rockies over Marias Pass, at 5,216 feet the lowest pass over the mountains between Canada and Mexico, and follow the Flathead River down the other side of the Continental Divide, the water alternating between flat and glassy with broad gravel bars and narrow and rapid with banks of sharp, acutely angled sedimentary rock.

The sun's down. The sky is brilliant blue, the wispy clouds bright orange. There's no horizon—you can only see up.

Five-thirty A.M. Running through a broad valley between low, brown hills. Ground-hugging sagebrush casts long shadows in the almost perpendicular orange rays of the brand new sun, alternating with orchards and verdant cropland irrigated by huge center-pivot sprayers that look like giant silver stick-bugs. We're in central Washington's Inland Empire, the twentieth-century cornucopia built on Columbia River water diversions and hydroelectric power plants that in mid-century brought the desert to life even as they virtually erased the last vestiges of the river-based indigenous cultures of the Columbia basin.

Suddenly, we're deep in the thick coniferous forests of the Cascade Mountains, then out again, descending along a narrow, sinuous valley. At Everett, a glint of blue, a finger of the Pacific beckoning us along the final stretch of the way west. Seattle and Puget Sound are familiar territory to both James and me, but the sight nonetheless quickens our hearts, although perhaps not quite as much as those of the millions who heeded Horace Greeley's call to "Go west, young man" in the great migration between the completion of the transcontinental railroads and the Second World War. Among these millions were various Thomson ancestors, following the lead of young Origen, from Indiana. The first of these was R.H. Thomson, who soon became Seattle's chief engineer and led the overhaul of the streets, railroads, and water and sewer systems that transformed the city around the turn of the century, and the last was our grandfather William Orville Thomson, who arrived in Seattle in 1912, went into the publishing business, married his second cousin Jesse Cox, and began to raise three Thomson boys and a girl, John, David, Peter, and Patricia, before losing his business, his marriage, and nearly his kids in the Great Depression. His last book couldn't have been more ill-titled or ill-timed: *Thomson's Manual of Pacific Northwest Finance*, published just after the stock market crash of September, 1929.

Finally, skittering along the fractured edge of the continent, this latest generation of Thomson wanderers sees the blue and white Olympics come into view, glittering across Puget Sound, the ferries and freighters that are the circulatory system of this region, and the forest of cargo cranes and skyscrapers that is the dense heart of Seattle, and then it all suddenly disappears again and we're in blackness under the city and the brakes are hissing and squealing in the tunnel until finally the giant steel snake exhausts itself just back out in the open by Pioneer Square, the center of the old downtown of lumberjacks, stevedores, prospectors, dreamers, and drunks. We emerge from the *Empire Builder* into a Seattle bathed in bright, cool sunlight.

•

Shapeless low clouds hang flat over the narrow channels and rocky shores of Washington's San Juan Islands, thick with arrow-straight cedars, the deep green broken here and there by a house, a patch of pale green lawn, or a hayfield rising toward the interior. For the first time since we set out nearly a week ago, I'm on my own for a few hours, and glad to be. James is back in the woods on Lopez Island, in a cabin without plumbing at the end of a road without a name, visiting friends from school, and I'm riding the ferry over to Friday Harbor, the biggest town among these small islands.

The ragged, rocky shores, the tall, dark conifers, and the narrow blue channels of the San Juans remind me of the coast of Maine, one of my favorite landscapes in the world. But mostly, despite my best efforts to forget, they remind me of my only other trip here, almost five years ago, Christmas. It was going to be the last time Emma and I would see each other before she headed back to Southeast Asia for another six months of anthropology fieldwork, from which she would return the following summer, when we were going to get married. I'd arranged the trip and was trying to put together a memorable holiday in a cabin by a rocky beach, but it was a disaster from the get-go, a week-long argument. She was cranky about everything I'd planned, cranky about the duck I'd cooked, cranky especially about going back to her island village, which, it ultimately became clear, was the precipitant of all her crankiness—her anxiety and deep ambivalence about her work there bubbling over and seeming to poison her entire being. It was awful, for both of us. The brilliant, magnetic, hilarious, and beautiful woman I'd fallen in love with like no one before had been replaced by a malevolent, acid cloud. I'd seen this happen before, but never for so long, never so completely. And when it did, I'd convinced myself that the very dark and scary place that she occasionally disappeared into was just a little basement in her soul with a door that I could coax her back through and that she could keep safely shut behind her most of the time, rather than a black hole that threatened to consume her and everyone around her. Here in the San Juans that Christmas, I still wanted to believe that, but I began to fear otherwise. Now here I am back, on a trip made possible only by the hole blown in my life by that explosive relationship. I'm getting to live the dream of millions, getting to go places and do things that I never thought possible, getting to measure the world in the rotation of steel wheels, propeller spins, footsteps, and heartbeats and to stare down into its deepest blue eye. Would I trade this adventure of a lifetime for that marriage working out better?

In a heartbeat.

•

James and my original plan was just to go to Alaska for a month or so. From that grew the idea to just keep going west, straight on to the Far East and Russia. So we set out to find a boat from somewhere in Alaska across the Pacific. A freighter, a fishing boat, a kayak. And if we'd had more time and determination, we probably could've found such a boat, someone to take us on as paying passengers, crew, stowaways. But we didn't have a lot of time to look, and we weren't so attached to the idea that we'd let ourselves get hung up on it. So when we couldn't find one, we settled for passage across the Pacific from the Lower 48. But we stuck to the plan to get there by way of Alaska.

•

July 21, Georgia Strait, British Columbia

A week out of Boston, eighteen hours out of Bellingham, Washington, morning fog gives way to brilliant sunshine illuminating whales and eagles and the sunglasses and brimmed hats of more than 400 humans crowding the decks of the *M.V. Matanuska*, plying the Alaska Marine Highway's three-and-a-half-day route along the Inside Passage between Bellingham and Skagway, Alaska. By afternoon, the broad open water of British Columbia's Georgia Strait narrows into labyrinthine channels through a seriously crumpled coastline draped in thick forest. North America broken into little shards of rock, the crumbs of a continent. The unseen helmsmen pivot the ship ninety degrees west, then full north again, veer a bit east, then northwest and west again, then again north, and it goes on like this most of the day and into the fog and drizzle of the night. I imagine the first European and Russian explorers trying to make their way through here, perhaps taking decades and hundreds of dashed vessels to chart the region and find the best routes and build the body of knowledge that allows us to get through today with thousands of oohs and aahs but never a moment of fear.

Inside Passage, Day 3, North of Ketchikan, Alaska

There's a break in the cold rain, and the deck of the *Matanuska* has filled with a chorus of splatters as James and I and the dozens of others who began this voyage by setting up camp out here all wring our tents and belongings out after a miserable, soggy night. Whose idea was it, anyway, to pitch tents on an impermeable steel deck of a ship sailing through a rainforest? Ah, but this is the great tradition of this route in the summertime—a floating campground, tents from rail to rail. Not that we had much choice—it was either pitch a tent on the deck or squeeze into a spot on the floor inside. The *Matanuska* was pressed into service after a fire disabled the much larger ship that regularly serves this run, and it's packed. Inside, where the rain and fog have forced all but the most intrepid or foolhardy, every few minutes the PA crackles with an ever-more-frazzled voice, urging diners to move on from their seats in the cafeteria when they're done eating, reminding those seated in the lounges that they can't save their chairs when they leave them, warning everyone to watch their step on the wet floors, and less and less gently reproaching antsy kids not to run in the hallways, which has its desired effect for about thirty seconds.

Still, the squeeze and the weather don't seem to have dampened anyone's enthusiasm for their adventure.

"It's like one big slumber party," says Chuck, a burly fisherman from Michigan on his annual pilgrimage to work the canneries of Ketchikan, sitting where he slept in the crowded forward lounge. "I love it." A dozen or so teenage Christian missionaries from Texas are a mass of restless excitement, wearing grins as big as their state at the memory of yesterday's whales and eagles and all those tall trees and open water. A divorced grandmother from Colorado hobbles around the ship like a dogged wind-up toy, bobbing stiffly on legs damaged at birth by cerebral palsy, but eager to take in everything she can on her annual

trip to a new part of the country. An eloping couple from New Orleans are giddy with excitement, while an ancient wisp of a man on a solo trip from Los Angeles by train and boat to visit his great-grandchildren in Juneau watches the crowd and whatever dramatic landscape he can see with a serene enthusiasm. And then there is Jacob, a squinty-eyed ten-year-old with tousled black hair, who's traveling with his parents and two brothers to Anchorage, to meet the man who found the message in a bottle that Jacob threw into Puget Sound months ago. And I thought our adventure was improbable.

I learn about all these people not because this voyage has suddenly transformed me into an extrovert, sidling up to strangers and striking up conversations, but because I've put on my Extrovert costume—my headphones and microphone—a disguise intended to fool only myself and that allows me to, well, sidle up to strangers and strike up conversations. I realized years ago that in journalism I'd chosen an enterprise that cuts sharply against my own grain in that it requires me to engage people in intelligent and purposeful conversation when at my core I've always felt shy and slow-witted. I told myself I did this because journalism is fundamental to the workings of democracy and that it was my solemn duty to help inform the citizens of these United States about important issues and events before them, blah, blah, blah, but what I realized years later is this: Being a journalist forces me to engage with people with whom I might otherwise never figure out how to start or maintain a conversation. It allows me to move beyond myself and find out what other people think and feel, to hear their stories and learn how they make sense of the world. And it requires me to face up to the irrational fear and awkwardness that otherwise so often tyrannize me, and to tell myself, *Sorry, gotta do this. It's my job.*

Inside Passage Day 4, North of Juneau

I've nodded off in a lot of bars, but this is the first time I've spent the whole night in one. Yesterday's rain got worse, and by evening the ship's crew invited soggy campers into the *Matanuska*'s cocktail lounge. By 10:00 P.M. the bar's tinkling piano music had been replaced by snores wafting over its vinyl armchairs and crimson carpet.

We emerge from the dark bar into a bright, dry day and almost deserted decks. Nearly half of the ship's passengers disembarked at the 5 A.M. stop in Juneau, and it feels like the rest of us are stragglers at a party who crashed on the couches while everyone else went home, and are now left in the glare and stupor of the next morning to help clean up the empty bottles, crushed chips, and cigarette butts.

Among those still on board are Jacob and his family, and every time I turn around, he's back with a round of questions, determined, it seems, to turn the tables on me, the reporter. "How come you're traveling with your brother? How come he's so much younger than you are? You had to sleep in a tent? On the floor? It was wet? Oh no! How come you're taking a boat across the ocean? Do you have any pets? . . . " all of which I'm more than happy to answer. Perhaps it's because he's not yet old enough to have picked up on the faux world-weariness of so many of today's American kids, or he hasn't yet had all the curiosity squashed out of him by unimaginative teachers, or he's lucky enough to have parents who haven't told him not to pester strangers with rude questions, but I've really taken a shine to this inquisitive, slightly eccentric kid. He's the best advertisement for *Homo sapiens* that this world-weary adult has encountered in weeks.

The *Matanuska* slips into its dock in Skagway in the shadows of two monstrous cruise ships, floating cities that dwarf our modest little 400-passenger craft. Skagway is at the head of the last fjord on the Inside Passage, a place born to service the hordes of miners drawn north by the Klondike Gold Rush toward the end of the nineteenth century and reborn to service the hordes of tourists drawn north by the new gold rush of the Alaska cruise ship trade toward the end of the twentieth century. In port, Jacob invites James and me to stay with him at his family's hotel. He invites us to accompany his family to Anchorage. He invites himself to come with us to the Yukon and Fairbanks. And a few days after we see the last of him, I'll get an email from his father, Don: "We are now in Haines. Jacob claims that the ferry ride just isn't the same without you. . . ."

•

The White Pass Railroad labors from Skagway up over the steep Coast Mountains, traversing the same narrow ravines and precipitous slopes climbed by thousands of hopeful Klondike miners, most of whom returned empty-handed, if they returned at all. From the terminus of the railroad, it's a day-and-a-half ride to Fairbanks by bus over the mountains and broad valleys of Alaska, British Columbia, the Yukon Territory, and finally Alaska again, passing along the way through the metropolis of Whitehorse, on the Yukon River, population 19,000, and the resort community of Burwash Landing, population 81; stopping to sleep and play miniature golf in the never-quite-dark of an outpost that you decide is called Mosquito Links, and crossing some of the most entrancingly desolate country you will ever see, a ghostly landscape of silver lakes and jagged mountains, gray glacial outwash, and purple lupines and fireweed.

And then, you get to Fairbanks, and you wonder why you came.

Our uncle John Thomson lived in Fairbanks for a few years in the 1950s. Later, our grandfather wrote of his relief at John's return to the Lower 48, "My older son . . . came out of Alaska two years ago after a four-year hitch in the 49th state, where he served two years as a reporter on the Fairbanks *Times-Miner* [sic] and two years as public relations director of the University of Alaska. He made no mistake coming out. . . ." This is only my second visit to Fairbanks, and when I leave I will have spent a total of about four days here, so it really wouldn't be fair of me to say that nothing seems to have happened to change our grandfather's estimation of this place. But nothing does seem to have happened to change our grandfather's estimation of this place.

There are one or two pleasant restaurants in Fairbanks, a friendly bookshop, the beautiful Tanana River that meanders through town, and a good university that's a leader in research on cold climates and global warming. And there's certainly no shortage of access to wilderness, big sky, and solitude. Many people lead quite happy lives here. But to these two outsiders, with no ties here, Fairbanks feels very much like what it actually is: the end of the road, the place where the country with the most miles of pavement on the planet finally ran out of reasons to lay down another inch. The city is ramshackle houses and battered cars sinking into driveways, listless kids sitting in the middle of the streets, empty storefronts and bingo halls, and Eskimos, Indians and Anglos staggering in and out of bars, all seeming to carry with them stories of broken lives, damaged communities, lost cultures, shattered families, and dashed hopes. It feels more than anything like a displaced persons camp, a profoundly lonely place inhabited largely by human screws that have popped out of the works of society and rattled off into this dismal corner.

This last paragraph is probably the most unfair characterization of a place that I've ever written, and I may rightly be taken to task for it. So let me offer the more tempered appraisal of my more charitable brother: "I wouldn't recommend coming here unless you're on your way someplace else."

•

There is, of course, a hopeful side of Fairbanks. It can be found in places like Dogpatch, a little community strung along a dirt road north of town, where you'll meet people like Celia Hunter. Celia is among the last of a breed, an Alaska pioneer who landed here nearly sixty years ago, carved out a life for herself, and left a profound imprint on the landscape and the culture. And Dogpatch is the neighborhood that she and her longtime companion Ginny Wood share with a bunch of friends, named after the hillbilly town in the old Al Capp comic strip *Li'l Abner*.

Celia first came to Alaska during World War II, flying planes up from the West Coast on their way over to Russia. In the 1950s, she and Ginny and Ginny's then-husband Woody founded a wilderness camp in the backcountry near Mt. McKinley, a place called Camp Denali that was an early model of what would later become known as ecotourism, in an area that would later become Denali National Park. And in a place that at the time seemed nearly infinite and inexhaustible, Celia was among the few to sound the alarm about Alaska's vulnerability to unchecked resource and tourism development. She's since been involved in every major land battle in a state in which land battles are the only major league sport, helping push through national legislation that more than doubled the size of Denali National Park and Preserve and that established virtually all the state's other national parks, preserves, and wilderness areas, including the still much fought-over Arctic National Wildlife Refuge. Look at any map of Alaska and you'll get an idea of how important her efforts have been. At eighty-plus, she's still both revered and reviled here, but pretty much universally respected as someone who's devoted her life to protecting the place she loves most.

Our uncle John rented a cabin from Celia when he lived here in the '50s, and they've remained friends since. I met her on my first visit to Fairbanks three years ago, and on this trip James and I spend two afternoons in her Dogpatch cabin, listening to stories of her life here.

•

From Fairbanks, the Alaska Railroad's gleaming old yellow and blue cars descend through the state's vast interior plain and across the broad Yukon River to Denali National Park, almost 10,000 square miles of protected wilderness surrounding North America's highest peak, a mammoth white sleeping abominable snowman of a mountain looming over the surrounding terrain of crumpled brown and green; then on to Anchorage, Alaska's only real city, sprawling above the tidal flats between the Chugach Mountains and Cook Inlet, and finally on to the port of Whittier, squeezed onto the edge of a narrow fjord at the westernmost edge of Prince William Sound. James and I will travel every inch of it, more than 400 miles altogether. We'll stop and hike and camp and visit with friends and see remarkable things along the way, and a big part of each of us will wish we could stay here, but we've made plans to be somewhere else a lot farther from home still, so we keep moving.

•

Kayaks and kittiwakes chase our little ferry out of Whittier on a brilliant August day when the water sparkles like a sea of sapphires, when the gulls squeal and cling to their rookery on a sheer rock face turned almost pure white by their guano, when a hundred snoring sea lions bask on a gravel beach as our captain cuts the engine and we slip almost noiselessly by, when the gigantic Columbia Glacier strews icebergs of dirty gray and luminescent blue in our path, when we're made dizzy by a swirl of dolphins, uninhabited islands, and mountains like massive arrowheads plunging into the sea, when it seems impossible that this place ever could be anything less than perfect. But no one can cross Prince William Sound, or even think about it, without also thinking about Good Friday, 1989, when a supertanker laden with Alaska North Slope crude veered off course to avoid icebergs and hit a well-known and well-marked reef, and suddenly hundreds of miles of pristine Alaska coastline were smeared in thick, black, smothering oil.

The *Exxon Valdez* oil spill shocked and enraged America. Images of oil-soaked otters, seabirds struggling to free themselves from an ocean of black tar, and space-suited men blasting oil off rocks with fire hoses seared themselves into our collective consciousness and remain imprinted on our culture and our politics today. In a way, the disaster quickly became the Vietnam of the environment, a universally understood symbol of worst-case scenarios and our inability to predict or control the outcomes of our actions, despite all assurances to the contrary. *It can't happen here*, we were all told, *we've made sure of it*. But it did. And as one local fisherman told me when I first came to this part of Alaska a year and a half ago, as the tenth anniversary of the spill approached, a huge swath of one of the most beautiful and ecologically productive pieces of America's Last Frontier is "forever changed."

Exxon says that eleven years later the Prince William Sound ecosystem is on the mend and has proved to be a lesson in nature's resilience. This is certainly true. But it's equally true to put it another way: The *Exxon Valdez* disaster is proving to be a lesson in the long-lasting impacts and wide-ranging ripple effects of environmental carelessness. Many scientists say it may take decades more for the region's ecosystem to completely rid itself of the effects of the spill, if it ever does. And certainly, the human communities here can never regain what they've lost. As the tenth anniversary of the disaster approached, local residents told me of black oil still lurking just beneath the surface of area beaches and the subtle damage that it likely continues to do to wildlife. They told me of a silent sea where the water was once afroth with everything from herring to whales, and of worthless fishing businesses in a salmon market that never recovered from the spill. They spoke of lingering anger, depression, divorce, suicide, and the destruction of age-old traditions in native communities. And they told me of the hollow feeling that they get when visitors tell them how beautiful the sound looks—a superficial beauty, they said, masking a darker reality.

I think of all this as I pass through some of the most stunning and emotionally compelling landscape I've ever seen, and especially when I see the steel tower marking Bligh Reef—"Hazelwood's Stick," some locals mockingly call it, after the ship's disgraced captain—the spot where the assurances of an industry and a government went hard aground, the promises proving to be as hollow and vulnerable as a wayward single-hulled tanker. And then I think about that other storied body of water that still awaits me on the other side of the world, one even more unique and perhaps even more vulnerable, and I think about what I've heard about it—*infinite . . . powerful . . . resilient*—and about the assurances that have been made there, and I wonder what lessons Prince William Sound could teach Russia and the world about taking risks at Lake Baikal.

•

I could tell you about Cordova, the remarkable little town I found when I came to Prince William Sound last year to report on the tenth anniversary of the *Exxon Valdez* oil spill, tucked at the edge of the sound between steep forested hills and a small harbor protected by tufted green and white islands, a community still licking its terrible wounds from ten years before but very much alive even in the dead of winter, displaying an extraordinary spirit and pluck as it wrestled with its radically changed present and uncertain future. I could tell you about the vibrant and feisty blend of Anglos, natives, Mexicans, and Japanese, rednecks, radicals, newcomers, old-timers, leave-me-and-my-land-alone libertarians, and never-allow-a-shovel-to-hit-the-ground greens who all stop to exchange neighborly greetings at the supermarket or the bookstore-cafe, who beat back seasonal depression and cabin fever with an annual mid-winter Ice Worm festival and parade and laugh in the face of danger and of a ravaged fishing industry with a survival suit race, in which residents dive into the frigid February harbor in equipment that they would otherwise wear only in the direst of emergencies at sea; who curse the fact that you can only get to their town by one of the few daily flights into Mudhole Smith Airport or the slowpoke little ferry across Prince William Sound, or who wield their town's isolation as a shield against an assault from the outside world; and whose ambivalence about the new tourism economy is on display in the postcard rack of a local bed and breakfast, which features only multiple copies of a single image: the *Exxon Valdez*, aground on Bligh Reef. I could tell you all of this—and about the Copper River, the massive and untamed ribbon of green water that unfurls out of the Wrangell-St. Elias Mountains just outside of town, and about how, if you're lucky, you might meet a renegade Indian environmental activist and his hippie writer-river guide friend, who might take you on a hallucinogenic, week-long float down the river, shared only with salmon, seals, and grizzlies.

I could tell you all this, but then I'd have to kill you.

I I

The Great Circle

In which we slip through the Golden Gate,
follow the whims of earlier Thomsons out to sea,
and say goodbye to the world as we know it

The Port of San Francisco, once one of the world's most celebrated ports of call, has been reduced to this: a quarter-mile of bare, worn asphalt between a chain link fence and the bay, a couple dozen oblong cargo containers stacked like a set of playroom blocks, and one huge gray cargo crane that looms over the water like the skeleton of some Stanford student's monstrous robotic dog. A few miles to the north, the Embarcadero and its ripsaw ridge of angled piers, once the pulsing heart of the city's commercial port, is today a palm-tree-lined recreational waterfront of restaurants, bars, condos, and t-shirt vendors, while here to the south of downtown, huge swaths of abandoned waterfront lie fallow, awaiting the next wave of redevelopment. The San Francisco Bay itself remains a major Pacific port, but virtually all of its cargo traffic now moves through the modern container terminals of Oakland, across the bay. In the city of San Francisco itself, there remains only a single active cargo pier, and this is it. Pier 80.

Lashed to the far side of the sea of asphalt is a ship, of modest size by contemporary standards but its sheer bulk impressive nonetheless—a hulking mass of emerald green steel looming three stories above the tarmac, a pale yellow superstructure rising eight stories above that in the stern, and a wall of red and blue containers stacked six high above the forward decks. The ship looks awkward and ungainly. It looks like it may well challenge the principles of buoyancy and displacement. It looks like nothing that neither James nor I have ever trusted his life to before.

Our hallucinatory float down the Copper River is ten days behind us. We've reentered civilization in Anchorage, visited friends in Seattle, finally met Gary Cook of Baikal Watch and our Russia-specialist travel agent Debbie, and made other last-minute arrangements here in San Francisco, and now we're riding across the acres of asphalt in the back of a battered yellow van and our friend Eleanor, who drove us down here, is repeating, as if a mantra, *Oh my god, I can't believe you're getting on this thing.... Oh my god, I can't believe ...*

I think it was in the back of *Harper's*, or *The Nation*, that I first saw a tiny ad for a company that could book you passage on a freighter, to just about any port in the world. I'd had a notion to do such a thing since I saw my grandfather off from Boston on an old hybrid cargo-passenger ship bound for Europe when I was six or seven, and I was surprised to find that it was still possible thirty-some years later. But it turns out that passage on cargo ships is a thriving little corner of the international travel market. A quick online search turns up dozens of outfits that will match up travelers with a taste for the unconventional with shipping companies that have unused berths on their vessels. It ain't cheap, it certainly isn't fast, and the uncertainty posed by storms and port delays and other variables requires a degree of flexibility not shared by most travelers these days. But if you've got a thing for going by ship, it's just about the only way to cross the Pacific aside from joining the merchant marine or building your own replica of *Kon-Tiki*. So just before we left Boston, James and I booked passage on the *Pacific Champion*, a 180-meter container ship that was sailing from San Francisco to Pusan, South Korea, in late August. This meant we would have to fly from Anchorage to San Francisco and ditch the idea of doing the entire trip without leaving the surface of the earth, but we convinced ourselves that this wasn't truly a deviation from our original plan, since the flight would carry us not just south but also a bit east, so all of our westward progress across the meridians would still be made by land and sea. So, we rationalized, we could build in this little hiccup and still lay legitimate claim to *All the Way Around, On the Ground*.

Now here on Pier 80, the van drops us by the *Pacific Champion*'s gently sloping hull, we say our thanks and farewells to the still-stunned Eleanor, and our footsteps clang on the open metal stairway as we ascend to the ship's deck. And we, too, are both thinking as we leave terra firma behind for the next two weeks, *Oh my god, I can't believe we're getting on this thing....* But perhaps I'm thinking it more than James because while he's sailed on tall ships and crossed the Atlantic on the *Queen Elizabeth 2*, the only ocean-going vessel I've ever set foot on was the *Queen Mary*, which long ago had her boilers ripped out and won't be going anywhere unless a typhoon tears her from her permanent dock in Long Beach. So this is it. Six weeks into our journey, finally time for something completely different.

•

Long Way Home Journal, September 3

At 2 A.M. we're pushed back from Pier 80 and into the bay by a single tug under a low sky glowing in the lights of the sleeping city. To starboard, other container ships lie at anchor awaiting a berth in Oakland, and beyond them the lights of the East Bay climb the hills into the mist. To port, the lights of the freshly unwrapped Pacific Bell Park, still proudly illuminated hours after the last out of tonight's Giants game, and beyond, the huge, gilded dome of City Hall and the skyscrapers of downtown San Francisco.

Ten minutes or so takes us under the Bay Bridge. Here on the bridge of the *Pacific Champion*, more than eight stories above the water, I feel I can almost reach up and touch the car decks. It still pulses with traffic at 2 A.M.

Past the Ferry Building and Treasure Island, I look east to the forest of lights climbing the hill, to get a fix on Berkeley. I follow the avenues west and north and more or less locate my own neighborhood and street—what used to be my neighborhood.

My excitement at starting this voyage, at being here on this ship, at seeing San Francisco and the East Bay from this vantage point, is tempered by my sorrow at once again leaving this place. It's been with me every day since James and I arrived here, as real and tangible as another traveling companion. And, really, it hasn't left me since I closed the door to our house for the last time and drove away last November.

I went home to Boston for a lot of *very sensible* reasons. I wanted to be around my father while I still could. I felt I should help take care of my mother again. And I wanted to commit myself to a place that I had a history with, and where it felt like my presence could matter. I hated California's fractured politics and its relentless pursuit of the good life. I missed New England and my friends and family. I missed winter. I missed the Red Sox. And I couldn't stay in my house. I couldn't afford it alone, and even if I could have, it was too haunted—by Emma and us and by the hope and faith and life energy spent and squandered there.

And yet I left with an intense ambivalence. Despite feeling drawn home, and despite the things I had come to dislike about California, I still felt a deeper visceral resonance with the Bay Area than I've ever felt with any place. I loved the landscape and cities, the diversity and exuberance of the culture, and the access to the rest of the West, which I was having a blast exploring and reporting on. I had made great new friends here, and rediscovered old ones. Since I left I've missed all these things and all these people, sometimes almost unbearably. But most of all, I've missed the feelings of hope and commitment and excitement and re-creation of my life which brought me here and which are inextricably bound up for me with this place, and probably always will be.

This feeling of loss has barely receded since I left, and it washed back over me upon my return. And in a way, I've realized that my deep ambivalence about having left here is one of the reasons for this trip. I couldn't resolve myself to settling back in Boston, and as the months slipped by, I came to think that maybe it wasn't yet time to settle. I told myself that the divorce had given me a once-in-a-lifetime opportunity to do something like this. What I didn't realize was that maybe I also needed to do it—to shake up my life, get away from both places and just about everything and everyone I've ever known, and see how I feel about things when I'm done.

So here I am, shipping out, on a twelve-day Pacific crossing, arcing northwest between Alcatraz and Angel Island, and then sweeping back southwest toward the Golden Gate Bridge. The bridge's two massive red stanchions stand in stark relief even to the black night sky.

As we pass beyond the bridge and into the open water of the Pacific, I can faintly make out the wail of the foghorn off Baker Beach. From land, it's impossible to miss its warning call—its deep tone reverberates off every cliff of the Golden Gate and every drop of fog it hits. But out here, among its intended audience, its urgent wailing seems utterly lost and insignificant, barely audible above the hum of the ship's engine.

We pass through a narrow channel in the open water, green flashing lights to starboard, red to port. Half an hour or so beyond the bridge, at about 3:30 A.M., the local pilot puts on his coat, descends the eight stories from the bridge, and climbs down a rope ladder from the deck to a small boat that's pulled up alongside us. We are now officially beyond San Francisco's sphere of influence. I head down to my cabin and watch the last lights of the city, now just a distant shimmer off the stern, recede into the blackness.

•

The world is gone, terra firma and the sum of all human endeavor reduced to twenty-five souls clinging to a speck of flotsam adrift on a blue infinity. San Francisco, North America, everything that once was, has fallen off the edge, and all there is is us and the sea and the sky. From the bridge of the *Pacific Champion*, the world reverts to a time before time, to the unmeasured days before the Abrahamic God/G-d/Allah or the Polynesian deity Io or the Mayan creator Hurakan or whoever you think it was conjured up solid ground, separated it from the sea and the sky, and plopped humans on it. Out here, the ocean is all and only and forever. And yet this universal sea is in no way uniform or unchanging. The play of light and clouds and wind alters the form, texture, and temperament of the sea and sky from day to day and hour to hour. And with a cadence a good bit slower and subtler than that of the thirty-second ads that have shaped the modern attention span, this world is utterly entrancing.

From the bow, where an aperture called the hawsehole allows us to see directly down to the point of impact between roiling ocean and surging metal, the power of both sea and machine are palpable, the unending clash between the two producing a hypnotic, rhythmic surge of spray and foam. At the ship's long side rails comes the most palpable sense of movement across the expanse; the ship's hull is rigid and stationary against the undulating liquid rushing by at eighteen knots below. And yet without a single landmark by which to measure your progress, this movement apparently accomplishes nothing—it seems only an illusion of motion, a sensation akin to walking up a down escalator. And it's on the wings of the bridge, extended almost as if in flight nearly a hundred feet above the sea, where I feel most completely vulnerable, and completely alive. Slip over the railing here and you're gone. Sure, they've got life buoys and emergency sirens and rescue craft aboard, but by the time anyone even notices you're missing, the likelihood of actually finding you and bringing you back alive would be almost nil. Every night, I head out onto the wings, into the darkness and the wind, and stare down into the churning waves of mesmerizing black below, just to get my blood flowing again on this cramped ship, and I have to hold on tight. Not because I fear being tossed overboard but because I fear I might jump.

The *Pacific Champion* is a 180-meter microcosm of the global economy. It's owned by a German company, it was made in Poland, and it's registered in Antigua and Barbuda. Its twenty-three crew members are Polish, Romanian, and Filipino, and its common and official language is English. The ship plies a roughly forty-two-day route around the Pacific Rim, from Los Angeles and San Francisco to Pusan, then on to Manila and the Chinese ports of Xiamen, Yantian, Hong Kong, and Kaohsiung before heading back to Los Angeles. From Asia to the U.S., the ship's first mate Andrew tells us, it carries "everything"— clothing, electronics, consumer goods of all kinds. On the return trip, he says, it carries "nothing"—some paper products and chemicals, but mostly just empty containers on their way back to the Far East to scoop up more stuff. The U.S. trade deficit, writ small. James and I are the ship's only passengers.

And of course, not every moment at sea is spellbinding. Not long into the twelve-day voyage, exhilaration is often muted by the mundane rhythms of everyday life on board. The dull throbbing of the engines and slow swaying and creaking of the ship. The long hours spent writing, reading Melville and Dostoyevsky, and studying Russian. The dull meals in the officers' mess. The walks to the bow and back, beneath the creaking and groaning containers, a thick salt crust on every surface. Drinking cheap whiskey and singing sentimental karaoke in the crew's mess. Climbing the eight stories from the main deck to the bridge half a dozen times a day, plotting the ship's course, watching the weather, watching the sea for whales, dolphins, albatross, other ships, anything beyond its own great emptiness.

The soft hours of a maritime hanger-on are also spent in long talks with the ship's officers during their twice-daily shifts. Captain Panzeka is a jovial Pole who carries out his duties in shorts and flip-flops. Andrew, the first mate, is a garrulous fellow with whom I discuss weather, navigation, life at sea, life in Poland, languages, and sports (volleyball is big in Poland, baseball is not). Second mate Segundo tells us about his peculiarly Filipino version of Catholicism, his life at sea, and his hope that his family won't forget the sacrifice he has made for them by spending so many long years away from home. And then there's Argie, the thirty-one-year-old Filipino third mate. Quiet and thoughtful, he offers me tea and talks about his life and family with a heart-wrenching earnestness and melancholy. Like virtually every other Filipino on board, Argie doesn't have much fondness for the sea, with its lonely watches and its interminable months away from home. But his is a good job by Filipino standards, so he tries to make the best of it. During his daylight shifts, he pores over manuals on maritime safety and medicine, studying for the exams that he hopes will help him move up the maritime ladder. At night, a friend from the crew comes up to keep him company on his watch, and together they stare silently into the black void beyond, with rarely a ship's light or even a star to be seen. Almost every night, Argie sits in the faint green glow of the radar and says to me, "This is the life of a sailor. . . ." One night another crew member brings up a guitar, and we play and sing together. Simon and Garfunkel's "The Boxer," John Denver's "Country Road"—songs of loneliness and longing for home.

We have befriended other members of the crew, as well. James, the Filipino third engineer, is at something like forty-eight the oldest member of

the crew save the captain, and tells a harrowing tale of surviving a shipwreck years ago, floating on a piece of debris for two days before being rescued. Marcel, the Romanian chief engineer, has the ashen complexion of a man who spends most of his life below decks and the haunted eyes of someone who's been on board a little too long, as his already long-

overdue liberty keeps getting pushed further and further back. He's seen every movie in the ship's library of action films, hard-core pornography, and sentimental tear jerkers several times, it seems, and after sitting through one for the third or fourth time he says to me, "This one is particularly awful. If you are thinking of suicide, watch it. It will push you over the edge." I imagine him hosting a Siskel and Ebert-type TV show, "Movies with Marcel," the "Thumbs-Up/Thumbs-Down" rating system replaced with "Suicide/Not Suicide."

And as we sail, I also think occasionally of our uncle David Thomson, who, we discovered after we had already booked this voyage, worked this very route, San Francisco to Pusan, while in the Merchant Marine in the early '50s. On one passage, David's ship ran into trouble in Korean waters, he was given

a month's liberty in Japan, and he met a woman named Hideko, whom he would later move to Japan to marry. David died a few years ago, but near the end of our trip we'll visit Hideko—who later took the name Maria—in Spain, where she and David and their children later moved.

•

Looking at a flat map, the shortest distance from San Francisco to Korea is due west. But on a globe, it's actually an arc swinging far north toward Alaska and the Bering Sea, then south again toward Russia's Kuril Islands and Japan. This deviation from the "flat map" course is the norm for pretty much all intercontinental crossings, whether by boat or by plane. It's called the Great Circle Route, and this route provides us with one of the most memorable parts of our crossing.

Six days out, the emptiness of the sea is breached by our first sighting of land since the Golden Gate—a ghostly gray chunk, which emerges from the mist and floats for the better part of the day on the northern horizon. A consultation with the navigator's chart puts a name to this apparition: Amatignak Island, the southernmost of the Aleutian Islands, the great volcanic chain that swings in a 1,000-mile arc from Alaska almost all the way to Russia. Ragged and bleak through our binoculars, a gigantic shard of primordial rock, Amatignak appears utterly inhospitable, literally the ends of the earth. And a glance at the ship's copy of *Bering Sea and Strait Pilot*, carried in case of the need for an emergency anchorage, reveals it to be only slightly less inhospitable than I imagine:

> The coast of this rugged island is mostly steep and fringed with rocks.... The NW and W sides are steep-to; elsewhere foul ground extends to 6 cables offshore ... in 1978, a wreck was visible on the S side.... Ulva Cove indents the E side.... At the head of the cove there is a boulder beach and a cabin.... A small, deep cove on the NW side affords the best protected landing place....

A cabin? Who the hell built a cabin on such a god-forsaken place?

And yet, despite being a place of such few charms for a shipwrecked mariner, or perhaps because of it, I can hardly take my eyes off the island, until it eventually slips back again over the horizon and into the seamless gray.

•

Toward the second half of the voyage, we start watching the weather faxes as a tropical storm develops in the East China Sea and moves slowly northwest toward Korea—our destination. We're heading straight for it. Within a couple of days, our daily "newspaper"—a single sheet of headlines that comes over by satellite—brings a report of five dead in Japan and thousands flooded out of their homes by what has now become Typhoon Samoai. Second mate Segundo begins charting alternate routes to and from Pusan, and upon entering the Sea of Japan the boat begins big time pitching and rolling on swells created by winds rushing southwest toward the center of the storm. The crew is ordered to secure all hatches and lash down everything on deck as the wind howls at better than gale force, the sea grows white with foam, and little wind-tossed birds take refuge under the eaves of the bridge.

Mercifully, for us, the storm stays south, leaving us on its dry side, and our southeast heading keeps the *Pacific Champion* running with the wind and the swells rather than against or across them, both of which help spare us Samoai's worst effects. Still, as we near Pusan word comes that the port has been closed. Captain Panzeka orders the engines cut to one-quarter speed, and we head for calmer waters in the lee of the big Japanese island of Honshu, where, after eleven days of the constant motion of the sea and throbbing of the engine, we spend an oddly calm and quiet night. After an eighteen-hour delay, we approach Pusan during a lull in the storm the next afternoon.

Korea rises up out of Samoai's swirling clouds all at once, a brooding mass of steep green hillsides sprouting forests of towering white apartment blocks. After twelve days at sea, it's jarring to suddenly be smacking up against land and civilization again. Amatignak Island was just a ghostly apparition on the edge of the world, and the Japanese archipelago, which we've been sailing by these last couple of days, has remained well on the periphery of our consciousness, never approaching close enough to the little bubble in which we've been floating to threaten popping it. But now the landmass of Asia has planted itself directly in our path, and there's no getting around it—this bubble's about to burst, and we're about to get tossed ashore.

It's strange how quickly this big metal bucket, which seemed first so utterly foreign and then so utterly insubstantial on the open sea, soon became our terra firma. And now here we are again, facing the stirring unease of departure as we're about to hop off our known world onto another unknown shore. Especially since two nagging little uncertainties have just popped up like evil little jack-in-the-boxes. We've just gotten word from Pusan that even though the commercial port is open, Samoai has likely knocked out the overnight ferries to Fukuoka—our plan A for getting to Japan. And we didn't make a plan B. In fact, we didn't even bring a Korean guidebook, just a little pocket phrase book that might get us dinner, if we're lucky. We could well be stuck in Korea, literally without a map, for God knows how long. But that's a minor disruption. A somewhat more major one is that the problem we've only now discovered with our Russian visas: they were issued for the wrong dates, and they're set to expire three days after we enter the country. This could be a major glitch, as Russians are not known to be especially flexible on such matters. So as we sail into Pusan harbor, I'm riding a buzz of adrenaline and anxiety.

The entrance to the harbor is marked by two converging jetties, creating a needle's-eye aperture through which returning and departing ships pass at full throttle, and close enough to each other to smell the tobacco on the other captain's breath. Beyond the jetties, Pusan Harbor itself is remarkably small for what I've been told is Korea's busiest port, a natural cove hemmed in tightly by the steep hills. But it's swarming with the largest mass of container cranes James and I have ever seen, jostling for space on the docks like a herd of gigantic parched beasts at a desert watering hole. And then the city itself comes into focus through the cranes—a throbbing jumble of neon and concrete, industrial noise and car horns. The quiet desolation of the sea already seems a distant dream.

At the rim of the cramped inner harbor, a tug helps our ungainly ship execute an awkward 180-degree turn into its berth, its bow facing back out toward the sea. And once the ship is secured, the local agent arrives and tells us that indeed the ferries to Japan have been canceled, and that he's booked us into a downtown hotel, where it looks like we'll have to wait out the storm. And maybe buy a better phrasebook. After twelve days at sea, we climb back down off the *Pacific Champion* and into Asia. As we set out, some of the sailors are also heading ashore to enjoy three or four hours of liberty. They invite us to join them, have a drink, and maybe "find a girl." I quickly try to imagine a port-side brothel in Pusan, and conjure up a thick, rank haze of whiskey, sweat, cheap perfume, and fleeting human contact . . . now *that* would be something to write about. Another time, perhaps. We thank them for their invitation but decline, intent instead on figuring out how we're going to get to Japan. We bid them farewell and head out into the city.

Typhoon Samoai has weakened long enough for the *Pacific Champion* to make landfall, exchange part of its cargo of containers, and deliver James and me safely to the Far East. But the storm is supposed to regain strength again tomorrow, and the port is scheduled to close again at six in the morning. And since it's safer for ships to be in open water during a big blow than tied to a pier, the ship will head back out to sea before then. We assume that she and her crew will make it safely to Manila, her next port, but we'll never find out for sure.

I 2

Zigzag to Russia

*In which we experience the wonders of Japanland,
ponder what it is that propels us safely around the planet,
and are bailed out by a midnight phone call back home*

The Fukuoka train station feels nearly asleep as the clock heads toward 11:00 P.M. Perhaps the station in this small city on Japan's western shore always feels nearly asleep, no matter where the clock is heading, but we hope not to have to find out. There's a train leaving for Kyoto in a few minutes, and we hope to be on it.

We had no idea when we left Korea whether there actually was an overnight train from Fukuoka to Kyoto, but the way I figured it, it's Japan, the place that's supposed to have the best train system in the world—there has to be. And now here we are in Fukuoka and we've found out that I'd guessed right, and we've caught the snappy little bus that was waiting outside the terminal to take us to the station, hauled our stuff off the bus, quickly tried to ascertain from the kaleidoscope of Japanese signs and strange symbols which way the ticket lobby might be, and turned to head in that direction. What we still have no idea about is whether we'll be able to find out if there are any seats left on the train, get our rail passes validated, get tickets, and find our way to the platform before the train slips off into the warm September night in less than half an hour—especially since it quickly became apparent that few people out here in the Japanese hinterlands speak English. And now as we hitch up our backpacks and take our first steps toward the lobby, a voice comes from behind us, a female voice in heavily accented but well-practiced English, and it's saying, "Can I help you?"

We turn back and where not a moment ago there was nothing but still night air there is now a beautiful young woman and, I'm pretty sure, the fading swirls of a puff of smoke. Out of nowhere has materialized our own little Glinda the Good Witch, only Japanese, and without all the glitter and lace. She tells us that her name is Momo and that she's just getting off her job as a salarywoman for an airline, so I suppose that maybe she saw us on the bus looking like the disoriented *gaijin* that we are and that maybe that puff of smoke was nothing more than exhaust from the bus, but whoever she is and wherever she came from, Momo is our guardian angel of the moment. She spends the next half hour making sure that we get our passes validated, get what turn out to be the last two seats on the train, find the right track, and even have food in our stomachs before we depart, perhaps none of which we may have been able to do without her. We thank her for her trouble with a little bottle of maple syrup. And then she's gone.

We might've been content to wait out Typhoon Samoai and wander around Pusan for a couple of days until the ferries started running again, but an email check at our hotel revealed that our Japanese friend Aso-San in Boston, who had told us he might be able to give us some ideas about where to stay in his country, had in fact set up an entire itinerary for us, including a series of rendezvous with friends and colleagues. And because the storm had made us late to Pusan, the clock was already ticking. People we didn't even know were already waiting for us. We were also surprised to learn that while Samoai had knocked out all the boats, we could still fly to Japan. We wondered about the wisdom of flying up and over a typhoon that we knew had already killed several people on the ground, but only for a minute or two, after which we cast off any such concern, along with, for the second time, our attachment to staying at ground level. Here again, we rationalized that flying to Japan from Korea would not violate the spirit of our endeavor because, as from Anchorage to San Francisco, we would be flying backward, toward the east. Our westward progress would remain earthbound. So we found ourselves a couple of cheap plane tickets that would take us out of Korea before the sun had set for a second time.

September 15, 2000

Dear—

  Pusan reveals shades of Hong Kong and Manila. Behind the façade of modern high-rises, Hyundai-choked boulevards and state-of-the-art ATMs, James and I have found an enduring urban core of grime and sewage, labyrinthine back streets and tiny stalls jammed with cheap shoes and CDs, strange fruits and vegetables, salvaged mechanical junk and pigs' heads. Our short-term anxiety about our next move has been more than assuaged by the sumptuous digs in which our ship's agent set us up—an elegant but inexpensive establishment with a marble bathroom, big down pillows and a panoramic view of the port. Further relief from our weighty concerns came when we ducked into a tiny restaurant for dinner. As soon as we entered, the woman behind the counter, as if complying with some local law about proper behavior in the presence of Americans, got up and changed the channel on the TV from Chinese soaps to American baseball. It was the Red Sox. They were playing the Indians in the second game of a double-header, and they were going down hard after having lost the first game too. They'd been struggling to stay in contention when we left the U.S. and now they're clearly out of the race. And I am greatly relieved. The only thing worse than them going to the World Series and losing again would have been for them to go and win for the first time in nearly a century— and for me to miss it completely. I can now travel worry-free.

      Love from Korea,
      the Vagabond Brothers Thomson

As I fell asleep in Pusan, on solid ground for the first time in two weeks, I felt my bed still pitching and rolling. The next day we caught the last plane out of Pusan to Seoul, where a JAL 747 crammed with 500 Japanese shoppers carried us into the dark and turbulent skies and across the Sea of Japan to Fukuoka in less than an hour.

  And then we got to Fukuoka, and there was Momo waiting for us.

          •

Like many other nine-year-olds in the U.S. in 1968 or so, one of my favorite songs was the Monkees' "I'm a Believer." I would sing it to myself while walking to school, working on my *Apollo* spaceship models, playing with my sister and her horrible little blue- and pink-haired trolls. Sometimes I secretly still sing it to myself. But the truth is that right around that same time is when I realized that I'm really not much of a believer at all, that I could find no reason to believe in any of the things that others seemed to cling so strongly to at the time—God, astrology, psychic powers, marriage, the benevolence of the U.S. government.... I was quickly becoming the biggest little naysayer around.

As a grown-up I'm still not much of a believer, but sometime after I reached thirty—actually, I remember exactly when, it was when I was thirty-two and in the middle of a nasty relationship crisis—for the first time in my life I consciously decided to believe in something that I didn't have clear evidence of, and to act accordingly. I took a leap of faith.

I suppose, as with so many people, that this was partly a desperate grasp for something to hold me up in a difficult time, but I think it was also because I was finally coming to understand that having faith in something can actually affect its likelihood of becoming true, that the way you think and act can influence, in a very small way, how the world works.

Perhaps this is all obvious to most normal human beings, but it hadn't been to me.

Now don't think for a minute that this epiphany instantly transformed my life. I'm still not one of those people who believes that you can change the world by just thinking good thoughts, that war and violence and greed and blind self-interest will suddenly disappear when enough people just *Visualize World Peace*, as the old bumper sticker used to urge us to do. The part of me that is an inveterate naysayer was not dislodged by this realization, nor was my stubborn adherence to sometimes-destructive habits of mind vanquished. But both of these have been somewhat softened, and in the years since my blind dive back into that relationship, I've tried to base decisions in my life less on fear and more on hope; to practice, when facing terrifying uncertainty, again making a leap of faith. And sometimes I've succeeded. Exhibit A: my decision to get married. (OK, so things don't always work out—a leap of faith might enable good things to happen, but it doesn't guarantee that they will.)

And I think this change helps explain this journey, too. Sure, you can't up and haul yourself around the world without money or the ability to make it along the way, without time and some sense of how to navigate unfamiliar places. But I'm realizing as we get farther away from home and farther into the unknown that James and I have also taken a gigantic leap of faith. We left Boston with tickets in hand that would get us, with reasonable certainty, only as far as San Francisco. Beyond there, the sky to the horizon was filled only with clouds in the shape of question marks and our path was marked only by a chain of hypothetical humans, some with names, some whom we still can't even imagine. We were able to climb the metal stairs lashed to the *Pacific Champion* only because a big part of each of us trusted in the strength of this untested human chain and held a fundamental, if not yet articulated, belief that if you're open to the possibility of good things happening, people and opportunities will open themselves up to you. We had faith that one way or another, things would work out—or that maybe they wouldn't, in which case something else would happen, perhaps even more interesting than what we'd imagined. Sure, we'd also need a good dose of common sense and intuition, the ability to sort out meaningful opportunities from the random clutter that the universe throws at you, and yes, a bit of practical planning—after all, as Branch Rickey, the general manager of the Brooklyn Dodgers, once said, "Luck is the residue of design." But without that faith, I think I'd be home sitting behind a desk right now, comfortably weighed down by doubt and anxiety masquerading as my usual good sense.

So thank God for excruciating relationship crises. That which does not kill me makes me better able to jump off the edge of the earth.

Of course, James and I are hardly alone here. The faith that you'll survive all those ominous question marks is what sustains most independent travelers, people who tend to travel with a backpack rather than a cart full of suitcases. That and the belief that surprises and leaving a certain amount to chance are a big part of the reason for going in the first place. If you want to know how everything's going to work out ahead of time, take a Carnival cruise. Or stay home and watch *Perry Mason* reruns.

So what does all this have to do with Fukuoka and Momo? Just this: Good things happen. Kind strangers present themselves. Faith is rewarded.

•

Sometimes, fast is too fast, and well-thought-out slowness can be just the ticket.

Japanese trains are known the world over as fast and sleek, epitomized by the country's ultramodern Shinkansen bullet trains, which, more than thirty-five years after their introduction, remain the standard against which other modern trains are measured. The overnight train from Fukuoka to Kyoto, on the other hand, is neither fast nor sleek—it's perhaps more like a pebble sprung from a slingshot than a bullet from a rifle. But just as sometimes a slingshot is just the right tool for the task, so too this pokey little train is perfectly suited to its job. It carries its passengers across roughly 500 kilometers of southern Japan in eight hours, a positively nineteenth-century average speed of roughly sixty kilometers an hour, and delivers them to downtown Kyoto rested and in time for work the next morning, a positively twenty-first-century idea.

The last two spots on the train are reclining seats in a charming little car graced with soft pink lights and soothing sage green upholstery, a tiny blanket and a pair of tiny slippers for each passenger, green tea vending machines, and a ficus tree that shakes gently with the train's every rumble and sway. Before long the soft snores of the somewhat smaller people for whom these small seats, slippers, and blankets were designed begin to waft over the whoosh of the train as the lights of sleeping Japan flit by beyond the windows. As a kid, my mom read me a children's book about Japanese brothers with magical powers, but half-lying half-awake as I float through my first night in Japan, I imagine being in a children's book about this train, an enchanted vessel carrying misty-eyed passengers to all kinds of magical adventures. I am enthralled. And this is just a train.

This wondrous little vehicle will carry us to the old Japanese capital of Kyoto, and then another will carry us to the even older capital of Nara and another on to the modern capital of Tokyo, and here's some of what we will see in these parts of this new world: A tiny wooden home in a dense neighborhood, filled with rice paper screens and tatami mats and occupied by a seventh-generation antique furniture restorer, his wife, and his grown son, an eighth-generation antique furniture restorer. An urban plaza of neon and skyscrapers that looks like all of Manhattan compressed into a half-kilometer radius. A plateful of foul-smelling sea urchin roe and gelatinous sea cucumber that are certainly the most unpalatable substances that anyone has ever suggested I put in my mouth but that we must eat in order to be polite. A six-stool private bar, where we will sing American pop and sentimental Japanese country and western karaoke with three young Japanese businessmen and their father while a man named Junji, wearing a cowboy shirt and a Cheshire Cat grin, pours us round after round of whiskey and a clear liquor called A Thousand Years of Sleep. A live baby octopus, staring back at us from a platter. A small building clad in gold that looks like the home of the sun, in the middle of a pond filled with water lilies. Huge wooden temples with roofs the shape of eagles' wings. Small rocks and boulders surrounded by fields of gray pebbles meticulously raked in circles and swoops and swirls. An immense dark brown wooden shrine as big as a city block filled with a three-story high Buddha, huge bronze flowers, and towering statues of scowling warriors. Complexes of buildings and intricately sculpted environments that evoke a deep sense of calm and harmony and perfection in a way that's usually achieved only by extraordinary places in the natural world.

And here's what we will understand about these people, places and things: almost nothing.

In a way, exploring new places really is like experiencing the world as a kid again. Every step and turn is laced with both anticipation and disorientation, every encounter fraught at once with the possibility of embrace and danger, discovery and disappointment, every moment extended, every sensation heightened. You're having to relearn the world, divine the significance of new objects, interpret the meaning and context of unfamiliar words, gestures, and facial expressions. You're trying to figure out all over again how people feel, what they think, how they experience the world, whether or not you can trust them, and how you fit into it all. I heard once that humans learn ninety percent of what they'll ever know by the time they're two years old, that everything after that is just details. Who knows whether this is actually true, but when you're traveling you sure can imagine it to be true, because suddenly you feel like you don't know anything at all, all over again, as if you're suddenly having to refill that ninety percent of your brain that's just about basic orientation in the world, and you just know that you're not going to do it before it's time to leave. And it's frustrating and scary and exhausting and often overwhelming, but it's also exhilarating, which is why we do it. The whole world is new again, and you're new in it.

Of course, sometimes, amid all this newness, you are just filled with an anxiety that gnaws at you like something bad you ate for lunch a few days before.

Before the squashed Manhattan district, before the businessmen in the private bar and the still-twitching octopus, our first stop in Tokyo is the Russian embassy. Our visas are giving us heartburn. We can only hope the embassy might be able to provide us with some diplomatic Rolaids.

The process of getting a Russian visa by itself can stir up a little anxiety in those already prone to it. First, you have to find someone within Russia who will issue you an official invitation to visit the country. Then you have to fill out a zillion-page application rife with questions that make it clear that they are not all that happy to have visitors in the first place. Then you have to decide what to put in the box that says "occupation" that will not be a lie but will certainly also not be the whole truth, which is that you're a journalist, since word is that they are even less happy to play host to journalists. Then you have to send the application and the invitation and your passport itself off to the consulate and hope that the notoriously slow Russian bureaucracy gets everything back to you before you're actually due to leave for their country.

Fortunately, we were assisted through this process by Gary Cook at Baikal Watch, the human master key who helped unlock just about every door between us and Baikal. When he finally handed the visas to us in San Francisco before we shipped out on the *Pacific Champion*, we stashed them in our bags right away, not thinking to ask whether he'd looked them over to make sure that everything was in order. Of course he had, we figured—he'd done this a million times. Nor did we look very hard at them ourselves, since we couldn't yet read a word of Russian and even the numbers looked weird. But then we did start to study Russian aboard the ship, and to test his new skills James decided to have a look at the visas. It was then that he discovered the problem with the dates, and those little spots in our stomachs started to tighten. We'd be lucky if they'd even let us into the country with visas that were due to expire in three days. And if they did, we knew that getting an extension in Vladivostok would be a belabored process, one that would leave us stranded for who knows how long and throw a huge wrench into the works of the rest of our trip. That was not an option. On the other hand, we'd been told by every authority from Gary to our *Lonely Planet* guide that traveling in Russia without your visa in order was something you just did not want to do. You could be stopped anywhere, anytime, we were told, by virtually any person in uniform—and Russia is overflowing with people in uniform—and asked for your papers. If your papers were found to be out of order—and what constituted "out of order" seemed itself to be very sketchy—they could fine you, detain you, confiscate your passport, demand a bribe, kick you out of the country, prevent you from leaving the country, or, it seemed, do pretty much whatever they wanted.

We would have to deal with this before going to Russia, somehow.

The visa office of the Embassy of the Russian Federation in Tokyo is a stark little room that resembles a bank branch office in a dying Midwestern town, minus the plastic flowers and feed store calendars. It is not the busiest place in town, with just a couple of anxious Russians ahead of us, and after just a couple of minutes we're beckoned toward the counter by an indifferent man of about forty with an ashen complexion. His English is good enough, and our problem simple enough, that he quickly grasps our request: May we change the dates on our visas to what we originally asked for? He looks over our papers, gives no audible response, and disappears into the next room. We wait several long minutes, drumming our fingers, glancing at the strange city out the window, refraining from continuing our "what if" discussion before he returns, expression unchanged, to deliver the verdict.

"It is not a problem to fix the dates," he says, still with no affect whatsoever. "We can do that for thirty dollars. . . ." And suddenly it's as if the skies have cleared after a tornado watch and we can come out of our bunker and be on our way.

"... But—"

There's more.

"—these visas are not valid. All visas must now be issued from Moscow. These were not issued from Moscow. You must reapply."

Our relief after two weeks of anxiety has lasted all of three seconds, and now, just as quickly as it gathered itself back up, our entire Russian trip is again crumbling before us. It looks like Gary, or someone, has screwed up big time, and we may not be able to recover. It takes weeks to get Russian visas, and before you can even apply there's the matter of the invitation. Gary had finagled our invitation from a colleague somewhere in Siberia. We have a copy of his letter, but really have no idea who the man is or how to reach him, and we're reluctant, for obvious reasons, to admit that. And we have already been told that we can't procure invitations from other contacts we've developed in Russia, including our guide, Andrei, for reasons that will remain forever murky. Starting over will mean finding a travel agent who can procure us an invitation from a tour operator in Russia. Only we have no intention of taking a tour—we're going to be traveling on our own and staying in people's homes. And then there's the little detail that despite being in possession of tourist visas, we're also in possession of two full sets of recording equipment. But Gary has advised us that under no circumstances should we ask for journalist visas. And we've bought train tickets with specific departure dates, which, we've also been told, are almost impossible to change. We have booked time with Andrei and know that the window of opportunity for exploring Baikal with him is rapidly closing as the Siberian winter approaches. Standing here in front of the man who holds our fate in our hands, we realize that we have built our trip with very little margin for error and that we are looking at a very big error. Our human chain has broken. We are screwed.

Thoughts of China and Southeast Asia and India flash through my mind, places I've always wanted to go but haven't made any effort to research for this trip. Meanwhile, Baikal flickers like a busted neon sign, about to flash out altogether.

With little hope of finding a sympathetic ear, I ask the man if there is anyone else we can talk to. He disappears again without a word and returns a few tortured minutes later with a somewhat older woman with short black hair, more stylish clothes, a more engaged manner, and a considerably better command of English. She even sounds somewhat apologetic about her country's labyrinthine bureaucracy as we recount our dilemma and ask, with as delicate a balance of courtesy and urgency as we are able to strike, whether there isn't something she can do. And even amid our desperation, with the appearance of this new character I suddenly feel as if we're acting out a hackneyed old Hollywood cliché: innocent Americans rescued from an undeserved fate at the hands of a soulless and badly dressed Russian bureaucrat by a more humane and cosmopolitan female superior who—it always works this way in the movies—speaks much better English.

But, it seems, there will be no happy ending to this tired little scene.

"I'm sorry," she says, looking back at the documents, "my colleague is correct, your visas were issued in Buryatia and are invalid."

With nothing to lose, we continue to plead with her. She again listens patiently and again tells us that there is nothing she can do. We come at her again, from a slightly different angle, and on the third or fourth approach a crack opens up. "Try to find the man who issued your invitation," she says. I'm not at all sure what good that will do, but I take more hope from her next statement: "Then I'll see what I can do." Something tells me that this woman, who I suspected is quite glad to be working for the Russian embassy here in Tokyo rather than back in the motherland itself, just might come through for us.

There's a pay phone outside. It's still morning in Tokyo, which means that it's not yet evening in San Francisco. We take a stab, our only hope: Gary. He answers the phone. I blurt out the details of our predicament as well as I can in my near-frenzy, trying hard as I do not to sound accusatory about this jam that he seems to have gotten us into.

Gary, as usual, seems unfazed.

"Those idiots," he says, or something to that effect. "They don't even know the rules of their own country." He goes on to explain that he specifically got us invitations from a friend in an autonomous Buryat enclave within the Irkutsk region because the area has been given a special exemption from the new mandate that all visas be issued from Moscow. The region has its own special status, which the people at the embassy are clearly ignorant of. He asks if there is anyone he can speak to.

James rushes inside, emerges with the dark-haired woman, and we put her on the phone. She listens intently, exclaiming an occasional "*da, da,*" or "*nyet.*" After a few minutes, she hands me the phone, goes inside, comes back with a map, and gets back on the line. Neither James nor I have taken a breath since we first put her on the phone. After another minute she hands me the phone, looks at me, and says, with a look nearly as astonished as I'm sure my own is, "He is correct." She takes the visas from us, motions inside and says, "We will fix the dates. It will be thirty dollars each."

I get back on the phone to tell Gary that we owe him more than we could ever repay for setting the embassy official straight. "She works for the embassy?" Gary asks, with an air of astonishment of his own. He'd thought she'd been just another Russian civilian, with business at the embassy, and he'd launched into a tirade about the stupid embassy officials, who couldn't even be bothered to learn the geography of their own country or keep up with the news from home. And she had listened patiently and politely, calmly assessed what he had to say, and admitted that she and her colleague had been wrong. We had found perhaps the one helpful, patient, and unoffendable Russian embassy official in the entire world.

Baikal flashes back on. Our trip is back on track.

13

Power in the East

In which we find a ghost ship in a lost port,
touch Russian soil for the first time,
and contemplate the benefits of going Soft

On the western coast of Honshu, Japan's main island, there's a tiny town called Fushiki. It doesn't appear on many maps. Its dusty, somewhat unkempt streets make it feel more like the Philippines than sleek, modern Japan. Maybe there's a boat that sails from there to Russia, and maybe there isn't. After six days in Japan, we'll find out.

Our travel agent, who specializes in getting to and from Russia, had never heard of this boat. And the guidebooks I'd consulted had said the ferries from Japan to Russia had gone out of business years ago, when they lost their subsidy from the Russian government. But a couple of hours on the Web had turned up a lead, and a fax to a number in Vladivostok had brought a cryptic response. Perhaps the ship was still running after all. I gave our travel agent the coordinates, and she went to work. A few days later, she reported in the affirmative—it seemed that there was a boat, and she'd made the arrangements. But we would have to pick up our tickets on the dock. We had no confirmation of the sailing, no receipt from the company, no physical evidence that the boat really did exist.

The overnight journey from Tokyo to Fushiki is more like traveling through time than through space. A Shinkansen bullet train whisks you at 175 miles per hour from the pulsating megalopolis of year 2000 Tokyo to a transfer station in Yuzawa, where you catch an only slightly less astonishing express train to the spotless but eerily empty western city of Toyama, where you spend the night. The next morning, you board a still-more ordinary train for a twelve-minute ride to the even smaller city of Takaoka, with a decidedly older and shabbier downtown—the Japan, perhaps, of 1960. And finally, you find your way onto an unkempt two-car shuttle train, perhaps the only remaining diesel train in all of Japan, which clatters and chugs off through a maze of power lines, rusting cranes, and decrepit warehouses and creaks to a halt at a dusty little station, from which you emerge onto the forlorn streets of Fushiki. Sleepy little stores offer an uncertain selection of wares, there are few signs of any kind to direct visitors, and only an occasional car putters by, seemingly lost. Japan 1930, perhaps.

If you're looking for a way out of here other than the train you came in on, here's how you'll find it: Wander around until you notice a few signs in Russian. Then look for other non-Japanese on the narrow sidewalks. Head in the direction they're coming from. Round a corner, and you'll find that the ghost ship is real—the *Antonina Nezhdanova*, dowager queen of the Soviet Union's Pacific passenger fleet, her anchor hanging rust brown against a battered white hull.

The pier to which the *Antonina Nezhdanova* is lashed seems to be the only place in Fushiki with any buzz of life, yet even this has an odd sort of lassitude to it. Cars, bikes, and people move about like objects in space, on their own slow trajectories, barely interacting with those around them. This is our first test of our travel agent Debbie's arrangements, the first of a long series of rendezvous she's set up for us on which our entire trip between here and Helsinki rests. As we get closer to the ship, we spot a small trailer and head for it, and as we approach, a young Japanese woman emerges. "Hello!" she says, in English. "We have your tickets, but they are in the office. Please wait here!" "Thomson?" I ask as she turns to head back, but of course there's no need. Who else would these two westerners with backpacks be? A moment later she's back with our tickets. Debbie is one-for-one. We thank the woman and, before heading for the gangplank, ask what kind of currency they take on this Russian ship, rubles or yen.

"Dollars," she replies, "or yen. No rubles."

Currency aside, it suddenly feels like we already are in Russia. Other than the woman in the office, there's hardly a Japanese to be seen, just lots of Russians, mostly men in shorts and sandals a few women in tight pants and overcoiffed hair. The town, the pier, and the boat all feel worn out. And unlike every other place we've been in Japan, as we wander up the gangplank and onto the rusting, green deck, no one greets us, or even acknowledges our presence. *Welcome to Russia*, I think.

Passing through an open hatch brings us into the main cabin, suddenly cool and dark, both the walls and the carpeted floor a clotted scarlet. A robust man in the closest thing we've yet seen to a uniform, and with the closest thing we've yet seen to a smile, appears and greets us in English: "Hello! Please come this way!" He ushers us through glass doors into an even darker forward lounge, bedecked with chrome-trimmed chairs, a disco ball, and the setup for a small band, which, we will find, will remain unused for the length of our voyage. The man tells us to leave our things and be back to meet with Japanese immigration in an hour and a half.

James stays behind while I wander back to town in search of a grocery store to stock up on supplies for the two-day crossing and find a sad little neighborhood with a big sign in Japanese, Russian, and English welcoming visitors to Fushiki's special international shopping district. It's as deserted as the rest of the town. A single Russian guy floats by on an old bike, passing empty stores offering cameras, appliances, clothes. In a small grocery shop I gather up bread, juice, bananas and carrots, dehydrated soup, and Oreos, and spot the Russian from the bike, stocking up on toilet paper.

Back on board, I find that James has made the acquaintance of a young Japanese guy who's also taking the Trans-Siberian on Sunday. Soon, three more Japanese passengers appear, along with a young Englishman who's also taking the train, heading back home after a year teaching English in Japan. Suddenly we feel a little less alone. After a perfunctory immigration check, we follow a young woman two decks down a spiral staircase, stepping over the half torn-up, battered old carpet and the only slightly less worn-looking new carpet being put down in its place, to our cabin, where we drop our stuff and sit down on the beds, still a little stunned.

The wallpaper is peeling, the veneer on the bunks and desks is chipped and cracked, the light bulbs missing or casting only a cold, halfhearted glow. But the sheets are clean and pressed, the wool blankets warm, the down pillows fluffy, and the mattresses comfortable. And from just below our porthole, the sloshing of the water of Fushiki harbor casts ripples of reflected sunlight onto our ceiling.

The scheduled departure time of 4:00 P.M. comes and goes without notice. Back up on deck, passengers push bicycles or haul used washers and dryers up the gangplank, while on the dock below a Japanese man off-loads new appliances and stereos from a van into the arms of Russians. Above us swings a huge crane. When we boarded, we'd noticed a few cars in the forward cargo hold. Now, the crane is depositing cars on corners of the deck. And over the next few hours, with the sun sinking lower in the western sky and 4 o'clock just a memory, the faded gray planks of the ship's decks slowly disappear under the wheels of used Toyotas, Nissans, and Subarus. It becomes clear that the lost government subsidy for this ship has not been made up for by some boom in recreational passenger traffic. The *Antonina Nezhdanova* has found a new life as a seagoing used car lot.

The loading continues on into the evening. When the decks are half covered with cars, I begin to worry about the ship's stability and load capacity. When we go to sleep at 11 o'clock, the cars are still coming, and when we awake the next morning, under sail in the middle of the Sea of Japan, every available square meter of deck space is occupied by a vehicle. There are three cars in the swimming pool.

The *Antonina Nezhdanova*, we will learn later, was named for a great Russian opera singer of the early twentieth century, and despite its ragged carpets, its rusting hull, and the humiliation of having its once-gleaming decks start to rot and be covered with castoff Japanese vehicles, the ship manages to maintain some of the dignity appropriate for its namesake. Among these vestiges of its earlier days is the restaurant, where the tables are elegantly set, the food is served by prim waitresses in crisply pressed uniforms, and the mashed potatoes always have an exquisite little swirl in them. And every table, even the three-quarters of them that forever remain empty, feature lovely little salt and pepper shakers and a sugar bowl, each monogrammed *АНТОНИНА НЕЖДАНОВА*. I have to restrain myself from pocketing a set of them.

The food itself isn't at all bad, if you have a taste for bologna steak and sautéed sea cucumber. We won't be needing those Oreos and dehydrated soup after all.

The *Antonina Nezhdanova* did not sink and dump us and its floating used car lot into the Sea of Japan. The second morning out of Fushiki, we spot land—our first glimpse of Russia.

•

Back in high school, I took a class in Russian history and culture, called Things Russian. It was taught by an eccentric guy named Mr. Mitchell. He was said to be a terrific teacher, with a real passion for his subject. Just as important to me at the time, he was said to give all of his students A's—a capital *A* if you did well, a lowercase *a* if you didn't. But he would also ask you what grade you thought you deserved. I was an unindustrious student, and I knew it. I told him I thought I deserved a C. I got a C. This was the apex of my formal study of Russia and the Soviet Union.

Still, it would've been difficult to have been born into the age of the Cuban Missile Crisis, grow up in the time of Richard Nixon's détente, come of age in the era of Ronald Reagan's "Evil Empire," and watch the historic transformation of the Soviet Union under Mikhail Gorbachev without developing some genuine interest in our one-time arch-nemesis. Viewed largely through the popular press, Russia was dark, ominous, and fascinating, sort of like the farthest reaches of my subconscious, except that this was a place that I actually wanted to visit someday.

I finally catch my first glimpse as I'm in our cabin, reading Dostoyevsky's *Crime and Punishment*, the one piece of Russian literature that the clerk at San Francisco's City Lights Bookstore said I should bring with me to Russia if I could bring only one. I glance every few minutes out the porthole to the horizon. *Nothing. Splash. Nothing. Nothing.* Then suddenly, *something.* Dim, featureless, but it can be nothing else. James and I and our Japanese and English compatriots gather on a small patch of open deck not occupied by Toyotas to watch the approach. But the Russian coast teases us. For the next two hours, it seems to get no closer, just hovering in the distance, as if considering whether or not it wants to invite us in.

Signs of life eventually emerge—a few small fishing boats, a complex of antennas on the shore, a few scattered buildings. Finally, in the early afternoon, we can start to pick out the cranes, apartment blocks, and communications towers of Vladivostok.

Russia fought numerous wars to gain and keep control of this area. The Pacific coast was vital to the nineteenth-century empire's status as a continental and aspiring global power, and Vladivostok—the name roughly translates as "Power in the East"—was the linchpin of its presence here, a rare deep-water port that was free of ice for all but two months of the year. After the 1917 revolution, the Soviets were determined to keep it, too. The Russian Far East was a beachhead for international counterrevolutionaries and a last hold-out of the Whites, the allied forces of the monarchists and the social democrats opposed to the Bolsheviks, and even as they struggled to consolidate the revolution and recover from the devastation of the First World War in the Russian heartland, the Soviets fought for control of Vladivostok and the Far East, nearly

6,000 railroad miles from Moscow. Ultimately, in 1922, the Reds defeated the Whites and regained control of Vladivostok. Lenin is quoted as having said, "It's a long way away, but it's ours."

For decades, the only Westerners to lay eyes on Vladivostok were spies. It was the home port of the Soviet Navy's Pacific fleet, and so of the utmost strategic importance, and in 1958 it was declared a closed military city, reopened to the world only in 1992, after the dissolution of the Soviet Union. But sailing into the city today, it almost seems as if the Soviets kept the place closed not so much to protect their secrets as out of embarrassment. Approaching Vladivostok by sea, almost before you can distinguish any particular features of the landscape, you can sense the decrepitude. The shoreline and hillsides are strewn with crumbling buildings, rusting ships, and ghostly concrete apartment blocks.

The old city is built on two knobby fingers of land that jut south from the mainland. As we turn north into the narrow gap between the fingers, named after Istanbul's Golden Horn Bay, the skeletal cranes of archaic old container terminals rise up like long-forgotten sandbox toys. Ragged piers and ware-houses are jammed onto the shores of the harbor, rusting and half-sunken ships lashed to their sides. The only thing in sight that looks as if it's been touched by human hands within living memory is the shiny new tugboat that chugs out to greet us.

As the tug shepherds us toward the crowded inner harbor, the city's downtown rises before us—dismal high-rises, sooty city blocks, the bleak Soviet-era ferry terminal. Vladivostok reveals itself in all its glory, a symphony in gray. Two gems sparkle amid the dreariness, though, the pride of the Russian Far East and symbols of Moscow's continuing power here: a set of three spit-shined, fresh-out-of-the-box warships and the regal, turn-of-the-century yellow train station with its elaborate wrought-iron tiaras, the terminus of the Trans-Siberian, the world's longest railroad, and the start tomorrow of our journey across the continent.

"Citizens of the Russian Federation May Go First." So reads the sign by the border control booth in the ferry terminal. It's the first example of a peculiar sort of Russian chauvinism that we'll yet see a good deal more of. "Russians aren't prop-erly respected elsewhere," the sign seems to suggest, "but on Russian soil you will get the respect you deserve." Or perhaps it's to make up for the indignities that lie ahead for many returning Russians. As we'll find out, it seems that traveling within Russia, no one is treated with less respect than your average Russian. We move on through customs, get our passports stamped, and look

through the glass door to the outside world, to Vladivostok, to Russia. And on the other side stands a young man holding a sign: "Peter Thomson, James Thomson." Debbie is two-for-two.

Vladivostok is one of those places that always seemed impossibly far away, as likely that I would visit as, say, Uranus. And frankly, as with Uranus, Vladivostok was never high on my list of destinations. But this is where Russia and the Trans-Siberian begin, so this is where we have landed. And as we begin to adjust to the atmosphere and the landscape, a city with a surprisingly familiar and comfortable texture begins to reveal itself. It's dingy and dog-eared, but it's very much a little European outpost here on the far cusp of Asia.

We head out from our hotel, a featureless concrete plug just over a hill from downtown, into air that's moist and warm under a thick canopy of trees. We cross behind a solitary car chugging up the hill to a bluff that looks over a broad bay beyond. In the distance, there's a huge tall ship at anchor, and closer in, a few languid little day sailers, floating on an almost imperceptible breeze. On the shore below us are the crumbled remnants of buildings of probably long-forgotten purpose, and a few people swimming from patches of dirty beach.

At the base of the bluff, our path merges with a promenade thick with late-summer Saturday afternoon strollers. We'd been expecting weather that was well on its way toward winter—this was going to be Siberia in late September, right? What did we know. It turns out that Vladivostok's climate is far more temperate than that of the interior. So where we expected maybe fur hats and overcoats, we instead find skirts, short-sleeve shirts, and ice cream vendors.

We join the parade—people of all ages, but certainly not all types. From its founding in 1860 through the first part of the twentieth century, Vladivostok was a bustling international city, built by Korean and Chinese laborers, settled by European merchants, and a port of call to sailors from around the world. But the revolution and the ensuing Stalinist paranoia changed all that. By the 1930s the region had been purged of most foreigners—hundreds executed, thousands deported, others merely having fled. Of course, the Soviet Union itself contained hundreds of ethnic groups, and even today, having lost much of that diversity, Russia remains a land of many nations. But few of them seem to be represented here either—no dark-haired Buryats, Evenks, Altais, Yakuts, Chukchis, Tuvans, Chechens, Dagestanis, Circassians, Abkhazians, Kumyks, Ossetians, Nogays, or Balkars yet to be seen here in this metropolis of 700,000, the biggest in the Russian Far East. Only *Russian* Russians are evident, with hair ranging from blonde to brown to bright tinted red and orange.

We walk past a rickety little amusement park and a dinky aquarium, among families, couples, old folks, kids, single men, women in pairs or groups but none alone, most of the younger women wearing a good deal of makeup and dressing in a fashion that might make even Madonna or Britney Spears blush. In our first transaction in rubles, we each buy—what else—a Coke, and head off toward downtown.

Away from the shore, we pass haunting blocks of dirty yellow and beige stucco, their lower floors filled with small shops, head up through a street market stuffed with stalls of cheap clothes, cosmetics, and cassettes and emerge onto *Ulitsa Aleutskaia*, Vladivostok's main thoroughfare—a rutted street with twisted, seemingly impassable streetcar tracks and no working traffic lights. The avenue is lined with buildings in nineteenth-century Russian Baroque style, weary and soot covered but whose elegant doorways and huge casement windows manage nonetheless to retain some of their original majesty. Every so often the buildings shudder as a dilapidated streetcar lumbers by, a thundering, red and white hulk of corrugated tin. But despite the pervasive patina of decay, downtown is as vibrant as the park by the water. Fruit vendors, grocery stores, and bookstores all do a brisk business, and a telephone and Internet center with cheap, fast connections is buzzing with Russians exploring the world through their electronic portals. Meanwhile, scattered throughout the city are icons of the lost Soviet society—a monument of huddled peasants being shielded from danger by courageous revolutionaries, a memorial to the Great Patriotic War (World War II, as we know it), and, of course, Comrade Lenin, boldly gesturing to the birds across the street from the train station. The station itself is by far the most elegant and well-kept building in town, testimony to the reigning importance of the train in a sprawling country with no through highway connecting east and west and a shaky air travel system that most residents can't afford anyway. Built in 1912 as the capstone of the grueling, decades-long effort to link east and west by train, the station's grand arches and spires, its spotless yellow and white plaster and stone walls, and its ornate, wrought iron crests and *ВЛАДИВОСТОК* sign seem untouched by the century that's been so cruel to the rest of this city and country.

For dinner, we choose a place called Cafe Nostalgia, across the street from Comrade Lenin, in exactly the opposite direction from which he's pointing. Which is most appropriate, because the nostalgia the name refers to is for the tsars. The place is done up in full imperial style, with red velvet walls, waiters in bow ties, and portraits of Nicholas and Alexandra, the last of the Romanovs, along with what look to be the entire slate of imperial officers who went down with them. I suppose a long era of hardship and repression under the callous and brutal communists was enough to make people here nostalgic for the previous even longer era of hardship and repression under the callous and brutal tsars. Whatever, the place is said to have the best authentic Russian food in town. Certainly, our first meal on Russian soil—crab and cabbage salad, *borshch*, a cabbage roll stuffed with something that might be pork, Greek salad, and baked eggplant—is, to our palates, anyway, far superior to the fried bologna and sautéed sea cucumber of the *Antonina Nezhdanova*.

After dinner, James and I walk up over the hill back toward our hotel under dim streetlights and the soft clattering of brittle yellow leaves. We like this place, despite its dinginess, its feeling of having been crumpled up and stuffed in a drawer for the last century or so. Together with our voyage across the Sea of Japan, it's a wonderful way to ease into this complex and challenging country.

•

"Train Number One—Rossiia—Vladivostok-Moscow." Twenty-four hours after our arrival in Russia, James and I hear the announcement crackle through tinny speakers as we sit alongside freshly groomed soldiers and restless families in the luminous, green-tiled waiting room of the Vladivostok station. We shoulder our bags and head downstairs, and as we approach the platform, our train emits an occasional hiss and shudder, like an impatient horse in its stall, itching to get out and let loose.

Russia's trains play a vital role in the economy and culture of this giant, fractious, and underdeveloped country. And the transcontinental trains hold a very special place within the train system. The name and route of this one are announced by an elegant metal sign mounted neatly on the outside of each car. And while most of the other trains we'll see in Russia are a drab green, the cars of the Trans-Siberian are a distinctive crimson and blue. Lace curtains and a vase of fake flowers adorn each window as we pass along the platform.

At the entrance to our car stands a stern looking woman in a light blue

shirt and navy jacket and skirt, with blonde hair and piercing blue eyes. Stern, that is, when she's looking at us. Otherwise, when greeting the Russian passengers ahead of us, she seems perfectly friendly and chatty. To us, she just gives a cold smile and gruffly checks our tickets and passports before waving us aboard. She is our *provodnitsa*, and for the next three days she'll be our conductor, cleaning lady, chambermaid, samovar attendant, and gendarme. Her name is Svetlana.

Our new home is the center cabin of the center car of the nineteen-car train. Its two berths are crisply made up with red checked wool blankets and massive down pillows. A fold-down table under the window is laid out with a linen tablecloth and topped with its vase of fabric flowers, in front of the lace curtain. On the floor is a little woven throw rug. All of these efforts at delicacy and grace, meanwhile, are strangely offset by heavy, awkward metal fixtures and hardware. You get the feeling that no one could break anything in here, no matter how hard they tried, and that the train itself would survive a nuclear war. Which, I suppose, may have been the point. Finally, the key feature of the cabin, the window, which we've come thousands of miles to see thousand of miles of Siberia through, is thick with dirt and permanently fogged up with moisture between the panes.

If the window seems the key feature at the moment, we've been told that soon we'll come to appreciate another feature of this cabin: It's private. We're traveling the Russian version of first class, what's known here as Soft class. Having been for more than seventy years an officially classless society, it seems that even the different levels of accommodation on the trains couldn't be ranked but that they could be described by vague "qualities"—hence Soft class and Hard class—and, as we will later find out, what you might call Gulag class, the level of accommodation enjoyed by your average Russian on shorter range trains. Soft class costs perhaps half-again as much as Hard class, a premium that we were told is well worth paying unless you have a real stomach for vodka and bodily odors. There are no showers on these trains, but there are plenty of opportunities to buy vodka, and lots of time to do not much else but drink it. And we've been told that it's very rude to decline an offer to drink with Russians, just as rude to stop once you've accepted, and impossible to outdrink them. We've also been told that just being able to lock the door on this train, at least from the inside, is well worth the extra fare. Further tales from reasonably reputable sources ranged from just getting stuck with an unpleasant cabinmate to incidents of theft on a scale from simple pilfering of bags to stabbings and even gassing of passengers in order to clean out their compartments. Perhaps these tales were merely well-circulated apocrypha, Trans-Siberian legends akin to the wet poodle in the microwave. Perhaps we should've scoffed at the suggestions that we ride Soft class and opted for a more authentic Russian experience. Perhaps Soft is really shorthand for *Soft Americans afraid of really rubbing shoulders with average Russians and having to deal with challenging but really not-so-dicey situations.* But frankly, James and I are quite content to ride Soft.

The train is due to depart at 3:14 P.M., although to an unenlightened eye, the schedule suggests otherwise—it lists an 8:14 A.M. departure. What you need to know to understand the discrepancy, and perhaps to understand something more fundamental about the unchanging soul of the Russian state, whether it's nominally democratic, communist, or monarchist, is that all train arrival and departure times, for every remote corner of Russia, now as a hundred years ago, are listed in Moscow time. Here in Vladivostok that means you have to add seven hours to the listed time to get the actual, local time of departure. In Irkutsk, you have to add five hours. If you don't know how many of Russia's ten time zones separate you from the capital, well—you'd better know, or you walk. We'll hear varying reasons for this peculiarity of Russian life, most of which seem merely to be varying ways of saying the same thing—that all power in Russia, and all standards for time, culture, and thought, emanate from the seat of the Russian government.

At 3:10, a thin voice crackles over the PA announcing the imminent departure of *Train Number One*, and then suddenly the platform resounds with martial music, blaring through the tinny speakers. This every-other-day event is not just the departure of a train—it's a moment of national pride. At precisely 3:14, a metallic thunder ripples down from the front of the train, through our car and on toward the rear, as the train slowly stretches out and the cars' couplers pull taught. Almost imperceptibly, the Trans-Siberian begins to creep out of Vladivostok.

14

Across the Sleeping Land

In which we set out on the world's longest railroad,
behold the melancholy landscape of the Russian Far East,
and start to stick our toes into Russian culture

Siberia is the Sleeping Land, a huge subcontinent barely awakened by the first nomads who arrived here uncounted millennia ago, and still, toward the end of the nineteenth century, so devoid of people that in much of it you could travel hundreds of miles in almost any direction and see no evidence that humans had ever existed. Yet the aim of Tsar Alexander III in committing Russia to carve the longest railroad in the world across this great nowhere was not primarily to provide an avenue for settlement by immigrants from overcrowded and often impoverished European Russia. A hundred years after the railroad's completion, Siberia remains today one of the least-populated places on earth. No, the primary purpose was empire building. It was a way to gain better access to the region's dazzling natural riches, which were the property of the tsar; to protect the eastern flank of the empire against Chinese and Japanese designs and provide a launching pad for Russia's own designs to the east; and to bind together a string of Russian settlements flung out over a contiguous land mass larger than that ever claimed by any other single entity.

To accomplish its goal of uniting Vladivostok on the Pacific with Moscow and then St. Petersburg on the Atlantic, Russia had to do something that nearly all engineers at the time judged impossible—carve a passable corridor through a continent's worth of forest, bog, permafrost, stone, and swamp. The work was done by free peasants, imported labor, and prisoners wielding wooden shovels, specially designed machinery, dynamite to blast through permafrost, and bonfires to melt it. Workers had to contend with plague and cholera, searing arctic winters and blistering summers, and attacks by insects, tigers, and bandits. It took twenty-five years from the first felled tree to the last spike, it cost roughly a billion rubles all told, or perhaps as much as seven billion in today's dollars, and by the time it was done in 1916, the empire was nearly bankrupt and on the verge of collapse. But to a large extent, the effort to bind together at least Russia itself, if not the larger empire, succeeded. The political geography of the Russian Empire and its successor states, the Soviet Union and the Russian Federation, has always been tremendously complicated, but it's likely more than incidental that while the country has fought a civil war and two world wars and has cracked apart twice, all in less than 100 years, no region through which the Trans-Siberian runs has gone its own way.

3:14 P.M. The clatter of its iron couplings rolls through the Vladivostok terminal as the Number One train stretches out like a monstrous segmented worm, beginning its seven-day crawl across Asia and Europe. The elegant yellow station, with its regal, wrought iron crests, recedes beyond our dirty window, and just as soon the whole of downtown Vladivostok is eclipsed by a tunnel, out the other side of which it almost immediately feels as if we've passed into another world. However shabby the city center has become, it still feels vibrant, active, lived in. But the territory beyond downtown feels merely survived. We pass rusting and broken factories, industrial zones strewn with rubble, and monstrous gray housing complexes that seem to have been dropped from the sky and left slightly crumpled from the impact, with a few disconsolate souls wandering on dirt paths and train tracks between them.

I station myself at the open window in the hallway outside our compartment, where I'll spend much of the next seventy-six hours, and fill my lungs with the musty, already cooler air. On the far fringes of the city, the rubble slowly segues to thin forest, fields, and small settlements, but the slices of life we pass still seem random and disconnected. Gardens of dark soil growing cabbage, cosmos, and sunflowers. Piles of garbage and abandoned cars. A man drawing water from what I can't help but think must be a poisoned well. Big old Orthodox churches. People living in old train cars. More abandoned factories.

Hay fields. A squadron of old fighter planes, partially hidden behind a set of earthen berms. Purple wildflowers. Rows of planted birch trees. A family having a Sunday afternoon picnic next to a small pool of murky water next to an abandoned factory. A goat. A cow.

Before long, the settlements begin to spread out, clustering along hillsides and ridges as magpies and herons float overhead. Inside the train, a young man with a slightly menacing smile of silver teeth appears at our door hawking cheap magazines and books. Others soon follow offering beer and fish.

We are not yet in Siberia proper but a section of the Russian Far East known as the Ussuri region, bounded on the east by the coastal Sikhote-Alin Mountains and on the west by the Ussuri River, the border with China. Our guidebooks tell us that this is the last refuge of the Amur tiger, what we know in the west as the Siberian tiger, of which there are perhaps fewer than 500 remaining. I imagine one of the huge predators lurking behind the trees, in the scrub forests of fir, ash, maple, and birch, their just-turning leaves brilliant in the late afternoon sun.

In the early evening, passengers spill out of the train onto the platform at the town of Sibirtsevo, to stretch and fill their lungs with fresh air or, as many prefer, tobacco smoke. Women vendors are spread out in front of the station with buckets of peppers, potatoes, and eggplants, tables laden with *bliny*, tomatoes, and *pirozhki*. This is the first of dozens of market stops we'll make as we roll west from the Pacific. Any time a train here stops for more than five minutes or so in the daylight or evening, locals—almost all women—line the platforms offering whatever they can grow, raise, cook, catch, or gather, and even early in the long trip passengers are glad to have it. James and I venture out into the crowd one after the other, so as not to leave our compartment empty, and return with *pirozhki* and *bliny*—fried dumplings filled with meat and vegetables and rolled up pancakes filled with cheese or sour cream—and back underway we lay out a dinner of these plus supplies purchased in Vladivostok—cheese, sausage, bread, and awful tea. For dessert, our Oreos from Japan.

As we roll on and I peruse my copy of Bryn Thomas's *Trans-Siberian Handbook*, I find an excerpt from a travelogue entitled *The Real Siberia*, in which the British writer John Foster Fraser writes that locals do good business on platforms along the Trans-Siberian selling "dumplings with hashed meat and seasonings inside . . . huge loaves of bread, bottles of beer, pails of milk, apples, grapes and fifty other things . . . " and I'm struck by how quickly the kind of scene we've just experienced for the first time became a fixture along this route, and how little it seems to have changed since. Fraser's book was published in 1901.

We're passing alongside hundreds of rail cars loaded with raw logs, almost certainly headed out of the country to serve the insatiable markets of eastern Asia and the West.

The four Japanese guys and the English kid we met on the *Antonina Nezhdanova* are all riding in the car ahead of us, Hard class, four to a cabin. The Japanese guys speak varying degrees of English, from quite good to none at all, but no Russian. One, Kunihiko, is maybe twenty-five, jovial, and wears an almost constant sort of sweet, innocent smile. He's going to Moscow, Prague, and Greece, and I wonder how he's going to fare. He speaks only halting English and, I think, no other European language at all. And he likes to drink, which at least doubles my concern. In the evening he comes by our cabin and enthusiastically struggles to tell us that barely four hours into the trip he and his Russian cabinmates have already consumed two bottles of vodka and consulted the schedule to figure out when they can get more. Later, James goes by for a visit and reports that he has not had a great deal of success, but a lot of fun nonetheless, trying to speak Russian with Kunihiko's cabinmates. I stay behind, mindful of the admonitions we've received not to leave our cabin empty or get into a vodka-thon, and ensconce myself with tales of Russia and Russians real and imagined—*Crime and Punishment*, Thomas's *Handbook*, the Lonely Planet's Russia guide, and an online account by journalists Gary Matoso and Lisa Dickey of their journey from Vladivostok to Moscow five years ago called *The Russian Chronicles*, all of which I'm reading at once. Upon his return, James brings the encouraging news that he managed to discreetly drink just one glass of vodka amid the bedlam of Kunihiko's cabin.

We stay up reading well into the night, James exclaiming every now and then at some outrage revealed in David Remnick's *Lenin's Tomb*, about the last days of the Soviet Union, I at once engrossed in and repulsed by Dostoyevsky's story of Raskolnikov and the old crone. When we finally do turn in, sleep is difficult. The train lurches and rattles. Every time it changes speeds, the cars' loose couplings slam into one another or jerk apart. We're tormented by Russian mosquitoes. But as with the *Antonina Nezhdanova*, the blankets are warm, the pillows soft, and the berths comfortable, and when I finally do fall asleep, I don't sleep all that badly.

Overnight, we're awakened at long station stops by the soft, almost musical pings and plinks of men with hammers testing the wheels and trucks of our train for cracks. They sound like the work of a minimalist avant-garde composer, like a gamelan slowed to a crawl. They will form a hypnotic, ethereal soundtrack for our journey of three nights to Irkutsk, and then four more on to Moscow and St. Petersburg.

•

We emerge from the dark cabin to yellow birch trees blazing through the corridor window. I open it and let in cool, damp air, full of the decay of fall. It smells wonderful. It smells like October in New England, a melancholy whiff of home. There's mist over low hills, the landscape is boggy and peppered with white-bark birches and dark, pole-straight larches, their needles turning from fresh, bright green to orange before our very eyes.

Overnight we passed through Khabarovsk, on the banks of the Amur River, named after the brutal seventeenth-century Cossack Yerofei Khabarov, who conquered the Amur region for Russia. Our guidebooks say it's actually quite a nice city, well worth stopping. Next time, perhaps. And from our northerly route along the Ussuri we've turned west, and for the next day or so will be running parallel to the Amur, which forms the border with China for hundreds of kilometers west of the point at which it merges with the Ussuri. We're finally approaching Siberia proper, although it's hard to say where the region actually begins. Coming from the east, there's no particular geographic feature that tells you you're there—not even a low mountain range like the Urals in the west. Some sources actually consider all of this part of Russia, from the Urals to the Pacific, to be Siberia. Others say Siberia ends at the eastern edge of the Chita region, 1,500 kilometers or so from the Pacific. Our Lonely Planet guide puts the line about halfway between these two, just west of the city of Belogorsk, which we'll pass this afternoon. I imagine in any case that Siberia is demarcated not so much by a line on the map as by a feeling you get, an unmistakable shiver.

Late morning has us in the small town of Obluche, just inside a place on the map called the Evreiskaia Avtonomnaia Oblast. The Jewish Autonomous Region. Huh? I've just read about this place in *The Russian Chronicles* and am amazed to find that it ever existed, that it still exists, that there are still Jews here even today. It was set up in the late 1920s as an internal homeland for Soviet Jews, five thousand miles from any place any Jews had ever called home, as part of the Soviets' effort to prove that they were not anti-Semitic. It never proved especially popular, though—something about the land being awful, the winters bone-chilling, the summers mosquito-infested. And the fact that not long after it was founded, all Jewish institutions and the use of Hebrew were banned. At its height, there were perhaps forty thousand Jews here. But by the mid-'90s there were only about fifteen thousand left, and many of those have since emigrated to Israel. But the few who remain cling to the only place some of them have ever called home, where many of their loved ones are buried and where, in the relative openness of post-Soviet Russia, Jewish culture is reemerging.

At the short stop in Obluche I scan the station for signs in Hebrew or Yiddish, which I've read that I might see. I want very much to get off and spend some time in this haunting place, one of the most intriguing I'll hear about among the thousands of mysteries hidden under the soft folds of this lonely landscape. Perhaps there really will be a next time.

Twenty of twelve local time brings us to Arkhara, just north of the Chinese border. To my surprise, we're running precisely on schedule. So far it seems that while the trains might be slow—we've been averaging less than fifty kilometers an hour, or about thirty miles an hour—they do run on time. On this point, at least, Russia is well ahead of the U.S., where the trains are slow *and* late.

Arkhara is a long stop, and the platform is lined with vendors, mostly babushkas in overcoats and kerchiefs, with a smattering of younger women dressed stylishly in leather coats and fur boots, tasteful makeup, and nicely done hair. James and I venture out to buy *bliny* (one ruble each—about four cents), a couple of bunches of small red grapes (five rubles), and salad (three rubles). Also, potato dumplings (two rubles), a newspaper cone of sunflower seeds (two rubles), and two kinds of cakes (a bank-breaking ten rubles each). Others procure fish, chicken, eggs, beer in huge two-liter plastic bottles, cigarettes and, of course, vodka. The crowded platform is thick with voices, tobacco smoke, and the smells of grilled meat, baked goods, and garbage.

It's at stops like this that you really get a feeling for the Trans-Siberian as a community. Under way, the train is just one long chain of discrete pods, basic units of only two to four people, with little interaction between them. You don't get much of a sense of being part of a shared experience. But out here on the platforms it's a whole little Russian city—young and old couples, groups of young men drinking beer, a smattering of dark-haired, obviously *non-Russian* Russians, a few glaring foreigners like ourselves, and over all far more men than women. People wear T-shirts and plaid button-downs, jeans, sweat pants. There's a lot of black leather on the men and a few, in a touching throwback to earlier times, are even dressed in their finest traveling clothes. And barely a day into what for many is a seven-day trip across the continent, many of the residents of this community are already starting to look a little rumpled. Svetlana and her colleagues, however, are not among this latter group. The *provodnitsy* look as sharp as when we left Vladivostok—not a wrinkle on their navy blue skirts and jackets, not a hair out of place under their prim caps.

The mist has lifted and the day has warmed. People squint in the sunlight.

West of Arkhara, we pass through thin forests in full fall color—bright orange, yellow, even a bit of New England red. At Bureia, beds of orange and yellow marigolds at a clean and well-kept station. Beyond Bureia, freshly cut hayfields.

Early in the afternoon, our Japanese friend Kunihiko returns to our doorway, his usual smile broader than ever and his head topped by a new feature—a Russian soldier's cap. He's also looking a little cross-eyed. "You must come visit us!" he blurts out. "Drink vodka! Speak with Russian friends!" We promise that we will, and he disappears. But soon, while James is off playing his harmonica at the end of the car, Kunihiko is back, with three of his Russian friends in tow. I invite them in.

The Russians are Kostia, Pasha, and Victor, each no older than twenty, all soldiers, and in their very broken English and my dozen or so words of Russian I learn that they're all heading home on leave from a base in Sibirtsevo, a journey of at least five days for each of them.

Kostia is beefy and cock-eyed, with blonde stubble on his recently shaved head, the kind of guy you think is trouble, until he lights up his dis-arming smile. Pasha, on the other hand, is a wisp of a guy, with wavy brown hair, bright eyes, and a wonderfully expressive face with exaggerated, almost cartoonish features. Victor hovers in the background, a blur. Pasha's English isn't very good, but it's the best of the group, and he's eager to try to use it with an American. His search for words and phrases is punctuated with constant exclamations of "Oh!", "However!", and "Just a minute! Just a minute!" We manage to establish that he knows the Beatles, the Rolling Stones, and Nirvana. But he's more interested in what I know of Russian culture. He was born in Uzbekistan, he says, "but Russia is best country." He's passionate about his homeland, and he almost demands that I be, too. "Do you know—?" "Have you read—?" he stammers. I offer him Gogol and Turgenev, Chekhov, Tchaikovsky and Prokofiev. He seems surprised that an American would have read some of Russia's great writers and heard her composers. And when I show him my copy of *Crime and Punishment* and manage to translate its title, his exuberant face somehow lights up even more. I am at the very moment reading a sacred Russian text, and he seems nearly in tears. I instantly feel that I've risen significantly in his estimation.

The Russians have brought vodka and repeatedly urge me to drink it with them. My polite refusals are met with protestations—"To Friendship!" "To our country!" "To your country!" "You must!" Finally I lie—*I can't drink*, I say, *doctor's orders.* Suddenly their expressions turn serious and their entreaties come to a halt. This they respect. But they still want to drink themselves, so before long they say their goodbyes and head back to their own cabin.

When James returns, we decide to take a chance on leaving our compartment empty for a bit and head down to visit our new friends. In a cabin in the middle of the next car, we find Pasha and Kostia, another young Russian guy with gold front teeth, and an attractive young woman, whose dark hair and round face suggest she's a Buryat, looking slightly uncomfortable amid the boisterous young men. Pasha makes the introductions—"This is Lena. However, she is married!"—before enthusiastically resuming his effort to break through the linguistic and cultural walls between the Russians and the Americans. We pass the phrase book back and forth, leaf through it for crucial words, and blurt them out. Before long, Kostia is again offering us vodka, along with potatoes and dumplings, and two more of his friends have joined us, including a shirtless, wall-eyed, tattooed guy named Nikolai who is clearly plastered. *Menia zovut Pyotr, ochen priiatno*, I crib off my flash cards. *My name is Peter! Nice to meet you!* They love that I am Peter—"The, the Great! Petersburg!" They again offer vodka—"Russian friendship!"—and again I politely demur, feeling like a coward even as I do. But James is less burdened with this affliction, and since the bottle is almost empty, and they say it's all they have, he takes a small glass.

The four-person cabin is jammed with at least eight by now. The guy with the gold teeth is quietly trying to read a secret agent novel, smiling politely amid the mayhem, he and Lena jammed into a smaller and smaller space. The air is stuffy and sour with sweat. Nikolai is completely blitzed, sweaty, red-faced, and rattling on loudly about I know not what. James and I are eating a tasty dumpling, and I am just starting to think that maybe it would be OK to have just a little bit of vodka after all when suddenly an older woman with a stern expression appears at the door and speaks sharply to Nikolai. His demeanor instantly changes. He becomes very serious, gets up, goes away, and comes back with a shirt on, chastened. Pasha tells that us the woman was angry, that Nikolai was speaking too loudly and using bad words.

With Nikolai's scolding, the group's sprits are considerably dampened—except, perhaps, for those of Lena and the gold-toothed reading guy, for whom things might be finally looking up. The landscape beyond the window slows as we pull into a station. "If we stay only a few minutes in station," Pasha declares, "we stay in room. If we stay longer, we go out, and come back." We quickly learn that it's a market stop, and the cabin empties. End of party.

The town is Belogorsk. A silver statue of Lenin strides toward the glorious, historically inevitable future in front of a spotless blue station. Below him, residents of that future smoke filterless cigarettes and buy more cheap vodka and beer. Great Father Stalin was long ago obliterated from the cultural landscape of the Soviet Union, but nearly ten years after the demise of the country he founded, we will find that Lenin remains nearly ubiquitous in Russia.

The highway west from Vladivostok terminates just south of here, at the border city Blagoveshchensk. From here on to Chita, 1,000 kilometers or so west, you get through only by train or plane.

On the platform we run into Dave, the English kid heading home from Japan. He tells us that his two cabinmates last night kept trying to get him to drink with them, and got very unfriendly when he wouldn't. Finally he consented, but his effort to appease them left them still unfriendly, and him angry. He was much relieved when they got off the train this morning.

Back underway, an hour or so past Belogorsk, Kunihiko again appears in our door, but instead of his usual grin he looks pallid and unsteady. "Oh! Hello!..." he blurts out. "The three Russian mens in my cabin, we are drinking more vodka.... In my cabin we have lots to drink...." He staggers slightly and slumps against the wall, holding his head in his hands. He begins to mumble. "Maybe I should go first class.... Maybe I should stay in Irkutsk.... They are also  going to Moscow.... I should go first class...."

We ask if he's OK, to which he answers, "I am not OK...." I offer him some water. He accepts, thanks us, and drinks it slowly.

In a moment he looks up, his head slightly steadier. "That refresh me," he says. "Thank you. Come to my cabin again. There are many people there...."

More than ever, we are happy to be traveling Soft.

The afternoon takes us through the late-autumn fields of the Zeisko-Bureinskaia Plain—"the main granary of the Russian far east," Thomas's *Handbook* tells us, "the most populated area of the Amur region ... (growing) barley, soya, beans and melons...."

In the late afternoon the fields give way to thicker forests of birch, larch, and black-barked pine. The white bark and golden leaves of the birch glow iridescent in the late afternoon sun, the larch wispy, gold-tinged green. The air is cool again.

In the evening we visit again with Victor, Pasha, Kostia, and Nikolai. English Dave tells us that barely a day into the journey he's almost finished his last book and is already starting to get bored, with six days still to go to Moscow. But he also says he's been playing chess with another Russian and playing his harmonica to keep himself distracted.

Pirozhki and dehydrated soup for dinner again, our soup and tea made with water from the samovar at the end of the car, an incredible contraption sprouting a forest of levers and gauges and valves and a detailed diagram on the wall next to it that makes it look like the core of a nuclear reactor, only it's fueled by coal from a bin by the exit. All this just to boil water. A key element of Russian culture is starting to reveal itself: simple need, archaic and needlessly complex solution.

•

Day three brings thin sunlight, birch trees stripped of nearly all their leaves, and Svetlana in an overcoat on the platform in the town of Mogocha. One night, and it seems we've moved a month later into fall. A glance at the *Handbook* tells us that overnight we've crossed the administrative border between the Amursk and Chitinskaia regions, and left Russia's Far East territories behind. Wherever we were before now, there is no argument from this point west. The trees feel it. Svetlana feels it. We feel it. We are now definitely in Siberia. And the handbook welcomes us almost with glee. Mogocha, it says, is an "ugly railway settlement... probably the harshest place to live on the Trans-Siberian.... In winter the top 10 cm of earth that thawed over the summer freezes over again in temperatures as low as −60 °C (−87 °F), killing all but the heartiest plants while the intense summer sun singes most shoots." I cross Mogocha off the itinerary for my return trip.

Around Zilovo, a small town with a big rail yard, we pass through what was once a gold mining region, the mines owned by the tsars and worked by slave labor. For a time, the slaves scoured an average of almost 4,000 pounds of gold a year out of the ground here. The empire of the Romanovs, built of fur, gold, and blood.

Thinking about the Trans-Siberian before we actually set out, I envisioned a single track of steel and gravel cut through a vast, unbroken forest, with bears, perhaps, more common beyond the windows of the train than humans. But the reality here is that it's the presence of humans that's nearly unbroken. Villages and towns of dark timber houses and drab concrete apartment blocks cluster along the rails like beads on a silver chain, the gaps between filled with plowed fields, power lines, and the requisite abandoned factory. Beyond the ridges south and north of the rail line, I'm told that Siberia and the Russian Far East unfold as I envisioned them, the great emptiness, the Sleeping Land. But in an unforgiving place settled by people with few resources, humans cling to this chain like a lifeline. It's the only way in, the only way out, and the only link to the rest of Russia and the world beyond. And if you have your wits about you, you don't want to stray far from it.

After two days, the largely unchanging landscape is starting to lose its freshness, and I'm hardly the first to feel this way. "I drive on and on and see no end to it. I see little that is new or of interest," Anton Chekhov wrote, on a much more interminable journey across this same terrain, before the first mile of railroad had been laid. "But," Chekhov continued, "I feel and experience a great deal." And so do I. Whenever I step away from the window to read, write, or play cards with James, something draws me back, and again I'm transfixed. By mid-afternoon it's a new river, the first west-flowing one we've seen, bounded by big deciduous trees in full golden foliage that remind me of the billowy and comforting cottonwoods that line rivers and creeks in the arid American west. Now, yellow hayfields, being cut by horse-drawn reapers, a scene that could have come right from the Great Plains of Abraham Lincoln. At Shilka, a large farming town in a broad valley between low hills, a little girl hangs off an iron walkway above the tracks and watches our train creep by beneath, her blonde ponytail catching the last rays of the afternoon's sun, her imagination hopping aboard and riding west with us. Just past dark we roll into Karymskaia, a "small industrial town first settled by the Buryats," according to our handbook, where the platform in front of the grand station is lined with vendors, including the first non-European Russians we've seen other than Lena, up in the next car. We buy rolls, sweets, and water from two exceptionally beautiful women with the same round faces and sleek black hair as Lena's. There is smoke in the air, and the last faint light of the western sky throws itself in silver bands off the siding rails as we pull out. At Darasun, where mineral springs promise healing waters, only two passengers disembark. And late in the evening we reach Chita, the largest city since Khabarovsk, where a dark cloud of waiting passengers scurries as one down the unlit platform to the far end of train, jostling for position. The cold night air holds a muted stampede of shoes scuffing on asphalt, murmuring voices, and the thin crackling of loudspeaker announcements.

•

On the morning of the fourth day, Kostia and Pavel's cabinmate Lena steps off into the embrace of a slender Russian in fatigues and a world drained of all color, even black and white. The massive station at Ulan-Ude seems cast of ash, the air above it is heavy with mist, and the world seems to disappear completely just beyond the ends of the train. Ulan-Ude is the capital of the Buryat Republic, the semiautonomous homeland of the largest remaining group of indigenous Siberians, and this is our sneak preview. We'll return here in a few days to meet Andrei Suknev and explore the eastern shore of Lake Baikal.

Overnight we passed through Mogzon, where, our handbook says, "there are a number of heavily guarded prisons." After the tsars, after the Soviets, Siberia remains a land of punishment and exile.

Clearing the Ulan-Ude station, we pass a decrepit set of sewage treatment ponds, what we call primary treatment back home but likely the only treatment given to sewage from this city of 360,000 before it passes into the Selenga River. Just past the city center, neighborhoods stretch out along the track, somber houses of dark timber, most with chalky blue- or green-painted window frames and shutters, corrugated tin roofs, and a big garden plot, surrounded by a wooden fence. A bit farther west we cross the Selenga, a broad river split into channels by large islands. The water runs gray-brown and is laced with swirls of foam. Baikal is a hundred or so kilometers downstream.

West of Ulan-Ude, Svetlana comes through and cleans the railing in the passageway, leaving the strong smell of chlorine filling the compartment. The world beyond our windows might be untidy, but Svetlana is determined not to let the same fate befall her domain on the Trans-Siberian. This is part of her daily routine, as is her appearance straightening the curtains, flattening the rug, vacuuming the corridor and, on her hands and knees, the floor of our compartment. For each task, she wears a different outfit.

Suddenly, a couple of hours beyond the city, a glimmer of blue-gray flashes through the woods to the north, the first significant change in the landscape since we left the Ussuri River. I move out to the corridor window as the lake we've traveled so far to see slowly comes into fuller view, and I'm quickly joined at the windows by perhaps half the passengers here in Soft class, with their cameras, tea, and vodka, singing a sentimental ballad. The only word I can make out is *Baikal....*

I spend most of the next three hours or so at the window as we hug the descending edge of the great blue crescent. Behind me to the south, steep mountains rise up close to the lake, the southern rim of the great Baikal rift basin and the first real mountains we've seen in Siberia. Eventually, a menacing forest of metal and concrete rises up on the shore—the infamous Baikalsk Pulp and Paper Mill, the biggest single source of pollution in the Baikal basin. If we're lucky—lucky!—we'll soon get back here to visit the plant.

At Sliudianka, at the sharp southernmost tip of the lake, there's an imposing and starkly beautiful stone station—"the only built totally from marble station in the world," by one account—with high, arched windows and topped off with a sort of grand imperial helmet with a tall spike at the apex. Beyond it the train swings through a broad arc in the shadows of the mountains, ducks through a tunnel, and begins to climb north, up the ridge that forms the lake's far southwestern shore. Until the 1950s, the route continued alongside the water's edge below to the mouth of the Angara River, a stretch that required the construction of dozens of tunnels and bridges. The "Circum-Baikal" route, as it's known, is said to have been the most difficult stretch to build of the entire Trans-Siberian and, between the shoreline itself and the handiwork of Italian masons, the most beautiful. But when the Irkutsk dam raised the level of the lake and the river, part of the old track was submerged, and this new stretch was cut along the ridge above. The Sliudianka station is said to be a monument to the workers who built that now vestigial route. This new one rises quickly from the thin edge of the lake and for a few minutes before we disappear into a heavy mist, passengers have spectacular views down a steep incline covered with golden birches to the blue slate beyond.

As we rise through the clouds, Svetlana comes through with her vacuum and motions to me, gestures that I struggle to divine the meaning of. Eventually she takes my wrist and points to 3:00 on my watch, the time at which we're due to arrive in Irkutsk. *"Da, da,"* I blurt out, making it clear that I understand. Then she motions toward the bedding: *time to gather it up.* But before she does she cocks her head, puts her hands together under her cheek and closes her eyes. This sign language seems universal: *"Do you plan to sleep any more?"* Then she opens her eyes and smiles a blonde Russian beauty queen smile, the first smile we've gotten from her in four days.

"*Nyet, nyet*," I reply, "*spasibo*"—*thank you*—and she is back to her gruff old self, hastily gathering up the bedding and stuffing it into the bins under the beds. Then she is gone.

Kunihiko, recovered from his binge of yesterday, comes by to say his goodbyes. He's decided to stick with his plan and continue on to Moscow, despite his qualms about his cabinmates. Then we head up to the next car to bid farewell to Pasha, Kostia, Victor, Dave, and the rest. Back in our own car, the standard-issue Soviet dreariness rises back up beyond the windows as we approach Irkutsk. We cross a wide river—the Irkut—just above its confluence with the Angara. Soon we approach the Angara itself, bearing the water of Lake Baikal north and west toward the Arctic ocean, and across it we can see downtown Irkutsk. For one of the largest, oldest, and supposedly most sophisticated cities in Siberia, it looks pretty insubstantial. A couple of white spires rise above the yellow trees, the largest building a massive, gray Soviet-era *Inturist* hotel near the riverbank. But it also seems to be less sullied by the grim, ash-colored apartment blocks we've seen in every other city so far.

We arrive in Irkutsk at 3:12, three days and 4,004 kilometers from Vladivostok, precisely on time.

15

Angels and Ghosts in Irkutsk

*In which we stumble around Siberia's finest city,
stumble upon two new guardian angels, and stumble into
a drinking match with two young Russians*

For thousands of the tsars' political enemies in imperial Russia, the bad news was that they were being stripped of their wealth, their civil rights, and their aristocratic privileges and exiled to Siberia, perhaps never to return home. The good news was that they were being sent to Irkutsk. In the continent-sized freezer and prison camp that was Siberia, Irkutsk was a place where formerly dignified and refined Russians not only might survive but might even be able to live with something approaching the dignity and refinement of their lives back in St. Petersburg or Moscow.

"The best of all Siberian towns is Irkutsk," Chekhov wrote on his way east to report on the prison camps of Sakhalin Island in the Pacific in 1890. The city is more than 5,000 kilometers from Moscow, 250 kilometers from Mongolia, and twice as close to Beijing's Forbidden City as to the Kremlin, and even after the first road was cut from Moscow in the 1860s, it took a month of miserable travel to get here under the best conditions. It's also a place where it was said that you could hear a symphony or an opera as good as any in St. Petersburg, or attend the theater in a hall that would grace the most elegant streets of the Russian capital. Where, today, you can walk down tree-lined sidewalks fronting elegant commercial blocks with well-stocked shops and cafes serving the best coffee west of San Francisco. Where green and gold spires descend to ornate white Orthodox churches and poplar-shaded log houses with gracefully carved eaves and window frames extend for what seem like miles in every direction.

Irkutsk was founded in the mid-seventeenth century as a Cossack *ostrog*, a fort at the confluence of the Irkut and Angara rivers, and by the mid-eighteenth century it had become the administrative center of Eastern Siberia as the Russian Empire pushed its frontier ever eastward. It had also become the economic hub of the region, "the warehouse of Russia," as the contemporary writer Mark Sergeyev puts it, where, he says, quoting a Russian proverb, "everything was on sale except pigeon's milk." It was a major transit point along the trade routes that carried such valued goods as tea, silk, grain, silver, household items, and iron works between the Far East and Europe, and it was the westward embarkation point for all the riches vacuumed out of eastern Siberia, from furs to rare woods to gold. The merchants of Irkutsk were said to be the wealthiest in all of Siberia, and they invested a good deal of their haul in schools, hospitals, and cultural and scientific institutions. Some of these schools instructed merchants and diplomats in Far Eastern languages in preparation for expeditions to points much farther east, which were also organized in the city. Among these were the expeditions of the Danish navigator Vitus Bering, the first European to sail through the strait between Siberia and North America and for whom it was later named; Grigory Shelikhov, the "Russian Columbus," who established the first permanent Russian settlements in North America; and the Russian-American Company, which carried out most of the trade that followed. The region also became the destination of generations of troublesome aristocrats, scholars, writers, revolutionaries, and others whose continued presence in European Russia became inconvenient for the tsars, and whose presence in Irkutsk brought a level of intellectual, cultural, and political sophistication unseen elsewhere east of the Urals. The last waves of exiles here included a number of future Soviet leaders, including Viacheslav Molotov, who would later become one of Stalin's most notorious henchmen; Sergei Kirov, who would later become one of Stalin's most famous victims; and Iosif Dzhugashvili, who would later become Stalin himself.

All of this rich history has earned Irkutsk a special place in Russian consciousness, a city as closely tied in the minds of many to its part of the world as Moscow is to European Russia. "Like England created London and France,

Paris, Siberia created Irkutsk," the nineteenth-century writer and dissident Nikolai Shelgunov wrote of the city in a now widely quoted pronouncement. "Not to see Irkutsk means not to see Siberia."

Of course, growing up in the U.S., I knew nothing of all this. Irkutsk was just an empty green space in eastern Asia on the Risk game board, a spot that had to be captured in order to conquer the world.

So here we are, James and I, ten weeks and 10,000 miles from home, and on the threshold of Lake Baikal, staking our claim to *the best of all Siberian towns.*

Our arrival in Irkutsk comes on a cool fall afternoon, with deep yellow sunlight casting long shadows over the city. We leave our new friends and stern Svetlana behind and emerge from the Number One train into a spare and chaotic mid-Soviet-period waiting room filled with the ubiquitous mist of smoked fish, cigarettes, and perspiration. Before we left the U.S., we'd booked a room at a hostel here called the American House, and had also arranged to be picked up. But I realized as we made our way here that I'd given them the wrong arrival date and that we were showing up a day early. There will be no welcoming party. But I do have directions scrawled somewhere in my notebook, courtesy again of Gary Cook. I pull it out, we tighten up the straps of our backpacks and head out.

The streetscape in front of the station is a frenzy of taxi drivers and touts, buses and vans maneuvering for space three and four deep from the curb, passengers lugging heavy bags, tiny kiosks jammed with food and CDs, old men and women in frayed overcoats, young men in black leather drinking beer out of bottles, and nearly everyone, it seems, smoking cigarettes. The same thundering trams we'd seen in Vladivostok roll along the same twisted rails past the station.

We follow the tracks up a crumbling and rutted sidewalk beside a crumbling and rutted road and quickly leave behind anything that looks remotely like what we would call a city, as I had suspected we might from the part of the directions that reads "Take the fifth dirt road on your right. . . ." We're ascending a hill that climbs the western bank of the Angara, away from the old downtown on the far side of the river, and suddenly we're walking through a neighborhood full of the familiar haunting dark timber houses that we'd seen from a distance as we'd passed through Ulan-Ude and other towns to the east, stalwart structures whose brooding mass is offset by the simple but elegant geometry and the powder blue or green and white of their window frames and shutters. Barely feet up the hill from the station, it feels like we've slipped 200 years back in time.

Ten or fifteen minutes up the hill, the spell of the past fades a bit as the log houses slowly intermingle with houses of brick, some quite large and new, and the ubiquitous smell of coal smoke begins to intermingle with the whiff of something not caught wind of since Japan—money. Some local residents are clearly making it. Of course, this isn't reflected in any way in the public realm— the streets still have no signs, the main road looks like it hasn't been paved in decades, and all the side roads are dirt. In fact, sometimes we can't tell what's a street at all, as opposed to just a dog path—which normally wouldn't concern me, except that we're looking for a street with a name, a certain number of streets above the last main crossroad, so names, numbers, and distinctions between streets and dog paths are of some interest today. Eventually, we decide to just head down what clearly is a road and see if anything that looks like the American House presents itself, not at all sure we'll recognize it if we do see it. But as the homes that seem to be too new and fancy fade into others that seem too old and dingy, we decide that whatever it is that we're looking for, it's not here, and we turn around and head back. And as we do, we notice some-one standing at the corner of the main road from which we've come, looking our way.

When you know where you're going, or when you're at least trying to look like you know where you're going, you exude a sort of confidence that can encourage others, say, potential muggers or con men, to take their business else-where. We left that air of confidence on Pier 80 in San Francisco. And certainly, having just turned around and abandoned course, it would be clear to anyone watching that these two guys with backpacks do not know where they're going. And this guy has been watching.

James and I both slow our step a bit, wary of whether his intentions are good or ill. Is he, like Momo in Japan, a good witch? Or is he the sort of bad witch that travelers everywhere fear encountering, or not a witch at all? In any case, as we approach him—because there's certainly no turning back down this dead end road—he does seem not to be a Russian. He's wearing a blue synthetic jacket, whereas most Russian men favor black leather, and he has a red bandana around his head, whereas a Russian man wouldn't be caught dead with such a thing. His greeting clinches it—he speaks in English, with a French accent. And he asks us, "Are you looking for the American House?"

His name is Etienne, and he's from Montreal. He was walking up the hill, and seeing a couple of backpackers ahead of him wandering aimlessly in the neighborhood, he figured it was a pretty good bet he knew where we were headed. Etienne, it turns out, is another very good witch. He will help us find everything we need in Irkutsk—our hostel, the main market, the Internet café, the bank machine, the best tram routes and, perhaps most crucially, the best coffee in town. Another chance encounter with the person best able to help us.

Etienne has been in Irkutsk for three days, on his way from Moscow to Ulaanbaatar by train. He, too, is traveling around the world, also mostly by surface, but in the other direction—west to east. He left Montreal on a freighter bound for England via the St. Lawrence River, and after a month in this country he's in love with Russia and Russians. He tells us that they're the most passionate and kind people he has ever met, particularly Russian women, and that he'll be lucky to get out of the country without marrying at least one of them. But he also seems like the kind of guy who thinks that about every country he's ever visited, and every one he will visit before his travels are done. This garrulous and animated Québécois is, it seems, in love with everything he sees.

And he's staying at the American House—which, he tells us, we missed by one block. He escorts us back down the hill and around the corner to a newish brick house with an iron gate and nothing at all that would have helped us to know it even if we had found it ourselves. Not that there would have been anyone home to let us in anyway, because, as I said, we were a day early. But Etienne has a key.

The American House is run by a Russian woman named Lida, who was married to an American guy who had come to Irkutsk as some sort of military liaison or something in the late 1970s or early '80s. As we enter, we find the walls covered with photos of their wedding and newspaper clippings celebrating the marriage as an example of the great friendship possible between these two great rival nations, and suggesting that the couple opened their house to travelers as much to help advance the cause of peace and harmony as to augment their meager Soviet earnings. If I sound a bit vague on the details, it's because the American man is long since dead, and it turns out that Lida, whom everyone has told us will be a standout character on our Russian excursion, is away. The place has been left in the care of her son by a previous marriage, who, when we meet him later, will seem not at all to share his mother's enthusiasm for bridging cultures. He will speak perhaps three words of English and won't seem at all happy about having to share his house with strangers and look after things in his mom's absence.

For now, with no one else here, Etienne takes it upon himself to get us settled in. We lug our stuff into a big room in the basement and collapse on the two beds. Despite having exerted virtually no energy on the train over the past four days, James and I both feel ragged and run down, like maybe we're coming down with something, so it's definitely nap time. In an hour or so we're back upstairs with Etienne, who in the meantime has been joined by his current traveling companion, an Australian guy in his twenties with a look of perpetual complaint on his face, a sort of sour snarl that immediately makes one think about looking for company elsewhere. As best I can tell the only things in the world that this fellow finds remotely interesting have to do with war and weapons. He's served in the Australian army and is now on his way home from a stint with the British, and is planning to go from here to Mongolia via a highly restricted military border crossing that he is not authorized to visit. When we ask him what he'll do if he's turned back, or worse, his reply is something along the lines of *"fack 'em."* He's all in a lather because he's supposed to be on the train this very night but the *facking* clerks at the *facking* train station won't sell him a *facking* ticket for reasons that he can't *facking* comprehend—a common and frustrating occurrence here, one which we ourselves have taken pains to avoid, but which in this case elicits absolutely no sympathy at all. You get the feeling that he wishes he'd brought one of Britain's tactical battlefield nuclear weapons with him to Russia. After five minutes in his presence we're already deeply worried that he won't be getting out of town tonight.

I wonder what sweet and charming Etienne is doing traveling with such a world-class jerk, but we'll soon find out that what he's doing, at this very moment, is trying to shake him. They were thrown together by the fates on the train from Moscow, and it turned out they were both staying at the American House and both had planned to ship out toward Ulaanbaatar on the same train. But Etienne is telling him now that he isn't feeling very well and he's decided to rest up a while longer, of course at the same time secretly hoping that the Aussie will somehow get a ticket for tonight's train and get the hell out of town.

Which, to everyone's great relief, he will do. I wonder which prison camp he ended up in. In the nearly six months of our trip around the world, through fifteen countries and over twenty five thousand miles, our fifteen minutes with this walking pit of misanthropy will prove to be the only truly unpleasant encounter that we'll have.

A young German couple has appeared at the American House only long enough to pick up their gear before catching the afternoon train west, and James, Etienne and I grab the opportunity to part company with Mr. Black Bile and head back down the hill with them. At the station, we hop one of those rattletrap old red and white trams heading across the river toward downtown. The tram is a decrepit box of sheet metal and plastic loosely held together with rivets, groaning and squealing on its lumpy rails, stoic passengers shoehorned into every square centimeter of its narrow aisle and doorways. Like so much else of Soviet design that we'll encounter between Vladivostok and St. Petersburg, the tram seems designed to kill the spirit, yet just a minute or so into the ride a figure emerges who defies this cynical intent. Floating almost effortlessly between the stubbornly passive passengers is a young woman with long, bright red hair pulled back in a neat ponytail, bright red lipstick and a stylish leather jacket. This Technicolor human being amid a sea of dreary gray is the tram's ticket lady. She's collecting three rubles each from the passengers and passing out tiny scraps of paper in return, and succeeding at the remarkable feat of making this menial job in this soulless context seem dignified. It's a theme that we'll encounter time and again in Russia, perhaps an essential quality of this country—people determined to maintain their dignity in the most undignified circumstances.

Across the river, we spill out of the box onto a narrow street under a thick canopy of yellowing poplars, head up a side street, into a darkened doorway and down a set of stairs to a basement. There's no sign, no indication whatsoever, other than a couple of gloomy-looking teenagers hanging around by the door smoking, that we are entering the lair of Irkutsk's techno-geeks—the Internet café. The stairs empty into a dark room where there's a little bar serving beer and *bliny*, a rack of standard-issue fantasy and mayhem video games, and a bank of fifteen or so computers. The keyboards are in the Latin alphabet rather than the Russian Cyrillic, with just a few of the letters in unusual places. Our fingers quickly get their bearings, tap out a Web address, and boom, we're connected, straight through the earth's core and out the other side to Boston, home, wherever and whomever we want to be in touch with. We went online in Vladivostok and Tokyo with just as much ease, but I remain in awe of the reach of this revolutionary technology, which we're still not quite used to even back home in this final year of the twentieth century. We've traveled halfway around the world to just about the farthest spot on the map I'm ever likely to reach, and here's a casual note from my father, mundane memos from colleagues, news of the end of another disappointing Red Sox season, missives from friends—*no need to rush back, it's the same as it ever was*—and I can write back in the blink of an eye. And only now is it hitting me how profoundly this technology is changing the nature of travel, for better and for worse. It allows you to stay in close touch with almost anyone and so feel less isolated and lonely when you're far from home, to shrink distance and time to almost nothing, to look over the horizon and plan your course several steps ahead. And at the same time, it distracts you from where you are, dampens the rush of being entirely on your own somewhere entirely new, and encourages you to leave a little less up to chance than you might have otherwise. It's a very mixed bag. But one that, despite our ambivalence, we've totally thrown our lot into. The Internet café will become a regular stop as we float in and out of Irkutsk over the next couple of weeks.

Next stop, another technology that's new to Irkutsk and transforming travel, the ATM, safely housed in a big stone vault of a building on a quiet promenade by the river, known as Bulvar Yuri Gagarin. Yuri Gagarin, by the way, was the first man in space—which, the more I see of Russia, the more I think was an incredible accomplishment. I imagine him hurtling upward at a thousand miles an hour at the tip of his retrofitted nuclear missile, crammed into something much like the bathroom on the Trans-Siberian, with huge, crude, overengineered knobs and dials and switches on the dashboard in front of him, beneath him a hole open to the planet racing away from him, the stages of the rocket slamming back and forth against each other as the whole ungainly contraption lurches skyward, straining to escape not only Earth's gravity but also, perhaps more powerful, the weight of Russian engineering and bureaucracy. I can't believe he made it up there. I can't believe he made it back. I don't believe he ever made it to Irkutsk, but he's got a street named after him anyway. And on it is the Alfa Bank.

When traveling in Russia, you have two choices for acquiring rubles. Choice one: Go to a teller at a bank and inquire in broken Russian whether the exchange booth is open; then, if you're able to understand from the teller's muffled reply that it is, discretely go to a corner of the bank and extract a few crumpled American twenties from your money belt under your clothes; stand in line for half an hour or so awaiting your turn to enter the private booth all the while trying to flatten out the bills because you've been told Russians won't accept anything but crisp, new greenbacks; enter the booth, fill out a stack of paperwork requiring everything from your passport number to where you're staying to when and where you entered and will leave the country, pass everything under a thick glass window, wait while the teller counts your dollars three times, calculates the conversion, counts out the rubles three times, then fills out more paperwork, and finally curtly passes the rubles back under the bulletproof glass and waves you out of the booth. Choice two: walk up to a bank machine, stick in your American bank card, punch in the amount of cash you want, wait fifteen seconds, take your card and rubles and leave. It's bizarre, really. Right here in the bank, within inches of each other, exist two parallel universes—the belabored, tightly controlled, bureaucratic universe of old Russia and the Soviet Union, and the fast, efficient, technological universe of the west. *Matter, antimatter.* It's a wonder that they don't neutralize each other and disappear in a little puff of cosmic dust.

•

Not to see Irkutsk means not to see Siberia. And so, perhaps, this is Siberia, tucked in between Bulvar Yuri Gagarin and Ulitsa Karla Marxa, a haunting place that draws you instantly into a time so far before bank machines and the Internet that you wonder how they could've been created by the same species. And you wonder, as well, whether this place and these kinds of things might in fact not be able to coexist in the world of *Homo sapiens* much longer, whether the kinds of change and progress that you were reveling in just moments ago might not wash all too soon completely over this city.

The streets between the Angara and the heart of downtown Irkutsk are broad and straight, like a modern metropolis, but they feel like no streets I've ever walked on. Steel and concrete have yet to be invented here. Bricks and mortar are too scarce to use for anything other than chimneys. Stone doesn't exist, and plaster and stucco are rare luxuries. What there is is wood—dark, brooding, endless, and all-enveloping, a forest not so much cleared as rearranged, turned horizontal rather than vertical, but still very much a forest.

We've seen similar buildings across eastern Siberia, and even in our first glimpse of Irkutsk this afternoon up the hill past the train station, but here, instead of standing apart as in a village, separated from each other by gardens and fences, these houses are jammed together cheek by jowl into the dense, unbroken blocks of a city. A city of logs. Squared off or raw and round, intricately notched and wedged together or simply stacked like Lincoln Logs, painted a weathered and peeling green or as dark as the Siberian earth, the timbers out of which these houses are hewn all seem barely transformed by the human hands that felled them. The log walls form a dark corridor rising two and three stories above the street, the eaves and rooflines cutting sharp against the sky and the stark timbers broken every meter or so by tall casement windows. And it's here at the edges, where the wood gives way to air and glass, that austere Siberia finally allows for a carefully constrained expression of human craftsmanship and whimsy. Ornate fretwork hangs from the eaves in tendrils, swoops, and spears that mimic the ice crystals that form on window glass here every winter. The windows themselves are framed in exquisitely carved casings and filigreed moldings that reflect the lace curtains behind the glass, and every now and then wild turrets and sharp gables jut from the roofs into the sky, topped by wrought iron spires. The stark contrast between the elemental wooden walls and the elaborate embellishments, meanwhile, is mediated by heavy shutters adorned with simple geometric shapes and painted soft hues of blue, green, yellow, and white.

Some of the houses are slumping into the permafrost, others seem to stand as straight and solid as the day they were built. A few seem long abandoned, while most display flowers and other telltale signs of life in their windows. All are more than a little ragged and weather-beaten, having gone a human lifetime, perhaps, without so much as a new coat of paint, but all also seem proud to stand so long after their birth and bathe themselves in the rose-colored late afternoon Siberian sunshine filtering through the yellow poplar leaves.

And as you walk beneath the eaves of these homes and run your fingers along their timbers and their blistering paint, you might suddenly feel the weight of a great overcoat on your shoulders and a tall fur hat on your head, and your ears might fill with the muffled clop and swoosh of a team of horses drawing a sledge over fresh snow and your nose with the smells of coal and wood smoke and horse manure . . . and then you might stumble over a root breaking through the sidewalk and be jolted out of your daydream and back into your life as an American traveler on the cusp of the twenty-first century, and you might suddenly remember what a German visitor to this place once wrote, "I am far from nostalgic but in such a city I am moved with every sign of the past," and you might find yourself wondering how long this extraordinary place, this place with such power to transport a visitor, can hold out. Because you know that ATMs and the Internet are just the leading edge of not just new ways of doing things but of new ways of thinking, in which the values of tradition and continuity are pitted ever more against those of ease and efficiency. You sense that places like these neighborhoods could easily become collateral damage in today's collisions between a troubled history and an uncertain future, between extremes of poverty and new riches, stifling bureaucracy and freewheeling markets, authoritarianism and impunity. And you've heard the whispers that these blocks of timber houses are archaic and unfit for human habitation and that bulldozers should just finish what the great fire of 1879 began, when much of old Irkutsk was destroyed. And you find yourself wondering, too, whether these voices might not be right, whether these ancient houses in which residents likely shiver through life without modern heat or plumbing or proper wiring aren't in fact hopelessly obsolete and shouldn't give way to more modern dwellings.

But you also know that if these places conjure up such vivid images and strong emotions for visitors, they must have an even stronger pull on the sense of place, history, and belonging of the people who know them far more intimately. You know that these houses, these starkly beautiful monuments to the sort of psychic truces that people in less technologized times made with their environment, are part of what makes this place still worth living in and worth caring about. And you know that this might well be the only place on earth like this, that *to see Irkutsk is to see Siberia*, and that when it's gone, it will be gone forever. And you might suddenly realize that, in a way, Irkutsk is a human analog to its neighbor, Lake Baikal, allowed to follow its own idiosyncratic course in only distant conversation with the rest of the world, becoming an utterly unique place, and now contending with a breach of its isolation, and potentially with challenges to its very nature. And you wonder again whether

Russia and Russians will be able to see their way through these challenges to a society that provides for the needs of real, live people and places today, without sacrificing too much of what's been handed down from the past, and can help sustain it into the future.

•

There's another Irkutsk, and then another. Beyond the enchanted forest of log houses spreads a vivid city of lovely and sometimes fantastical eighteenth-, nineteenth-, and early-twentieth-century buildings, boulevards, and plazas, distant outcroppings of urbane, imperial European Russia with occasional overlays of East Asian, South

Asian, and Moorish flourishes, and beyond that, a city of dreary and monolithic Soviet-era construction that's not really worth going on about. And at some point as you explore this enchanting, contradictory, and dog-eared city, you'll want to get something to eat.

As evening falls on Irkutsk, Etienne leads us up a flight of stairs off Ulitsa Karla Marxa, through a darkened second-floor doorway, and into a small room where a few men sit on high stools by a bar, nursing beers and cigarettes. Small knots of young men in the usual black leather and young women in the usual way-too-tight skirts sit at a handful of tables. A video jukebox belts out Euro pop and Russian techno. Dim track lighting above the bar casts the room—the Café Tête-à-Tête—in a permanent dusk.

From the new homes going up near the American House to the Benetton shop on Ulitsa Lenina, the presence of new wealth is evident in Irkutsk, and it's likely that the city has a number of swanky nightspots where the possessors of this wealth gather, members of the five percent of Russian society known as New Russians who, depending on your point of view, are either successfully adapting to the new market economy or sucking the wealth out of the country while the other ninety-five percent become ever worse off. The Café Tête-à-Tête is not a haunt for members of this elite. But it sure wants to be.

We park ourselves at the bar, and Etienne tells us the routine: It's well stocked with favorite western brands, from Chivas Regal to Absolut Peppar, but as in the rest of the country, the drinks of choice here are Russian vodka and beer. Among the beers, he tells us, there are seven choices, all the same brand—Baltica, with numbers roughly corresponding, he says, to their alcohol content. Baltica 1 seems to be for those with the weakest constitutions and who probably would be better off ordering chocolate milk, while Baltica 7 is for those able to stand toe to toe with Boris Yeltsin. James and I, always boldly striking out for the safe middle ground, each order a 3. Etienne orders a 5. The bartender refuses to serve us. He's a heavyset guy, square-faced and with a glint of gold in what I take to be a vaguely menacing smile. It takes me longer than it should to realize that he's joking, and when I do, the quality of his smile immediately changes from menacing to a sort of dopey adolescent pranksterism. Menace is in the eye of the beholder, and I am a prisoner to my jaundiced eye.

Before long, we find ourselves sitting at a table amid the knots of young Russians, in front of plates festooned with crab and corn salad, potatoes, and stuffed trout, and are quickly finding it to be the best meal we've had since we left Japan. And as we eat, two young men at the next table keep peering over at us, one of whom eventually comes over and introduces himself in halting English. "Excuse me," he says, in a thick accent and deliberate manner, "we have both studied English but have never had the opportunity to speak with others who aren't Russian. May we join you? My name is Misha, this is Dmitri. . . ." My jaundiced eye is untempered by its inability just moments ago to detect the real fellow behind the grin at the bar. I remain mistrustful, my brain having been poisoned by too many cold war movies and stories about scams perpetrated on travelers in Russia. But I restrain my darker impulses, and if James and Etienne have any, they do too. We invite them to join us. They bring their vodka.

Misha is a short, round-headed guy in a collarless white shirt under his black leather, his thin lips and narrow eyes adding up to a blank and inscrutable face. His companion, Dmitri, is tall and lean, with close-cropped golden hair, a white dress shirt buttoned to the top, and an innocent, relaxed expression that seems almost the exact opposite of his companion's. I wonder what they're doing together. It fleetingly occurs to me that what they're doing is attempting a tag-team, good-cop, bad-cop con, that earnest Dmitri is going to set us up and sinister Misha is going to take us down.

Of course, the first order of business when they join us is for them to order up more glasses, pour us each a few fingers of vodka, and immediately have their carafe refilled. All of the admonishments we'd received before we left rattle around in my head once again: *Never drink with Russians, because if you start, you can't stop. . . . To a Russian, an empty glass is an insult. . . . You can never outdrink a Russian. . . .* On the train, these kept me from raising a glass with the soldiers, but for some reason here I am more willing to start down this darkened street. Maybe I'm loosening up. Or maybe it's because in just these few hours, I've learned to trust Etienne's judgment, and he seems to have learned a thing or two about how to handle situations like this. In any case, over the course of the next ninety minutes or so, the tap will stay on—every time one of our glasses gets less than half full, Misha will fill it up—"*Choot choot!*—Just a little more!"—and every time there isn't enough left in the vessel to refill every glass, he'll motion for the waiter to replenish it. As we drink, Misha and Etienne engaged in lively, if disjointed, debate about life in Russia and why it is the way it is—Etienne full of bold assertions about Russia and Russians, most of which Misha parries with cool skepticism. And as they talk and drink, their conversation takes on more and more of an edge, at least on Misha's part. Both of them clearly like to challenge people, but as the evening progresses Misha seems to be getting more agitated, even slightly angry, while Etienne remains relaxed and good humored. Dmitri, meanwhile, remains as earnest as ever. He quizzes James and me about our trip, about life in the U.S., about English and verb conjugation and word usage. I finally really believe that he has never spoken with a native English speaker.

The vodka is tasty—clean and smooth as any I've ever had—but to my surprise, it seems to be having little effect on me, or James, Etienne, or Dmitri. But it slowly becomes clear that Misha is getting sloshed. He grows ever more frustrated with his inability to bridge the language and culture gap between himself and us, and he seems to disagree ever more sharply with just about everything Etienne says. It doesn't seem that they're trying to scam us after all, but I am starting to get concerned about what this drunk and agitated Russian might do. I'm starting to scheme up exit strategies when, without warning, Misha abruptly closes his eyes and leans back, and his tense expression dissolves into a sleepy smile. Eyes open again, he slowly reaches over, turns the empty vodka carafe on its side, and says, "I think it is time to go."

Our new Russian friend has drunk himself nearly into a stupor and surrendered, and we are still standing. They said it couldn't be done.

Barely able to get to his feet, Misha offers to drive us home. "*Spasibo,*" we say. *Thanks, but we'll take the tram.*

•

I am intoxicated by Irkutsk, enthralled by the prospect of our imminent excursion to Lake Baikal, fascinated by the swirl of contradictions and the challenges of post-Soviet Russia, and still amazed to be here at all. And I am also: Lonely. Anxious. Fearful. Homesick. All of these things despite the constant, reassuring presence of my brother. This is always the way it is when I'm traveling, always the way it is but never the way I tell it. This nagging fear and anxiety is the backdrop of my life, ebbing and flowing through travel, work, relationships.

My email box at the Internet café is full of notes from friends, family, colleagues. They tell me how envious they are, how exciting it must be to just drop everything and take off around the world, how brave and bold we are to just go out and book passage on a container ship, ride the Trans-Siberian, jump off in the middle, and see what fate throws our way. I sure don't feel brave. For the most part, I don't even feel excited, but instead just a sort of dull and muted sensation pressing through my thick and desensitized rind, the way I've felt—or not felt—about everything, even about my mother's death, for the last year and a half or so, since things finally crumbled with Emma in Berkeley and left me completely tattered and spent. Truth be told, I don't even feel particularly adventurous. I don't feel like I'm exploring the world with confidence and purpose, like I'm sure my grandfather William Orville on the bus in North Africa did, and my other grandfather Jack on his bicycle in France did and my great-great whatever Origen crossing the Continental Divide with his wagons and cattle did. I feel like we're doing this the easy way, cautiously stepping out only as far as the next extended hand, which will then grab hold and lead us safely to the next chaperone. And even so, much of the time I hate it. I feel intensely ambivalent about this entire enterprise, like the four-year-old who asked to be allowed to walk to school alone and then was really sorry that he did. This feeling has been here for weeks, and I know it won't really ebb again until I get my feet back on the ground in the U.S. There's nothing here to envy, I tell myself. But I don't tell them, my friends and my family. I don't tell anyone. I barely mumble it even to James. I want to go home.

But where is home, anyway? And what am I homesick for? I have no home. The demise of my home is recorded in a file cabinet at the Alameda County Courthouse in Oakland, California, case number 6060-842. I realize now that since I handed my keys back to my landlords in Berkeley nearly a year ago, I've basically been a vagabond, casting about for some kind of connection and dressing up my turmoil as boldness and adventure. Reveling in my aloneness as I drove back from San Francisco to Boston, but stopping to visit just about every person that I'd ever met along the way. Jumping when I got there from one awkward and short-lived relationship to another, determined, but utterly unable, to just get on with my life. And now this, a spur-of-the-moment trip around the world, officially and self-mockingly dubbed on our Web site "The Long Way Home." My feeling of being at least psychically homeless was so overwhelming that I could barely even recognize it. So I made a little joke of it, renewed my passport, and headed off. What I thought I was doing, to fall back on a hackneyed fortune cookie truism, was turning a problem into an opportunity, using my divorce as a springboard to something fantastic that I would never have been able to do otherwise. But what I've realized I am doing is more like what we used to say when we had to polish up a weak story and put it on the air—"making chicken salad from chicken shit." If I'm going to feel untethered, cut loose, displaced, I might as well live it. See what it brings me, and where.

But why has it brought me here? Why have I chosen Lake Baikal, this ancient piece of earth? Because it seems permanent and unchanging, in the face of wrenching change nearly everywhere else, including in my own life? Because it, too, is faced with possibly wrenching change, and somehow, along with whatever professional skills and knowledge I've gained, there's something about my life that might help me understand this place? Because, as with the challenges of my family and my marriage, I can't compel myself to just walk away and say that there's nothing I can do? Because, driven around the world by a profound feeling of dislocation, I might somehow locate part of myself here?

All of this. None of this. I don't know.

Asleep at the American House, I dream of train-ships, of me and Emma back in our Berkeley bungalow, and of my mother back among the living. I dream of the things that propelled me here and the things that I left behind.

•

"You have learned all the important Russian words," Olga Baksheeva says to me in English, with a wry smile, as if she somehow understands that I've struggled for weeks to master the simple phrase I've just uttered and knows that it still has utterly failed to come to mind when I really needed it, for instance, with Russians who speak no English.

"*Dobroe utro*," I managed, without flashcards, as she walked through the door of the American House. "*Menia zovut Pyotr, ochen priiatno.*" *Good morning. My name's Peter, nice to meet you.*

Olga stands not much more than five feet tall, a storm of brown hair on her head, oversized glasses framing a broad and somewhat impish face. Simply put, she cuts a modest figure, but to my eyes she may as well be another Atlas, carrying James's and my world of the moment on her shoulders.

I've been told that Olga is an excellent interpreter, that she's well connected in the Irkutsk area and well versed in the constellation of issues surrounding Baikal. But I hadn't known until we arrived in Irkutsk whether she was going to be available. Nor was I certain that I could trust the source of the recommendation—it had come from her sister, whom we'd met at Gary Cook's house for maybe three minutes a few nights before James and I shipped out from San Francisco. But I hadn't really had time to look much further. So as with so much else on this trip, it was going to be Olga or nobody. I dropped her an email before we left the U.S. and then gave her a call as soon as we hit Irkutsk yesterday. "Yes," the voice on the other end of the line said, in the best English we've heard in Russia, "thank you. My sister told me I should expect your call." The first tumbler of the lock had fallen into place. Olga was available. And if I'm going to try to do any serious business here at Baikal, she's the key.

At the big table in the American House's front room, I give Olga a wish list of the kinds of people I'd like to try to talk to about Baikal—officials at the Baikalsk paper mill, scientists, environmental officials, and activists. I've gathered a few names, but I figure that if she's all we've been told, Olga will have others, probably better, more representative of the key voices echoing around the lake.

Our conversation suggests that Olga is indeed quite knowledgeable about Baikal issues and personalities. She speaks with a touch of irony and dark humor about her homeland and the challenges of making arrangements and getting around in this part of the world. She is warm and friendly and seems to truly enjoy her work with visitors to the region. James and I like her right away. But will she come through for us?

"I'll see what I can do," she says, and then she says goodbye and disappears in her waiting taxi.

James and I will soon head back east to Ulan-Ude for our still uncertain rendezvous with Andrei Suknev and visit to Buryatia and the eastern shore of Baikal. We don't yet know that before the week is out Olga will send us an email with a detailed itinerary encompassing nearly every item on our wish list, and then some. We don't yet know that she will introduce us to a rich cast of characters and places and will be able to translate not just their words but also their meaning. We don't yet know that she will help us put our encounters with these people into a context that would otherwise take us months of study to develop, if we ever did at all. In short, we don't yet know that with Olga, our latest shot in the dark, we have hit another bull's-eye.

PART THREE

BAIKAL, TOO, MUST WORK

October–December, 2000

Don't spit into the well water—you'll need to drink it later.

—Russian proverb

16

One of the Best Enterprises in Russia

*In which we confront the legacy of Soviet
industrial development of the Baikal region,
visit an infamous paper mill on the shore of the lake,
and meet with residents who are trying to create new choices*

The Angara River races out of Lake Baikal like a daughter fleeing her angry father for the arms of her lover. So goes the legend of the powerful river that is Baikal's only outlet. Until the 1950s, you could see a huge rock near the mouth of the river that was said to prove the legend—the rock hurled by father Baikal toward his recalcitrant offspring, hoping to block her way as she ran off to join her beloved Yenisei, the great river to the west. Today, only a tiny tip of what's known as Shaman Rock is still visible. Powerful Baikal could not block his daughter's way and tame her energies, but humans could. They captured daughter Angara behind a series of hydroelectric dams and put her to work for the good of the Soviet people. One of the dams raised the level of Baikal by a meter and submerged most of the great rock in the river.

Isolated in the middle of sparsely populated Siberia, its colossal depths and unique ecosystem enclosed behind its barrier of mountains, it would be easy to imagine that Baikal remains a world unto itself. But today that would be just an act of imagination. The lake may have stood apart for millions of years, but in the last 100 years, humans have speeded up time and collapsed space, and Baikal can no longer blithely follow its own, idiosyncratic course.

Some changes were already evident early in the twentieth century. The Barguzin sable, source of so much wealth over more than 200 years, was on the verge of extinction, its long decline punctuated by Nicholas II's belated decision to protect it with the Barguzinsky Nature Reserve. The limits of the limitless lake itself were starting to be tested, too—Baikal's populations of omul and sturgeon were crashing as human populations rose, spawning habitat was disrupted, and new fishing technology was introduced. And along its southern shores, workers were clearing, blasting, flattening, and filling in, laying the path for the needle that would truly puncture Baikal's bubble of isolation, 250 years after the arrival of the first Russians. The railroad was the thin edge of the dramatic changes that the century would have in store for the entire world. It brought new people and communities, new technologies and industries, new markets for the region's raw materials, new invasive species hitching their way from Europe and the Far East, new clearing of land for farms and timber, new erosion along Baikal's banks and sedimentation of its tributaries and shallows, and new wastes being flushed into the lake. And then came the war.

It was the Great War that convinced the Soviets of the need to put daughter Angara, Father Baikal, and other Siberian waterways to work, despite the region's still-sparse population. Factories in European Russia were devastated by German assaults during the war, and much of what was not destroyed was literally picked up and moved beyond the range of German guns and aircraft, east of the Ural mountains, to Siberia. After the war, the Soviets were determined to keep as much of the country's industry as possible out of harm's way again. Siberian factories and hydropower helped lift the USSR out of the devastation of the war and propel it to its greatest economic and technological heights in the 1960s and '70s. With its three massive dams producing electricity for a bank of huge aluminum, petrochemical, paper, and airplane factories, the Angara corridor beyond Irkutsk became the industrial heart of eastern Siberia, barely fifty kilometers from Baikal.

Unlike much of Russia's industry, which itself has collapsed since the collapse of the Soviet Union, much of the industry of the Angara Valley continues to be economically viable. But like elsewhere in the former Soviet Union, the economic progress achieved here has come at a tremendous environmental cost. The factories and fossil-fuel-fired power plants in the cities of Irkutsk, Shelekhov, Angarsk, Usole-Sibirskoe, and Cheremkhovo have created a contaminated hot zone along a swath of the Angara more than 200 kilometers long and 100 kilometers wide, right up to the shores of Lake Baikal. A 1993 study by the California think tank the Rand Corporation found that the region has been "irreparably damaged" by pollution and development. And a 1989 study by a Soviet researcher found that this contamination of the region has led to "increased illness and shortened life expectancy."

As if out of a lingering loyalty to her spurned father, daughter Angara carries the heavily polluted water from these plants away from Baikal and toward other unfortunate places downstream to the west. But she can do nothing about the pall of pollution that these factories cast into the air. According to a Soviet government study, in 1988 stationary sources in the city of Angarsk alone, population roughly a quarter of a million, emitted more harmful air pollution than those in all of Moscow, with its more than ten million inhabitants. Little has changed in the region since—the Russian government recently reported that the cities of Irkutsk, Usole-Sibirskoe, and Cheremkhovo still suffer some of the worst air pollution in the entire country. And every day a plume of waste from these cities' industries is carried by the prevailing winds southeast up the Angara Valley toward Baikal, sixty kilometers away—a noxious cloud variously containing such substances as carbon monoxide, sulfur dioxide, and hydrocarbons; organochlorines like dioxins and PCBs; heavy metals including mercury; nitrogen oxides; particulates; and a whole lexicon of other pollutants. By some accounts, as much as twenty percent of the air pollutants from the Irkutsk-Cheremkhovo corridor reaches the lake. The Rand study found that Baikal suffers "acutely" from air pollution from the Angara corridor and other sources.

To the east of the lake, a second river corridor presents a reverse image of the Angara. The Selenga River is by far the largest of Baikal's 336 tributaries, carrying roughly half of the water flowing into the lake. The watershed of the Selenga drains Mongolia's main agricultural and industrial centers, home to seventy percent of the country's population. It carries human and industrial wastes from Mongolian cities, factories, and mining sites, including what's likely a large amount of highly toxic mercury from the site of a mining accident in the 1950s. And it picks up pesticides, fertilizers, animal waste, and soils running off Mongolian farmland, likely including such notorious pollutants as DDT. Downstream in Russia, the Selenga is the repository for the runoff and waste of similar human activities and communities, including a significant dump of inadequately treated industrial waste and municipal sewage from the nearly 400,000 residents of Ulan-Ude. And toward the end of its journey, the river passes through its agricultural delta and a paper and cardboard plant in the town of Selenginsk before finally disgorging itself into Baikal.

In this inverted version of the Angara, the air pollution from the cities and industries in the Selenga watershed is generally carried east, away from the lake, but the waterborne cargo of human, agricultural, and industrial waste flows west, downstream, toward Baikal. And although much of the Selenga's contamination settles out along its hundreds of kilometers of river and in the broad delta where it meets the lake, by most accounts the Selenga still delivers the largest overall pollution load into the Baikal system.

Meanwhile, an uncountable number of smaller sources, from farms to towns to illegal logging and mining operations, are flushing untold volumes of nutrients and chemical pollution into the lake. Largest among these is Severobaikalsk on Baikal's far northern rim, a new city built in the 1970s to support the construction of a new spur of the Trans-Siberian and that has since become a significant source of sewage and industrial pollutants flowing directly into the most pristine part of the lake.

This daily assault might be enough to kill an ordinary lake. And in fact, some critics say that's exactly what's happening. Among the news articles I unearthed before heading out from Boston was one bearing the headline "The Killing of Lake Baikal." It quoted Greenpeace Russia as saying that Baikal was "close to a catastrophe." But as we've heard, Baikal is no ordinary lake, and there are others who dismiss such hyperbole and say that the nastiness coming into Baikal amounts to little more than a couple of mosquitoes, pestering powerful Father Baikal but presenting no real threat. The argument heats up considerably when it turns to a sullen jumble of machinery and smokestacks near the sharp southern tip of the crescent, right on the shores of Baikal: the Baikalsk Pulp and Paper Mill, producer of more than 100,000 tons of pulp and paper a year and for more than thirty years the largest and most notorious single source of pollution in the Baikal basin.

•

A smudge. A clumsy mistake. A knocked-over ashcan that has spilled its contents onto the shores of Baikal. The town of Baikalsk feels like all of these, and less. You wonder why, when Soviet planners dreamed this place up, mighty Baikal didn't hurl his giant rock at them, instead of at his wayward daughter. To a visitor on a dank October morning, this town—if a place such as this can be called a town—feels like a slur against the lake and on the 17,000 souls who manage to muster up the daily energy to inhabit it.

James and Olga and I stumble onto the barren platform of the Baikalsk train station as the clack and hiss of metal rolling on metal follows our train away from us. The air is damp and cold and laced with the acrid smell of sulfur. At a morose hotel, an apathetic clerk takes fifteen minutes to register us and has to check several times on which are the correct rooms for what may well be the place's only guests. At the town's only open restaurant, the menu features only dumplings and sandwiches, but today it's just dumplings, because the owner didn't show up with the tomatoes and cheese for the sandwiches. On the town's main street, rows of chalky cement buildings lurk like half-hearted ghosts, and the only sounds other than the barking of dogs, the hollow buffeting of the wind against concrete, and the lonely chirping of a few lost birds are the forlorn wailing of a kitten thrown from a doorway and the distressed voice of a woman on the other side, declaring "I told them I cannot take it, I'm sorry...."

The town of Baikalsk seems a perfunctory afterthought, a shoddy barracks thrown together when the ministry in Moscow suddenly remembered that they needed workers to run their new factory. And an appendage it is. The town was built to serve the plant, and it could not exist without it. The two are entwined like the fungus and algae that form lichen, a single, symbiotic, organism.

The red-and-white striped smokestacks of the Baikalsk Pulp and Paper Mill rise above the lakeshore at the edge of town like candy canes laced with strychnine. At its main gate, workers and visitors are greeted by bold and colorful murals of hearty laborers, technicians, and managers working side by side in a spotless modern factory, pumping out massive rolls of gleaming white paper. In front of the murals, real-life workers in shabby jackets shuffle through a darkened security gate, carrying brooms made of twigs and shovels with handles made of branches into a gloomy mass of decaying steel and concrete.

The story of the Baikalsk plant recapitulates the basic elements of much of Soviet industry: The stubborn single-mindedness of the command economy. The overarching power of the state and the military. The almost total disregard for the environment. The fantasy of superior, state-of-the-art production giving way to the reality of inferior goods.

The plant was dreamed up in the 1950s as a source of super-high-quality cellulose fiber for military aircraft tires. To make this super-tough fiber, the military said it needed cellulose pulp produced with super-pure water. Baikal had that water. It also had access to boundless forests and a direct rail link to the rest of Russia's military-industrial complex. A grand factory would rise in the Siberian wilderness on the shores of the country's great lake, to help protect the motherland. Such symbols were a deeply engrained part of life in the Soviet Union at the time. A program of rapid industrialization beginning in the 1920s had squeezed the century-or-so-long industrial revolution of Europe and North America into a few short decades, and images of smokestacks belching dark clouds into the sky had become glorious

homages to the progress of the workers' paradise, even emblazoned in mosaics on the ceilings of the Moscow subway.

But to the surprise of Soviet leaders, the cultural power of Baikal was nearly a match for the monolithic economic and political power of the Soviet state. The proposal for the pulp mill on Baikal's shores—an outcropping of one of the world's most notoriously polluting industries on the banks of one of the world's most famously pristine and unique bodies of water—prompted something that was rarely seen in the country before or after: sustained public opposition. A chorus of influential scientists and intellectuals went on record criticizing the plan, risking their careers, their homes, perhaps even their lives. The Siberian branch of the Soviet Academy of Sciences joined the fray, and eventually even *Pravda*, the official paper of the Soviet Communist party, published an essay challenging the reasoning behind the plant. "Every time nature's interests are disregarded," *Pravda*'s correspondent wrote, "it answers with dead rivers or lakes." Soviet leader Nikita Khrushchev is said to have dismissed these opponents as being interested only in fishing and swimming in the lake. In the effort to build and protect the country, Khrushchev is reputed to have said, "Baikal, too, must work."

And of course, the Soviet leaders ultimately prevailed. The lake went to work. The Baikalsk plant went on line in 1966, delayed, but not stopped, by the cries of protest. But the promise of the plant was broken before it even opened its doors—the super cellulose fiber it was designed to produce was already obsolete. Located on the shores of an utterly unique lake, the plant ended up producing materials that could have been produced just about anywhere. It currently produces newsprint and bleached cellulose pulp.

The unprecedented concern voiced about the plant's impact early on wasn't completely ignored. When it opened, the Baikalsk mill had more sophisticated waste treatment facilities than most others of its time in the USSR. But the waste system was never fully tested, and it failed to work as designed. Within five years of its opening, a commission of the Siberian Division of the Soviet Academy of Sciences found that concentrations of waterborne pollutants regularly exceeded projections, sometimes by as much as twenty times or more. Emissions above federal government standards remain a regular occurrence despite improvements in the decades since 1966, and even the Russian government—still a minority owner of the plant—acknowledges that the system is still insufficient. Reliable, independent data for specific substances is hard to come by, but a conservative estimate of its total releases of wastewater since 1966 is somewhere in the neighborhood of a billion cubic meters, or one cubic kilometer of inadequately treated effluent. The contaminants are typical of dirty old paper mills: sulfates, organic compounds, and suspended particles, all of which can disrupt the biological processes of aquatic environments; phenols, which can damage the organs and nervous systems of animals and possibly humans; heavy metals like mercury, which can disrupt the nervous system and brain development; and highly toxic organochlorines, which have been linked to cancer and serious disruptions in the developmental, immune, and reproductive systems of animals and humans. And unlike most other paper mills, the unholy brew here even includes highly elevated levels of the nasty gastrointestinal bacterium *E. coli*, since the plant's waste treatment system also receives the town's sewage. Today, depending on how you measure it and who's doing the measuring, the impact of the plant's waste can be detected in the water, the sediment, or the lake's bottom-dwelling animal and plant communities over dozens or even hundreds of square kilometers of the lake, and perhaps even much farther away—cellulose fibers from the plant have been found on the shores of islands more than 200 kilometers to the north. Meanwhile, leaks in the system have contaminated the soil around the plant, contaminating part of the local water supply and leaching into the lake, and highly toxic sludge from the effluent sits in crude settling ponds on the shore, barely protected from the elements.

The plant also releases thousands of tons of airborne pollutants a year from its smokestacks—depending again on who's doing the counting, between 7,000 and 40,000 tons of such contaminants as lung-clogging particulates, toxic dioxins, mercury, and hydrocarbons, forest-destroying nitrogen oxides and sulfur compounds, and chemicals that contribute to the formation of asthma-inducing smog and ground-level ozone. By some reports, certain airborne emissions at times exceed permitted levels by a factor of ten and have affected an area from 500 to as much as 2,000 square kilometers around the plant. A government report on the emissions says they have caused "intense and even (in certain areas) irreversible degradation" of some local forests. In the summertime, some of these smokestack emissions float away from the lake to settle elsewhere, but in the cold months—most of the year here in Siberia—they're often held in the lake basin by the kind of thermal inversions that sometimes occur over places like Los Angeles. Cold air above and mountains to the sides trap the pollution over the lake. In the winter, it's said, there's often a noticeable cloud of smog hanging over Baikal's entire southern basin.

On this day, it's impossible to tell where the plumes streaming from the Baikalsk plant's stacks end and where the heavy gray sky above begins. And to an untrained eye, it's also difficult to distinguish the mill itself from the dozens of abandoned factories that we passed in the wilds along the Trans-Siberian. Inside its fences, only the dull groan of machinery and the occasional somnolent worker suggests that this place is any less derelict. A network of skeletal black cranes and elevated conveyors that hauls logs of Siberian larch and pine to the chipping mill looks like a ride at the devil's amusement park.

The cavernous structure where the logs are chipped and boiled looks like it would be knocked down by a good wind—or a modest earthquake. With each step inside the plant, I feel more and more like one of the characters in the Andrei Tarkovsky film *Stalker*, being guided by a haunted man through a forbidden Soviet-era industrial wasteland, every structure rotting, every trickle of water poisoned, the air itself malevolent. No paper mill on earth will ever be mistaken for a chocolate factory, and the production of paper in general is one of those dismal industrial processes on which we all depend but would just as soon not get too close to or know too much about, but this mill seems even grimmer than most.

But against this stark background, plant officials are unapologetic. Natalia Parfenova, the head of the plant's Department of Nature Protection, stands in the dreary courtyard between two of the mill's disintegrating buildings, turns the fur collar of her long wool coat up against the raw October chill, and declares, without a hint of irony, "We local people who live on the shores of Lake Baikal are sure that our enterprise is one of the best in Russia."

I wonder if Ms. Parfenova is deliberately blowing smoke. I fear that she's hopelessly naive. I shudder at the thought that she might be right.

Maybe I'm letting appearances get the best of me—maybe my visceral reaction to the reports I've heard, the statistics I've read, and the unbearable shabbiness of the place itself are clouding my ability to see it in a more positive light. Maybe on a verdant June day, or under a softening blanket of snow, it would take on a different cast, would feel less ominous. Or maybe it's just a matter of perspective. From hers, anyway, Ms. Parfenova says things have never looked better here. ("But please," she tells James as he snaps pictures of the buildings and equipment, "no more photographs. We can give you nice photos of plant back in the office.")

"Much effort has been taken in past ten years to improve the technological cycle," Ms. Parfenova tells us, with Olga translating. Wastewater discharges are down more than forty percent, she claims, and toxic sludge is now incinerated rather than dumped into the ponds along the shore. "We are doing our best to introduce a closed cycle for water so there are not any discharges to Lake Baikal in future," she says. "Of course, there should not be bleached productions, no chlorine usage."

Chlorine bleaching of paper poses a significant environmental threat the world over. Elemental chlorine can react at high temperatures with natural substances in wood pulp to form dioxins, a group of organochlorine chemicals that are notoriously difficult to detect in the production systems of paper mills, that pass through even the most sophisticated treatment systems, and that are believed to cause serious health effects in wildlife and humans, which is why environmentalists have been pushing to ban chlorine bleaching everywhere. But even the most profitable Western paper companies have resisted getting rid of chlorine, which is why I'm surprised to hear Ms. Parfenova's promise about getting rid of it here. But I also know that as we stand here, it's only that—a promise. No plans have been approved, no financing has been found. Whatever the continuing environmental challenges of the plant, though, Ms. Parfenova says they would be relatively easy to resolve were it not for more vexing challenges. "In my opinion," she says, "the greatest problems that the plant is facing are related to political issues, rather than environmental ones."

Her colleague Natalia Miller, from a family of German immigrants to Russia and the plant's public relations chief, joins the conversation. She agrees that cleaning up the plant isn't a question of technology. "Total upgrading of enterprise could have started many years ago," Ms. Miller asserts. The process, she claims, has been held up only by opposition from environmentalists. "The environmental experts say that the emissions should be zero. But this is not possible in any technology." And by insisting on a pristine plant, she says, environmentalists have prevented it from being made considerably cleaner.

Besides, Natalia Parfenova adds, offering a refrain that will become a chorus as I inquire further into pollution here, "Baikal is capable of purifying itself from some of the elements of human activities."

A kilometer or so to the east of the mill buildings, three dark pools stretch out along the shore. These are the settling ponds that are the end of the plant's waste treatment system, the last stop before the wastewater is discharged into the lake, 150 meters out and thirty-five meters below the surface. As our driver pulls his car up by the last pond and we open the doors, the air is thick with the familiar paper mill stench of sulfur—even stronger here, it seems, than in the plant itself. When I ask her about it, Ms. Parfenova insists that it's nothing, really. "*Minimalny zapakh*," she says, "the smell is minimum. It is not the pond that smells. The smell comes from the plant, because wind comes here." But there is no wind, and I'll be told later that there rarely is, that before the town was built and dubbed Baikalsk, this place was known as *Mertvy Veter*—Dead Wind. Down the shore I can see the plume from the candy cane stacks going straight up into the churning gray sky, not toward us.

At the edge of the pond there's a concrete platform, with a metal trap door covering the spillway through which the water rushes on its final dash toward the lake. James stands over it and tells me to stick my nose down into the cracks between the concrete and the door. "It just reeks," he says. I open the metal cover and the smell bursts out.

"Unfortunately there is no cup to extract water," Parfenova continues. "Sometimes they advise the visitors to drink it, to taste it."

James and I both laugh. Well at least she's got a sense of humor about this, I think.

"You should not laugh," she admonishes us, "you should not be sarcastic about it. The treated water meets all the standards of drinking water in Russian Federation. I've seen people drinking it and they say normal, no taste at all."

I decline her offer nonetheless. But I do briefly stick my hand into the stream of water, and when I shake it off it smells strongly of sulfur. The smell will persist until I finally wash my hands hours from now.

Paper companies everywhere tend to play down the effects of the chemicals they use and release from their factories, including hydrogen sulfide and the other chemicals collectively known as reduced sulfur compounds. But the U.S. government warns that even at low levels, these sulfur compounds can affect the eyes and the respiratory system, and that chronic exposure can cause headaches, dizziness, memory loss, and other cognitive problems. Children are especially susceptible to the effects of airborne toxins like hydrogen sulfide gas because they breathe more air per unit of body weight than adults do, and simply because children are shorter and hydrogen sulfide accumulates close to the ground. And hydrogen sulfide in the atmosphere forms sulfur dioxide, a notorious contributor to acid rain, which can harm fish, trees, and other organisms. I didn't bring any testing equipment, so it's impossible for me to know precisely what's in the air and water here at the moment. And, again, I've been told that it's difficult to get reliable, independent information on the precise substances and amounts being released here, so it may be impossible for anyone else to accurately gauge what's coming out of these effluent pipes and those smokestacks, either, and to estimate what the risk might be to local people and the environment. But whatever the specific emission levels and risks might be, I'm more concerned that the stuff is here at all when the plant's Director of Nature Protection is telling me flat out that it's not. I wonder what else is getting through the system that Ms. Parfenova assures me is not getting through.

"You know," she continues, motioning over to the point where the wastewater empties into the lake, "children used to come here, they go fishing. Children like it because the waters are warmer there, and fishes come to this warm place. So fishing is very good there."

This comment delivers another shudder. I know that many of the most toxic contaminants in paper mill effluent accumulate in the tissues of fish, especially organochlorines like dioxins, and that fish from Baikal is a staple of the local diet. Reflecting on our host's words later, Olga will tell me that there are many local media reports of immune system problems in children in the area. She knows that immune problems are often linked to pollutants found in the Baikalsk plant's plume. I wonder what the plant's officials know.

I don't push the Director of Nature Protection any further on this stuff because, well, frankly, there are just some gaps of understanding that even the best translators can't bridge. And how much further could I go with it when she's already asserted that her company's mill is top-notch, blamed environmentalists for standing in the way of the last few tweaks of their system, declared that the best place to fish in the vicinity is right by the plant's outfall pipes, and pretty much dismissed any lingering concerns by invoking Baikal's mystical powers to take care of itself? Would Ms. Parfenova be more forthcoming if I pushed her on the well-established link between the kinds of organochlorine pollution known to be released by the plant and significant health problems in wildlife and humans? Would she drop her official line if I could tell her, as one British scientist reviewing recent research will put it, that "it has been shown that the Baikalsk mill caused locally enhanced levels" of these pollutants? Would her certainty waver if I pressed on about the widely recognized evidence that fish consumption is a significant mechanism for the transfer of these kinds of contaminants to humans around the world, and the recognition even by organizations such as the World Bank that this is happening here at Baikal? Would her unshakable façade show the slightest crack if I were able to mention what I'll learn later, that even by official Russian government statistics, Baikalsk residents suffer disproportionately from serious health problems, many of which have been linked to a variety of common pulp and paper mill pollutants? Somehow I doubt it.

I wonder what the plant's officials know, and later on I'll learn a bit of what they certainly should know, because it's from their own records: Over the last five years, the mill's annual waterborne emissions significantly exceeded Russian Federation standards for an average of eleven regulated pollutants. Among the violations last year, in 1999:

- Twice the allowed amount of suspended particles, which cloud the water and can reduce photosynthesis
- Seven times the amount of sulfates
- Eighty-four times the amount of lignin, a chemical residue of raw wood that has been linked to developmental toxicity in fish and invertebrates
- One hundred forty-seven times the amount of detergents
- Forty-seven thousand times the amount of organochlorines

•

The outcry that preceded the construction of the Baikalsk plant has continued sporadically right up into the present. In recent years, Greenpeace Russia and other environmental groups within and outside of the country have targeted the mill, and some protestors have even marched on it and symbolically tried to shut it down. Even the Irkutsk regional government has unsuccessfully sued the mill's owners for environmental damages. Critics say that while there are many places people can work and live, there is only one Baikal, and that the mill presents a clear and present danger to both the lake and the local human community. I ask Natalia Parfenova about this argument as we stand on the rim of the lake between the settling ponds and the outfall pipe.

She parries my question with one of her own: "Do you consider your great American lakes as unique ones?"

Point taken—I think. The five North American Great Lakes are also a unique ecosystem, also home to a fifth of the world's fresh water, and over the last century their shores have been home to not one or two but thousands of factories that have dumped untold millions of tons of pollutants into the lakes' waters and the skies above. We North Americans have defiled these lakes and by a generation ago had nearly killed at least one of them. The 1969 image of Cleveland's Cuyahoga River burning as it flowed into a filthy Lake Erie—*a river on fire!*—instantly became an indelible example of something gone terribly wrong in America. Who are we to talk?

But I'm afraid that Ms. Parfenova has taken exactly the wrong lesson from our experience with our American lakes. We didn't learn how much environmental damage we can get away with doing and still be able to clean up later. We learned what we shouldn't be doing in the first place, and the limits of our abilities to fix what we've broken. The pollution of Lake Erie and the rest of the Great Lakes system helped spur a profound awakening of environmental consciousness in the U.S. and helped lead to the passage of some of the most important antipollution laws ever put into place anywhere, including the Clean Water Act. More than a generation later, the Great Lakes, and Lake Erie in particular, are much improved, but they're still nowhere near the same ecosystem that they were before we began messing them up, and there are signs that they're once again losing ground. Does Russia need to make similar mistakes at Baikal? Can they afford to push things as far here as we did there?

And it's not just us, not just Americans who have criticized the Baikalsk plant and called for it to be shut down. Russians have always been in the forefront of the campaigns against the plant, and in extolling the unique virtues of Baikal. *Yes,* I reply to Ms. Parfenova, *our American lakes are unique, but not as unique as Russians tell me your great lake is. They say it's the purest, the deepest, it has the most endemic species—everything! And that it's the most beautiful.*

"Yes, that's correct," she replies in turn, "we believe that it's the best in every respect, and it really deserves its place on the World Heritage Site list. But still, our opinion is that such chemical plant operations are possible here.

The main requirement is that there must be new, sophisticated technologies used, and of course the air emissions and these bad smells should be addressed properly."

"And you know," she goes on, "if the enterprise is closed, it will cause many very serious social problems."

She has played the plant's trump card. Baikalsk is an old-fashioned company town. The mill directly employs some 3,000 of the community's 17,000 residents, and most of its remaining jobs support the plant or its workers in one way or another. The plant also provides eighty percent of the town's taxes, Ms. Parfenova says, along with all of Baikalsk's hot water, central heating, and sewage treatment. The town and the mill are like Siamese twins who share crucial organs. Few people can imagine one staying alive without the other, and no one with any authority to do so is saying that the plant should be shut down, whatever its impact on the lake may be. "Yes," Russia's top environmental official in the Irkutsk region will tell me later, "in terms of the ecosystem, it would be far better if there is no enterprise at all of that type on the shore of Lake Baikal. But," he will go on to say, "it is the reality. There are no talks about the complete closing of the plant."

Russia's new Law of Baikal states that "environmentally hazardous economic units in the Baikal natural area shall be liquidated or converted to other operations." So here at Baikalsk it's this second option that's being discussed, and discussed, and discussed. In fact, such discussions predate the Law of Baikal and even the new Russian state that adopted it. As long ago as 1987, under Mikhail Gorbachev, the Soviet government adopted a plan to convert the plant to benign operations within five years. Five years later, with nothing yet accomplished, the government of the new Russian Federation under Boris Yeltsin reiterated the commitment. And the discussion continues under new president Vladimir Putin as we visit the plant another eight years on, in the form of a years-long study of alternatives to its current operations. The preferred choice, if one is ever actually implemented, would likely be to replace the plant's antiquated production systems with modern, chlorine-free, European technology for producing higher quality pulp as a raw material for other paper mills, which would significantly reduce its emissions of toxic compounds and its consumption of wood, water, and electricity. Meanwhile, a plan to disentangle the wastewater systems of the town and the plant by building a separate municipal treatment system is working its way through the regional government. And the plant's owners have been ordered to clean the contaminated groundwater around the facility.

As we head back toward the plant's gates and its murals depicting the nearly fifty-year-old myth of immaculate production here, Natalia Miller urges me to spread the word that her paper plant and the lake can coexist. "We are grateful for your visit," she tells me, "and we really hope that you will support the way the plant goes in its improvements." I tell her that I'm not sure it's my role as a journalist to support or oppose anything. I say this, even as I'm thinking, *It's a fucking pipe dream, it'll never happen, there's no redeeming this hideous place. Shut it down and at least keep things from getting worse.*

I don't think I'm lying to her, saying one thing and thinking another. For the most part it isn't a journalist's role to support one agenda, one outcome, over another, so much as it is to try to represent the facts and their context as fully and accurately as possible and then let people make up their own minds. But neither are journalists empty vessels for carrying pure, "objective" information. Their values, judgments, and levels of expertise inevitably come into play in deciding what to report and how to report it. And, of course, along with conveying knowledge fairly, journalism is also about raising difficult questions, challenging questionable assumptions and false assertions, identifying problems, and trying to help light the way to solutions. So there's an inherent contradiction between the role of values and judgments in journalism, on the one hand, and the need to pull personal biases and agendas out of the story, on the other. It's a constant balancing act.

But the fact is, despite what my gut is telling me, if it was my job to take a position on this place, I still don't know what it would be. Russia has painted itself into a corner here. There are no good choices. The last good choice was foreclosed when they flipped the switch and the first log was chipped, boiled, and pulped here thirty-plus years ago. It's easy to say now that this paper mill shouldn't be here, but it is here, and the question is, what's the best way forward? To summarily shut the factory down, at least without some new economic engine to replace the lost jobs, would destroy a community that, despite its oppressive dreariness to an outsider, is a place that 17,000 people call home.

On the other hand, to allow the plant to stay open with the always-renewed promise of an upgrade might well continue to provide false hope for the lake. Plans to improve and orders to clean up are easy to come by in Russia, but the resources and will to achieve real environmental progress are considerably rarer. As it has for at least the last thirteen years, the promise of progress could merely lead to more of the same—more pollution being pumped into the Baikal ecosystem every day, for years to come.

Ultimately, the end to the story of the Baikalsk plant may come about not through official condemnation or triumphant renewal, but through a natural death, the plant's archaic production system no longer able to compete with the ever-greater efficiencies and ever-lower costs of the global market. Which would, perhaps, be the worst outcome of all—the town of Baikalsk left in the lurch, and the sludge ponds and pollution plume untended to, toxic time bombs left ticking, since bankrupt companies don't often pick up after themselves and there's no big pot of public money in Russia like America's Superfund. So uncertainty hangs as dark and thick over this place as the clouds that snag on the mill's smokestacks as we bid farewell to our hosts and drive away on this raw October day. And it may well be that the only really significant question about the Baikalsk plant will end up being not when this toxic smudge will be cleaned up, but how much it will matter if it isn't—whether the lake's powerful immune system can protect it against whatever damage this place can inflict. It's a question that I'll spend the rest of my time here trying to find an answer to.

•

If there is a flicker of hope here in Baikalsk, it's a small flame being tended in a windowless back room with a few beat-up desks and antiquated computers.

Evgeny Starostenko has the impassive manner of a man who has lived a life of low expectations. And it's easy to see why in a town where you can't even expect to be able to get a tomato and cheese sandwich, whatever the menu says, a town where time seems to have stopped decades ago in the stifling days of Leonid Brezhnev. But Starostenko does not accept that life in Baikalsk can never change. Change is slowly washing over much of Russia, and he is doing his best to generate a few ripples here himself.

"Local people are interested to have job," Starostenko says, "but there are some other local people who are not happy with the existence of the plant here, because it spoils the landscape." He counts himself among those who wish the paper mill had never been built, but he doesn't directly get into the debate about whether it should be shut down or upgraded. Those questions are too far beyond his control. What he is trying to take on is the challenge of creating an alternative. An alternative that could help to wean Baikalsk off of its utter dependence on the paper mill and make it easier for local residents to envision a future without the plant.

Like Andrei Suknev in Ulan-Ude, Starostenko believes the heart of this alternative is low-impact tourism—especially here in the Baikalsk region. Shabby town and brooding mill aside, this part of the Baikal shoreline, running from the southern tip of the lake more than 150 kilometers to the east, has the best road and railroad access anywhere on Baikal. Interest in the region is growing, he says, and already, every weekend, hundreds of cars are lined up along the shore, carrying thousands of local people. Starostenko says most of these people are "wild" tourists, at once a problem and an opportunity. "They use the forest like a toilet," he says, "make fires—you can imagine what is going on." But with properly trained tour guides, innkeepers, excursion boat operators, and the like, he believes that tourism here could be directed toward environmentally responsible activities, to the benefit of both the environment and the local community. The missing ingredient in the recipe for a new economy here isn't potential customers—there are plenty of them, Starostenko suggests—but a lack of knowledge, skills, resources, and the ability to unravel the tangled knot of Russian bureaucracy.

That's where this dark little office comes in. It's the home of a fledgling little outfit called the Baikalsk Business Incubator.

"It's not a secret that here in Russia it is very difficult to start your own business, no matter how small or large," Starostenko says. And even if it were easier to find loans and capital, to get the proper papers and keep abreast of the ever-changing laws and regulations, he says, most local people just wouldn't know where to begin. A few years ago, he and some of his neighbors began talking with people outside of their community about how to broaden their economic options and break out of their dependence on the mill. Among these folks was an environmentalist from Irkutsk, one of the most vociferous opponents of the plant—a surprise to some, but not to Starostenko. "Environmentalists have come to the understanding that extremist measures are not adequate," he says, that they have to help forge alternatives and provide solutions rather than just criticize.

The incubator got seed money from American foundations and the U.S. Agency for International Development, and in 1999 it rented this office and opened for business, providing training, small loans, and administrative assistance to aspiring local entrepreneurs. In its first year, Starostenko says, 125 people took part in classes, and 100 of those registered their own businesses. "So people start to work. And new job opportunities have been created already." And it's not just tourism, he says. Among the new businesses is a company processing local berries, and there are plans for a small producer of sports uniforms and children's clothes.

I ask how many of these new enterprises are profitable—it's one thing to start a business, quite another to actually make a go of it. "Maybe it is too early to speak about successful businesses," Starostenko replies. In fact, in its first year, none of the firms hatched by the incubator has made money. So the results of this effort may take a while to play out, whether it helps to provide a real alternative to the paper and pulp mill or becomes just another failed expression of opposition to it. Certainly, the challenges are formidable—the specific problems presented by Baikalsk's geographic, economic, and cultural isolation, piled on top of the generic difficulties of the larger Russian economy. And despite Starostenko's expressions of hope, the voice of his colleague at the incubator, Olga Gamerova, carries a hint of desperation. Like Natalia Miller at the mill, Gamerova too pleads with her visitors from America to help spread a positive message about her operation to people outside of Russia. Even with the incubator's links to American institutions, she confesses, "We are in a sort of darkness. Nobody can provide us good advice. And we need some advice to go further."

•

Baikalsk has disappeared into its sulfuric fog as the train climbs the loops and switchbacks through the mountains along the lake's southwestern shore and I am glad to be leaving the soul-numbing little town and all of its wrenching contradictions behind. It's the kind of place that as a journalist you're drawn to because it's an important and compelling part of the story of this place, but as a human being, especially one who's trying to leave stories of slow-motion catastrophe behind for a while, you don't even want to think about it. It creates too much psychic dissonance. I'm trying to remember everything I saw and heard and felt there, and I'm trying to forget it all at the same time.

James and Olga and I are riding a Transit train, a string of third-class cars that travels something less than the seven time zones between Vladivostok and Moscow and so is considered a local route, and I'm realizing that this is so much greater a challenge to human dignity than the Hard class berths our friends rode west from the Pacific that our decision to ride Soft seems selfishly trivial, and I'm realizing at the same time that this is almost certainly the way that most Russians cover the great distances they must cross to get anywhere in their immense country.

Our car is a fetid olfactory swamp of sweat, tobacco smoke, dirty socks, fish, and beer. Passengers are lying or slumped on berths that are not quite high enough to sit up straight in if you're a normal-sized Russian and too wide to sit on in comfort no matter how big you are. The berths themselves are arranged in open compartments that resemble human self-storage bins, but with no door or wall separating them from the passageway and the noises, smells, and intimacies of their sixty or so neighbors, most of whom are more yellowed and wrinkled after a day or two squeezed in here than the sheets beneath them. Climbing onto one of these trains and searching for a spot to park yourself is a lesson in Hobbes's concept of the "war of all-against-all," as new passengers squeezing themselves and their bundles through the narrow passageway come face to feet with passengers still trying to sleep on upper berths and knock into others at floor level, many of whom stand arms crossed and stone-faced in the narrow space between the berths, defending their territory against newcomers who might have designs on it. No one talks to anyone else as people shuttle anxiously up and down the car until at last, long after the train has pulled out of the station, most everyone finds at least a corner of a seat and things settle into a sort of uneasy calm. Some who've been defending their seats return to their upper bunks. Others shuffle their crumpled early morning selves off to the bathroom and return with a clean shirt and combed hair. Still others change their clothes right in the open, start up quiet conversations, pick up crossword puzzles, return to their *detektiv* novels, or wander off cup in hand in search of tea.

And suddenly, through this monument to socialist dystopia, wanders a tiny human, a beaming little black-haired Buryat boy of no more than three clutching a lollipop and a bag of chips, walking right up to strangers and peering at them with such a sense of sheer joy and curiosity through his wide brown eyes that he burns a hole right through their masks of indifference and can't help but leave them suddenly feeling that just maybe the planet or even this small part of it is not so awful after all, that just maybe the spark of engagement with the world and the utterly unrestrained love for everything in it that shines so brilliantly in this freshly minted person won't be stamped out before he and others like him grow to adulthood and can start putting it to work in the world. The kid's smile fills up the compartment as his eyes move from person to person. He studies the cushions and blankets, investigates the luggage stuffed under the berths, scrutinizes the scraps of food and empty plastic beer bottles on the table, and then takes himself and his lollipop back around the corner where he came from, but the smile and the eyes remain and carry me all the way back to Irkutsk.

17

Righteousness, Uncertainty, and the Point of No Return

*In which we meet a rabble-rouser, hear a litany of sins,
and consider when we know enough to take action*

Life in Russia is littered with small humiliations and labyrinthine obstacles to everyday tasks, and seems to have always been. And when you notice this, which is pretty much right away, you begin to understand the fatalism and stoicism that permeates this country.

To get to the offices of the Baikal Environmental Wave, you have to squeeze into a cramped and rattletrap city bus, which hurtles along a dusty avenue through Irkutsk's drab Akademgorodok, or university district, on the western bank of the Angara. Above the kerchiefs and caps bobbing around you, you might notice a color-coded route map, and you might initially be surprised at this little flash of consideration for the rider—we don't even have route maps on the buses in Boston. But as the crowd shifts and you move closer, you discover that this speck of civility is merely an illusion. Instead of Russian, the names on the map are in German, and instead of Irkutsk, the bus system depicted is that of Potsdam. The bus is second hand, a castoff from Russia's former satellite state of East Germany, no less, and local officials didn't even bother to try to disguise the fact.

Getting off the bus, you spot your destination—a new building that's not yet finished but already looks old, sprouting up amid a scattering of other older structures that look as if they were never completed. You've been told that the office you're looking for is toward the front of the building, right next to the street, but to get to it you have to take a circuitous path up the side and around the back, through the courtyards of neighboring buildings, under a darkened archway and through a construction site to an unmarked side door. You feel like little Billy Whatshisname from that insipid Sunday comic strip *The Family Circus*, forever taking the most roundabout route home through whatever trouble and mess he can get into, except that here you're certainly not looking to get into trouble, but there is no short, straight line to your destination, and you're pretty sure there never will be. Finally, passing into a stairwell and climbing up one story, you leave this tangle behind and enter a room filled with the precarious jumble of files, books, charts, posters, and half-empty tea and coffee cups that will be familiar to anyone who's ever been involved in, or reported on, any kind of activism. And presiding over this controlled chaos you find a somewhat frosty and certainly determined woman named Jennie Sutton.

Now, you could've been paying even less attention than I was in my Things Russian class and still guess correctly that Jennie Sutton is not a child of the Russian heartland. But if you were to go on to argue that this British subject therefore has no business sticking her nose into debates over part of Russia's patrimony, as some here do, you would get a stiff, if polite, rebuke. Despite how Russians—or my neighbors back home in New England, for that matter—might feel about supposed newcomers to their part of the world, a quarter of a century intimately involved in the life of a place gives you a claim to a certain legitimacy. And besides, there is only one Baikal, and echoing Andrei Suknev across the lake in Buryatia, Jennie Sutton says that it belongs not just to Russia but to all of us.

Natalias Parfenova and Miller at the Baikalsk Pulp and Paper Mill politely refrained from naming any particular environmental activists whom they believe have stood in the way of improvements at their plant, but Jennie Sutton is no doubt high on their list. The Baikal Environmental Wave was founded in the early 1990s to advocate for protection of the lake and its watershed. Sutton is one of four directors, but she seems to be the first among equals. With her longish gray hair, her Queen's English, and her single-minded devotion to one of nature's most singular creations, Sutton seems something of a Siberian Jane Goodall, motivated by as undying a devotion to Baikal as Goodall has to the chimpanzees of Tanzania. Of course, it's a comparison that the modest Sutton will have none of.

Jennie Sutton came to Irkutsk from Britain in 1974 to teach English—the first such outsider in decades, she says—fell in love with the region, and finagled a way in those rigid times to stay. In the '80s, she threw herself into the peace and disarmament movement, and then jumped from that wave to the cresting environmental movement, given new impetus in the USSR by the Chernobyl nuclear power plant meltdown in 1986. And since she helped get the Baikal Wave going, Sutton has become one of the lake's most ardent defenders. The movement to protect Baikal is a broad one, encompassing everyone from Evgeny Starostenko in Baikalsk to Andrei Suknev in Ulan-Ude to Greenpeace Russia in Moscow to activists abroad like Gary Cook, but just about everyone says that if you're interested in the lake and you're going to Irkutsk, you have to talk to Jennie Sutton. And, she seems to concede, she probably has to talk to you. She receives me with the kind of curt friendliness characteristic of many activists who understand the need to spend time talking with media types but who feel that they have many more important things to do at the moment.

We settle into a small office stacked high with videotapes and ragged piles of paper. Her words, like her manner, are deliberate and straightforward. She doesn't soliloquize on the majesty of Baikal, or speak in rhapsodic language about its spiritual powers and its singular place in nature and the Russian soul. She leaves that to people like Siberian writer Valentin Rasputin, who has written a raft of passionate essays on the lake. To Sutton, Baikal's virtues are self-evident, the threats to it are clear, and the need to be unflinching in its defense is unarguable. And she seems to have little patience for those who don't share her way of seeing things. Present her with the proposition, for instance, that the Baikalsk paper mill has been cleaned up enough to be considered safe, or ever could be, and she'll reply, with an air of well-mannered indignation, "I'm sorry, it might be better than some old-fashioned mills in other countries, but it's certainly not fit for Baikal."

Despite her dearth of flowery rhetoric about the lake, though, Sutton is not averse to invoking religious imagery in talking about Baikal. She calls it the "sacred sea," as Siberians have for centuries, and speaks of the Baikalsk plant in particular as something akin to a blasphemy against it—not the only one, but certainly the most egregious.

Her list of the plant's sins against the lake is long and detailed, beginning with its long history of direct water and air pollution—the nearly thirty-five years of releases planned and accidental, which, she tells me, continue to violate regulatory standards regardless of the periodic upgrades to the plant's waste systems. Nor, she says, have the changes done anything to address the threat from three and a half decades of toxic sediments accumulated on the lake bottom and in the sludge ponds along the shore. The ponds were built in the narrow coastal plain between the lake and its surrounding mountains, which, Sutton says, makes them especially vulnerable to flooding and having some or all of their highly concentrated waste washed into the lake. And she fears an even more calamitous result when now-napping Baikal next shakes itself awake, something that could happen at any time, as the endless series of earthquakes that created the Baikal basin continue to this day. Since the 1950s, two quakes below the lake have registered above magnitude nine, and one in 1862 dropped 200 square kilometers of shoreline three meters below water level, creating a whole new bay. Sutton fears that a quake in the vicinity of the plant could cause the sludge ponds and the plant itself to crack open and disgorge their entire toxic contents into the lake, and that even an upgraded "closed-loop" production system might be vulnerable to such a disaster. She contends, with an air of barely restrained exasperation, that there just shouldn't be any chemical-intensive industry of any kind near the lake, no matter what.

But it's not just potential catastrophes at Baikal that frighten her. Sutton fears a disaster may be in the works already, the result of decades of daily, chronic impacts on the lake and its watershed from not just the Baikalsk plant but also the host of other sources of contamination and environmental disruption in the region. Her litany of ominous trends and warning signs includes the high levels of dioxins, PCBs, and other organochlorines that are showing up in the lake's ecosystem; illegal logging in the watershed, which she says is increasing the rate of flooding and runoff of sediments and nutrients into the lake; wastes from farms and human communities, which are contaminating the lake with increasing levels of nitrogen, phosphorus, and dangerous bacteria; and the loss of scarce and crucial shallow-water spawning habitat following the construction of the Irkutsk dam two generations ago and the subsequent increase in water levels. And hovering in the near future, she says, is the specter of oil and gas development and new mining operations in the watershed, which could bring whole new waves of contamination.

Sutton sees the fingerprints of these and other environmental changes on such things as falling fish populations, local declines of the crucial epischura and a corresponding increase in nonnative species of crustaceans, and those three recent instances of mass deaths of nerpa seals. But she also fears that something more subtle, and even more significant, is under way here—that all of the unnatural forces already at work in Baikal are combining to change the lake's unique chemical composition and biological processes, to alter the habitat for its narrowly adapted native species and to put the health of these species and Baikal's entire unique ecosystem at risk.

Her list of known impacts and concerns for the future is frightening, not to mention exhausting. And when she speaks of them it's as if Sutton were connecting scattered dots on a page and drawing a previously hidden and ominous picture out of an otherwise hazy background, a picture now so obvious that no one could miss it. But others could connect the same dots to form a different picture, or not connect them at all. And as I listen to her litany, I wonder if things really are as threatening and urgent as she suggests. It's the age-old question about anyone sounding the alarm about something that others aren't concerned about—is she, along with her fellow Baikal crusaders, seeing more clearly what others are missing? Or is she just overreacting to relatively manageable problems? To put it more bluntly, is she a visionary, or a crank? Even if the Baikalsk plant is as bad as Sutton says it is, as bad as I sense it might be, even if the toxic stews coming into the Baikal basin from the Angara and Selenga river corridors are causing real trouble in some areas, even if there are other significant problems in the watershed, does all this truly spell serious trouble for a lake as huge as Baikal? Compared to its size, the amount of contamination flowing into Baikal is still relatively small. Much smaller bodies of water have been hit with much bigger doses of pollution and seem to have bounced back. And none of them share Baikal's powerful natural filtration system. Are Jennie Sutton and the Baikal Wave just a bunch of Chicken Littles?

Yes, Sutton concedes, this place is different. "Baikal is a mighty lake, and it has the resources, it would appear, to cope with changes up to a degree." But the vital question, she says, is, up to what degree?

"We don't know," she says. "Scientists can't say for sure, have we come to this point of no return or not."

Uncertainty pervades environmental debates the world over. It nearly defines them. Even the simplest desert or tundra ecosystem is far more complex and dynamic than humans currently have the ability to analyze and understand. And much of the time, the picture only becomes murkier when human-generated changes are introduced into these environments. Determining the complete and precise impact of a substance or a factory or a subdivision on a particular environment is virtually impossible, especially when multiple changes and impacts have been introduced. Cause-and-effect relationships can be identified in the simplified conditions of a laboratory, and associations can be established in the real world, but these connections provide only the simplest and sketchiest answers to the infinite number of questions posed by environmental challenges. This is true even when millions of dollars and the best scientists in the field are thrown at a problem, and it's even more difficult when money, expertise, and modern technology are scarce, as they are here.

But a few general principles have been established as environmental problems have slowly revealed themselves over the past couple of generations. Human-induced changes in the environment, from the introduction of a chemical to the alteration of a landscape or of the distribution of species, can have unforeseen consequences, sometimes subtle and sometimes far removed from the original impact. Problems can ripple through an ecosystem and wash up on unexpected shores. Effects can overlap and interact with each other. And small changes can reverberate in big ways. So it's not far-fetched for Jennie Sutton and others to see a constellation of problems at Baikal pointing toward significant, underlying changes, whether or not their hypotheses have been put to a rigorous, scientific test.

Of course, we've also learned that not every environmental impact is as significant or as dangerous as some people feared at first that it might be, that you can't assume that the worst-case scenario will play out. So in the absence of scientific certainty—an impossible standard in any circumstance—how are we to evaluate the scale and scope of a problem, establish a threshold of concern and a point at which action is necessary? And even if there is a high degree of scientific certainty, science can't tell us what's right or wrong, what we should or shouldn't do, what's an acceptable level of disturbance. At best, it can only give us a pretty good idea of what is or isn't happening now, and what's likely to happen in the future. But people still have to decide what, if anything, to do about it, where to draw the line. Which is why environmental debates spill inevitably from the realm of science into those of values, ethics, and politics.

And perhaps along with the environmental impacts that she sees and fears, this, too, is a reason for Jennie Sutton's pessimism and impatience. She and others who warn of serious losses in Baikal's ecosystem are also losing in the realm of human debate. From her office here in Irkutsk, Sutton has been watching ominous signs rise over the western horizon, from Moscow and the rest of Russia.

"The political atmosphere in the country today is very anti-environment," Sutton says. As we meet, Russia's economy remains mired in a deep recession caused by the collapse of the ruble in the late 1990s. There's little interest within the government or the population in any policies that might restrict economic activity, and there's little money for environmental research, especially if it might strengthen the argument for stricter controls. And a collective shiver went down the spines of Russian environmentalists when President Putin recently decided to disband the State Committee on Environmental Protection, roughly Russia's EPA, and merge its responsibilities with the ministry in charge of developing the country's natural resources.

"We see this as a grave danger," Sutton says of Putin's decision. "It's a sort of green light to industrialists and developers to do what they want without any control." Putin has promised Russians that the government's commitment to the environment won't falter, and the Law of Baikal implicitly promises to the world that no harm will come to the lake. But such assurances, as with assurances that the Baikalsk plant will be cleaned up, do not mollify Jennie Sutton.

"No one believes promises," she says, "not in Russia today."

Politically, Sutton and other environmentalists here are playing a lot of defense these days. Among other things, they've joined a campaign to hold a national referendum on the dissolution of the state environment committee, hoping to roll back Putin's decision. But rather than focusing most of their attention on what they see as, at best, an indifferent government in Moscow, they're trying to win the hearts and minds of local residents. Like Andrei Suknev, they're trying to help create an economic and political constituency for greater protection of the lake. Toward this end, Sutton says, Baikal Environmental Wave runs an outreach project that brings mobile libraries with books on Baikal and environmental issues to cities and rural areas throughout the region. They distribute a quarterly journal to 3,000 schoolteachers, university professors, and environmental workers. And they've founded what Sutton calls a "voluntary inspectorate," in which local residents investigate possible violations of environmental laws within the Baikal watershed and officially register them with the local authorities.

None of these programs is likely to produce a groundswell of concern about the lake anytime soon, but this is the way that most movements start—a small core of dedicated people working to slowly educate others and to convince them of the importance of the core issues to their own lives and of their ability to actually start to change things. Of course, movements don't build often or easily. Most are catalyzed by some kind of obvious, grave injustice or calamity—the oppression of a whole class of people, like women or blacks or workers; a war, like Vietnam; or a sudden disaster, like the Cuyahoga River fire, the *Exxon Valdez* oil spill, or the Chernobyl meltdown. More subtle problems tend to generate more muted responses. And despite its history of grave injustices and calamities, Russia has never been fertile ground for broad social movements. The apex of social activism here was the 1917 Revolution, but however deep and widespread the suffering of the average Russian was at that time and for hundreds of years before, the Revolution was less the result of a mass uprising than of a small group of agitators moving against a war-weakened tsar. The demise of the Soviet Union came about in a similar fashion—largely the rotting of an unsustainable structure from within, rather than an assault from without. And even at its height, the upwelling of opposition to the plans for the Baikalsk plant in the 1960s came largely from intellectuals and academics, not ordinary people raised in the long shadow of Stalin and a centuries-old culture of submission to authority. So even in Russia's new democracy, the struggle for Baikal activists is likely to remain a long and difficult one—especially when local residents may be faced with the choice between working in a paper mill, poaching seals, or going hungry, and may see environmentalists as adversaries rather than allies.

All of this is partly why the Baikal Wave has recently begun a new initiative that has nothing directly to do with the lake. The organization realized that it's not enough to identify problems and preach the gospel of environmental purity—it also has to get involved in finding solutions and creating economic alternatives. It was this realization that led the Wave to found the Baikalsk Business Incubator. They helped Evgeny Starostenko and Olga Gamerova set it up, and they helped land funding for it from American foundations and the U.S. government. This was partly a strategic move—creating new jobs in Baikalsk will help wean the community away from its dependence on the paper mill and weaken the argument for keeping it open. But it was also a tactical move. "Environmentalists are always being accused of being against the local people," Sutton laments. She says they've even been accused of wanting to turn Baikal into a museum, in which there'll be no room for people at all, except as visitors. Sutton hopes that creating and working with the business incubator will help assuage residents' concerns. "We are not indifferent to their future," she tells me. "And we hope this will convince them of that."

Sutton believes that the only future that will protect the interests of both the lake and local residents is one built on carefully developed low-impact tourism, light industry for local markets, and sustainable agriculture. And she sees the challenges here at Baikal as no different from those facing the rest of Russia as the country struggles to build a modern human economy without undermining the natural economy that supports it. "There are two obvious ways ahead," she tells me, before I leave her to turn her attention back to her stacks of reports and proposals. "One is a destructive way, losing your head and going for heavy exploitation of natural resources. The other way, the sustainable way, requires great foresight and good thinking from all sections of society. It may be slower for economic development, but it will be more sound."

Jennie Sutton is determined to try to help lead Russia down this second path, propelled by a righteousness of vision, a deep passion for Baikal and Russia, and sheer chutzpah and determination. But none of these qualities should be confused with optimism, with illusions that many of her adopted countrymen will follow her lead. "Unfortunately," she says, in a matter-of-fact tone that betrays barely a hint of the sadness that I know must underlie such a statement, "there's no sign that this will happen in the near future. We may have to make some very drastic mistakes first."

•

I have come to Baikal at least in part in search of something new in the world and in myself—a place that inspires a kind of hope and optimism that's been in dangerously short supply in my life and work. I have been talking with one of the lake's most ardent defenders, and I have found myself wondering if even in her pessimism Jennie Sutton still isn't being too optimistic. Perhaps, she says, only a dramatic mistake will shock Russia and Russians into adopting a truly "sustainable" development path at Baikal. And I am thinking, *Even big mistakes can get swallowed up by big places and big myths.* As shocking as it was to the entire U.S., the *Exxon Valdez* disaster, for instance, led only to marginal changes in the ways in which we transport oil and prepare for accidents. There was no fundamental reckoning with the routine dangers and ongoing environmental costs inherent in our society's insatiable appetite for petroleum, and no discernable change in the consumption patterns of individuals. The ultimate impact of the spill was muted in part by the very thing that caused the initial outrage—the huge and otherwise still largely pristine background against which it took place. Alaska—our idea of Alaska, anyway—was ultimately just too big and too perfect for it to be threatened by one oil spill, no matter how dramatic.

Similar thinking prevails elsewhere—just about everywhere, in fact, where geography and history and demographics have combined to create the idea of a frontier, and where culture has perpetuated it. The myth of the American West as a place of unlimited resources remains as powerful as ever, even as battles over water have become routine, mines and farms have poisoned rivers, forests have been transformed into tinderbox tree plantations, and salmon once as thick as cattle in a pen have ended up on the endangered species list. So, too, with the Amazon rainforest, suffering decades of degradation at the hands of immigrant farmers, loggers, real estate speculators, and wildcat miners. Those who hold sway over the place believe it to be just too vast for its basic ecological integrity to be threatened, even as evidence mounts to the contrary. And here in Siberia itself, the creation of huge uninhabitable swaths of land by Soviet-era nuclear and industrial disasters has not dispelled the centuries-old notion within Russia of a virgin territory of nearly infinite natural bounty.

"Siberia stood as . . . a storehouse that could always be opened in case of need, a force that could be mustered, a rock that could repulse any attack without fear of defeat," Valentin Rasputin has written in his essay "Your Siberia and Mine," an essay that could just as easily have been written about Alaska, the American West, the Amazon, or any number of other such places. "Whatever [Russians] might use up, wear out, or squander in their own economic sphere today, they would find something to replace it with tomorrow in Siberia," Rasputin writes. "Everything there was abundant." Russia has occasionally sobered up and felt remorse over the plundering of Siberia's resources, Rasputin writes, but for nearly 500 years, the myth of Siberia's inexhaustibility has continued to prove irresistible. And Baikal, perhaps, has the misfortune of fitting all too well within this narrative. *Endless forests, uncountable numbers of fur-bearing animals, mines that yield 4,000 pounds of gold a year, an unfathomable lake that makes pollution disappear.* In a land without limits, Baikal is a lake without limits.

This utopian myth of an exalted place of unlimited opportunities and inexhaustible resources seems as old and universal as humanity itself, but its grip on the imagination is perhaps especially strong in Russia. As much as any on earth, it seems, Russian culture is built on a profound sense of limits, scarcity, and suffering, all imposed by a harsh climate and an unforgiving land-scape, by a thousand years of repressive rule under khans, tsars, and Soviets, by a rigid theology that posited strict limits on how close humans can get to God here on earth, and by a steeply hierarchical social structure that left the vast majority of Russians largely destitute, dependent, and disenfranchised. In such a context, the idea of a place without limits has a powerful lure.

At the same time, almost paradoxically, Russian culture has also long been defined by a powerful sense of its own righteousness and an equally pow-erful belief in the unwillingness of others to recognize this. The very notion of Russianness itself was built in part on the belief that through Orthodoxy, Russians were upholding Christ's true church against the pretenders in Rome and Constantinople, giving Russians a sense of eminence and virtue that was further ingrained through centuries of conflict with hostile and invading neigh-bors from east and west. The power of Russia was constantly being challenged and often constrained, which tended in the minds of Russians only to confirm its fundamental truth. In later centuries, this notion of cultural superiority, or at least unacknowledged greatness, spilled over into the realms of art, science, and architecture, the kind of human achievements that are thought to repre-sent the pinnacle of a great civilization. From its medieval churches and icons to its eighteenth- and nineteenth-century palaces, literature, music, and science to being the first nation, in the twentieth century, to put a satellite and then a man into space, the achievements of Russian culture have been among the most magnificent anywhere. And yet Russians continue to have a deep-seated sense that the outside world denies its greatness.

But there's no denying the magnificence and supremacy of Baikal—it is, as Natalia Parfenova at the Baikalsk plant put it, "the best in every respect," the *biggestdeepestoldestclearestpurest* lake in the world. But more than all of its objec-tive, quantifiable qualities, perhaps the thing about Baikal that's most powerful for Russians is the one that's least certain—its power to maintain its own purity, and so too, perhaps, through a grand act of cultural transference, to maintain the purity of Russia and Russians themselves.

Could a dark and frightening truth compete with this myth?

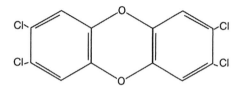

18

Connecting the Dots

In which we see dramatic evidence gathered by a modest woman,
meet an enigmatic man,
and get thrown the book on Baikal

Really, though—who among us, Russian or otherwise, isn't a sucker for a deft illusion? Who doesn't want to believe that the girl really has vanished? And in a time when talk of *The End of Nature* on our almost fully industrialized planet rings chillingly true, who doesn't want to believe that there are still a few scraps of earth left with the power to take the worst that humans can throw at them and turn it into nothing at all? Like I said, that's one of the reasons I came here—to witness the Great Baikal's awesome act. And the illusion is easy to get sucked into, because here's the thing: It's not just smoke and mirrors and nationalistic *Russky* hype. It's largely true—despite decades of hefty daily doses of contaminants from the Angara industrial corridor, the Selenga River, the Baikalsk mill, and other sources, there's been little discernable change in the overall chemistry of the lake—the vast majority of Baikal's twenty-three quadrillion liters of water remain as pure as just about any on earth. It seems that something remarkable really is going on here.

We know it's not that contaminants are just blending into Baikal's tremendous volume to the point of becoming undetectable. Scientists have detected miniscule amounts of industrial contaminants even far from the known hot spots, although nowhere near what they'd expect from the amounts they suspect are going into the lake. Nor is it that the lake is merely turning a trick on a grander scale that just about every body of water performs—using its plants and animals and microbes to metabolize and break down some pollutants. Normal biological processes here and elsewhere do destroy some contaminants fairly quickly, but many of the industrial pollutants coming into the lake don't break down significantly for years or decades, and those basic biochemical limitations are no different among Baikal's flora and fauna than anywhere else. And the water itself? Well, scientific tests prove it—it's just plain H_2O. It doesn't have unique properties that allow it to alchemically transform tenacious pollutants into harmless substances. It's just water.

So how does the Great Baikal pull off this impressive slight-of-hand? Well, if you've read this book from the beginning, you might already have picked up on Baikal's secret. *Epischura baicalensis*, the lake's unique and ubiquitous miniature shrimp, is the hidden compartment into which the Great Baikal slips its "disappearing" pollution.

Epischura, as we've heard, are filter feeders, animals that strain tiny bits of food out of the water. There are lots of kinds of filter feeders in the world, and there are hundreds here in Baikal alone. But when it comes to the disappearing pollution trick, the only ones that really matter are the lake's shrimpy little shrimp. Think of every epischura as a tiny vacuum cleaner about the size of a poppy seed, sucking algae, bacteria, and little scraps of debris from decomposing plants and animals into its little filter bag, and along with them—there it is—tiny specks of pollution that these things have picked up from the water. By itself, the impact of each one of these creatures on the lake is infinitesimally small. But together, their impact is enormous, because there are just so damn many of them—as many as three million below every square meter of Baikal's thirty-one billion square meters of surface area. You do the math. The zillions of epischura trawling Baikal at any one time are like a vast armada of aquatic vacuum cleaners, filtering Baikal's water with extraordinary efficiency. Grigory Galazy, the most famous of Baikal researchers, estimated that, together, all these little cleaning machines filter as much as a thousand cubic kilometers of water a year, or the lake's entire volume every twenty-three years.

So that's the trick—that's where it goes. Baikal's epischura are the living foundation of the "self-purifying system" that people refer to. They are, as Jennie Sutton puts it, "the heroes of the lake."

But like every good heroic story, it turns out that this one is laced with tragedy. And you can only avoid it, you can only maintain the happy illusion of supernaturally vanishing pollution, if you look no farther than Baikal's epischura. (For those of you wishing to maintain this illusion, please close this book now and wait for the forthcoming Disney version.) Because just as the filter bag of a real vacuum cleaner isn't the end of the dust story, the epischura aren't the end of the Baikal pollution story. In fact, the story from here on should be familiar to anyone who's ever read a children's book: *big fish eats little fish, bigger fish eats big fish*. Epischura are, so to speak, the littlest fish in Baikal, near the bottom of the food chain. They get eaten by the bigger larva of golomyanka and other fish, which are eaten in turn by bigger creatures like the omul, and on it goes, all the way up to the top predators—large hunting animals like nerpas, raptors, bears, and humans. And with each link in the chain, the concentration of pollutants in the animals increases. What starts as a virtually undetectable amount of toxins in the epischura concentrates exponentially as it passes up through each successive predator.

This process—known as *biomagnification*—was already well understood by scientists when it was first brought into public focus nearly forty years ago by Rachel Carson in her landmark book *Silent Spring*, and it's only been further documented since. In some aquatic ecosystems, concentrations of pollutants have been found to jump by several orders of magnitude from one link in the food chain to the next. And marine mammals in particular—animals such as seals—have been found to accumulate and store especially high concentrations of toxic chemicals—in some cases, more than ten million times higher than in the surrounding water.

Accumulation and concentration of toxic chemicals are functions of the ordinary workings of every ecosystem, including that of our otherwise extraordinary lake. And it's the force behind the nasty irony in Baikal's stupendous self-cleansing act: extraordinarily pure water, extraordinarily contaminated animals.

●

Evgeniia Tarasova reminds me of my grandmother—a wisp of a woman with the slenderest of hands, grayish hair cut so as to attract the least amount of attention, and a self-effacing, almost apologetic manner. Except I'm quite sure that my grandmother never used sodium sulfate and a solution of *n*-hexane:acetone to help identify polychlorinated biphenyls and polychlorinated dibenzo-*p*-dioxins and furans in samples of ground-up omul flesh. And she rarely said or did anything that would betray a sense of distress, or cause such a feeling in anyone else.

Dr. Tarasova's little office off a dark hallway in a musty concrete shoebox in Irkutsk's Akademgorodok district is cluttered with racks of glass beakers, plastic tubing, gauges, folders and notebooks, a jumble of tools, and data representing a lifetime spent studying Lake Baikal and its inhabitants. Today she's a senior researcher in the Institute of Geochemistry at Irkutsk State University, but she took her first samples at the lake as a graduate student nearly forty years ago, in 1961. It was a heady time for researchers all across Russia: the cold war was at its peak, and rubles were being shoveled into the sciences—not just those that could directly help the USSR compete with the west but also those that could help demonstrate the overall superiority of the Soviet mind and the Soviet land itself. Interest in unlocking the mysteries of Russia's unrivaled lake was high, and so was funding. "Many expeditions took place," Dr. Tarasova tells us as she ushers us into her office and toward her desk by the window. "We used to take samples every month, every year."

Of course, much has changed over the four decades of Dr. Tarasova's career, in Russian science and in Russia itself, especially in the nine years since the collapse of the Soviet Union. "Recently, such explorations stopped," she says. "We researchers do not have enough funding to continue monitoring, to carry out steady and regular research." And it seems that the scarcity of resources has come at an especially bad time, because the lake, too, Dr. Tarasova says, is not what it once was.

"There is a belief that Lake Baikal is stable," she tells me and James and Olga, illuminated by the pale, flat light of a cloudy October morning beyond her office window. "But it is not a correct point of view." The words carry the confidence of a veteran scientist, but the voice is barely more than a whisper. It has the quality of sorrow and trepidation of someone who has just received grave news about a family member and now has the excruciating task of telling everyone else.

Dr. Tarasova is devoting what are likely the final years of her career to a grim chore that she probably never could've imagined when she began her work—tracking and documenting the contamination of Baikal's ecosystem. She's become, late in life, less a pure researcher than a sort of *ekologichesky detektiv*, painstakingly tracking the path of industrial pollutants through the lake and the surrounding region. With the meager resources they have been able to muster, she and her colleagues have developed much of the evidence that activists are using to press their cases for more urgent action to protect Baikal, uncovering and connecting some of the dots out of which Jennie Sutton and others compose their bleak picture of the lake's future.

The research team has set its sights in particular on a group of toxic compounds known as persistent organic pollutants, or POPs—a set of mostly chlorinated hydrocarbons including dioxins, PCBs, and DDT that can be highly toxic, accumulate in the food chain, and remain active for a long time. "We studied the food chain up to the Baikal seal," Dr. Tarasova tells me, as well as the region's water, sediment, soil, snow, and human residents. And they found POPs at every turn.

This result by itself wasn't unexpected. Less than a lifetime ago, POPs were virtually nonexistent, but these days, they're just about everywhere. Since the first industrial organochlorines were created in the mid-twentieth century, their production and use have become nearly a defining feature of civilization, and from factories and farms they've spread via food chains and ocean and atmospheric currents to the farthest corners of the planet, blanketing the world in a sort of global haze that scientists now simply call "background levels." With so much heavy industry in the Baikal region, the researchers wouldn't have been surprised to find levels in the food chain noticeably higher than the background. What was surprising, Dr. Tarasova says, was how much higher some of the levels actually seem to be.

There's a slight tremble in the scientist's frail fingers as she sifts through a stack of documents on her desk, finds what she's looking for, and hands it to me. It's a set of scientific articles in English, including one published in a British journal in 1997 that summarizes what she considers one of the most significant studies she's participated in: "Polychlorinated Dibenzo-p-dioxins (PCDDs) and Dibenzofurans (PCDFs) in Baikal Seal."

"Our conclusion," she says of the report, in her grave near-whisper, "shows that the Baikal seal, in contamination, is similar to those of the Baltic Sea."

Yikes. The Baltic is one of the world's most heavily polluted seas, a shallow, nearly enclosed body of brackish water that's a virtual holding tank for pollutants from a northern European economy of nearly 100 million people. And Baltic seals are notoriously contaminated with POPs—they carry some of the highest body burdens found in animals anywhere.

Polychlorinated dibenzo-p-dioxins and dibenzofurans—a large family of chlorinated hydrocarbons that most people know merely as dioxin—form as unwanted byproducts of industrial processes such as waste incineration and chlorine bleaching of pulp and paper. They're produced only in extremely tiny amounts, but they also can be toxic in extremely tiny amounts. According to the U.N.'s World Health Organization, or WHO, dioxins have been found to cause immune, hormonal, reproductive, and developmental problems in laboratory animals at levels in the range of ten parts per trillion—a concentration roughly equivalent to ten grains of poisonous sand in a whole lakefront beach. The U.S. Environmental Protection Agency says that dioxins "can alter the fundamental growth and development of cells, [can have] adverse effects upon reproduction and development" and are a "likely human carcinogen."

Dr. Tarasova's team sampled the blubber of more than a dozen nerpas in the mid-1990s and then compared their dioxin levels to those that had been found in seals in other parts of the world. The lowest concentration found anywhere in recent years was two parts per trillion in two species of Antarctic seals, a level that might be considered the global background. Against that background, Baltic seals stood out a like a toxic Himalaya—concentrations in adults of two species ranged from 14 to 170 parts per trillion. And here in Baikal, the dioxin levels that Dr. Tarasova and her colleagues found in adult nerpas fell within almost precisely the same elevated range—from 15 to 175 parts per trillion.

Yikes, indeed. The dioxin levels in the average male nerpa in Dr. Tarasova's studies were thirty times higher than the global background and six times higher than the WHO threshold for health problems. The level in the most contaminated nerpa was almost ninety times the global background and more than seventeen times higher than the WHO threshold.

Dr. Tarasova hands me studies containing data on other POPs in nerpas, gathered by other scientists, and the results are similarly jarring. Levels of PCBs, a once widely used class of chemicals related to dioxins, overlapped only with the lower levels in the Baltic but were up to a hundred times the global background, well into the suspected danger zone for immune system and reproductive problems in various marine mammals and, at the high end, above the level considered under an international treaty to be hazardous waste. The restricted pesticide DDT and related compounds followed a similar pattern—levels also generally lower than in the Baltic but from roughly 10-300 times the global background and in most cases well above the level suspected of causing hormonal problems and tumors.

Three major organochlorine pollutants, three sets of results that place Baikal's top predator in dangerous territory. "Yikes" is nowhere near strong enough a word.

Dr. Tarasova doesn't suggest that these numbers show that Baikal itself is anywhere near as polluted as the Baltic. But the data do indicate, as she and her colleagues write in one of their studies, that "Lake Baikal must have experienced large inputs of PCDD/Fs, especially when its enormous volume and dilution potential is considered."

If they're reliable, the numbers point toward two chilling conclusions. The first, drawn from the absolute levels of POPs in the nerpas, is that there is clearly a significant load of these pollutants entering the Baikal ecosystem. The second is a more fundamental conclusion, drawn from the much bigger gap in Baikal than in the Baltic between the relative pollution loads in the water itself and in the seals: Baikal's unique self-purification process, by which the epischura filter the lake's water with such extraordinary efficiency, has the corollary effect of moving the contaminants into the food chain with extraordinary efficiency.

If these studies are accurate, they seem to blow the notion of Baikal's power to maintain its own purity right out of the water.

But there's that nagging question—are the studies accurate? Can the data be trusted? Getting a reliable fix on these substances in such minute concentrations requires levels of expertise and technology that are not at all guaranteed to be present in a scientific environment in which long-standing intellectual isolation is now compounded by a serious lack of money. And the scramble for funds has put Dr. Tarasova and some of her colleagues, in particular, in a potentially compromised situation. I notice that for two of the dioxin studies she's given me, she and her colleagues got financial support from Jennie Sutton's Baikal Environmental Wave. That's an automatic eyebrow-raiser, at least where I come from. In the West, accepting research funding from anyone who has an interest in the outcome is an invitation for close scrutiny of your methods and results.

Dr. Tarasova tries to assure me of the integrity of her numbers. "We have arranged our analysis in Germany with the use of the most sophisticated equipment," she says. "The best high-resolution system in the world provided these results. So these data are reliable."

I'd like to take her word for it, but ... I scan the articles for other information that might bolster their credibility.

What other kinds of company do the researchers keep? Along with the Baikal Wave, Dr. Tarasova and her colleagues have also received support for some of their dioxin research from research institutes in Germany and the MacArthur Foundation in the U.S., a major and widely respected philanthropy. They have worked regularly with researchers from major Western institutions, including the Canadian health ministry, and their results have been published in peer-reviewed journals in the U.S. and Britain.

How do their results compare with those from similar studies of similar compounds? The results of Dr. Tarasova's dioxin research roughly parallel data collected by other researchers on PCB and DDT levels in Baikal. And the credentials of those researchers? Scientists from leading American and Japanese institutions, supported by government agencies in both countries, with results also published in American scientific journals.

And finally, do any of the data stand out as just looking weird and improbable? Well, one of the studies, by the American team, does show an eye-popping leap in PCB concentrations from the water to the nerpa of as much as seven orders of magnitude—ten million times—and three orders of magnitude, or a thousand times, just from the water to the epischura. But as jarring as they are, these numbers aren't out of whack with anything that's been learned about concentration factors in other food chains, anything else we know about the Baikal food chain, or data in any of the other studies of Baikal.

The integrity and credentials of this community of researchers appear solid, and it doesn't appear that their results have been skewed to satisfy a funder. I'm no scientist, but to this layperson, these studies have the ring of truth.

Yikes.

Dr. Tarasova can only speculate what these levels of organochlorine contamination are actually doing to nerpas. Not all animals respond in the same ways to the same environmental contaminants—not even all closely related animals do—and laboratory test results can only be roughly extrapolated to the real world. So knowing, for instance, that lab rats were harmed by a certain level of dioxins, or that certain levels of PCBs have been linked to disease in St. Lawrence River beluga whales and Baltic ringed seals, or that a certain amount of DDT has been associated with lowered sex hormones in Dall's porpoises, doesn't necessarily allow you to predict that you'll see the same effects in nerpas facing similar levels of the same contaminants. And the uncertainty is made even more vexing when all these similar compounds with similar effects are found together in an ecosystem—it's virtually impossible to figure out which contaminant might be causing which problem, or whether they might even be working together to enhance the overall effect, as some scientists suspect.

But when scientists like Dr. Tarasova find similar amounts of similar contaminants in similar animals and then also see similar unusual problems that they know have been linked to those contaminants, they can be pretty sure that they're seeing cases of cause-and-effect. And that's what's happening when they compare the situation of Lake Baikal's nerpas to that of seals in the Baltic Sea and elsewhere.

In the last decade or so, populations of marine mammals around the world have been hit by mass die-offs, including one in the Baltic and the nearby North and Wadden seas in 1988 that killed as many as 20,000 seals and sent waves of carcasses washing up on the shores of northern Europe. In each case, the immediate culprit was found to be a virus that overwhelmed the animals' defenses. But a chain of evidence later fingered organochlorine pollutants as a hidden culprit that likely weakened the seals' immune systems and made them more vulnerable to the virus.

Here at Baikal there's been an eerie echo of these events—nerpas, like their cousins in Europe, have been succumbing to viral infections in large numbers. In 1987-1988, an epidemic similar to the one that hit the Baltic and North seas killed at least 5,000 Baikal seals. A decade later, in 1997, dozens of carcasses washed up on beaches near the Baikalsk paper mill. It happened again in 1999, and again, many were found near the mill. The location of these corpses may have been purely coincidental—no one has been able to link the deaths directly to the plant's effluent, and organochlorines generally don't do their dirty work quickly enough to suddenly affect migrating species like the nerpa. But the patterns of contamination and deadly epidemics in the seals were similar enough to what happened in Europe to convince Dr. Tarasova and others that, whatever their sources, the pollutants in the nerpas' systems played an important role in their demise.

There may also be echoes in the nerpas of the other health problems associated with high levels of POPs in other marine mammals—reproductive problems and tumors in adults, and developmental problems in embryos and pups, who get heavy doses of contaminants through their mothers' placentas and milk. There's no reason to believe that problems found in similar animals in similar circumstances in other places wouldn't also show up here. But there's also little being done to find out whether they are. The funding squeeze, again.

For their part, having made their splash with the nerpa research, Dr. Tarasova and her colleagues have turned much of their attention elsewhere in the Baikal ecosystem—because nerpas, she reminds us, aren't actually the lake's top predator. "This is a dangerous thing even for people," Dr. Tarasova sighs, and the already heavy weight she bears on her small frame seems to grow even more burdensome. Some local residents still eat nerpa meat and blubber and use the seals' oil as medicine, exposing themselves to the animals' high levels of POPs. But there's a more widespread danger to people. "We have also taken samples of fishes," Dr. Tarasova says, "and they also accumulate dioxins with age." Further research in the lake has confirmed that omul and other Baikal fish are a major source of dioxins for the local human population.

In the U.S., advisories are routinely issued warning people against eating more than a small amount of fish caught in waters polluted with organochlorines and other persistent toxic substances. Pregnant and nursing women are often told not to eat any at all. But no such advisories are issued here, and if they were, they'd almost certainly be ignored. To tell Siberians not to eat omul would be like telling Americans not to eat hamburgers. "Everybody eats omul here," Dr. Tarasova says, a fact to which James and I can attest. We've seen a brisk business in omul in every market we've entered and on every railroad platform we've passed. We'll be served it in every home we'll visit in the Baikal region, at nearly every meal.

So what kind of risk does eating so much dioxin-contaminated fish pose to people in the Baikal region? Neither Dr. Tarasova nor anyone else can come close to answering that question with any certainty. The science surrounding the impacts of different amounts of dioxins and other POPs in people and other animals is at once maddeningly sketchy and excruciatingly complex, in both the laboratory and the real world. At best, scientists in the field are able to talk only about such things as *the results of longitudinal retrospective studies, generally accepted paradigms,* and *comparison and extrapolation of end points*—all scientific jargon for educated guesses.

The educated guess of Dr. Tarasova's research team in response to my question comes from Elena Mamontova, a young doctoral candidate who's just appeared with a sheaf of papers from her office down the hall. She pulls a report from the bundle and directs my attention to some of her data, written in English.

"The day rate of dioxin is about two to three picograms per kilogram a day from all sources in the Irkutsk region," Ms. Mamontova tells me, using a standard measure of dioxin consumption: trillionths of a gram per kilogram of a person's body weight per day. "It is from forty-one to fifty-one percent from fish. And the health risk with the above-mentioned day dose makes about 410 cases of cancer out of one million people."

Four hundred and ten cases of cancer is roughly four times the number that Americans could expect from the average levels of dioxins in their diet, according to the U.S. government's latest assessment of the dangers of dioxins. But Dr. Tarasova suggests that the actual number of dioxin-related cancers here will probably be much higher, because the team's calculations were based an a very conservative estimate of the amount of fish people here eat—thirty-four grams, or a little more than one U.S. ounce a day, a piece smaller than a Hershey bar. "But you know," she tells me, "people who live on the shores of Lake Baikal eat more fish than this thirty-four grams a day." A good deal more, it appears, just from my own short experience here. And when they eat all this fish, they are exposed to more than dioxins. They likely ingest significant doses of PCBs and the rest of the long list of the bioaccumulating pollutants that are circulating through the Baikal food chain. And as with other animals, these pollutants present more than one serious threat to humans. There are strong indications that dioxins and other POPs can affect the human immune, reproductive, neurological, and endocrine systems, causing health and developmental problems that are more subtle than cancer, but often no less serious.

Somewhere else. Not our fault. Dr. Tarasova has heard the refrain from government officials and even some other scientists: *if Baikal does have a problem with the accumulation of things like dioxins and PCBs—and we're not saying it does—the stuff isn't produced locally. It's coming from somewhere else.* Fingers are pointed at Mongolia, at other parts of Asia, at the global haze of POPs. Never mind that the kinds of notoriously dirty industries active in the region would be the first suspects in cases of such contamination no matter where they took place. Never mind that scientists have documented toxic hot spots around known sources of pollution here for years. To many of the people here who matter most, the origin of whatever industrial chemicals may be in Baikal remains an open question.

But along with that of the levels of POPs in the Baikal food chain, Dr. Tarasova and her colleagues have set out to answer this question once and for all. A few years ago, the research team began sampling various stationary environmental media up and down the lake basin—things like soil, sediment, and nonmigratory fish. Previous samples of migratory fish, which move throughout the length of the lake, had showed no significant differences in contaminant levels, regardless of where they were caught, but Dr. Tarasova's research found that fish that spend their entire lives in one part of the lake showed a clear pattern: steadily increasing concentrations of POPs moving from the largely wild regions in the north and east of the lake toward the more industrial regions in the south and west. The soil and sediment samples showed the same pattern. In the lake basin itself, concentrations rose to their highest levels in sediment near the outfall pipe of the Baikalsk mill and in soil at the head of the Angara Valley, where the winds streaming up the valley from the factories in the Angara industrial corridor slow down as they spread out over the lake. From there, the researchers followed the trail along the river and found levels of POPs in the soil and in milk from local dairies continuing to rise toward Irkutsk, and ultimately Usole-Sibirskoe.

But like a team of bloodhounds tracking its quarry for miles and miles only to lose the trail in a confounding swirl of scents, this team of environmental sleuths has lost the trail of organochlorine contaminants just as it seemed to be closing in on the precise sources of the pollution. They're certain that the factories along the Angara are major sources, but the chemical stew bubbling out of the region's huge industrial cauldron is so far too complex, the possible sources of its ingredients are too numerous, and the information on exactly which facilities are using which substances in precisely what ways remains too sketchy to close the case.

The researchers have been similarly vexed by the evidence surrounding the Baikalsk mill. They can't quite correlate the mix of chemicals that they believe is coming out of the plant with the chemicals that they have been told are going in. And just to further muddy the waters, other researchers have found a spike in the levels of PCBs around the plant, pollutants that are not at all a usual product of paper making.

There may well be simple explanations for the inconsistencies surrounding the Baikalsk plant—information on its inputs and processes may be incorrect or incomplete, and perhaps PCBs have been released from other parts of the operation. And the remaining uncertainties aren't enough to dissuade Dr. Tarasova from her larger certainty about where the trail of evidence generally leads. "Of course," she tells us of the factories of the Angara corridor, the Baikalsk mill, and its sibling mill in the Selenga delta, "these are the major sources for dioxins." But as long as the evidence remains only circumstantial—until or unless scientists can draw an unbroken line of pollution from specific sources through Baikal's water and fish to specific health problems in nerpas and humans—the people with the power to make decisive changes may remain unconvinced of the need to do so.

Certainly to date, Dr. Tarasova says, this whole body of work has garnered little official attention here.

"We don't feel any support," she tells us. "You see that our decision-making bodies don't want to believe that Lake Baikal is not pure, that it is polluted. They don't want to believe it."

Her frail hands fidget with her stacks of documents as we near the end of our interview, her drawn face seeming less than ever like that of a detached senior researcher and more than ever like that of a distraught elder of a vanishing culture. "I can't understand what is going on," she continues, "because we have the experience of other lakes which are contaminated, like the example of the great American lakes." Her comments are an eerie echo of those of Natalia Parfenova at the Baikalsk plant, only she has taken a very different lesson. "It must be human nature that man has to go through all the stages to the very end, until some of the conclusions are made.

"If there were several Lake Baikals in the world, maybe the concern would not be that high. Unfortunately, there is only one Lake Baikal, and there is a threat to it. We live here and we observe this situation. But we don't know how to change the situation. If you could provide your help and assistance, it would be good."

Muted echoes of Dr. Tarasova's parting comments, with their now-familiar plea, bounce off the concrete walls and floor as we head back down the dark hallway from her office, follow us into the lurching, claustrophobic elevator, and swirl with the blowing leaves in the sunless October air outside.

•

The environmental standards in the Law of Baikal are vague, the time frames for implementing its mandates are not spelled out, and the consequences of violating the law are uncertain. But when you read the document, rife with references such as "unique ecological system," "mandatory government-sponsored environmental expert assessment," and "Maximum Permissible Volumes of Discharge," this much is clear: it is a testament to the wisdom and authority of science. In fact, like nearly every piece of environmental legislation the world over that isn't concerned solely with aesthetics, the document makes no sense whatsoever uncoupled from the underlying assumption that the qualities and benefits of a slice of the planet, the threats to it, and the standards of protection of it are all essentially matters to be determined by the impartial arbiter of scientific analysis. The Church, the tsars, and the Politburo have all relinquished their supreme authority in this land, and Russia, like most of the rest of the modern world, has at least officially turned to science to provide the closest thing it can get to Truth.

But science, of course, is a product of the human mind. Its imperfections and limitations reflect those of the people who practice it and the larger society in which they work. The legitimacy of its claims can be judged only through testing and comparison with other scientific findings, and with other ways of seeing the world. Its "truth" isn't self-evident to all who behold it. Ultimately, the pronouncements of science, like those of governments and gods, are something in which one must choose whether or not to invest one's faith and belief.

What else could possibly explain this? Mounting internationally supported, peer-reviewed, government-accepted science says that Baikal is in trouble. The chief Russian Federation environmental official in the Irkutsk region believes that Baikal remains "in a pure state."

•

The man in the dark blue sweater and heavy brown mustache sits in front of a Russian flag and a wall-sized map of Lake Baikal and the Irkutsk region and gestures with a smile toward his American visitors.

"Your questions, please!"

Anatoly Malevsky seems relaxed and welcoming, not at all the stereotype of the gruff and imperious Russian official that I brought with me into his brightly lit office in downtown Irkutsk. Mr. Malevsky is the chairman of the State Committee for Environmental Protection of the Irkutsk region, something akin to a regional administrator of the U.S. Environmental Protection Agency. He is the highest environmental official in the Baikal region, and he's eager to proceed with the business of our visit.

I'm here to talk about Lake Baikal, I remind him. *It's a U.N. World Heritage Site, and people around the world want to know whether it's being well taken care of.*

"It is known to everyone," Mr. Malevsky begins, "that Lake Baikal has been inscribed on the United Nations' list...." He goes on to deliver a lengthy recitation of the reasons for this inscription, the long list of well-known superlatives, but with a twist at the end: "Another unique feature of Lake Baikal is that it is capable of self-purification. So such a unique lake requires special protection. All of our efforts should be devoted to this, and we will do our best. We hope that it will be kept in the same pure state as it is today."

Baikal is capable of self-purification. I wasn't surprised to hear this assertion from an official of a polluting factory, but I am a bit surprised to hear it from someone at the highest official levels. And yet the lake also *requires special protection.* Somewhere deep in my brain, the voices of the two Natalias at the

Baikalsk Plant resonate like a sympathetic string on a piano—*There is not really any problem, and we are committed to fixing it.* And somewhere down there as well is a simple question, waiting to be asked of Mr. Malevsky: if his first assertion is true, why is the second necessary? It's a simple question, but it doesn't quite emerge through my cluttered brain. I follow up on only the first half. *So, Baikal remains in a pure state. What about the problems identified by people like Evgeniia Tarasova and Jennie Sutton?*

Mr. Malevsky parries each of the critics' thrusts as I begin to run through the list of their concerns.

Is he worried about the impact of the Baikalsk paper mill?

Certainly, he replies, the lake would be better off without the mill, but its impact is limited. "Based on the official, many times tested data, there is no impact of the plant outside the radius of fifteen kilometers."

And what about the persistent organic pollutants that have been found in nerpas—has he heard of this research?

Yes, it's true, he acknowledges, some dioxins have accumulated in the seals' fat. But the levels aren't significant enough to worry about.

OK, well, however much there is, where did it come from? Does he accept the evidence that most of the POPs flowing into the lake are coming from sources here in the Irkutsk region, the Angara industrial corridor, and the Baikalsk plant?

"That's personal opinion," Mr. Malevsky says. "Studies of the composition of this chlororganic matter have shown that the dioxin doesn't come from Russia. They are related to fertilizers. And this fertilizing component comes with the Selenga River into Lake Baikal. But we believe that it comes from Mongolia, because most of the water catchment zone is located in Mongolia."

Nothing else I've heard or read, or will hear or read, suggests such a conclusion. But whatever their sources, Mr. Malevsky has already said that there's no need to worry about the impact of dioxins on the lake. In fact, he expresses little concern about the effects of any industrial pollutants, from any sources, on the lake's ecosystem or its animal or human communities.

Perhaps his demeanor is relaxed and welcoming because all really is quite well with Baikal? In any case, it seems that Dr. Tarasova was dead on in at least one regard: as far as the Russian government is concerned, her team's research appears to be as valuable as yesterday's *Vostochno-Sibirskaia Pravda*. I wonder about Mr. Malevsky's choice of facts. And from the last of his assertions about industrial pollution, I wonder about his expertise, as well. Dioxin doesn't come from fertilizer, unless the fertilizer has somehow been contaminated. Maybe he's confused fertilizer with pesticides? And maybe he's confused dioxins with their chemical relative, DDT? Whatever the explanation, it doesn't inspire much confidence in his familiarity with such critical issues. And then there's this other assertion by the chairman of the State Committee on Environment Protection: "There is no bleached pulp production at the Baikalsk plant anymore. We were against bleaching, and we succeeded." Even the two Natalias didn't make this claim—they said only that the plant hoped to convert to a chlorine-free production system sometime in the future.

As with Natalia Parfenova in Baikalsk, I don't see much point in pressing Mr. Malevsky on these questions. I'm here to find out what and how he thinks, what positions inform and represent the Russian government from its environmental field office closest to Baikal, not argue about claims and counterclaims or which organochlorines come from which sources. Besides, our appointment is for only an hour, and half of that will be taken up by translation. We still have a lot of territory to cover.

We move on, and Mr. Malevsky describes further progress at the Baikalsk plant. A plan is being drawn up to build a new, separate sewage treatment plant for the town of Baikalsk, he says, which will then allow for a separate upgrade of the plant's system. And waterborne emissions of pollutants such as organic sulfur compounds and organochlorines have been cut in half in recent years. In these cases, both assertions roughly jibe with what I've been told elsewhere, and in fact, a review of data from the mill later will show that the reduction in organic sulfur and organochlorine emissions has been far greater than Mr. Malevsky's estimate. Emissions of organic sulfur compounds at the plant have been cut from a recent high of nearly 9,000 times the government's Maximum Permissible Discharge to only 314 times the limit. And emissions of organochlorines fell from a high of 118,000 times the government's maximum to, as we've heard, only 47,000 times the limit.

Progress, as they say, is relative.

Improvements are being made elsewhere around the lake, as well, Mr. Malevsky says, and he points as an example to the construction of a new sewage treatment plant in Sliudianka, the largest town on the lake.

But the environmental chief's assessment of Baikal's condition is not entirely blithe and cheery. Overgrazing by livestock is a problem in some areas, he says, which could lead to erosion of scarce topsoil and increased sedimentation of parts of the lake. "Another issue is that we have some problems with specially protected areas. Almost all the shoreline of Lake Baikal is included in nature preserves or national parks, but we believe that the current system of preserves and parks is not adequate." Without stronger protection of these areas, he believes, key tracts of land could fall into the hands of private owners and developers. And then there's the plan that Andrei Suknev told me about to drill for natural gas in the Selenga delta, one of the most ecologically sensitive parts of the watershed. "It is the opinion of the official bodies of nature protection that this project is forbidden," Mr. Malevsky tells me. But he says that the decision is up to the regional government in Buryatia, and they see it differently.

And the Buryatian authorities, he says, have signed a deal with the city of Moscow to develop the gas fields. So with powerful players from the nation's capital involved, he worries that the project has not yet been safely scuttled.

Perhaps Mr. Malevsky's greatest overall concern stems from the decision of his new boss, President Putin, to disband his agency and transfer its powers to the Ministry of Natural Resources, the agency responsible for developing Russia's forests, minerals, and the like. The plan has not yet been carried out—"not yet, fortunately!" Mr. Malevsky says with an apparently resigned chuckle—and on this issue, at least, he shares a bit of Jennie Sutton's concern about the future of environmental protection in Russia.

"This decision caused considerable reduction of our staff," he tells me, perhaps testing the limits of the definition of the term "considerable." "Before the restructuring," he says, "it was 131. When it is complete, there will be thirteen staff members only." Some of the positions will be moved to the city of Novosibirsk rather than eliminated outright, Mr. Malevsky says, but Novosibirsk is more than 1,000 kilometers away. "Here in the Irkutsk region," he says, "there are about 5,500 enterprises, and if you work with them directly, you cannot do that from Novosibirsk.

"It is not the idea of restructuring itself, but the method of implementing it. We really hope there will be some improvements and corrections of this decision, and that the Department of Nature Protection will be strengthened."

And yet—despite his concerns about the bigger picture—Mr. Malevsky does not believe that the disappearance of the State Committee on Environmental Protection into the Ministry of Natural Resources will spell trouble for Baikal.

"Luckily," he says, "the special federal committee on Lake Baikal will continue. We will keep our environmental laboratory in the city of Baikalsk." And tighter protections for the Baikal watershed are being drawn up in Moscow, he says. "We know that such limits will be very strict. So we are sure that as far as protection of Lake Baikal is concerned, we are as strong as we were."

"Much depends on how we are to live here, how we are to carry out protection of Lake Baikal as World Heritage Site."

Mr. Malevsky is responding to a question about the future. He has just told me, adapting a phrase for Russia's nascent democracy that has long been invoked in Washington, that "policy is the art of possible," and I have asked him whether I can take that to mean that he wishes it were possible that more could be done to protect the lake in the future. "Much depends," he says, "on if we—Irkutsk region, Republic of Buryatia, and Russian Federation as a whole—if we are alone here or if there will be support from the world community. Because at the moment, we can state that the fact that Lake Baikal has been inscribed in the World Heritage list does not change anything. It has not brought any financial impact.

"We believe that the most important thing would be if international business would come to this area to help in the development of the Lake Baikal region," Mr. Malevsky continues. "Many people in the West still believe that bears walk along the streets even in Moscow, and we think that they can imagine that somewhere in faraway country which is Siberia, in this taiga forest, maybe people still live in caves, together with bears!" He pauses, then adds, in English, "It is a joke!" Back to Russian: "Nonetheless, investments come here with great difficulties. We are too far away."

Certainly, if the rest of the world cares about this place, it also has a responsibility to help care for it. But Mr. Malevsky has got me wondering whether the Russian government saw the U.N. listing less as the beginning of a global partnership and more as a sort of global real estate development prospectus, especially as he goes on to recite a host of businesses ripe for investment: resorts, skiing, boating, construction of hotels and hostels, roads and airports. Beyond the lake itself, he'd like to  see electricity from the hydropower stations on the Angara and natural gas from fields northwest of the lake exported to China and Japan.

Power lines. Pipelines. Airports. Resorts. In his enthusiasm for outside investment, Mr. Malevsky sounds at the moment less like the region's chief environmental official than its economic development minister. He assures me that all development comply with the special protections of the Law of Baikal, that there would be no heavy industry within the protected area, and that nothing would be done that would harm the lake. But his vision for the Baikal area— large-scale tourism and resource development—nevertheless sounds like the worst nightmare of leave-no-tracers like Andrei Suknev and Jennie Sutton.

The assertion that development is the answer to the Baikal region's environmental challenges reflects that of many in the U.S. and elsewhere who espouse the almost universal virtues of free enterprise and limited regulation— that investment and economic growth will generate funds for environmental remediation and conservation and will create alternatives to environmentally damaging subsistence activities like poaching; that wealth, essentially, protects the environment. Others reply that this argument is based on vast oversimplifications and has the potential to result in more harm than good. Yes, these folks say, growing wealth can improve the environmental bottom line in some ways, but it also worsens it in others by generating waste, chewing up land and natural resources, and disrupting natural systems. Different experiences elsewhere bring different lessons, or at least different interpretations. But in this case, Mr. Malevsky's assertion of the principle seems based less on experience than on faith—the belief in things unseen, maybe even unprovable. The same faith, perhaps, that allows him to assert that Baikal is capable of self-purification.

And this, it seems, represents the bottom line in the fissure between those who are deeply concerned about the future of Lake Baikal and those who aren't. It's a question of faith.

If you believe, as an article of faith, that Baikal is fundamentally capable of self-purification, then insults to it can be forgiven, potential problems and threats lose their significance, pollution disappears. Baikal's exceptional qualities become so utterly extraordinary that the lake is not at risk for the same kind of dangers that affect other water bodies, not subject to the same chemical and biological processes that apply everywhere else on the planet. You have faith that no matter what, here, at least, all will be well.

If, on the other hand, you don't share this article of faith, if you believe that principles demonstrated and lessons borne out in similar circumstances are roughly applicable wherever those circumstances are found, then much of Baikal's uniqueness can look like a mirage, it becomes susceptible to similar dangers as other, less mythical places and it may require the highest vigilance and the most stringent protections. The two camps occupy two different worlds, each with its own way of seeing its world. And it seems that it may be a matter not so much of establishing the truth of this place as of deciding which truth you want to believe.

"We have said much and covered the most important topics," the chairman of the State Committee on Environmental Protection of the Irkutsk Oblast says, extending his hand toward mine as we rise from the table. Our hour has become an hour and a quarter, and now it's time to go.

I'm perplexed by this man at the other end of my microphone. He has swung back and forth between complacency and concern, between questioning his government's commitment and affirming it, between being reasonably well-informed and being surprisingly clueless. Might he really be less sanguine about the state of Baikal than he's letting on, but afraid to say so out of worry that he'll lose his job in the restructuring of his agency, along, perhaps, with whatever influence he has? On the other hand, he isn't afraid to state some concerns, or to criticize the restructuring itself. Is he truly committed to protecting Baikal but politically, intellectually, and perhaps bureaucratically isolated, or is he a self-serving hack, pulling his punches in an effort to save his skin? I like him, he's clearly smart and engaging, but he's opaque to me—I can't get a clear read.

I thank Mr. Malevsky for his time.

"Don't mention it," he says, in English. "It is my job." And on the way out, he hands me a small blue book, written in English. It has an outline of Baikal on the cover, and when I read it later, the enigma of Anatoly Malevsky will become even greater, as will my estimation of the credibility of Dr. Tarasova and Jennie Sutton. The book is the *Annual Report of the Governmental Commission on Baikal Lake, 1998*, which Mr. Malevsky tells me he helped to write. And it contains some remarkable data and conclusions about pollution going into the Baikal ecosystem and its impact on its animal and human residents—especially those of the town of Baikalsk—data and conclusions that in some cases directly contradict what the man who gave me the book has just told me. I cited some of the report's contents earlier. Here are a few direct—albeit somewhat tortured— quotes:

> On air pollution from the Angara River corridor:
> *. . . Air basin is mainly victimized by stationary sources of industrial facilities located in the cities of Angarsk, Usole-Sibirskoe, Shelekov, Cheremkhovo. . . . The situation is aggravated by climatic conditions not favorable for dispersion of pollutants in the atmosphere. . . .*

> On water and air emissions from the Baikalsk plant and the state of the facility:
> *. . . Chlorine organic compounds (up to 1.5 mg/l) form a part of wastewater pollutants, the discharge of which was prohibited by environmental regulations as far back as 1987. Without doubt, the lake ecosystem extremely suffers [even] from "safe" mineral substances, such as sodium, sulfates, chlorides which have been discharged for 30 years. . . .*
> *. . . Discharges and emissions are responsible for significant changes in the lake ecosystem, namely, a specific composition of phytoplankton (replacement of endemic Baikal species for all-Siberian ones), as well as for accumulation of super-toxic substances of the dioxin type in the lake's animals. Probably, this fact is the reason for weakening of immunological tolerance of some species, and first of all, Baikal seal. . . .*

. . . Stored substances pose a threat to Baikal Lake ecosystem in optimum situation, but they will provoke inevitable ecological catastrophe in case of natural cataclysm, first of all, earthquake. . . .

. . . Since the process equipment at BPPM is extremely outworn, the risk of emergencies is increasing with regard to leaks of chlorine, fuel or lignin sludge, and can result in disastrous effects for Baikal Lake ecosystems and population as well. . . .

. . . Investigations conducted in 1974-1986 demonstrate that BPPM air emissions cause intense and even (in certain areas) irreversible degradation of silver fur forests. . . .

On public health in the Baikal region and the town of Baikalsk:

. . . The trend has been toward changing for the worse relative to the health of population in Buryatia, especially regarding those diseases which somehow or other are caused by unfavorable environmental situation. . . .

. . . The industrial development of the region along with considerable amount of chemical enterprises result to a rise of nervous breakdowns and sense organ pathology. . . .

. . . Children who were born in the Baikal region are less happy in respect of their physical development (weight, stature) as compared with children from other regions of Russia. A proportion of such children is particularly profound (up to 60%) in industrial centers such as Bratsk, Shelekov, Baikalsk. . . .

. . . In 1998, the total morbidity level in Baikalsk was higher by 5% among children and by 32% among adults in comparison with these figures in the Irkutsk oblast. The frequency of oncological diseases among children, teenagers and adults happened to be 2.6, 6.2 and 3.1 times respectively higher. (It is conceivable that there is a definite relationship between air pollution and the increasing level of morbidity, as during the process of sulfate-cellulose production the atmosphere receives a huge amount of toxic emissions which negatively impact on almost all the metabolism components). . . .

. . . The unfavorable environmental conditions particularly victimize children. . . . The children whose mothers do not work at BPPM, but live in the town of Baikalsk, are assigned to "an increased risk group" as to their perinatal morbidity. . . .

19

Dr. Hope and Dr. Despair

*In which we travel to a small village with
no roads, meet two colleagues who embody two
opposing views of Lake Baikal, and visit a cathedral
of science where faith carries the day*

The road from Irkutsk to Lake Baikal, unlike the roads we traveled with Andrei approaching the lake's eastern shore, is smooth, straight, and well maintained. But in the first snow of the Siberian winter, it's almost impassible nonetheless, as it struggles on its arrow-straight trajectory to negotiate wave after wave of steep hills. Its stubborn course ignores the promise of an easier if somewhat longer approach were it to wander to one side or the other, dooming local residents to a treacherous journey for six months of the year, and it suggests the firm determination of a ministry chief in Moscow that the most direct road be built between the regional capital and the lake, no matter what. And in fact, I will learn after traveling this road that this is exactly what happened. In 1960, at the height of the cold war, the U.S. and the USSR brokered a deal for President Eisenhower to visit Russia. Included on his itinerary was to be a stop in Irkutsk, and a visit to Siberia's famous lake, sixty kilometers away. There was no modern road between the two, so Moscow commanded that one be built, and it was—in just two months. But Eisenhower never came. Just before he was to depart, Gary Francis Powers's U2 spy plane was shot down over Russia. The trip was canceled, and a new freeze settled over relations between the two adversaries. But, as imperfect as it is, the region did get a road between Irkutsk and Baikal, and after forty years local residents have gotten quite used to the sometimes white-knuckle ride.

Over forty years, I might get used to it, too.

The little white minibus into which James and Olga and I are now crammed with a dozen or so other passengers rises and falls like a roller coaster cart, except that this feels like even less sturdy and dependable transportation. Snow squalls are blowing through the Angara Valley, and when the bus isn't being buffeted by gusts of wind, it's straining to climb a slippery slope. We have approached Baikal from the east, with Andrei; we have approached it from the south, at Baikalsk; and now we are approaching it from the west, on our way to meet two scientists who work side by side in a tiny village.

As the road rises and falls through scruffy forest, we get an occasional glimpse of the wide blue ribbon of the Angara River, flowing northwest from Baikal. But there's no hint of what lies ahead until at last we crest a final ridge, and the black of the trees suddenly gives way to a dazzling blue that fills the earth below and stretches almost to the horizon beyond, rimmed by snow-covered mountains. On this frigid October morning, mist rises in sheets off the lake.

The minibus finally comes to a merciful rest in the community of Listvianka, a town of bunker-like buildings hanging onto steep hillsides where the Angara meets Baikal. This was once the center of research on the lake, the original home of the respected Limnological Institute of the USSR Academy of Sciences, now based in Irkutsk. It's the place where thousands of scientists have encountered the lake for the first time, and maybe felt their heart rates quicken with excitement. Ours certainly do, even though by now the lake has almost become a familiar companion. The van disgorges its passengers into an icy parking lot beside the lake, next to a dock at which just a few boats are tied up. James and I lug our packs into a small restaurant in hopes of finding a cup of tea or anything warm, while Olga goes to find out about our boat. It should go every day around this time, she says, but you just never know for sure.

In a few minutes, Olga is back. We're on.

The white and powder blue *Professor Kozhov* chugs through the chop of southern Baikal, and even though the sun has come out, it's still too cold to stand out on the deck for long, so we climb down into the cramped cabin below and watch the lake's steep shore pass by through small portholes. Listvianka soon diminishes to just a few lonely buildings hugging the bluffs above the lake, then disappears completely and only the bluffs remain, topped by yellowing larches and random patches of white. Through the far portholes, the sun illuminates mountains topped in snow, as if they've ripped the bottom layer off the last bank of low-hanging clouds. The water between us and the mountains is a vast pool of cobalt, and today Baikal reminds me of my grandmother's favorite ring—a big sapphire encircled by tiny diamonds. After forty-five minutes or so, the groan of the engine slows and we head back up on deck as the boat sidles up to a long wooden dock. Beyond it, a couple of dozen houses of brown and green and white speckle a shore of brown and green and gold. We hitch up our backpacks once again and follow Olga off the boat and into the village of Bolshie Koty.

Bolshie Koty, the tiny town of Big Shoes, the exact origin of the name lost to memory. While Baikalsk, across the lake, seems stuck in a Soviet-era time warp, Bolshie Koty is a relic of a still earlier age. Its frame and log houses and bare wooden fences seem to have been unmoved by the Ten Days that Shook the World back in 1917, and its handful of tiny farms seem too insubstantial to have come to the attention of the collectivizers who followed. The automobile hasn't yet made it to Bolshie Koty, since no roads have yet made it here either, and on the world's largest body of fresh water, even the advent of the power-boat seems almost accidental—the few vessels that inhabit the shore look as if they washed up here in a storm, dilapidated and rusting, resting on their sides high above the waterline. For much of the year, the boat we've just stepped off of is the only regular link to the outside world. In practice, it's a ferry for residents and the occasional visitor, but its official purpose is as a research vessel. It carries samples and scientists to and from two tiny Baikal research stations that sit side by side in the village—the domains, we will learn, of Dr. Hope and Dr. Despair.

The air as we head up the shore from the dock smells of dirt and fennel, summer's last remnants pulled from now bare gardens. A few indolent cows sit in the grass behind wooden fences, their eyes circled with big, brown spots. What seems to be the only store in town seems to be closed. Perhaps it's just because it's October, and Siberia is about to freeze solid, but Bolshie Koty seems to be suspended between a past that is certainly gone and a future that has yet to declare itself.

At the far end of this wisp of a town rises a hint of this future: a hand-ful of new houses, including the one we're heading for—a hostel with accom-modations for maybe a dozen visitors. The houses are built of fresh, yellow logs, and suddenly, with your back to the lake, this corner of Bolshie Koty looks almost like a hillside of freshly minted second homes in Colorado. I wonder which future this outpost of the new leisure economy will grow into—Andrei Suknev's future of small-scale, low-impact tourism or Anatoly Malevsky's future of capital-intensive, infrastructure-heavy tourism—because it will certainly not remain motionless for long. Later today, I'll wander back through town from this outcropping of its future and find it bookended by a solemn but proud outpost of the past—a small cemetery of modest white headstones and wooden crosses, most graced with a red star, a wreath of plastic flowers, and a solemn black-and-white photograph of the person entombed beneath.

•

The Hydrobiology Laboratory of the Institute of Biology of Irkutsk State University is in one of Bolshie Koty's more distinctive buildings, but behind its pale-green picket fence it still looks more like a hunting club than a laboratory, its dark clapboards and sharply peaked white windows resting under a steep, rust-red metal roof. On the landing between rough wooden pillars, the institute's director, Boris Pavlov, leans on metal crutches, squints through thick glasses, and looks out over the shimmering lake.

"I am an old person and maybe should be thinking about God," Dr. Pavlov says, in a measured and weary cadence, "but I'm trying to attract as much attention as possible to Baikal."

Dr. Pavlov is part of a family of prominent Baikal researchers. His recently deceased wife, Olga Kozhova, and his late father-in-law, Mikhail Kozhov—the Professor Kozhov for whom the boat that brought us here was named—devoted their lives to studying this place, and his stepdaughter, Dr. Liubov Izmesteva, now carries on the family legacy. Professor Pavlov himself began his first research project in the watershed more than forty years ago, and despite his own declining health and recent losses, he remains intently focused on the lake.

The old man's heavy frame teeters on his crutches, his face and shoulders are losing their battle with gravity. He seems literally unable to bear the weight of what he has seen here in recent years.

"I feel," he says, "a great sorrow."

Even after so many years studying the region, Dr. Pavlov says he still can't say that he knows Baikal well. The more he learns about it, he says, the more mysterious the lake's ecosystem becomes. But he says that he and his family and other colleagues have worked here long enough to be able to identify disturbing changes—changes that, like those tracked by Evgeniia Tarasova, help fill in the sketch provided by Jennie Sutton and give weight to her fears.

While Dr. Tarasova and her colleagues track the presence of toxic chemicals in the lake's ecosystem and assess their likely impacts on its animal and human communities, the Pavlov-Kozhova family and their colleagues have tracked changes in the health and distribution of Baikal species themselves—what is actually happening to the lake's animals and plants. They have looked at the lake as a whole and at specific areas, like that around the Baikalsk paper mill.

Within five years after the paper mill opened, Dr. Pavlov says, ninety-five local species disappeared. In particular, he says, the number of species of mollusks fell by more than half in the vicinity of the plant's discharge pipes, from fifty-two to twenty-four. And among individual mollusks that he's tested over the years, he's found something else: *"perestroika khromosom"*—changes in the animals' chromosomes, or DNA. Chlorinated chemicals like those thought to be released by the plant have been associated with mutations and developmental problems, and Dr. Pavlov believes that's what's happening here. He says these changes have been found in mollusks in the vicinity of the wastewater discharge pipes at levels up to twelve times higher than average, and still twice as high up to thirty kilometers away.

But a more widespread and ominous trend, Dr. Pavlov says, is changes in the lake's phytoplankton and zooplankton—its community of tiny floating plants and animals. In particular, over the last dozen years or so, he says, Baikal has suffered increasing numbers of algae blooms—explosions in the concentration of algae—in some of its near-shore areas and shallow, enclosed bays. At the same time, populations of epischura have declined slightly throughout the lake. It's entirely possible that these phenomena are unrelated, that the decline in epischura is due to other factors—an increase in predators, perhaps, which could in turn be due to overfishing of the fish species that prey on the creatures that eat epischura. But Dr. Pavlov fears that the trends may in fact be related.

Algae blooms can reduce the oxygen content of the water, and that can kill off other organisms, including creatures like the epischura that have a limited ability to swim away. Fewer epischura in turn mean less filtering of the water, which leaves more algae, setting the stage for what scientists call a "positive feedback loop"—more algae can lead to fewer epischura, fewer epischura can lead to more algae, and so on. The process isn't linear or inexorable—it can be influenced by factors such as light, temperature, currents, and the ebb and flow of nutrients into the system—but Dr. Pavlov fears that the increasing number of algal outbreaks is tied into changes in "the whole biochemical situation of the lake," with potentially grave consequences. It can't be stated too often—*Epischura baicalensis* is Baikal's bedrock species, vital to the overall health of the lake, both as the mechanism for filtering its water and as a key element in the food chain. If there's a significant decline in the number of epischura, Dr. Pavlov says, a decline in other species will follow, including those on which humans directly depend, like the omul.

What Dr. Pavlov believes he's seeing would by no means be unique to Baikal. Algae blooms and the die-offs of fish and other aquatic animals that often follow are a common result of nutrient pollution. Increased levels of nitrogen and phosphorus from human wastewater, agriculture, and some forms of industry are basically fertilizer for algae and other aquatic plants. Just as in your garden, more fertilizer leads to better plant growth. By itself, this isn't necessarily a problem. In fact, under normal conditions, algae are an important part of an aquatic ecosystem, providing food and producing dissolved oxygen. But algae *blooms*—in which the concentrations explode by an order of magnitude or more—bring an accompanying population explosion of aerobic bacteria. The bacteria decompose the algae and in the process use up dissolved oxygen. Sometimes the process is so accelerated and the populations so concentrated that aquatic animals can literally suffocate for lack of oxygen. This is what causes massive die-offs of fish in such places as the dead zone in the Gulf of Mexico at the mouth of the Mississippi river.

Nothing close to this scale of problems is afflicting Baikal—the algae blooms have been isolated, they haven't caused noticeable fish kills and they haven't yet affected the open waters of the lake well offshore. And away from local nutrient pollution hot spots along the shoreline, there's not even any measurable change in nitrogen or phosphorus levels. As with other contaminants, it seems that Baikal is so huge, and mixes so thoroughly, that these additional nutrients are virtually undetectable in the open water.

Still, Dr. Pavlov is deeply concerned that the decline in the epischura is linked to the increase in nutrients running off from shoreline settlements—in effect, that the epischura and other exquisitely sensitive Baikal organisms are responding to extremely subtle changes in the lake's chemistry. Proof has been elusive, though. And that, he laments, leaves scientists empty-handed when it comes to getting the authorities to pay attention. "It is very difficult," he says, "to convince the government bodies that the efforts need to be taken to minimize the discharges in the lake."

And yet if Dr. Pavlov is correct in his suspicion that undetectable amounts of contaminants are disrupting Baikal's ecosystem, it raises an ominous possibility: that what's thought of as the lake's extraordinary power masks what is in fact an exceptional vulnerability and sensitivity to disturbance; that its unique, natural protective blanket may actually be woven out of extremely thin strands, and that once they start to fray, it could quickly lead to an unraveling of the whole fabric.

This counterintuitive notion is not actually a new one. Amid the assertions of Baikal's supreme strength and resilience, a few voices have long warned otherwise. As far back as the 1950s, in the debate over the construction of the Baikalsk mill, a prominent Soviet scientist warned that "in nature there exist very precisely established biological equilibria whose mechanisms contemporary science does not yet know. But we do know that comparatively small factors can destroy this equilibrium and that then the consequences are capable of assuming a catastrophic scale." But today, as forty years ago, this proposition is not finding receptive ears within Russia. Like Evgeniia Tarasova in Irkutsk, Dr. Pavlov says that the Russian government just doesn't seem interested in research that suggests that any serious problems may be ahead. The policy at the moment, he says, is to develop the economy and worry about the environment later. "But even if it may be possible," he says, "when we get the improved economics, we won't have anything to protect."

Dr. Pavlov sees this attitude reflected in such things as the dissolution of the federal environmental protection committee and the plan to explore petroleum deposits on Baikal's eastern shore. "All these oil and gas investigations that are being carried out in the Selenga delta," he says, "they violate three federal laws. First, the Law of Baikal, then the water code of the Russian Federation, then the law on nature protection of the Russian Federation."

"A collapse of the whole system of environmental protection is taking place right now," Dr. Pavlov says. "And I cannot see that now in Russia there are any powers that can stop this powerful attack on the environment."

Dr. Pavlov pushes a heavy sigh from his thick chest and shuffles his weight on his crutches. "My grandson will not see everything that I have seen," he laments. "You know, Lake Baikal can be considered a natural laboratory. It is as if our Lord himself has created such a laboratory for these experiments. And I feel a great sorrow that such a unique and pure place is being changed and is coming to resemble a garbage area."

•

A cobalt shadow rises from the mountains behind Bolshie Koty, deepens as it crosses the sky, and locks itself in place on the far side of the lake. Across a tufted field of brown and silver-green in front of our hostel, Baikal fades to a sheet of metallic blue. Smoke rises from a *banya* below the hostel, and inside James and Olga and I dine on fish, beets, potatoes, and salad while our host Slava Maksimov, Jr., helps his young daughter with her homework and his wife Lena talks on a scratchy radio telephone. After dinner, there is a *banya* under a black sky, sans flogging and swim but with periodic respites on the porch outside, where our lungs fill with the smell of wood smoke and dead leaves. On a midnight walk on a glittering frosted path to the outhouse, the air is still and silent and cuts like sharp steel on my skin. Half awake and half dreaming, I half remember where I am and wonder again what I'm doing here, and I recall something that Dr. Pavlov told us this afternoon: "The longer you live, the more questions you have with no answers."

•

Yesterday, the snow-topped mountains across the water glimmered like a ring of diamonds. Yesterday, Baikal stretched nearly to the horizon, the iridescent blue of a Steller's jay. Yesterday, the steep, dark green hills above us cut a sharp line across the clear Siberian sky. Baikal was bold and sure of itself. Today, a gray sky hangs heavy over the lake, the ashen water barely stirring as it meets the crescent shoreline. Today, Baikal is misty-eyed and sleepy, seemingly ready to be taken into the folds of the descending blanket of winter.

Lazy snowflakes drift from the low sky onto the thin beach and dark pines and settle onto the wool hat and gray beard of a man standing on a set of wooden steps.

"*Zdravstvui!*" the man calls to his granddaughter down the shore. "Hello! I love her very much," he declares, "and I would like her to live forever. I want all of us to live forever here!" An elfish sparkle in his eyes illuminates the half-light

Slava Maksimov, Sr., it is immediately clear, is an optimistic man. He tells us that he himself plans to live for at least 200 years beyond the sixty he has already counted, and to spend as much of that long life as possible here at Lake Baikal.

"I am a loyal citizen, an aboriginal person here," he announces. "I am drinking Baikal water, eating Baikal fish, the air I breathe is Baikal air."

Dr. Maksimov has been drinking, eating, and breathing Baikal for nearly as long as his neighbor Dr. Pavlov—going on forty years. These days he is the director of the village's second small research institute, the Microbiology Laboratory, which occupies another small wood-frame building just down the beach from Dr. Pavlov's Hydrobiology Laboratory. The two scientists are neighbors here in Bolshie Koty and colleagues at the Irkutsk State University, but in their dispositions and their evaluation of the health of their beloved lake, it seems that they could not be farther apart. Where Pavlov is old and in failing health, Maksimov remains youthful and energetic. Where Pavlov sees nothing but darkness, Maksimov is unfailingly sunny. And he will have none of his neighbor's dire predictions.

How is the lake? I ask him.

"Baikal is in a perfect state!" Dr. Maksimov proclaims, his eyebrows raised in a gleeful grin. "It is huge, it is rich, it is healthy, it is wise, and it is not similar to any phenomena in the world! *Absoliutno blagopoluchny Baikal!*"

And he is off, on a lengthy and animated discourse on the pillars of Baikal's perfection and the delicate interworkings between them. "*Baikal is lucky to be in a cold climate.... Due to the anomalous properties of Baikal water, there is life in all parts of the lake.... Its microorganisms are the natural purifying system.... As long as they live at Lake Baikal they will consume everything that is polluting the lake, and they will keep it pure....*"

In my series of interviews with Russians here, I have learned to expect that even accounting for translation, the answer to my first question will be a lengthy one, stuffed like a Boy Scout's backpack with everything that might possibly be needed—exposition, background, professional qualifications and *bona fides*, philosophy, and a research library-full of facts, anecdotes, and assertions. And although he seems determined to cut against the grain of some of his colleagues in other ways, Dr. Maksimov stands apart in this respect only in his animated, almost mischievous manner. And before I can squeeze out a second question, he moves from his impassioned assertion of the lake's unique powers into a spirited denunciation of those who question them.

"It does not make sense to try to protect Lake Baikal!" he announces. "There is no need for that! However, there are specific groups of people who behave like parasites at Lake Baikal. They try to claim that not everything is OK, that it is in danger. Actually, these people are trying to make money out of this campaign! Or are seeking to become famous."

His critique of those who warn of trouble here begins at the same place that they begin their litany—the Baikalsk plant. Dr. Maksimov tells us that as a graduate student he helped to design the plant's original wastewater treatment system—the one that others have told us was quickly found to be utterly insufficient.

He says he has no illusions about the plant's usefulness. "That Baikalsk plant is absurd," he says. "It is a nonsense on the lake. From the very beginning it was evident that there is no demand for its products. But fortunately, it is of no threat to Lake Baikal." He categorically dismisses his neighbor Pavlov's reports of widespread mutations and species loss in the vicinity of the plant. "The impact of its effluents," he asserts, "is not found farther than six or eight hundred meters from the discharge zone." As evidence in support of this claim, Dr. Maksimov offers only this: that the clearest water in the lake is found only twenty-two kilometers from Baikalsk.

Dr. Maksimov similarly rejects findings of changes in the populations of plankton in Baikal as merely part of the lake's natural cycles. And he scoffs as well at concerns about industrial pollution coming into Baikal from else-where in the region. "There is no heavy chemical stuff in these waters," he says, flat out. "Most of the stuff that is brought by the streams is of natural origin," he says. What about Jennie Sutton's and Evgeniia Tarasova's concerns about dioxins concentrating in the food chain? "This is just stupidity," he says with a scornful laugh. "I will tell you openly that the concentration of dioxins in a species under investigation is in direct correlation with the involvement of the person in certain nature protection movements! Ha ha! Maybe one of the tasks of Jennifer Sutton is to show that Russian people are incapable, or maybe stupid!"

Dr. Maksimov suggests another, more venal motivation for such "stu-pidity" as well: that some environmentalists are tied in with Western bottled water companies, and that those companies are threatened by efforts to market water from Baikal. "There are people who are paid money so that they should tell that everything is bad at Lake Baikal," he says, again, offering no evidence. "Some of the environmentalists are trying to spoil the image of Baikal water, so that nobody will want to buy it." Which would be a shame, he says. "Even if every person living on the earth will get three liters of Baikal water every day, Lake Baikal would not even feel it. The amount of Baikal water is sufficient for the whole mankind.

"Please," Dr. Maksimov continues, "don't believe anyone from the green movements and environmentalists. They are just shouting. Most of the people who say that they are trying to protect Lake Baikal are incapable in anything else. They cannot work as agriculture men, they cannot go fishing, they cannot construct a house, they just can shout and claim about the threat to Lake Baikal, and this is how they attract attention to themselves."

It's impossible not to hear these last comments as a not-so-thinly veiled jab at Dr. Maksimov's elderly and infirm colleague next door. And in case we missed it, he makes sure to put a finer point on the distinction between him-self and his neighbor. "*Absoliutnye antipody*," he declares. "We are at absolute antipodes. Pavlov lives *at* Baikal. I live *in* Baikal. Pavlov cannot do anything by his hands. He cannot make an experiment. He is just thinking and writing his thoughts. My conclusions are based on my personal experiments, the things that I can really see.

"Since I live in Lake Baikal, if I would see anything that is threatening the lake, I would be the first to fight against it, and I will even start a war against this threatening factor, and I will make everyone join me. But it doesn't happen, luckily."

So everything is completely fine here, there's absolutely nothing to worry about?

Well, yes, Dr. Maksimov concedes, there is at least one problem: invasive species, especially in the shallow coastal areas and bays. Introduced algae, plants, mollusks, and fish are starting to compete with some of Baikal's own unique species, he says. Considering how vital endemic species such as *Epischura baicalensis* are to Baikal's ecology, one might consider this quite a concession. But Dr. Maksimov dismisses the importance of this trend, as well. "They are not of any threat to the deep

and cold lake, and the real Baikal is the very deep and cold body." Cold, he repeats, is the key to Baikal's health. So as long as it's cold at Baikal, and as long as the cold-loving epischura remain in the lake, he says, "they will consume everything that is polluting the lake, and they will keep it pure."

Dr. Maksimov wears a provocative grin as he speaks. In a land of deeply held orthodoxies, he clearly relishes the role of the iconoclast, debunker of the fantasies of the unscrupulous and the infirm. But who's upholding what myths here, I wonder, and who's trying to smash them? On the question of cold, in particular, it may be that Dr. Maksimov is truly whistling in the dark, ignoring one of the gravest threats to Baikal's future. Scientists have found that the average air temperature over the southern part of the lake has risen 0.8 degrees Celsius, or roughly 1.4 degrees Fahrenheit, over just the last ten years, and that the average period of winter ice cover on the lake is more than two weeks shorter than it was a century ago. This follows a trend of rising surface temperatures and decreasing ice cover in northern latitudes in general, due in part to the growing concentration of heat-trapping pollutants in the atmosphere. And scientists project that if current trends in greenhouse gas emissions continue, global average temperatures will continue to rise significantly over the next century and beyond. Cold, as we've heard, is a defining factor in the health of the Baikal ecosystem, but Baikal is likely to continue to become less and less cold for perhaps centuries to come.

No one knows precisely what this trend may mean for Baikal, just as no one can know now whether the other warnings being issued about Baikal by people like Dr. Pavlov, Dr. Tarasova, and Jennie Sutton will prove prescient or alarmist. But wise policy and practice are increasingly based not merely on what we know but also on what we don't know, incorporating a significant measure of caution as a buffer against uncertainty.

But here again, I'm at a loss for just the right question to pose to Dr. Maksimov. How do you pierce the membrane of the self-enclosed world of someone as sure of himself and his beliefs as our host? Especially when you're a stranger in it, separated by language and history and culture and when he's so disarmingly blunt and oddly charming? As we speak, I have a peculiar sense of having slipped into a fairy tale world. We've been talking in the chill of the advancing Siberian winter for more than an hour, but I am not getting cold. The snow continues to fall, but there seems to be no more of it on the ground now than there was an hour ago. And then there is Dr. Maksimov and his cartoonish characterizations and rather outlandish narrative. It's almost as if James and I have passed through the dusty wardrobe in that big old English mansion and entered C.S. Lewis's fantastical realm of Narnia, where time stops and it's always winter, and callow visitors are entranced by a charismatic stranger offering irresistible nuggets laced with a powerful intoxicant. I am under Dr. Maksimov's spell. I know he's largely talking nonsense, at least when it comes to the presence of contamination in the lake. Like a see-no-evil monkey, he's not finding it because he doesn't want to. But I can't help but be captivated by him, by his sly wit and roguish manner, by his deliberately provocative language, and, not least, by the power of his vision of Baikal. *Baikal is perfect. Its perfection is secured by cold, depth, and a tiny, unique creature, all forces of nature. And nothing humans could do can disrupt that perfection.* It's a wonderful, soothing story, which exalts the lake even as it frees humans from their responsibility to care for it.

Dr. Maksimov ushers us from the snow into his little laboratory, and whistles merrily while he leads us around its three small rooms. There's not much to see, just a few instruments for preserving and analyzing samples from the lake and some old photos. The most unusual piece of equipment in the place is something Dr. Maksimov designed and built himself. "*Anti-evoliutsiia,*" he says as he positions it on the floor by a rough plaster wall—his anti-evolutionary device. Two columns of wooden blocks nailed together, with an old vinyl cushion atop each column.

"This device has been patented," Dr. Maksimov says with a grin as he leans over, rests his shoulders on the cushions and thrusts his torso and legs into the air. "We always keep our head upright," he blurts out from between the blocks, his upside-down face crimson from the rush of blood to his head. "This is why some pathology may occur in our head, there is some stagnation in your brains.... We should stay for some period of time like this, with your head down. Just try yourself...."

He tumbles back over, and I shed my bag and recording equipment to take his place. "So this helps shake up your thinking," I ask from my upside-down repose?

"*Da, da, da*, that's correct," he says. Two hours a day.

"And it helps you live forever?"

"At least 200 years! But of course this is not the only device for the eternal life. You need to keep your heart active, you need your immune system to be strong and powerful. But the most important thing is you should learn how to love people."

I resume my normal stature slightly dizzy, we leave the anti-evolutionary device by the wall and walk across the snow and pine needles outside to the institute's little one-room museum next door. This tiny archive has actually made it into our Lonely Planet guide, but only to be dismissed as "sad," a description that of course only piqued my interest. Seeing it for myself, I would've written something else, something like "humble" or "quaint," which would've then left room for "kinda cool"—if you're into such things as photographs of long-dead researchers, strange fish and crustaceans floating in jars, and tables and shelves cluttered with tiny stuffed musk deer, Barguzin sables, and all other manner of inanimate beasts.

The room smells of dust and formaldehyde, and as he shows us around, Dr. Maksimov reels off what by now have become the standard statistics about life in and around Baikal—the size of the lake, the number of known endemic creatures, the most important species—all in a suddenly dry and passionless tone, until we come to a jar on a shelf, in which is suspended a small, opalescent fish, tail over head. "This is the natural position of this little fish," Dr. Maksimov tells us. "Golomyanka can fly like angels in the sea."

The snow outside the institute is not so much settling onto Bolshie Koty as Bolshie Koty seems to be settling into it, remembering the reassuring feel of it, like the comforting embrace of your own bed or of a returning lover. "Today you are experiencing the best weather in Lake Baikal," Dr. Maksimov tells us, and he graciously thanks us for bringing it. "You must be very nice people."

Like the lake, so too does Dr. Maksimov seem in his element, as if he were himself an epischura, a hero of Baikal's cold water, catching and filtering out whatever contamination is thrown its way, except that the contamination he sees is of the mind, not of matter—insults to Baikal's virtue and efforts to besmirch its character. Despite their stark disagreements, Dr. Maksimov is no less a defender of Baikal than Boris Pavlov or Jennie Sutton, no less, in his own way, a patriot of the lake than Andrei Suknev.

And however shaky their basis, it's become clear that Slava Maksimov's fundamental assumptions about Baikal have broad currency here. He himself seems to occupy a position something like that of the climate change naysayers in the United States, scientists who are in a small minority and often speaking far beyond their own area of expertise, but who are listened to because they say things that powerful people want to hear. As we say our thank yous and farewells and prepare to head back to his son's hostel down the shore, Dr. Maksimov produces a clipping of an article he wrote for *Komsomolskaia Pravda*, Russia's largest newspaper, dismissing any pollution threat to the lake. "There is no need to be much concerned," he beams once more. *"Baikal absoliutno blagopoluchny!* It is perfect! So you can take this, read it, and think it over. Please tell people in America that Baikal is well protected!"

James, Olga, and I leave Dr. Maksimov behind and walk along the beach amid big Ivory Snow snowflakes. The air smells of wood smoke and frost, the only sound is the lonely bark of a single dog and the muffled crunching of tiny ice crystals beneath our own feet. The lake itself seems utterly content, lapping gently at its soft white rim, harboring its beloved offspring in a vast ark beneath its infinite surface, working its eternal magic on itself, and on us. There's no suggestion here in Bolshie Koty that Baikal is anything less than what Dr. Maksimov says it is—utterly sound, serene, eternal, and unaffected by the presence of humans. Perfect. *Blagopoluchnoe.* And there is no doubt about this: It is seductive. It's hard in a place such as this not to see what you want to see, not to believe what you want to believe. And you want to believe what Dr. Maksimov believes. To think that this place is anything less than perfect does seem an affront—not merely to Baikal but to the very idea that there are some things more powerful than humans, some things that are beyond our capacity to diminish, debase, or destroy. Not to have faith in this place—well, it might not be a sin, but it would certainly be a tragedy.

And yet . . . and yet here we are, the very thinkers of these thoughts, walking this shore, leaving our own tiny trace in this village and this lake, leaving our garbage and our poop, contributing to the demand for new buildings and services. We are only three, but we are far from alone. And here, as we approach Slava Maksimov, Jr.'s new hostel, is another new house, and there are two men digging a ditch and laying a pipe from it right down into the lake. One can only fear what will come out of that pipe, and others like it being laid elsewhere along the shoreline. People are coming to Baikal. People are here. People are having an impact.

Which would be more tragic—to lose the myth and all it represents, or to cling to the myth and lose the lake itself?

•

The *Professor Kozhov* parts lace curtains of snow and indifferent gray waves on its return from Bolshie Koty. When we reach Listvianka, we learn that the two or three inches of snow on the ground has made the road to Irkutsk impassable, and that the buses back to the city are not running. "It is too early," we are told. "It shouldn't snow for another two weeks." Even in Siberia, they are not ready for winter.

Olga hadn't planned for an overnight in Listvianka but still quickly rustles us up a place to stay, in a tiny flat with a woman named Lena, who, in the midst of these very hard times in Russia, traded a good career as a cartographer in Irkutsk for work as a secretary here in Listvianka because her ill son needed to get away from the dirty air of the city. We will pay her 400 rubles for the night plus dinner and breakfast for the three of us—$14 and change—and I can't imagine it's worth her while, disrupting her life for unexpected guests, cooking six extra meals, cleaning up after us, washing the bedding, until I find out that her monthly salary is 850 rubles, or about $31, and that from this short visit she'll make the equivalent of nearly two weeks' pay. From the moment she opens her door, Lena is apologizing—for not being ready for guests, for the modesty of her accommodations, for greeting us in an apron, for the quality of the food she prepares. And yet the food is delicious and plentiful, the beds are comfortable and the rooms kept with obvious care and pride, and she is a gracious host.

Lena's secretarial job is at the Limnological Institute, which maintains a small presence in its old building here even though its main offices have moved to the city. The institute was the first Baikal research station, and some credit it with actually inventing the science of limnology—the study of lakes. Evgeniia Tarasova and countless other Baikal researchers began their careers here, and the institute's former director, Grigory Galazy, was one of the best-known advocates for the defense of the lake; he risked his career and perhaps even his institution in his unsuccessful campaign against the Baikalsk paper mill. But Galazy was forced out of his position back in the 1970s, and the institute is said to have since lost its leading edge. Back in Irkutsk, Jennie Sutton told me that while it still conducts good basic research on Baikal's flora and fauna, the institute shies away from examining toxins in the environment because it wants to market Baikal water. I'd hoped to be able to talk with someone from the institute, but this was one of the few interviews that Olga wasn't able to set up for me. Normally, without independent corroboration and an opportunity for response, a comment like Sutton's would stay in my notes. But Maksimov had made a mirror-image charge in Bolshie Koty: that environmentalists sounding the alarm about toxins in the lake are fronting for foreign water merchants who want to scuttle any competition from Baikal water. Whatever the truth of these charges and countercharges may be, they seem to highlight not just the bad blood between people who might seem natural allies, but also the likelihood that a fight is brewing over the potential sale of some of Baikal's liquid assets.

The institute's offices are closed today, but its museum is open, and after settling in at Lena's, we head for it. It's in the basement of the institute's building, a dusty old turn-of-the-century box shrouded by evergreens, on a bluff overlooking the mouth of the Angara, the place where daughter Baikal begins her long journey to meet the Yenisei and ultimately the Arctic Ocean. We pay our foreigners' entry fee of thirty rubles—about $1.10—and enter a space that's a good deal bigger and brighter than Dr. Maksimov's little place in Bolshie Koty but built upon the same nineteenth-century style of presentation that we'll find from Barguzin to St. Petersburg—a haphazard jumble of artifacts. Haphazard but, again, captivating. The walls of its two rooms are plastered with maps and charts. Models of research ships stand next to remnants of actual ships pulled from the lake. Display cases are crammed with rocks, minerals, and mollusks. Plant and insect specimens are pinned to cork mats, and long-dead animals stare blankly at us from pedestals and jars—deer, birds, cats, fish, worms, tiny epischura, and dozens of other varieties of crustaceans, and a nerpa, the only one we will see, alive or dead. And running continuously in the background, on a TV screen in a prominent spot by the entrance, is a video. The film takes viewers soaring over the lake, climbing through its uplands and diving into its depths, and finally, as it gently sets the viewer back down at water level, an empty glass appears in the foreground, and then a hand, holding a plastic bottle with a label that reads—in English—*Baikal WATER*. The hand turns the bottle over and begins to pour. The glass slowly fills. The crystalline water sloshes enticingly toward the top, crests, and begins to overflow. The bottle and the hand remain steady, the water continues to flow. And flow. And overflow. And the screen fades to black. A message that one need speak no Russian to understand, that one needs no astute interpreter or dictionary of obscure words to appreciate. Baikal is limitless, infinite, inexhaustible. Perfect. *Blagopoluchnoe.*

Even in this old cathedral of science, faith prevails.

Blind Love Is a Dangerous Thing

In which we resume our westward journey, sample the glories
of the Russian/Soviet Empire, and wonder
whether we can really ever leave Baikal behind us

The sky is a blinding white and blue, and the little minibus from Listvianka to Irkutsk flits over the folds of the Angara Valley like a bumblebee, slightly ungainly and, to an observer, perhaps not quite in control of its trajectory, but confident in its own path and in the completion of its journey.

We've seen our last of Baikal. One last run alongside daughter Angara and James and I will get our final glimpse of the lake's cobalt water, bearing northwest for the turbines and factories of the Angarsk industrial corridor and then, slightly tarnished, on to her rendezvous with her beloved Yenisei and finally the Arctic ocean, 2,500 river kilometers downstream. One last pass through Irkutsk, and we'll be back on the beast-machine bound for Moscow and beyond, and a world more familiar if still not known. We've seen our last of Baikal, but I'm pretty sure that I, anyway, am not leaving it behind, that it will never quite stop flowing through me. Blood has the same salinity as the ocean, someone once told me—we never really left the sea, we just carry it around inside us. Alas, this little detail of life turns out to be just too exquisite to be true, but it sure works as metaphor—we all carry around a biological memory of where and what we come from, from the water that makes up roughly sixty percent of our bodies to the ninety-eight or so percent of our genes that we share with chimpanzees. And so it is with Baikal—the lake inseparable from the people who love it in so many complex and ambiguous ways—I'll carry a piece of it around in every part of me, like a new strand of DNA that has spliced itself in with mine and changed ever so slightly who I am and how I live in the world.

For our last couple of nights back in Irkutsk, James and I stay in a downtown hotel, for about three times the cost of the American House, where, Olga tells us, we can finally get our visas properly registered. "Certainly," the clerk tells us when we check in, "we can do this, no problem."

"No," the same woman unapologetically tells us when we check out two days later, "we cannot do this. You should have done it already, when you came into country. It is too late. This is rules."

"There is no such rule," an exasperated Olga tells us, not suggesting, I'll realize later, that our problem likely could be taken care of with the offer of a small gratuity. But Olga has been to Europe and America, and perhaps now, in a small act of silent protest, she refuses to engage in the usual petty corruption that greases the wheels of her own country. In any case, she doesn't suggest a bribe, and we naively don't think of it, the clerk and the manager remain unmoved by Olga's arguments, and James and I will continue to lug around our anxiety about not having our papers in order.

We say a warm goodbye to Olga as we did to Andrei, the chance we took on each of them having paid off more than we ever could've imagined, but in Olga's case having learned almost nothing about our somewhat eccentric guide and interpreter herself. How did she become so proficient in English? How did she get so plugged into the political and scientific circles of Irkutsk Lake Baikal? What became of the father of her twelve-year-old daughter? We are left only to wonder.

At the basement Internet café, we peer through the wormhole, over the horizon west again. We've reached the apex of The Long Way Home—halfway around—and from here it's pretty much just a long, slow coast down the back side of the planet. We have tickets as far as St. Petersburg, where we'll get our first whiff in three months of the sea that on its far side laps on the wharfs of our own hometown, the shore on which, provided we get our papers in order and are actually able to slip through what Peter the Great envisioned as Russia's Window on the West, we ourselves expect to wash up two and a half months or so hence. But between the two fringes of the Atlantic, we have no real plan. We don't even know how we'll get home. We'll find a ship, is all we know, from somewhere on the eastern shore of the Atlantic to somewhere on the western shore, sometime before the end of the year. In the meantime, we'll bob around like bumblebees ourselves, following the scent of something alluring to wherever it takes us but, like bumblebees, also confident that we'll find our way home.

•

Train Number Two: Baikal-Irkutsk-Moscow—is a stream of iridescent blue that pours out of the Irkutsk rail yards and down the Angara Valley like a sliver of the river itself, carrying a memory of Russia's great lake westward toward the country's heartland. And for the three days along this stretch of the Trans-Siberian, there will be little to divert passengers from that memory, or from any other thoughts. Watching the natural and human terrain beyond the windows between Irkutsk and Moscow is like seeing reruns of a once-riveting TV show—what was novel and compelling now just feels stale. *I drive on and on and see no end to it.* . . . We will see our ten-thousandth blue-shuttered timber house, our one-hundredth Lenin leading the way to the workers' paradise, our three-billionth birch tree, the infinite, mournful, and monotonous terrain of Siberia continuing to unfold and unfold and unfold. If you've traveled the eastern stretch of this great railroad and have been captivated by the austere beauty of its landscape and the human stories that lie beneath it, well—the western stretch affords plenty of time to think.

I find myself thinking again, because this is just the way my brain works, about Berkeley and Boston and the fractured life that I left behind and am now closing in on again around the other side of the world and about which pieces I'd like to try to pick back up and rebuild, which ones I'd just as soon leave behind, and what new pieces may yet present themselves when we finally come to rest back in New England. I'm thinking about what lies ahead down these tracks in Moscow and St. Petersburg, each city stuffed with potent images and symbols of the Russia that we in the U.S. learned from the arts to love and from the news to loathe. I'm thinking—because, like I said, this is the way I am—about being turned back at the border and having all our stuff confiscated and our money stolen and dying of cold and starvation in some last outpost of the Gulag only because we are missing a couple of little smudges of ink on our passports. And I'm thinking about Andrei and Olga, both trying in their own way to build relationships with people beyond the far borders of Russia that will enrich their home here in Siberia. About Sergei and Tania and that other Olga in her Audrey Hepburn hat, all making their peace with the narrow borders of their small world in Barguzin. About self-sacrificing Lena and crusading Jennie Sutton and mournful Dr. Tarasova and the two Natalias, the Baikalsk mill's own Tweedle-Dum and Tweedle-Dee. And about the entwined lives of Dr. Hope and Dr. Despair—the inveterate optimist and the incorrigible pessimist—flesh-and-blood incarnations of Russia's eternal yin-and-yang and, I've realized, of my own. And about the animated Old Believers and placid Snake Bay and its *banya* and serene little Bolshie Koty and dreadful Baikalsk and transfixing Irkutsk and the nerpas we never saw and the dive into the abyss we never took and the parts of the lake we didn't get to and the peo-ple we didn't meet and all the new questions I've just accumulated that have no answers, so many that they're falling out of my head and I'm leaving a trail of them along the crushed stone of this 6,000-mile path across Eurasia, only I doubt that I'll ever be able to start picking them up again and following them back to Lake Baikal.

I'm thinking about Emma, and about whether I'll ever be able to fill that hole in my life.

I'm thinking about faith and trust and belief in the ultimate power of benevolent forces, or at least the ability to survive whatever the world throws at you, and how without a good deal of each of these things I would never have gotten married and James and I would never have set out from Boston, and how despite the always uncertain outcome I want to create more of these things in my life, but how at the same time these very same powers of mind may well be pushing Baikal toward the same cliff over which so many other irreplaceable places have fallen.

And I'm thinking about a story I edited a few years ago at *Living on Earth* about the Ganges River.

The Ganges is one of the world's great rivers, carrying the melting snows of the planet's highest mountains in the Himalaya more than 1,500 miles to the Bay of Bengal and the Indian Ocean, through one of the most densely populated regions of the world in India and Bangladesh. To the hundreds of millions of Hindus in South Asia, the Ganges is holy—*Gangama*, they call it, "Mother Ganges." Hindus revere the Ganges, make pilgrimages to it for ritual cleansings, and send the burning bodies of their loved ones on to their next life on its currents.

The Ganges is also horribly polluted, carrying a huge load of waste from industry, agriculture, and human communities. But, our reporter Richard Schiffman found, many of the millions who worship it are unable to accept this truth. Even to suggest that their holiest river is polluted, he said, would be a blasphemy. Reverence for the object keeps people from seeing the object in its true light, and from taking action to protect and restore it.

As in India, so too is the case here in Siberia. "Russians are deeply moved by Baikal," Jennie Sutton told me back in Irkutsk, something that had been obvi-ous from our first encounter with it on the train, when most of the rest of the car's passengers brought their tea and vodka to the window to sing and pay tribute to the lake. "But this love," she had continued, "is not always with its eyes open. This sort of blind love is a dangerous thing."

Russia has built the principles of exceptional caution and care into the laws and policies concerning its great lake. Official documents and rhetoric reflect a growing recognition that Baikal needs a greater level of stewardship than has been afforded most other parts of Russia—more, even, than has been afforded most of the rest of the world. But as is usually the case not just in Russia but most everywhere, practice and culture have proven far more resistant to change, and how Russians actually act in regard to Baikal seems mostly to ignore the wisdom gained from experience elsewhere—the wisdom that we should be alert for warning signs, that complex ecosystems can sometimes mask profound changes, that it's almost always more expensive and more challenging to try to undo damage than to prevent the damage in the first place, and that, sometimes, before we can even imagine what we've done, it can be too late to undo it. Here at Baikal, belief in what's possible obscures the reality of what may actually be happening; the power of the lake is legendary—*it cleanses itself of pollution.* But the legend of the lake is even more powerful—*it cleanses people of concern about pollution.* A small truth about Baikal is transformed into a big myth, and something profound—the belief in the transcendent power of nature and of this singular place—is transformed into something corrosive.

Who knows, maybe the fears of Dr. Tarasova, Dr. Pavlov, and Jennie Sutton will yet be proven baseless and Baikal will show itself to be so powerful and unique as to be the exception, the one place on earth where processes of degradation that pertain everywhere else do not apply. Maybe God will finally show his face here. Or, short of an outright miracle, maybe the great lake will prove at least strong enough to resist threats to its basic integrity. Maybe some endemic but unloved species of clams or worms will disappear under a blanket of toxic muck, but the rest of the ecosystem will remain more or less intact. Maybe the nerpa will fall victim to compromised immune systems, poaching, and shorter winters, or the golomyanka to small changes in Baikal's temperature, but the Baikal epischura will remain and maintain the water's extraordinary purity and clarity. Or maybe even the epischura will disappear, and the purity of the water will diminish with it, but the great chasm itself—*the very deep and cold body*—will remain, an eternal, gargantuan, ever-widening abyss.

And certainly in the long run, after the blip of human civilization has passed and there are none of us left to remember how we once felt about it and what we did or didn't do to it, Baikal will be what it was before we came along— old and huge and restless and full of the creative forces that drive evolution. It will keep rumbling and widening and reshaping itself, and the climate around it will go through its irregular swings, and new conditions and habitats will give rise to new species, and then in a hundred million years or so it will slowly crack open to the global sea and everything will change, but only in roughly the same way as has happened uncountable times over the half-billion years or so that there has been life on earth. In the long run, we'll be gone and Baikal will still be here, doing what the earth has always done.

But we are here now, and we have to ask, what makes Baikal a place that so many humans care so deeply about? What defines it as a place to be so astounded by, to be worth writing—or reading—a book about?

Is it, in its essence, just that great chasm, awesome in its depth and breadth? Is it the uniquely pure and cold water that fills the chasm in such an astounding amount? Is it the *Epischura baicalensis* and the other tiny creatures that were born of that cold and pure water and now help maintain its purity? The golomyanka and the nerpa and the hundreds of other kinds of animals and plants that have never known any other home? Is Baikal some of these things, some strands of this web, which might continue to exist even if others are lost or frayed? Or is it all of them together—not just the strands, but the whole web? And if we lose or diminish just some of what nature has created here, might not something essential about the whole be lost? How much can this place be changed and still remain what it was?

No ecosystem is static, no place unchanging. Baikal is here to create unanswerable questions because of change, eons of change, sometimes imperceptible, sometimes cataclysmic. And you could argue that humans are just another agent of change, maybe even as natural and inevitable in their impacts as the ever-shifting climate and continental plates—all is fluid, dynamic, and we are merely part of that dynamic process. You could argue this. Some do. You could also argue that our capacity as humans to affect widespread, long-term, and even permanent change in nature exceeds anything other than nature's most calamitous events—a massive volcanic eruption or a meteor impact. And that while those cataclysms are random, truly without design, the impacts of human actions on the world around us are the result of the conscious actions of a species with a wide range of possible choices, and so are preventable. The earth itself and the laws of physics have no intelligence. Even other intelligent animals don't have anything close to our ability to learn from our mistakes. And as far as we can tell, nothing else on this planet shares our capacities for ingenuity, self-awareness, and wisdom. You could argue that because we can do things differently, we should. Other animals fight and kill, the earth consumes its inhabitants in fire, nature delivers them plagues and inundates their homes. What separates us from other creatures and natural processes are supposedly the very things that make us human. So you could argue that knowing what we know, having learned the lessons of our corrosive actions elsewhere, it would be one of the finest achievements of human civilization to stay out of the way of the rest of nature at Baikal—to try to fix what we've done and do no more.

And on the scale of challenges that we as a species have solved, even on the scale of challenges that Russia has solved, this would be a breeze. Baikal's is not an ecosystem under assault because millions of people have moved in, as is the case in much of the world today. The livelihoods and consumer needs of millions don't depend heavily on the region's factories, farms, and forests. The contamination of the lake and its ecosystem is in all likelihood not yet so great that it will require billions of dollars and decades or more to undo. No, the human presence and impact here relative to other places are still extremely limited. And we know as a human community how to live here in a way that is far more sustainable that what has been practiced at Baikal and most everywhere else. It's merely a matter of lining up the right resources, calling upon the best available knowledge and technology, creating and maintaining the right kind of institutions. The question is not, *can we*, the question is, *will we*. And I say "we" because it's not just Russia that's responsible for the future of Baikal. Baikal is no longer Slava Maksimov's snow globe bubble of Russian perfection and serenity. It's part of a global exchange of goods and ideas, of benefits and costs. Within the last generation, geography has become almost meaningless as a barrier—to people, capital, pollution, almost anything. So, too, is there an increased understanding that nature's great creations are not the heritage of only one national or political entity, but that they exist for all to share, enjoy, and care for. Andrei Suknev would get little argument in his characterization of Baikal as "property of all world." Nor would Anatoly Malevsky, in his assertion that the future of Baikal depends at least in part on resources from outside of Russia. If the world is going to enjoy the benefits of Baikal—even if those benefits come, as Wallace Stegner said of wilderness in the U.S., merely from knowing that it's there—it must also share the responsibilities of caring for it.

I'm thinking, as Baikal recedes miles, time zones, half a continent away, that there is still time to do things differently at the world's great lake, to learn from our experiences elsewhere, to make the right choices. Even Jennie Sutton, deeply concerned about Baikal and by her own admission not especially optimistic, believes that there is still reason for hope—that the waste products of human society can be reduced and kept out of the lake, that people's understanding of their relationship with their environment can be improved, that the short-term costs of changing our impact on Baikal will be far outweighed by the long-term benefits. But she also believes that, given current trends in Russia and the world, there's little time to waste. "We need to convince people that we need to start acting," she says, "and acting now. We need to get the message over that if you love Baikal, then you must behave appropriately. That when we love something, like when we love someone, it always demands sacrifice."

•

James and I dive back into our books. We sleep a lot. We muse about ideas and plans for the road ahead. We play marathon games of rummy, which I always win handily, and cribbage, in which James retaliates fully, and we bicker about the rules. We watch three more days of mostly flat western Siberia rise before us, and three nights of a huge yellow moon rising through the clouds over eastern Siberia behind us. We read about the tsars and their barbarity from first to last and wonder how it was that unlucky Ivan IV got saddled with the moniker "The Terrible" rather than merely "The Perhaps Just Slightly More Terrible Than the Rest, or Maybe Not Even." We barely interact with the other passengers. We are accompanied again by the ever-present *bangclatterslamsqueal* of the train, the noise intermittently replaced overnight by the musical pings and plinks of the crews working beneath the train at long stops, just as incongruously delicate and haunting as before and imprinting themselves forever on my brain. We smell the tobacco smoke, grilled meat, and damp earth at each lonely stop, and even the growing cities seem lonely, even though our guidebooks insist that many of them are not.

A day west of Irkutsk we arrive at Novosibirsk, on the Ob river, not even a town before the coming of the railroad and today Siberia's biggest city, with nearly two million residents, and home to the biggest opera and ballet theater in all of Russia. Now Omsk, just north of Kazakhstan, population 1.3 million, where Dostoyevsky was imprisoned for four years, was nearly flogged to death, and wrote *Notes from the House of the Dead*. And here, in the foothills of the Ural mountains, is Yekaterinburg, one and a half million, named for both Peter the Great's wife and Russia's patron saint of mining, site in 1918 of the murders of the last tsar, Nicholas II, and his family, and in Soviet times renamed Sverdlovsk in honor of the man likely responsible for the murders, a name that Russia's railway system has yet to give up. Just west of Yekaterinburg and roughly two days out of Irkutsk we cross over a low pass over the barely discernable Ural mountains, where a little white obelisk marks the fictitious continental boundary of Asia, and into European Russia. Late in the evening we pass through Perm, population one million, supposedly the unnamed city from which Chekhov's *Three Sisters* hoped to escape and renamed in Soviet times in honor of the foreign minister who signed the infamous Molotov-von Ribbentrop Soviet-Nazi nonaggression pact and, in earlier days, invented the Molotov cocktail. And the farther west we go, the more the landscape ever so slightly fills up with chalky gray apartment buildings, brick Orthodox churches, roads, and power lines, and the more sorrowful many of the station vendors become—a weary man of somewhere between thirty and seventy in a knit cap offering a single, huge cabbage; an old woman with a tiny dog, wearing a colorful plastic bag for a rain hat and struggling on bad knees over three sets of tracks to offer apples to disinterested buyers; two younger women finding no takers for a pair of garish electric light fixtures; a young girl with a bright pink hat hawking who knows what from a crumpled, rain-soaked box—more sorrowful, perhaps, because the closer to Moscow, the greater the overall level of opportunity and so the even greater marginality of those working the lowest rungs of the informal economy. Somewhere back around Omsk, James had looked up from *Crime and Punishment*, which he's now reading, glanced out the window at the unchanging landscape, and declared, "I'm bored." A day later, now bearing down on Moscow, I declare myself sad and cranky and once again sick of Russia—sad about the harshness of life for so many of its people, sick of the nearly unrelenting dreariness of its cities and towns and the brusqueness of people in public places, cranky about the weight and anxiety of its bureaucracy and corruption, and the herking and jerking of this damn, interminable train. How can Russians survive a lifetime in this country? I'm not looking forward to another week here.

Now finally, nearly a day west of the Urals and three days out of Irkutsk, we cross the wide and lazy Volga, Europe's longest river, and the settlements on the still largely unchanged landscape are getting denser and the buildings bigger and the roads more numerous and the traffic thicker, and now all of a sudden there's the first outpost of Western commerce we've seen for six or seven thousand glorious miles, a set of those once-ubiquitous Golden Arches, and just like that, as if we've passed through some invisible membrane from one universe into another, we're in what is unmistakably a European metropolis full of Mercedes and grand plazas and people on cell phones, and the city gets denser and taller and then *pow*, after seven days of field and forest and bog and village and barely an hour from wide-open countryside, we're on a jammed platform at Yaroslavl Station in the heart of what was not long ago, to us in the West, the real-world Mordor, source of all that is nefarious, wicked, totalitarian, and freedom-destroying—Moscow, population nine million.

Our driver barrels along boulevards as wide as whole Siberian villages, past gold-domed churches and menacing Soviet-era government buildings, swanky shops and sidewalk soda-and-nut vendors, down lesser avenues and rutted side streets, under gigantic metal heating conduits snaking through complexes of dreary apartment buildings, and then down a dark alley at the end of which he leads us to a battered metal door leading in turn to an unlit vestibule where I am certain that he is going to crack us over the head with a crowbar, take our stuff, and leave us to die, unnoticed for weeks except by some feral dogs. When the man leads us instead into an elevator not much bigger than a coffin, whose single faint bulb casts only enough light to reveal that there is no ventilation or emergency hatch in the ceiling, pushes a black button, and the doors squeal shut and the box begins to groan and crawl upward more slowly than a legless man could climb the stairs, I am sure now that this is where we will die, stuck between floors and driven slowly insane with claustrophobia. Alas (at least from the perspective of one trying to construct a compelling narrative), no such dramatic fate awaits us, merely a two-night stay in a small flat with a middle-aged woman named Lena, about whom there is nothing much to say except that on her tiny porch overlooking more heating conduits she keeps crates of small, gnarly green apples that she grows at her dacha just outside the city and that may be the best that I've tasted since I picked apples for a living one fall after high school.

Debbie, our San Francisco travel agent, is three-for-three.

A few chapters back I mentioned how the fact that train schedules across Russia's ten time zones are all posted in Moscow time suggests that all standards for time, culture, and thought in this country emanate from Moscow. Well, it turns out that when you get to Moscow, you find the very spot—a small disk of bronze with the points of the compass, surrounded by totemic images of some of the vast country's most revered beasts—a bear, an eagle, a deer, a seal, a tiger—all embedded in the bricks of a plaza just meters outside the Kremlin. And even in the drizzle of a dark October afternoon, there's a constant stream of tourists, even certain forty-something Americans circumnavigating the world with their brothers who are loathe to think of themselves as tourists, waiting to stand on the spot from which all things Russian are measured and have their pictures taken.

Elsewhere throughout the plaza, young men in leather jackets hawk bogus Soviet-era wares to some of these same foreigners and more than a few wistful Russians—Red Army jackets and hats, badges with images of Lenin and Marx, red hammers and sickles and gold stars—and just beyond are the gates to Red Square, through which we can see the stark walls of the tsars' Kremlin, the audacious onion domes of St. Basil's Cathedral, and the final resting place of Lenin himself, architect of the revolution that consigned both the Russian monarchy and the Russian church to the dustbin of history, mercifully unaware in his permanent repose that all of his earth-shattering efforts have been reduced to a few hustlers selling cheap junk to nostalgic tourists.

We have traveled fifteen or twenty thousand miles, come two-thirds of the way around the planet, and seen works of nature and humans that we could never have imagined, and only now, as we walk through the gates beyond the focal point of all of Russia and into Red Square, does my taciturn brother James finally exclaim, "Holy shit!" This was the place, more than any in all of Russia, that symbolized the epochal twentieth-century struggle between East and West, images of which the Soviet government and our own used to instill in the hearts of Americans the defining fear of nearly our entire lives—of a nuclear Armageddon authored by our arch-rivals that could be averted only by threatening an even more horrendous nuclear Armageddon—until Gorbachev pulled his fingers out of the holes in the dike and the Soviet Union crumbled and washed away.

Red Square is all that twentieth-century propagandists, and perhaps also those under whose guidance it evolved over the centuries, conjured it up to be— vast, cold, and intimidating, reducing the individual to a speck no more significant than one of the millions of stones with which it's paved, the stones that channeled the blood of the state enemies executed here in the years before the capital was moved to St. Petersburg in 1712 and that still bear the broad white lines that we would see on our flickering screens back home, beneath the treads of the tanks and soldiers' boots parading across it every May First. It is also unexpectedly, stunningly beautiful. It's not merely the extraordinary St. Basil's at the far end, with its ten onion-domed towers sprouting like a cluster of hallucinogenic mushrooms in ostentatious colors and shapes and swirls, as wildly eccentric today as when they were dreamed up more than 400 years ago; not merely the monolithic Kremlin walls, nearly twenty meters high and the color of dried blood, with their malachite-green-roofed towers and the austerely elegant gold-and-white houses of government that rise behind them. It's not merely the stark modern pyramid of polished red and black granite that is Lenin's Tomb, or the ornate stone façade of the massive GUM State Department Store across the way, or the riot of spires, arches, and double-headed eagles of the Resurrection Gate and the State History Museum at the near end, or the expanse of gray stone bricks between all of these that looks like a restless sea in the quiet before a big storm blows in, or even the slight warp of the whole square, which creates an odd sense of disequilibrium, as if St. Basil's were a fantastical ten-masted ship slipping over the edge of this restless gray sea. It's the combination of all of these elements together—the way the textures, colors, patterns, shapes, periods, and functions interact, like the best public spaces everywhere, to create an emotional impact more like some grand work of nature than of mere humans, a man-made Yosemite, or Baikal.

If you have only a couple of days in Moscow, here are a few things you might want to do:

- Buy a ticket for the metro, hold on tight as you ride one of its dizzyingly fast escalators so deep below the city that you may feel you've ended up beneath New York rather than Moscow,  and marvel at the exquisite architecture and artwork of the station and of just about any other that the fast and frequent trains will take you to—among them Komsomolskaia, its arched ceilings sporting grand mosaics of Peter the Great and other Russian military heroes; Ploshchad Revoliutsii, where bronze statues honor the working people of the great Soviet Socialist utopia; and Barrikadnaia, featuring bas-reliefs depicting events of the revolutions of 1905 and 1917 in a hall of red and white marble.

- While entering and leaving the metro, keep your ears out for strains of music wafting through the passageways—it might be a boy of no more than eight playing gorgeously mournful songs on an accordion or a world-class string quartet playing Tchaikovsky for a few spare rubles.

- Poke around the museums and churches of the Kremlin long enough to sate a lifetime's appetite for icons, crosses, Fabergé eggs, gold, jewels, fur, and other staples of the Russian imperial class and then keep poking around until you find some of the less-celebrated and more wonderfully bizarre pieces of the tsars' collections, like the silver chicken-king, the elaborate little gold wagon carrying a potato-shaped pod stuffed with a maniacally laughing man pulled by an elephant bearing a gigantic clock, and the floating wooden priest bathed in pale green light and holding a small gold-domed church in his hand.

- Try to avoid eye contact with any members of two large classes of men: those sporting cuts, bruises, scars, and black eyes, most likely from drunken fights, of which there are many, and those sporting military and police uniforms, of which there are many more. Close contact with either of these will likely come to no good.

- Go to the American embassy, inquire about the proper regulations regarding visa registration and the consequences of getting caught without your visa properly registered, and utter a dark and anxious laugh when the embassy officials tell you that they don't know the regulations or the consequences except that maybe you will be "fined" the equivalent of one day's pay of whatever uniformed official stops you.

- Ditch your bought-in-New York muskrat hat with which you hoped to impress Russians but that you could tell by their response was at least three stories too short, and replace it with a black wool cap bought at the GUM, and ditch your daypack in favor of a plastic shopping bag, in order to look a little less like a clueless American who just might not have a properly registered visa.

•

On the Trans-Siberian there are Soft class and Hard class and Gulag class, and on the overnight train between Moscow and St. Petersburg there is what you might call Tsar class—spotless cars of two-person cabins with sumptuous crimson upholstery and curtains, porcelain teacups, crisply ironed hand towels, pillows stuffed with down that could only have come from geese with the finest of pedigrees, a fetching young woman knocking on your door offering sushi, canapés, and small bottles of expensive whiskey, and—perhaps the most remarkable amenity of all—a stopper in the bathroom sink. More than 150 years after this stretch of track was first laid and more than eighty years after the collapse of the monarchy, this car seems an homage to Nicholas I, who, legend has it, in a fashion similar to that of his Soviet successors in Irkutsk, commanded that a railroad be built between St. Petersburg and Moscow and drew an arrow-straight line on a map depicting his desired route. Today the "Nicholas railroad" still follows this almost unerring path, never wavering to accommodate the lowly residents of any of the towns that lay to one side or another between the two historic Russian capitals at the time of its construction. The ride is the smoothest and quietest of any we have had in Russia, and the bed the comfiest, on or off a train. Still, I sleep fitfully as we approach our last stop in Russia and the border to the West. Visa anxiety lingers.

Even here, on the finest cars on Russia's finest railroad—the tsars' own line—the toilets dump right onto the tracks.

•

"In Russia, before, we had very little money, even if you had good education. They would pretend to pay us, we would pretend to work!"

Over tea in her St. Petersburg kitchen, Mila Klepikova breathes new life into an old cliché about life in the Soviet Union. "At my factory, it was very important work, very well-educated engineers. We would go to work, first we have tea, that is maybe hour. Then the women go to put on makeup, the men they go to smoke. Then after maybe two hour, we start to work. But then we talk about shows, concert, what books we read. Then boss say, OK, time for work. Then it's dinner. We take one hour for dinner. Then we go shop. Then we come back, and talk about what we buy. Then boss say, OK, time for work. . . . It is like this almost every day, except maybe at end of month. At end of month, boss say, OK, time for work, we work hard for few days, then at beginning of month, back to regular."

Mila is a little ball of a woman, maybe fifty years old, less than five feet tall, with a sparkle in her eye that shines through thick glasses, a self-professed gift of gab, and a self-deprecating wit that doesn't quite disguise a deep loneliness. She lives alone in St. Petersburg, in the biggest apartment we have seen in Russia, with high ceilings and grand casement windows looking out onto a fine neighborhood not far from the Hermitage and Nevsky Prospect, the heart of the city. James and I are staying five days with her—another home stay set up through the efforts of our champion travel agent Debbie, who is now a perfect four-for-four—and in just our first day she opens up to me as if I am the first human being to wash up on her deserted shores in years.

"This is very special house," Mila tells me. "My father, before the revolution"—like many here, she calls the fall of the Soviet Union "the Revolution"—"he was very important, so government gave him this place, for his family to use for life. Now you see, one person, all these rooms. . . ." Mila's parents are dead, and her only child, a daughter, went off to the States for school and never returned. "When she finish, she do not want to come back, she is afraid. I say, it is not so bad now, but she stay anyway. She is in New York. Maybe she enjoy freedom—from her Mama! Maybe I could go live with her, but my daughter, she pretty, she will marry soon. I don't know, will her husband want to live with, what you call it, mother-in-law? So I stay here, I keep this place. Things are changing here, maybe she will come back."

Mila has been taking in guests for about a year and a half. She says she likes getting to use her English, bringing in some money. "And yes," she says, "I get to have company." She advises us on what tourist sites we should hit. She asks us about our religion. She tells us about the New Russians who she feels have taken over her neighborhood and brought in security guards and made her feel like a prisoner in her own house. And she talks.

"My time is over," she tells me, with an air more of resignation than sorrow. "I am trained in technical area, but I don't know computers! I know airplanes, and space. But the plant I worked in, it was closed. Now, I don't know! I have no one here. I have friend, we talk on phone, but she have own life. She is very busy, but I am always here. I stay in, I get very lazy!

"I am sorry, all this talk," Mila says. "The women, they like to talk. Would you like some more cake? What would you like for breakfast tomorrow? Where are your wifes? Why do you not travel with a woman?"

•

St. Petersburg, October 23

Dear—

This is the end of the line for us in Russia, the end of the 6,000-mile, battered and dusty Russian rainbow and here at the end is a big old dusty pot o' gold. St. Petersburg is one big museum—ragged and unkempt but crammed with jewels of all kinds, like this unexpected gem—"Lucy and Her Partner," by Kees van Dongen, c. 1911—at the Hermitage, stuffed in next to all those Rembrandts and Picassos and Monets and pillars of lapis lazuli and diamond-encrusted gold mechanical peacocks. Speaking of stuffed, for my money (15 rubles—about 60 cents) the real gem here is the Zoological Museum, heir to Peter the Great's collection of curiosities, jammed with preserved creatures of every conceivable variety from a blue whale skeleton to aphids to ten-foot parasitical worms to an oxymoronic "dwarf mammoth" dug out of the Siberian tundra.

A couple of days ago we looked for—and I think found—the building that was the setting for Raskolnikov's flat in Crime and Punishment—it looks and feels exactly as I imagined it and it's amazing that it's still here, unmarked, the courtyard and stairwell open to any and all. Even though the story was *fiction, the building comes closer than any of the city's "historical sites" to evoking real, lived history. Yesterday we went to a couple of the tsars' summer palaces outside of the city—Pavlovsk and Pushkin, among the most beautiful and opulent structures you'll see anywhere and built, of course, out of the blood and toil of countless millions of Russians who scoured the country's incredible mineral wealth out of the ground for the benefit only of this one family. Both palaces were bombed and looted by the Germans in WWII, and immediately after the war, with the country devastated, 20 million dead, countless millions more homeless and starving, its infrastructure destroyed, among the first things the Soviet government did was to begin rebuilding these places. When I asked our guide, a 26-year-old woman who knew all the facts but none of the context or meaning of the history of these places, whether Russians were resentful that so much of the country's scarce wealth has been put into restoring these places, she didn't understand the question, it didn't make any sense to her.*

Russia is more enthralling than ever but also as bizarre and vexing as ever. I'm especially disturbed by the country's obsession with its own greatness—its great history of great military victories, its great culture that Russians are certain is unappreciated by the West, its strange combination of chauvinism, inferiority complex and the worship by Russians of those who oppress them—especially here in St. P & Moscow, with their obsession with the glories of the tsars and the church even though they were all gained and built by the enslavement of most of the country's people, either as serfs or as forced laborers convicted of some petty or political crime. That didn't start with Stalin and the Soviets, that's for damn sure. And all of this obsession with their country's greatness seems only to lead Russians to ignore serious problems. Even with Baikal, it isn't enough that it's the mostest-everything lake in the world. They have to give it supernatural powers, which only ends up harming the lake by giving them an excuse to avoid dealing with real problems. I'm exhausted by trying to figure this place out and, I must say, even though I might never get back here, glad to be leaving tomorrow—hopefully. If you don't see or hear from me after the first of the year, inquire with the Russian Interior Ministry.

If I do get back, though, I'll tell you about Baikal.

Love, Peter

•

The landscape through the Karelia region northwest of St. Petersburg looks remarkably similar to most of what has passed before us since we disembarked from the *Antonina Nezhdanova* in Vladivostok eight time zones ago—flat and marshy, thinly populated, pushing up tall, spindly confers and wispy, white birches. But it feels remarkably different, if only because for the first time in weeks we are traveling without a heavy burden of anxiety. Finally, only yesterday, after a week of telling us they couldn't do it, the people from the travel agency that set up our home stays and transfers in Moscow and St. Petersburg did register our visas. The extent of our relief cannot be measured. And yet—if there is something nearly as bad as anxiety, it might be never knowing whether or not that anxiety was well founded. And if there is something worse than being shaken down, locked up, and embroiled in an international incident at the border for lack of an ink stamp, it might be not having this happen, and therefore having no story to tell.

We handed our passports to the uniformed officials as we boarded the train at Finland Station—where Lenin's famous sealed train from Germany arrived in the ferment of the spring of 1917—and now, just short of the Finnish border, another official has merely shrugged when we told him that we were not issued customs declaration forms when we entered the country, made a cursory pat of our backpacks, waved, and moved on. At Vyborg, the final stop in Russia, when our passports will be returned to us without comment, and the train begins to roll the final few meters toward Finland, I will find myself almost disappointed that we will never know whether not having our visas registered would even have mattered. And I will feel more than a little foolish for having wasted so much energy on the matter for so many weeks. And several months hence, when I will tell this nonstory to Gary Cook, the man who set our Russian adventure in motion, put us in touch with Andrei Suknev, and bailed us out by phone at the Russian embassy in Tokyo, he will give me a knowing look and tell me, "Russia is a wonderful place to travel, because things always work out. But you have to worry, because if you don't, things don't work out."

2 1

360°

*In which we skip like stones through Western Europe,
face the reality of going home,
and close the circle*

I f you missed the fences and the swath of open land in the woods that mark the border, you can't help but notice that you've finally left Russia because the human presence beyond the windows of the train is no longer disheveled. Finland shares a long history of tension with its huge and powerful neighbor to the east, but I wonder if having to share such a long border with Russia galls the Finns most of all because everything in their country is so orderly, while everything in Russia is such a mess. The immediate difference crossing between these two countries may well be more stark than between any two others on the planet.

We are out of Russia and into suddenly more familiar and comforting territory, and James and I are suddenly giddy and joking about everything—about how the damn Finns have a ridiculous word like *Hei* for hello instead of the far simpler Russian *Zdravstvuite*, about how the Finns must long for a life without lawn mowers, a social contract, and more than one color of paint, about how surprised we are that the Finns and the European Union allow Russian trains to use their filthy open toilets within their territory but have perhaps granted a special temporary exemption to trains originating in SDCs—*shit-dumping countries.* . . . Russia recedes beyond the Gulf of Finland, beyond the lovely decompression chamber of Helsinki, beyond the soothingly smooth and comfortable trains and beds of Western Europe and all its polite people who almost always seem to speak English, and with every passing hour and kilometer we are at once more relaxed and more glad to be rid of the place and more and more sorry that we are not still there. Russia grabs hold of you tight, and if it often feels as if it's choking the life out of you and making you want to flee, its suffocating embrace is also powerfully seductive. If it often seems to be going to extraordinary lengths to make itself infuriating and impenetrable—almost challenging you just to give up on it and turn your attention elsewhere—it also makes it impossible for you to turn away, and ultimately makes the whole exhausting and exhilarating encounter worth it. It is, in ways that I'm only now realizing, more than a little like Emma. Except that with every passing hour and kilometer, her gravitational pull wanes ever so slightly, whereas Russia's, much to my surprise, grows. I'm done with her. I don't think I'm done with Russia.

And now, having dived into the unending expanse of the Pacific, the cold and clear abyss of Baikal, and the murky and unsettled depths of Russia itself, James and I are relaxing in the shallow, warm waters of Western Europe, the wading pool of world travel for Americans. Not much learning to swim needed here, just a lot of lazy floating around. . . .

•

October 27, Northern Sweden

The little lake and the big sky behind it both have the texture of nacre, a mother-of-pearl sheen of pink and green and blue as the sun slips back below the horizon, barely having breached it this morning. We're on the far northern fringe of Europe and the far edge of fall, and in this place at this time of year, the cold comes on hard and fast. The air is clear, dry, and crisp, the pine and fir a deep, stoic green, the open water rippling in a soft breeze. By this time tomorrow, the air will be an impenetrable icy gray, the trees will be coated in a heavy silver-white glaze, and the surface of the lake will be frozen solid. With the abrupt end of daylight savings time, it will even be dark already—the sun will be out of sight by 3:30. Winter locks itself into place in twenty-four hours.

Even the few hearty items remaining in Elisa's garden by the lake won't be able to hold out against the killing frost much longer, so she prepares a final northern autumn feast for her visitors. "I'm usually a vegetarian," Elisa tells us, as we help her wash the last of her tiny carrots and potatoes and chop up the last of her kale and leeks in the kitchen of her well-insulated little wooden house. "But I also think it's good not to be rigid, and to eat what nature produces locally." Hence the snap, sizzle, and pungent aroma of sautéing reindeer meat rising from the stove across the room, which we'll have with tart, red lingonberry sauce. By the time we get home to Boston, we will have eaten famed Copper River sockeye right from the river, Tokyo's finest sushi, crepes and jam prepared in a stand at the base of the Eiffel Tower at midnight, and the best that the chefs of the Queen Elizabeth 2 can dream up, but this will have been our most perfect meal.

Elisa invited us here when we met at Baikal, traveling with Andrei. Here to Jokkmokk, Sweden, a small town just north of the Arctic Circle, in the part of the world known to outsiders as Lapland, where she runs an organization dedicated to protecting the boreal forests of the world's northernmost regions—Russia, Scandinavia, Canada, and Alaska.

After dinner, our feet crunch on the heavy frost as we cross the clearing in front of Elisa's house and duck into the sauna—the Scandinavian version of the *banya*—where we shed our clothes, bask in the blistering heat, and take turns dousing and scrubbing with warm water and soap.

Out on the sauna's landing, waves of steam float from our naked bodies into the black sky, mingling with the sheen of the northern lights and the shooting stars above and the shimmer of the frost below. I don't know how people survive the long months of cold and dark here, year after year—I guess it has something to do with vodka, which seems as popular here as in Russia—but at this moment, cold and dark seem the ideal human habitat. There's no more perfect place on the planet, and nowhere that I'd rather be.

•

November 14, Berlin

James and I have split up for the first time since we left the U.S. I left him in Prague, from which he's going on to Vienna and Florence, while I decided to come back here to Berlin for a few more days. I needed to slow down and try to get to know one city a little better—another Talking Heads' verse keeps rolling around in my head—*I'm tired of traveling, I want to be somewhere.* I think we both also finally needed a little time apart. OK, yes, there's also this girl, Vera, whom I met in a club the other night while listening to a man play a Chinese *sheng*. The Brothers Thomson Traveling Road Show resumes in Rome in a couple of days.

Berlin at the millennium is transfixing, full of dark and momentous history, now trying to remake itself for a new era without completely effacing its past. Every block, building, vacant lot has a story to tell about what was, what is, what should be; every rehab or construction project—and the city is one huge construction site—brings a debate over truth, memory, and responsibility. I've never been anywhere where history is so alive and present, the history that's shaped my life and that of everyone I've ever known. And the city is so alive and vibrant, especially the old East. It's the only place since we left San Francisco where I feel I could spend a good, long time. But for now, anyway, I won't. Duty calls me home.

On our first swing through the city, James and I stayed a couple of nights with a guy we met for 15 minutes in Irkutsk. He gave us his bed and slept on the floor.

Yesterday I found the old Jewish cemetery that a friend told me about years ago, just outside Mitte. It was all dark and overgrown, trees and vines twisting around headstones broken and knocked over by Nazi gangs. It wasn't enough for them to terrorize the living—they had to go after the dead, too. Among the stones that I could read was one of a man who died on January 30, 1933, the day Hitler came to power. *The last Jew to die a natural death in Germany*, I think to myself. I touched a broken headstone and felt something coming through it—a vibration? A shudder? The rumble of a U-Bahn train? It was eerie, powerful. And I don't even believe in that stuff.

Looming in the background here is the still-unfolding drama of our disputed presidential election back home, the news unavoidable, no matter how hard we try to keep it at bay. Gore won by half a million in the popular vote, but Bush is declared the winner. This is democracy? Things are getting very testy on the other side of the Atlantic, and we're on edge here, as well. . . .

From Rome it's on to Barcelona for Thanksgiving with our Spanish cousins and American parents—home comes to us, maybe before we're ready for it—then Paris, then Ireland. We're still not sure how we're getting back across the Atlantic. James is thinking of trying to sail. I'm thinking of trying to swim. I still have Russia on the brain.

•

Holyhead, Wales, Sunday, December 2

Dear—

The tempest over the Irish Sea has subsided long enough for me to do a bit of poking around Holyhead while stranded here waiting for storm to pass and the boat to Dublin to resume its crossing. Holyhead is a rather dreary place—lots of lottery shops and purveyors of cheap clothes and appliances—but anyplace looks more interesting with wind and rain squalls blasting across it.

And then there's this interesting reading in the Manchester Guardian—a front-page story revealing widespread, and apparently successful, efforts by Florida officials to keep blacks—Gore voters—from voting. Why haven't I seen anything about this in the U.S.-based papers and websites? WHAT THE HELL IS GOING ON OVER THERE?

James and I have diverged again. I left him in Paris, Amsterdam-bound, while I'm heading for the smallest town I could find in Ireland to sleep for a few days and try to rid myself of the bug I've been carrying around for weeks. We'll meet next week in Dublin. Then—our ship awaits us.

Love, PT

•

"This is a very small town," Pat told me when I arrived, "only six pubs. And only one worth going to!" And when we went to it on my first night in town, one of the only other patrons was the local vicar, with whom Pat traded niceties over pints of Guinness. Pat told me later that the vicar is his political nemesis.

I had a vague plan all along to come back to Ireland at the end of the trip, and way back in Irkutsk I emailed a friend, asking for the name of the town she stayed in last summer. A couple of days later I got a note back: "My friend Pat in Kilmihil is expecting you!" And now two months later I've gotten off the bus at the only gas station on what seems the town's only road and there's a guy walking toward me through the December gloom and it's Pat, and on his kitchen table in his house back up the street is a big steaming pot of Irish stew and he shows me to a room upstairs and tells me to make myself at home and stay as long as I like and I can tell that he really means it.

Pat's a gem of a guy—smart, wise, well read and well traveled, humble, funny. He works at the local power plant but sounds like he wouldn't be too sorry if he lost his job. "It's the biggest polluter in Ireland," he says. "If it shut down, we'd be in full compliance with the Kyoto Protocol."

A ragged green bluff rises up before us from the almost sheer cliffs above the mouth of the River Shannon. A lonely white lighthouse surrounded by a white-washed stone wall is the only thing standing against the gale barreling off the ocean. There isn't a tree to break the wind, the grass grows only in matted clumps, and beyond the lighthouse the bluff suddenly gives way without warning to the raging sea below. Pat and his son Rory and I tromp along the rim through a mad swirl of drizzle and salt spray. Pat apologizes for the weather, but I love it—it feels like the weather that created this place, raw and ragged and unforgiving. We keep ourselves a safe distance from the edge of the bluff, though—a rogue gust could catch you the wrong way and toss you right over. The sky is in shreds, tattered patches of clouds dangling toward the sea, holes ripped out revealing massive, towering thunderheads behind, brilliant canary yellow in the reflected sun against clear patches of blue. Below, the churning breakers hurl themselves against rocks just as tortured as the sky—jagged sedimentary layers thrust straight up here, twisted forty-five degrees there, then just a mad and convoluted frenzy, a landscape at war with itself. And even through the tempest here on the farthest western shore of Europe, I see a glimmer at the distant edge of the Atlantic, and if I squint my eyes I'm almost certain that I can see—yup—the tips of the tallest spires of Manhattan hovering on the horizon, the bright, shining promise that drew so many millions from this island over the last 150 years. This is part of the reason I wanted to come here. Even if I hadn't been able to get a ship back to the U.S., I would have felt like I'd nearly completed the circle on the surface anyway, come close enough to home to almost touch it.

•

December 12, Dublin

A cloak of depression is descending upon me as we draw closer to home. I'm growing more gloomy by the day, mentally sluggish, emotionally numb, my perhaps predictable state on this final leg only compounded by the news from the States. The Supreme Court will release its decision today on whether the Florida recount should proceed. If it's yes, the word is that Gore will probably win. If they say no, it clinches the electoral college for Bush. Odds are on Bush, as the court ruled 5-4 on Sunday to stay the recount, saying that Bush had a "strong likelihood" of prevailing. The loser will be the winner, and I fear for where that leaves our country. I dread everything that awaits me back in the U.S., except for my bottle of Prozac, which I purposefully left behind. I'm also still sick, going on three weeks now. My Irish rest cure didn't do the trick.

James has rejoined me here in Dublin. He isn't feeling much better than I am and is also full of homeward-bound anxiety. What a couple of sorry excuses for travelers we are.

I'm reading Joyce's *Dubliners*. His writing is as pure and perfect as Baikal water.

•

December 13, London

It's over. Our Council of Elders has selected Bush the Younger. He'll be officially crowned George II next month.

In my email inbox today:
> *PT! The Sox signed Manny Ramirez! We miss you! Come on Home!*

•

December 16, North Atlantic, 998 Nautical Miles West of Southampton

We awoke to rough seas and high winds this morning, the fringes of a big storm 700 or so miles to the north. I go stand on the upper bow deck for an hour in the bracing wind, virtually alone, nothing between me and the churning North Atlantic. A day and a half out and I finally feel like I'm really at sea. Five or six laps around the deck and I feel even more invigorated. For the first time in weeks I feel energetic, alive.

The Long Way Home has become The Posh Way Home. We've booked passage on the *Queen Elizabeth 2*. I was willing to load up on Dramamine and take on the wintertime North Atlantic in a freighter, but every one I looked into was leaving at the wrong time or going to the wrong place. But Cunard had a sailing right when and where I wanted it—from Southampton, England on December 14 to New York. We'll be home in time for Christmas. And this winter crossing is actually cheaper than any cargo ship we could find.

As one might imagine, the *QE2* is a somewhat different experience from the *Pacific Champion*. It's designed to efface the feeling of being at sea as much as possible, and to provide endless distractions in case you do actually feel the floor beneath your feet start to wobble a bit even before your first martini. Unlike the *Pacific Champion*, there is nothing intimate about this ship—in relation to the sea, the crew, or the ship itself. But not to complain—I am loving every minute of it. Even though I have yet to meet my Kate Winslet. Unless it might be that woman I saw playing Scrabble yesterday with her parents....

7:30 P.M. Winds gusting up to force 12—hurricane strength. In the Chart Room bar with three of the few other non-Tories on board, also sailing steerage, the walls, windows, ceilings, and floors creak and groan, and every so often the ship shudders as it rolls through the heavy seas. What would this be like without the

ship's stabilizers, the special structures designed to smooth out the rough wintertime North Atlantic? Maybe even more fun.

One very cool feature of the westward sailing across the Atlantic is that
we pick up an hour with each of the five time zones we cross, so all but one of
the days are twenty-five hours long. Why would anyone go the other direction,
when you'd have to squeeze your daily debauchery into twenty-three hours?

Met Scrabble Girl on the aft deck today. I'd figured her for her early 30s,
but she's actually—yikes—24. She's returning from a year in Africa working for a
development agency, and her parents have given her this trans-Atlantic crossing as a welcome-home present. She seems somewhat ashamed at the expense,
but it doesn't seem to be keeping her from enjoying the air and the ocean and
the swimming pool.

December 17, 1,620 Nautical Miles West of Southampton

Heavy seas and lashing winds again. Outside on the top deck, the wind wants
to push me and Scrabble Girl off the ship. We find a bit of shelter in the lee of
a cabin wall, but the spray still batters us like a sandblaster. The sea performs a
furious dance with the sky. We are transfixed, and drenched. And now a new
sound has joined the cacophony, a rattling through the whipping wind, roiling
water, groaning engines, and splattering spray, and tiny white hailstones are
swirling crazily across the wooden deck. Almost as suddenly, there's a new and
even more powerful blast of wind, and the sea disappears behind a wall of water
that flies up from—what, 75 feet below?—and engulfs us, even in our cleverly shel-
tered spot. Now we are truly drenched. There's water in our shoes. I'm ecstatic.
Scrabble Girl is now slightly frightened.

December 18-19, 2,200 Nautical Miles West of Southampton

Today we'll pass thirty-five miles south of the Titanic. At an afternoon Q&A
session with the captain, all that anyone wants to know about is icebergs.

2:00 A.M. Moonrise over the stern—white-orange final quarter. There's no horizon,
the moon's just hanging there, bobbing in the black void of sea and sky, like it's
the one that's moving, not us, white waves rushing toward it and disappearing.
Huge clouds of spray fly up over the top of the ship from the bow and rain down
on us—me, James, and Scrabble Girl, then just me and Scrabble Girl.

Behind us inside, there's still a big crowd on the dance floor—among
them a transvestite in a bright red dress and bright red wig. Great legs.

December 19, South of Sable Island, Nova Scotia

Last full day at sea. Now New York really is just over the horizon.

In the ship's cinema today, Richard Gere and Winona Ryder in *Autumn in New York*. Scrabble Girl asks me how I liked it, and I tell her that I'm sick of May-December Hollywood romances. And I guess I've just finally decided that they aren't the thing for me personally, either.

PT's Longwayhome Top Ten Best Places:

11. Temppeliaukio Church, Helsinki
10. New Reichstag dome, Berlin
 9. Barguzin Museum, Barguzin, Buryatia, Russia
 8. Big Buddha, Todaiji, Nara, Japan
 7. San Francisco
 6. Russian State Zoological Museum, St. Petersburg
 5. Pacific Ocean south of Amatignak Island, Alaska
 4. Jokkmokk, Sweden
 3. Junji's Bar, Tokyo
 2. Lake Baikal
 1. The Copper River, Alaska

Tonight, final night on board, final, excellent show by blues great Irma Thomas in the Queen's Room, final fraction of a degree of our 360, and I have finally nearly forgotten about George Bush, Florida, and the Supreme Court.

And I'm really wishing I hadn't said that thing about the movie to Scrabble Girl.

December 20, South of Long Island

7:15 A.M. Sailing into a stiff, frigid breeze, traces of snow and ice on the decks. The tropical ocean weather of most of the crossing has been replaced by a cold continental blast, a friendly greeting for the ninety percent or so of the passengers who seem to have spent the entire crossing indoors but who will likely now come out and watch our approach to New York Harbor. So far, only James and I and a few other foolish souls are out on deck. There's a thin sliver of land off the starboard bow, and soon dim, gray spikes and tall oblongs emerge behind it—Wow! Manhattan, rising behind Queens and Brooklyn! The vision I had on the cliffs of Ireland, come to life.

The ship slows and a pilot boat pulls up alongside, then falls away. We're back within the orbit of the United States of America, thrusters firing, gravity pulling us in. Prepare for reentry.

The dreary high-rises of Rockaway rise up and pass, and I have a flash-back to the *Antonina Nezhdanova*, now almost three months ago. Big metal skeletons and swoops of white and black appear on the shore, but they're not the dilapidated cranes and antennae of Vladivostok—they're the roller coasters and Ferris wheels of Coney Island. We're surrounded now by a growing flock of other ships paddling in and out of New York Harbor, and the deck is now jammed with the whole cast of characters from the last in our six-month series of ephemeral communities, and the flashbacks are to the *Matanuska*, deck jammed with its cast of characters snapping pictures of eagles, glaciers, and whales, and the *Pacific Champion* threading the needle into Pusan Harbor, and now the *Pacific Champion* sailing under the bridges of San Francisco Bay, because suddenly we're under the Verrazano-Narrows Bridge, and the ship's huge red and black stack against the bridge's silver and black span is an awesome sight, but this feels very different from our passage under those other bridges—that was all about leaving everything I knew and loved behind and a whole ocean and world of uncertainty lay ahead and it was the middle of the night and nearly silent and we were nearly alone and I was awash in heartbreak and excitement, but here the excitement and ambivalence are all about returning, closing this 25,000-mile circle, coming home, starting over, beginning some sort of new life in a place that's meant that for so many millions of people—New York Harbor, Manhattan, America. And here's the harbor, the Statue of Liberty, the Staten Island Ferry, and over there the bricks and stone of Governor's Island and Brooklyn Heights, and now right in front of us the steel and glass of lower Manhattan and the twin towers of the World Trade Center, and now the Hudson River and the West Village and Chelsea, and after a week of slowly unfolding nothingness beyond the rails of the ship, it's all suddenly coming so fast and I'm trying to take it all in and also keep connected to this freezing crowd and my new friends and there's a tremendous buzz and energy and I'm elated and not at all ready for this to be over and now we have slowed nearly to a stop, and the bow has pulled even with the pier at 49th Street, and a little squad of tugs has gone to work spinning the massive ship slowly on its central axis, nudging it into its slip, and James and I head below to finish our packing, and suddenly the interior of the vessel that I've gotten to know so well seems new and unfa-miliar all over again—stateroom doors wide open, halls littered with bags and linen carts, lounges and restaurants deserted, stairwells jammed with people—and we have said our goodbyes to Scrabble Girl and her family, to Irma and her band, to our dinner companions for the last week, and have made arrangements to meet up with others here in New York tomorrow, and we're through the cattle chute off the boat and suddenly surrounded by New York accents, and we're up on the parking lot on top of the pier and getting our first full view of the behemoth that has been our home for the past week and carried us across the Atlantic and brought us full circle, and I'm thinking that there's no better place to touch down from a trip around the world than New York, the world itself—minus Lake Baikal—in 300 square miles, and that I still don't know exactly where my home is here in the U.S., but I have no doubt that this is my home, no matter how much I'm drawn to other places, no matter how restless I am, no matter what happens with Bush and Cheney running the country, and James and I look at each other and we grin exhausted and exhilarated grins and we give each other a hug and we don't say much at all as we head up 49th Street to the A train downtown.

THE GREAT BAIKAL CHAIN

August, 2004

The world only spins forward. We will be citizens.
The Time is now.

—Tony Kushner,
Angels in America, Part Two: Perestroika

The Great Baikal Chain

*In which, four years later, the author returns to Baikal,
helps build a hiking trail, and reconsiders what's possible*

August 3, 2004, St. Petersburg, Russia

Have some vodka! (You know, you still cannot drink the water here.) Just a
little—a toast to our visitors! (Some people in the church now, they refuse even
to use the holy water, because, you know, it's really just ordinary water, and it's
polluted.) One more small glass—to friends from many nations! To writing!
To art! (But this makes other people angry—"It is holy water," they say, "it cannot
be polluted!") Just a touch more—*choot-choot*! To Lake Baikal!

•

August 10, Baikalsk

There's a thin swath of freshly cut dirt that slices through the wooded hillside
along the Babkha River a little ways outside of town, and stretched along the
far end of it are maybe two dozen people, maybe fifteen to fifty years old, men

and women, chopping at stumps and roots, unearthing boulders, filling holes, leveling, tamping, smoothing, and with each passing hour pushing the new Babkha Trail a little farther up into the Khamar-Daban Mountains on the southern shore of Lake Baikal, and one of them, a linguistics student from Moscow with a slender frame and a keen and thoughtful glimmer in her eyes, looks up from the meter-wide swath of fresh earth at her feet and flashes a satisfied grin. "What I like here," she declares—her name is Lena—"is womens and mens working equally! Not like in Moscow, for example. Here I can dig, I can saw— same as men!"

Of the dozen or so women on our work crew, Lena seems most enthusiastic about the work itself—getting dirty and sweaty, spending day after day at the always plodding and sometimes grueling task of reordering this small ribbon of earth. But Lena didn't come to Siberia just to find a rare taste of gender-equal physical labor. She came to help build a future for her country's great lake.

"I feel better that I can see people here who cares about Baikal," she says, her face illuminated by a beam of yellow August sun slipping through the canopy of poplar and fir. "Not only Russians, but Americans and other nationalities. Lake Baikal is epitome of Siberia. I come here by train. It takes me four days, but it's worth it. This place is very spiritual and very energetic, and when I came here and went to see Baikal Lake, I feel something special. When you touch the water, something like wind blows in your head."

I knew I had to come back. The book needed it. I needed it. But I couldn't come back just to see more of the lake, ask more questions, selfishly soak up more experiences. I already had plenty of mental pictures, and this time I wanted to leave more than footprints.

A couple of years after our encounter in Buryatia, I saw Andrei Suknev at a gathering at Gary Cook's house in Berkeley. We greeted each other with the big smiles and embrace of people who'd shared something memorable but who never figured on seeing each other again. We exchanged photographs and updates on James, Igor, and Andrei's family, and then he handed me a little brochure with big black lettering—Большая Байкальская Тропа—*Bolshaia Baikalskaia Tropa*. "We're starting to build trail!" he announced. "With volunteers, in different places around lake. You should come help!"

I'd never really expected that Andrei's *pirozhki* in the sky idea of four years ago would ever amount to anything, and I was still skeptical that it would get very far. But I promised him that if he really started to build the Great Baikal Trail, I'd come and be part of it.

August 11, Baikalsky Nature Reserve, Tankhoi

We're plucking blueberries from thigh-high bushes and ducking under huge spider webs hanging low over the trail, walking, and talking, again, me and Andrei.

"It was a big dream," he says, as we stop by the trunk of a huge old poplar, charred and split by a lightning strike. "Several time I try to start this project, but we need four years, and we need some conditions and then to meet right people."

The path unfurls through a rolling broad-leaf forest peppered with Siberian stone pines, larches, and silver fir and inhabited, Andrei says, by at least several hundred sables, those bearers of the golden fleece, still hanging on in these old woods. The air is as clear and dry and sweet and warm as a June day in Maine, and it fills every few minutes with the distant rumble of a train clattering along the Trans-Siberian tracks down by the lake, a couple of kilometers away.

The nearly four years since the train first brought me and James here seem now to have passed like nothing at all. Certainly Andrei seems unchanged—except, perhaps, that he's a bit more animated than when we first met. Because it's summertime? Because we're more comfortable with each other this time around? Because the work of his last four years is starting to pay off? Since that first encounter, he's given up his teaching position in Ulan-Ude, cut back on his guiding, and devoted himself almost exclusively to the GBT—the Great Baikal Trail project—raising money, finding partners, recruiting volunteers, writing reports. "Someday I would like to work on trail itself!" he says with a wry smile as we resume our hike. "Volunteers are doing real trail, and I am doing paper for trail!"

This particular stretch of trail was built a year ago, during the first summer of the project. It rises in the Baikalsky Zapovednik, the southernmost of Baikal's three strict nature reserves, about seventy kilometers east of Baikalsk and the Babkha Trail, and winds alongside the Osinovka River, a clear, shallow stream that cuts a jagged course through forest floor and bedrock on its way to the lake. Like the Babkha Trail, when it's finished the Osinovka Trail will roughly follow its namesake river up into the mountains, loop across the face of the Khamar-Daban range, and descend back to the lakefront several kilometers farther east, about a two-day hike. And eventually, in Andrei's grand scheme, the two trails will be drawn together in a network of several thousand kilometers, wrapping around the entire lake like a great ribbon.

Actually, Andrei tells me, the idea for something like the Great Baikal Trail has been kicking around for a lot more than four years. He and his friend Igor first dreamt up the notion of a network of hiking trails around Baikal as teenagers a quarter of a century or so ago. But it goes back further still, to a proposal by the local naturalist and author Oleg Kirillovich Gusev, who, Andrei says, once walked the lake's entire 2,000-kilometer circumference without benefit of a trail. "Nobody understood him thirty-five years ago," Andrei says. "Even now, there's lots of difficulties to explain to Russian people, what means trail building." Why bother to build a trail, people ask him, when you can follow one made by bears or by hunters, or just cut your own? But postcommunist Russia is slowly developing an appetite for new ideas, and Andrei and his colleagues have found a far more receptive audience recently when they've made their pitch for the environmental and economic benefits of a system of hiking trails linked with a network of bed and breakfasts, local guides, and other small businesses—a locally owned, small-scale tourism industry. The idea has won enough local support for crews to begin work in more than a dozen spots around the lake, and by the end of this second summer a total of nearly 500 volunteers and a few paid staff, from Russia and a dozen or so other countries, will have built or upgraded more than 200 kilometers of trail throughout the Baikal basin.

But Russia's growing openness to change isn't the only thing that's finally made it possible to start building the Great Baikal Trail. In the last few years, Andrei and several colleagues have traveled abroad to study everything from trail design and maintenance to fundraising and nonprofit management. And they've brought a sort of pragmatic idealism to their work that's not especially typical of Russia.

"It's a kind of ideology for Baikal," Andrei says of the GBT's approach. The organization explicitly links protection of the Baikal environment to the health of the region's communities, asserting to anyone who'll listen that neither can thrive unless the other does, too. It focuses its efforts on sites around the lake where it has the most local cooperation and the greatest opportunities for success, rather than on some predetermined list of priorities. And it will work with just about anyone who shares even some of its goals, creating a sort of grand coalition of supporters who might otherwise seem to have nothing whatsoever in common. The GBT may, for instance, be the only project ever supported by both Greenpeace and the Rotary Club.

Andrei and I have been talking almost unbroken for three hours or so, since we left the Babkha worksite and headed east in his white Toyota—he's got only one afternoon to spend with me before he has to get back to Ulan-Ude and his paperwork, and I have four years' worth of questions. But every now and then we stop for a minute or two and just look, listen, and breathe, remind ourselves of where we are, and why. Here the Osinovka turns from blue to white as it spills over a ledge of fractured brown stone into a deep, black pool, pauses a moment to gather itself, and then resumes its rush toward Baikal. Even this little river, no less than the great Selenga, is Baikal in the making, a small strand in the weave of the world's great lake. "You can't divide it," Andrei says. "Watershed of Baikal and lake itself, it's one body"

It's all connected—this, it seems to me, is what the GBT project is really about, the fundamental principle underlying its "ideology." When people don't see or understand these connections, both they and the lake suffer for it. When they do understand them, well—therein lies the hope. Andrei may be mired in the project's details, but he remains very aware of this big picture. "Trail is not just trail," he tells me. "It is opportunity to communicate with people, to strengthen people. It is chain."

The Great Baikal Chain. . . . Linking the fate of Baikal's human and natural communities. Connecting isolated communities around the lake with each other through the ongoing conversation about routes and work projects. Drawing local residents into the region's fledgling democratic processes as they debate the fate of development plans and land transfers. Connecting residents to the outside world as visitors come to help build the trails and hike on them. And linking those outsiders directly with the fate of the lake through their work, their dollars, and their own advocacy on its behalf.

It's a wonderful metaphor, the Great Baikal Chain. And, potentially, a powerful reality. Already, Andrei tells me, human links in this chain are having an impact beyond the growing number of trail kilometers being built. Local people involved in the effort have helped fight planned industrial projects that could have compromised the local and regional environment. And they've won, at least for the time being.

The trail is a chain. And the chain, Andrei tells me as we turn and head back toward the *zapovednik*'s headquarters and his car, in which he'll take me back to my work crew in Baikalsk—the chain is forged into something even more powerful. "It is," he says, "a kind of shield."

•

Report of the Bureau of the World Heritage Committee, United Nations Educational, Scientific and Cultural Organization (UNESCO), to the full Committee, April 2002:

XII.26 . . . The report from UNESCO/IUCN Monitoring Mission to this site noted that "the pollution load of the Selenga River is apparently still considerable. . . ."

. . . The UNESCO/IUCN Monitoring Mission noted a continuous decline in the Baikal seal population. . . .

. . . Pollution from the town of Severobaikalsk . . . remains an issue of serious concern to the integrity of the site. . . .

... *The Monitoring Mission report also mentioned that satellite imaging shows that considerable clear-cuttings went on in this area after the inscription of Lake Baikal in 1996. This issue remains unclear.* ...

XII.27 *IUCN noted [a few additional issues]: atmospheric pollution; fishing; state of reserves and artificial changes of the water table.* ...

XII.29 ... *The Bureau adopted the following recommendation for action by the 26th session of the Committee:*

"The Committee notes that there remain serious concerns in relation to the state of conservation of this site, particularly in relation to pollution impacts, including from the Baikalsk Pulp and Paper Mill, the lack of progress with the Federal Law 'On the Protection of Lake Baikal' ... and uncertainties about gas exploration and exploitation in the Selenga Delta. Having considered the report provided by the State Party and the comments by IUCN, the Committee decides to include Lake Baikal on the List of World Heritage in Danger. ...

The Environmental Situation of Lake Baikal, Greenpeace International, August 2003:

Lake Baikal is generally still intact, but under serious threat. ... *Phytoplankton species composition is changing and its biomass is increasing.* ... *The temperature of the upper water layer [is] increasing.* ...

... *Since the current administration came to power, enforcement of environmental regulations has weakened from an already poor and inadequate baseline and the scale of illegal practices appears to have increased.* ...

... *Research directed at the Lake environment is not intensive enough to allow many changes to be identified in a timely manner. It is likely that most change will be identified only retrospectively, after damage has been done.* ...

Tahoe-Baikal Institute Policy Brief: Lake Baikal Watershed, January 2004:

... *Agricultural pollution is assumed to be significant [but] data on its impacts has been sparse. Pollutants such as suspended solids, nutrients, organics, toxic organics, human pathogens, and inorganic salts are known to exist from the intensive agriculture and husbandry practiced within the watershed.* ...

... *Fishing and hunting [are] becoming bigger problems in centralized areas along the lakeshore, and within the larger watershed* ...

... The industrial sector remains the major contributor to Baikal's air pol-
lution, [but] the transportation sector ... is playing an increasingly significant
role....

... Recent legislation allowing housing developments around the shores
could bring a huge influx of development pressures on Baikal's shoreline. Once
constructed, it would be impossible to then reverse development trends towards
conservation priorities.

Despite the difficult institutional and economic situation within the water-
shed, progress has been made in protecting Lake Baikal and its watershed over
the last 15 years....

•

In 2003, the Russian government reiterated its long-standing pledge to help
clean up the Baikalsk Pulp and Paper Mill, and in 2004 it guaranteed a World
Bank loan of twenty million euros to the mill's owners to help finance the
conversion to a closed-loop production system. The promised completion
date is 2006. Or, perhaps, 2010, or 2015, depending on the source. Reports also
differ on what the converted plant would actually produce. In any case, work
has not yet begun, and plant critics are skeptical that the latest promises are
any more likely to be kept than those of the past. In 2003, Greenpeace Russia
and the Baikal Environmental Wave erected a "Failed Promises Monument"
on the highway near the plant. The monument was defaced, restored, and
defaced again.

There are rumors and reports of widespread illegal building on the shores of
Baikal, of plans for big tourist resort developments, including in supposedly
protected areas, and of big land transfers from the government to developers,
relatives of politicians, and other well-connected people. It's hard to know
what's true and what isn't. Russia is awash in rumors. Certainly Listvianka and
Bolshie Koty have seen a boom in construction of tourist facilities and second homes.

Since 2000, the world's growing demand for oil has emerged as a major threat
to Baikal. Russia's strong economic growth in recent years has been due almost
entirely to oil exports, and the government has announced plans to build a
pipeline from oil fields west of Baikal through the lake's watershed and eastern

Siberia to the Sea of Japan. Local opposition helped scuttle a proposed route through a national park on Baikal's southern shore, but the alternate route will still take the pipeline through a seismically active region of the watershed to the north, where it will traverse sensitive wetlands and fifty tributary rivers, including the Upper Angara.

Meanwhile, many observers now believe that the biggest threat to the Baikal ecosystem is climate change, driven by the burning of oil and other fossil fuels. The latest climate models from the Intergovernmental Panel on Climate Change, the leading international authority on the subject, predict that by the end of the century average temperatures in northern Asia will rise by somewhere between five and nine degrees Celsius, or nine and sixteen degrees Fahrenheit. Scientists predict that this warming will lead to a further reduction in the duration of winter ice cover by anywhere from two weeks to two months, "with a probable absence of complete freezing of Baikal in the second half of this century." Even the low end of these projections would have profound consequences for Baikal's ecosystem.

There's talk as well—although still just talk—of a pipeline to deliver Baikal water to increasingly parched China, and perhaps beyond. The prospect is reported to have currency among some local scientists, and even Andrei Suknev says it might not be such a bad idea. "Maybe it's better conclusion than fighting with China," he says of Russia's historic rival. "Just drink! Please, drink!"

After more than two years of discussion, the UNESCO World Heritage Committee has neither adopted nor rejected the recommendation to add Baikal to its list of World Heritage Sites in danger.

Olga Baksheeva continues to work as a translator, interpreter, occasional crack tour guide, and source of wry observations on Russian life for visiting scientists, officials, businesspeople, and journalists, and continues to travel outside of Russia whenever possible with her now nearly sixteen-year-old daughter. And each time she comes home to Russia, she remembers what she realized the first time she returned from abroad: "Oh, life doesn't have to be like this."

Should the latest promises fail and the government again be looking for new ideas for how to comply with the Law of Baikal and convert the Baikalsk paper mill to "other operations," Olga has three ideas: an international paper-making university, a museum of the papermaking industry, a museum of how not to build a factory.

Sergei and Tania are divorced.

Andrei has no news on Lena, Masha, and Pana, the Old Believers, but if they're still around, I'm sure they're still singing.

Evgeny Starostenko has left the Baikalsk Business Incubator and has gone over to work for the paper company, trying to help them expand into new businesses.

Olga Gamerova continues to run the incubator with her husband, Alexander Tokmokov, but after more than five years it has spawned only five successful businesses, and Alexander says they have come to a difficult real-ization: "Not a lot of people could handle running new business in Baikalsk." The incubator is now pinning its hopes almost entirely on ecotourism, and is a partner with the Great Baikal Trail organization in the Babkha Trail project. Alexander is also hoping that the U.S. government will send a stronger message to the Russian government about the need to carefully protect places like Baikal. "Our government listens to your government," he says.

Here's some of what our government has been saying: "Clear Skies" means allow-ing more air pollution. "Healthy Forests" means allowing more logging. Climate change is still too unproven to warrant action. *The Arctic National Wildlife Refuge, too, must work.* . . .

You no longer have to run a gauntlet of construction hazards to get to the office of Jennie Sutton and the Baikal Environmental Wave. The building is finished, and it actually looks quite good. But it seems that, for Sutton, that's just about all that looks good these days. Her pessimism of four years ago seems to have given way to bitterness and near despair.

Yes, she says, there have been some victories. She's proud of the local efforts to turn back both the oil pipeline through Tunkinsky National Park and the plan to explore for oil in the Selenga River delta. And after four years, she says, President Putin finally bowed to pressure and revoked his decree dissolving the state environmental committee. But for Sutton, each of these is a somewhat hollow victory. The pipeline route was merely moved farther away from the lake, not out of the watershed altogether. The Selenga petroleum plan may well return, she says. And the new federal environment agency remains just a promise.

And Sutton's growing list of grievances goes beyond the unresolved challenges to the lake. It includes an imperious government that harasses non-profit organizations like hers; the lack of serious, independent media; and the growing apathy and lack of responsibility of ordinary citizens. "I'm sure you'll find people being very proud of their lake," she says about Baikal. "I don't know whether it's those people, or maybe their neighbors, that throw all their rubbish onto the shores or the lake itself, but it's a fact that these two things go parallel.

"Quite frankly," she continues, "the sickness is not just with Russia. There are few countries in the world that can say, 'We're doing our best to preserve our planet for future generations.' The very reactionary position of the president of the U.S.A. is an encouragement for reactionary policy for Russia. So I wouldn't want to isolate Russia—I think things are going from bad to worse in the world as a whole."

And yet she continues with her work.

"Maybe I keep at it only for my own self-respect," she says. "I try to keep in mind what Gandhi said—at least in the movie!—'All empires come to an end.'"

Anatoly Malevsky has left the federal government and, according to a report in the Toronto *Globe and Mail*, has lost his faith in both the government's commitment to environmental protection and the future of Baikal. "Over the last few years," he told the paper in 2002, "we have seen a worsening of the ecological situation across the country.... Nowadays, enterprises can cause air pollution and water pollution and not pay at all."

Recent studies have found significantly lower levels of organochlorines in Baikal seals and fish, suggesting a decrease in local emissions of the chemicals. But these reports don't seem to have encouraged Evgeniia Tarasova, who continues her own work tracing the movement of pollutants through the Baikal ecosystem. I've been unable to set up a meeting with her, but Olga tells me that she's more pessimistic about Baikal than ever.

Boris Pavlov says that human impacts on the shore of the lake have gotten worse and that some of its near-shore ecosystems have been completely destroyed; that the mix of phytoplankton species in the deep-water system may be changing due to global warming; that funding and staffing for Baikal research have been cut drastically and that the Russian government is failing to meet its obligations to the United Nations to protect Baikal, but that he is nonetheless more optimistic than he was in 2000 about the lake's fate. The deep-water body of the lake, he now believes, will be fine—as long as the climate doesn't change markedly. Which, he also acknowledges, might already be happening. So what accounts for his new optimism? Maybe it's the weather. "The thing is," he tells me as he scales fish in his garden in Bolshie Koty, "last time when you were here, the day was gloomy, winter was coming. Today's a bright summer day—it makes its difference!"

Something has happened to Slava Maksimov, Sr. The animated scientist of four years ago, who would live forever alongside his beloved lake now walks with a halting, unsteady gait, a hollow look in his eyes, matted hair, and a tattered shirt missing all but its top button. His lab has lost virtually all of its funding, and he says that he and his wife now live mostly on what they can grow and catch in Bolshie Koty. He speaks of his own mortality. He is, people say, "in and out." But he remains proud and optimistic. "All transformations are just a test of our faculties," he tells me, "and we have overcome. Life is meaningful for me, and I will have many wonderful memories when the time comes for me to pass away." Nor has the professor lost his faith in Baikal. On this day, he remembers our last meeting four years ago down to the last snowflake, and in a laboratory of empty beakers and idle equipment, he repeats his mantra from that more hopeful time: "*Absoliutno blagopoluchnoe ozero Baikal!*"

Since returning with me to the U.S., James has served lobster and steamers in a New England seafood shack, worked as a resident naturalist in huts along the Appalachian Trail in New Hampshire and as an on-board scientist on a sailing journey from Tahiti to Hawaii, taught marine biology to school kids on California's Catalina Island and Washington's Olympic Peninsula, and become an instructor in natural building techniques in Oregon. He declined an invitation to return with me to Siberia. He, at least, has moved on with his life.

I have more or less settled back in Boston, channeled my penchant for rambling around and thinking too much into something approaching an independent living, and picked up the unofficial mantle of *Sibling in Charge of Generational Transition, Family Relations, and Land Preservation*. In the last four years, I have learned a lot about probate, real estate, conservation restrictions, the publishing industry, and temporomandibular joint syndrome and other interesting ways in which the body channels stress. And in the last week I have learned that those shovels with the handles made of branches that I saw workers at the Baikalsk paper mill carrying on my first visit to Baikal work just fine. And that it's possible to have grown up in the soul-crushing town of Baikalsk without having your soul crushed. In a few weeks I will travel from Irkutsk to Yaroslavl, outside of Moscow, and meet a Russian woman named Lutsia who will teach me three words that she says are vital to understanding Russians and Russia: *terpenie*, patience and forbearance; *smirenie*, humility; and *nadezhda*, hope.

The Red Sox, under new management, have continued their old ways, coming within five outs of vanquishing the hated Yankees in the fight for the 2003 American League pennant, only to have the weight of history once again prove unbearable. They are again in a heated race this summer and, I have just learned via the Internet at a computer center on Lenin Street in Irkutsk, have gone for broke in their eighty-six-year quest for a World Series championship by dumping their big-hitting shortstop and picking up two gold-glove infielders and a fleet-footed outfielder, a daring move that cuts against long-entrenched Fenway philosophy by sacrificing offense for defense and speed but will no doubt bring nothing but more tears and ignominy at the close of the 2004 season.

But what would we do if they won, anyway? We'd have to change our whole way of thinking about the world.

•

August 23, 2004, Irkutsk

Still We Believe. It's the name of a movie made about last year's Red Sox season and the fans who suffered through this latest cycle of renewed hope and crushing disappointment. I haven't seen it. I am not a masochist.

It might also be the name of a movie, if one were to be made, about the Great Baikal Trail organization.

With a few exceptions, the signs and trends at Baikal are no better in 2004 than they were in 2000, and in some cases they're worse. The GBT folks know this.

Still We Believe.

As with the Sox, if a long and sorrowful history is any guide, things will not improve; Russia will not soon become an enlightened liberal democracy with strong environmental values.

Still We Believe.

A rational person, a person who knows what's good for himself, would turn his attention to something more likely to succeed, would save himself the grief of failure.

Still We Believe.

Belief is still a difficult thing for me, accepting that something is true without any demonstrable proof, maintaining hope when all evidence and experience suggest that none is warranted. Maybe I'm a bad Red Sox fan. Certainly, I would be a bad Russian.

Ariadna Reida is a good Russian. As much as Andrei Suknev in Ulan-Ude and Gary Cook in San Francisco, Ariadna is responsible for making the Great Baikal Trail happen. She's a genial, thirty-fiveish biologist, a graduate of Irkutsk State University who has also spent a good deal of time in the U.S., getting a degree in environmental studies and working for nonprofits, including Gary Cook's Baikal Watch. With her range of knowledge and experience, she's a rarity in Russia—a perfect nonprofit manager, able to jump effortlessly back and forth between mission and logistics, between helping shape the vision of the organization and helping carry it out. She also seems to be unruffled when things don't work out exactly as planned, which is a good thing, since, this being Russia, a good deal has not gone as planned over the last two summers. Projects have been canceled, tools and food have been left in the wrong places, local leaders have proven unreliable, volunteers who speak no Russian have gotten off at the wrong train station and found no one to meet them (that was me), donated tents have leaked, cranky foreign volunteers have demanded vegan meals or have refused to pay what they'd promised to cover the costs of the operation. And yet neither this cascade of small failures nor the huge social and political obstacles seem to leave more than small dents in her confidence. She believes in the ultimate success of both the trail project and the grander goal of protecting Lake Baikal.

"Yes, sometimes I'm pessimistic!" Ariadna tells me on a gray August morning in the GBT's office at Irkutsk State University, the floor covered with drying tents and the walls with maps and photographs. "It's difficult, it really is! But why I feel confident? Because I'm working with wonderful people, and they have very good understanding of what they are doing, and why they are doing that. And we are working with young people, who will in ten years be in charge of things. They are not only biologists or geographers. They will be managers, people who do law work. We are building up the army of people who would protect the land by their own initiative."

I keep hearing on this trip, as I did four years ago, about the New Russians, the cynical young entrepreneurs and opportunists who have soaked up Russia's wealth in the helter-skelter post-1991 economy and hoarded as much of it as possible for themselves—yet another reason to have little faith in the future of this place. But it seems that Ariadna is another kind of New Russian, one of those who for the first time in generations have been able to go abroad to gather skills, experience, and perspective and then to bring them home to help make a difference for more than just themselves, who've had the opportunity to meld some of the best knowledge and ideas that the West has to offer with the hope and idealism that somehow survives in old Mother Russia. It's heartening and inspiring to meet her, to know that there are Russians like Ariadna.

For my part, I think I'll always be more the Jennie Sutton type—I see problems that look insurmountable, and I do what I can only so I can live with myself, and because I know that small victories do make a difference in people's lives. That's why I came back to be a part of the Great Baikal Trail project. That's why I've spent a huge chunk of my life writing this book. But in the big picture? I look at the challenge of saving Lake Baikal, one of nature's most astonishing creations, and I look at Russia, just about as much of a mess of a place as it's always been, and it just doesn't seem possible.

And then I look at Ariadna, and Andrei, and all the other dedicated and resourceful Russians I've met on these two journeys, and I wonder....

"There is one poem in Russia," Ariadna tells me as we wrap up our conversation and I prepare to leave the GBT office, Irkutsk, and Siberia. "It says that 'you cannot understand Russia with a common mind, you cannot measure with common measures, the only thing you can do about Russia is to believe in it.' So I really believe in Russia. I think we have really strong people, smart people, and now we have younger generation who can really stand for where they live and what they want to do here. So I'm optimistic about the future.

"Sometimes I'm like, no, it's impossible to change anything! But then you look at people around you and it's like, no, we can do it."

The world only spins forward. We will be citizens. The time is now.

Afterword

In October 2004, the Boston Red Sox swept the St. Louis Cardinals 4-0 to win the World Series for the first time in eighty-six years.

In January 2006, Russian Federation President Vladimir Putin signed a law tightening regulation of nongovernmental organizations. The law requires NGOs to provide detailed reports on their programs and finances and allows the government to shut down or curtail the activities of any groups that it deems to be involved in political activity or otherwise threaten the national interest. President Putin said the law was needed to ferret out extremist groups and keep foreign money out of Russian politics, and government officials said its requirements are roughly equivalent to similar laws in Europe and the United States. But the new law doesn't define such key terms as "political activity," and the leaders of many NGOs feared that it could open the door to a crackdown on government critics and independent activism. The law, the *New York Times* editorialized, "is broad enough to make all unofficial groups permanently vulnerable to the Kremlin's whims."

Shortly before President Putin signed the bill, one of his senior advisors resigned, saying that Russia had "ceased to be politically free."

In April 2006, Putin reversed a government decision to build a stretch of the new Siberian oil pipeline within a kilometer of Baikal's northern shore. The reversal came just weeks after the government had rejected the findings of its own scientific panel that this latest proposed route was dangerously close to the lake and vulnerable to earthquakes. That decision had prompted a warning to Putin from the chairwoman of the UNESCO World Heritage Committee that building the pipeline so close to the lake would result in Baikal being put on the list of World Heritage sites in danger. Soon thereafter, Putin ordered that the pipeline be rerouted at least forty kilometers to the north of the lake. In announcing his decision, Putin said "If there is at least a tiny chance of polluting Baikal, we, thinking of future generations, must do everything not only to minimize this threat, but to exclude it."

Following Putin's order, the pipeline company Transneft selected a new route that will take the pipeline roughly 400 kilometers to the north and out of the Baikal watershed.

By the end of the summer of 2006, nearly 1,500 volunteers from at least 18 countries had helped the Great Baikal Trail organization build or upgrade some 475 kilometers of hiking trails.

Acknowledgments

I n many ways, the long process of writing *Sacred Sea* unfolded much like that of the trip on which it's based. A modest idea treading familiar territory—in this case to produce a short radio documentary on Baikal—quickly ballooned into a notion for a far more ambitious journey into unknown terrain. The decision to pursue this bigger notion required a major leap of faith, followed by a good deal of fumbling around, a few targeted guesses, and an endless string of good luck. And the whole thing succeeded only because a host of people came forward to offer encouragement, advice, and resources.

I've tried to keep track of all of these people over the past few years. To those I've forgotten, I offer my sincere apologies and the faint hope that this book will garner enough recognition to someday warrant a second edition, in which I can make up for any omissions. For now, though, I offer my deepest gratitude to the following friends, colleagues, family members, and, before this project began, strangers. This book is your creation as much as mine.

If there is one person without whom this book almost certainly wouldn't exist, it is Clifford Mills, my original editor at Oxford University Press. Cliff believed in this project before I did. He rallied his organization behind it, provided invaluable guidance, patience, and prodding, and insisted that I share his unfailing confidence in both the book and myself. Once he had this book in his sights, Cliff refused to let me talk myself out of writing it.

Support of a wholly different but equally invaluable kind came from what you might call the Thomson Family Foundation. My father Peter and my stepmother Elizabeth embraced this project as if I were delivering them a grandchild (although with a considerably longer gestation period), and they helped provide the resources to make sure that it was properly raised. Together with the modest legacy of my mother, Anne Pearmain Thomson, they enabled me to make this project my job for long stretches of time. Their spirit has imbued it from before the beginning, and their love and generosity made it possible. I could never thank them enough.

And then there is James, of course. You've read about him, and I don't need to say much more except to thank him for his adventurous spirit, his faith in and patience with his older brother, and his willingness to turn down that research assistant job that awaited him after graduation, as well as the use of his beautiful photographs.

Others who provided indispensable assistance from nearly beginning to end were Gary Cook, at Baikal Watch in San Francisco, and Olga Baksheeva, our guide and interpreter in Irkutsk. Gary was the springboard for our journey to Baikal, and Olga laid the foundation for the journalism at the heart of this book. I don't believe they've ever met, but together their fluency in the language, culture, issues, and logistical challenges of Russia and the Baikal region—not to mention their warmth and generosity of spirit—made the crucial difference between the personal lark of two brothers and something worth writing about.

The more than two dozen friends, colleagues, and professional critics who read or listened to various drafts or parts of the manuscript served as a sort of editorial board for *Sacred Sea*, and I'm indebted to all of them for their blunt comments, subtle insights, and kinds words, for challenging me to think differently about my choices at every step, and for generally helping to keep me sane and motivated. Among these ad hoc committee members were my friend and agent Karen Nazor and her husband, Peter Rutten; Kathy Brister, Gwen Shafer, Timothy Thomson, James Thomson, and Edith Buhs; Brad Land, Tracy Winn, and Catherine Sasanov; Susan Tweit and Betsy Leondar-Wright; Henry Aaron, Alan Garganus, Mort Horwitz, Lars Kallings, Soyini Madison, and Eduardo Rabossi; Gary Cook; and Mark Hertsgaard, David Baron, and Bill McKibben. Professors Fred J. Alsop III, Chris Gibson, Lev Yampolsky, Roman Zlotin, and Gregory C. Knight all lent their vital professional expertise as early outside readers for OUP, and Oxford's Jeremy Lewis brought fresh eyes and an open mind to the manuscript's final review and approval.

Several readers deserve particular gratitude. In the summer of 2002, George Hicks, Leslie Hummel, and Scott Klinger each asked to read the pile of words about Lake Baikal that I had created six months before, had failed to sell to any magazines and then had stuffed in a drawer, and each of them then told me that they thought it was the nucleus of a book. Without their interest and advice, I might've just stuffed it back in its drawer. And much later on, Chris Arnold, Jenny Schmidt, and Karen Polinsky all provided the invaluable combination of critical assessment and support that can only come from people who are at once close friends and trusted colleagues. Together, the three of them pulled me out of one very deep hole.

Finally, among readers, I am most deeply indebted to Marianne Moore and Thomas Hodge of Wellesley College and Laura Arnow of Oakland, California. I don't think that Professors Moore and Hodge, of the Wellesley biology and Russian departments, respectively, had any idea what to expect when I cold-called them, told them about my book project, and asked if they would share their reading lists for their class on Baikal. They nonetheless responded with more openness and generosity than I had a right to expect, offering me a treasure trove of source documents, volunteering their students as research assistants, and offering to review a late draft of the manuscript. Their reading list broadened and deepened my understanding of the science, history, and culture of the Baikal region beyond measure, and their detailed comments and corrections were absolutely vital to the ultimate credibility of this book. Laura Arnow, meanwhile, heard me read an early draft of the first chapter in a small northern California bookstore and made it her mission from then on to make sure that the rest of this stranger's book actually got written, and written well. Her comments on successive drafts were a litany of challenges to sharpen, clarify, focus, broaden, excise, and rethink. And along with her missionary zeal, she brought the knowledge of a professional naturalist, the experience of a seasoned traveler, and the wisdom of someone who understands the power of a good story.

I'm grateful, as well, for the advice and support of fellow journalists and writers Bill Allen, Bob Braile, Dan Glick, Barry Lopez, Sandy Tolan, Nancy Lord, Christy George, Bruce Gellerman, Steve Curwood, and Frank Allen.

And once it was started, *Sacred Sea* may well never have been completed without the generous support of the Common Counsel Foundation's Mesa Refuge, in Point Reyes Station, California; the MacDowell Colony, in Peterborough, New Hampshire; and the Rockefeller Foundation's Bellagio Study and Conference Center, in Bellagio, Italy. There may be nothing more valuable in the creative process than quiet time away from the distractions of home and in the company of others following similar pursuits, and together these three sanctuaries provided me fourteen weeks of this precious solitude and fellowship. I will always feel honored and privileged beyond words to have been among those chosen to join these communities.

The Writers' Room of Boston provided a similar haven here at home, a quiet place filled with other creative minds, with a door behind which I could shut the rest of the world. If writing this book was my job, the Writers' Room was my office. I'm grateful for the organization and indebted to those whose support helps keep it open and affordable. Every city should have such a place.

Thanks also to the dozens of other friends and strangers who contributed knowingly or otherwise to this endeavor, and whose friendship and generosity have helped make the last few years the most relentlessly remarkable and heartening of my life—from people like Stephan Franz, Pat Maholly, and Igor and Vera Biron, who welcomed a traveling stranger or two into their homes in Berlin, County Clare, and St. Petersburg, to Tom Menihan and James Hatfield, who contributed their artistic talents at considerably less than fair market value. After what I've received from them and all those previously mentioned, I owe the world an awfully big debt.

Finally, special thanks are due to my uncle John Thomson, a former journalist and avid reader and traveler, for his enthusiastic support; to my brother Bill Clift for his seasoned artist's perspective on my design for the book, to my sister Sandra Thomson for her encouragement and that copy that she gave me years ago of J.I. Rodale's *Synonym Finder*; and to my sister Gwendolyn Thomson, who once told me that I'd write a book someday, a notion that I immediately dismissed.

Illustration Credits

CHAPTER 6

p. 54   *Listening, Cold Place*, James Thomson, used by permission.
p. 60   *Ivolginsk Datsan*, James Thomson, used by permission.
p. 62   *Selenga River*, James Thomson, used by permission.
p. 65   *Lena, Masha, and Pana*, James Thomson, used by permission.

CHAPTER 7

p. 68   *Chivyrkuysky Gulf 1 and 2*, Peter Thomson.

CHAPTER 8

p. 76   *River Barguzin*, Boris Konstantinovich Utekhin, 1958. Reproduction courtesy of Gelos Auction House, Ltd., Moscow.

CHAPTER 9

p. 85   *Barguzin Sky*, Peter Thomson.
p. 89   *Sergei and Tania Filippov*, Peter Thomson.

CHAPTER 10

p. 93   *The Lake Shore Limited*, James Thomson, used by permission.
p. 99   *Inside Passage*, James Thomson, used by permission.
p. 106   *Copper River Beach*, James Thomson, used by permission.

CHAPTER 11

p. 107   *Pier 60, San Francisco*, Peter Thomson.
p. 111   *Pacific Ocean, September 2000*, James Thomson, used by permission.
p. 113   *Crew's Mess 1*, Peter Thomson.
p. 114   *Crew's Mess 2*, James Thomson, used by permission.

CHAPTER 12

p. 118   *Big Buddha*, Peter Thomson.

CHAPTER 13

p. 128   *Power in the East*, James Thomson, used by permission.
p. 131   *Sea of Japan, September 2000*, James Thomson, used by permission.
p. 136   *Vladivostok Terminal*, James Thomson, used by permission.

CHAPTER 14

p. 139   *Sleeping Car, Train Number One*, James Thomson, used by permission.
p. 141   *Ussuri Tiger, 50 Kopeks, 1977*, USSR Ministry of Communication.

p. 147   *Bunkmates, Hard Class*, James Thomson, used by permission.
p. 151   *Sliudianka Station, 1905*, unknown photographer, image courtesy of Mikhail Krainov.

Chapter 15

p. 153   *Irkutsk Window*, Peter Thomson.
p. 155   *Anton Chekhov, 30 Kopeks, 1940*, USSR Ministry of Communication.
p. 160   *Uri Gagarin, 10 Rubles, 2001*, Bank of Russia.
p. 163   *Irkutsk House*, Peter Thomson.

Chapter 16

p. 171   *Baikalsk Pulp and Paper Mill*, James Thomson, used by permission.
p. 175   *Industry, 10 Kopeks*, USSR Ministry of Communication.
p. 185   *Mural, Baikalsk Pulp and Paper Mill*, James Thomson, used by permission.

Chapter 17

p. 189   *Dirty Train Window, Baikal Shore*, Peter Thomson.

Chapter 18

p. 199   *2,3,7,8-Tetrachlorodibenzo-p-dioxin*, Peter Thomson.
p. 215   *Anatoly Malevsky*, James Thomson, used by permission.

Chapter 19

p. 219   *Hydrobiology Laboratory, Bolshie Koty*, Peter Thomson.
p. 223   *Boris Pavlov*, James Thomson, used by permission.
p. 229   *Slava Maksimov, Sr.*, James Thomson, used by permission.

Chapter 20

p. 235   *Baikal Water label*.
p. 244   *ALWAYS READY!*, Young Pioneer organization of the Soviet Union.
p. 246   *Moscow Metro, 10 Kopecs, 1938*, USSR Ministry of Communication.
p. 247   *Red Square*, James Thomson, used by permission.

Chapter 21

p. 252   *Wall, County Clare*, Peter Thomson.
p. 262   *New York Harbor, December 2000*, James Thomson, used by permission.

Epilogue

p. 265   *Late-Day Light, North of Listvianka*, James Hatfield, used by permission.

Source Notes and Further Reading

The primary sources for *Sacred Sea* are recorded interviews, notes and journals, and correspondence conducted during the author's travels between July and December 2000 and in the months before and years since. Sources of corroborating information, general background, emerging or still unsettled science, further quotations and citations, and other obscure bits of information are listed below.

PRINCIPAL SOURCES

Baikal Web World, Comprehensive Data About Lake Baikal in Siberia (Irkutsk). [Online.] Accessed October 12, 2005. Available: www.bww.irk.ru/.

Belt, Don, and Sarah Leen, "Russia's Lake Baikal: The World's Great Lake," *National Geographic*, vol. 181, no. 6 (June 1992), pp. 2-39.

Billington, James H., *The Icon and the Axe: An Interpretive History of Russian Culture* (New York: Alfred A. Knopf, 1966).

Burgis, Mary J., and Pat Morris, *The Natural History of Lakes* (New York: Cambridge University Press, 1987).

Damstra, Terri, Sue Barlow, Aake Bergman, Robert Kavlock, and Glen Van Der Kraak, eds., *Global Assessment of the State-of-the-Science of Endocrine Disruptors* (Geneva: World Health Organization International Programme on Chemical Safety, 2002). [Online.] Accessed December 4, 2004. Available: www.who.int/ipcs/publications/new_issues/endocrine_disruptors/en/.

Danilov-Danilyan, V.I., A.F. Poryadin, A.K. Tulokhonov, and A.A. Shekhovtsov, eds., *Annual Report of the Governmental Commission on Baikal Lake, 1998: Lake Baikal Preservation and Efficient Natural Resources Management in the Baikal Region* (Moscow: Russian Federation State Center of Ecological Problems, 1999).

Dinar, Ariel, Peter Seidl, Harvey Olem, Vanja Jordan, Alfred Duda, and Robert Johnson, *Restoring and Protecting the World's Lakes and Reservoirs*. World Bank Technical Paper no. WTP 289 (1995). [Online.] Accessed October 15, 2005. Available: www.wds.worldbank.org/servlet/WDS_IBank_Servlet?pcont=details&eid=000009265_3961219120345.

Dudley, Nigel, Sue Stolton, and Jean-Paul Jeanrenaud, *Pulp Fact: Environmental Implications of the Paper Cycle* (Gland, Switzerland: WWF International, 1996).

Goetz, Philip W., ed.-in-chief, *Encyclopedia Britannica*, 15th ed. (Chicago: Encyclopedia Britannica, 1989).

Feshbach, Murray, and Alfred Friendly, Jr., *Ecocide in the USSR: Health and Nature Under Siege* (New York: Basic Books, 1992).

Forsyth, James, *A History of the Peoples of Siberia: Russia's North Asian Colony 1581-1990* (New York: Cambridge University Press, 1992).

Galazy, Grigory Ivanovich, *Baikal v voprosakh i otvetakh* [*Baikal in Questions and Answers*] (Moscow: Mysyl Publishing House, 1988). (Unpublished English translation by J. Sutton).

Greenpeace International, *The Environmental Situation of Lake Baikal* (Amsterdam: Greenpeace International, 2003).

Hingley, Ronald, *Russia, a Concise History* (New York: Thames and Hudson, 1991).

Knyazev, Alexander, and Mark Sergeyev, *Irkutsk* (Irkutsk: Irkutsk Department of the Russian Cultural Foundation, 1995).

Lagasse, Paul, Lora Goldman, Archie Hobson, and Susan R. Norton, eds., *The Columbia Encyclopedia*, 5th ed. (New York: Columbia University Press, 1993).

——. *The Columbia Electronic Encyclopedia*, 6th ed. (New York: Columbia University Press, 2003).

Lake Baikal Homepage. (Irkutsk) [Online.] Accessed October 12, 2005. Available: baikal.irkutsk.org/.

Lensen, George Alexander, ed., *Russia's Eastward Expansion* (Englewood Cliffs, N.J.: Spectrum/Prentice Hall, 1964).

Matoso, Gary, and Lisa Dickey, *The Russian Chronicles* (FocalPoint f/8/World Media Network, 1995). [Online.] Accessed June 15, 2000. Available: www.f8.com/FP/Russia/index.html.

Matthiessen, Peter, and Boyd Norton, *Baikal: Sacred Sea of Siberia* (San Francisco: Sierra Club Books, 1992).

National Geographic. *National Geographic Atlas of the World*, 8th ed. (Washington, D.C.: National Geographic, 2005).

Nebesky, Richard, and Nick Selby. *Russia, Ukraine and Belarus, Lonely Planet Travel Survival Kit* (Oakland, Calif.: Lonely Planet, 1996).

Newby, Eric, *The Big Red Train Ride: A Ride on the Trans-Siberian Railway* (New York: St. Martin's Press, 1978).

Peterson, D.J., *Troubled Lands: The Legacy of Soviet Environmental Destruction* (Boulder, Colo.: Westview Press, 1993).

Rasputin, Vladimir, *Siberia on Fire* (DeKalb: Northern Illinois University Press, 1989).

Richmond, Simon, and Martha Vorhees, *Trans-Siberian Railway: A Classic Overland Route* (Oakland, Calif.: Lonely Planet, 2002).

Thomas, Bryn, *Trans-Siberian Handbook*, 4th ed. (Surrey, U.K.: Trailblazer Publications, 1997).

Ware, Timothy, *The Orthodox Church* (New York: Penguin Books, 1983).

Weiner, Douglas R., *A Little Corner of Freedom: Russian Nature Protection from Stalin to Gorbachev* (Berkeley: University of California Press, 1999).

World Lakes Network, *Global Lake Database*. [Online.] Accessed November 4, 2002. Available: www.worldlakes.org/lakes.asp.

CHAPTER 2

PAGE 22

Creation Wonders, cited in *Baikal Web World: Legends of Baikal Origin*. [Online.] Accessed April 2, 2004. Available: http://www.bww.irk.ru/baikalorigin/baikallegends.html.

Brunello, Anthony J., Valery C. Molotov, Batbayar Dugherkhuu, Charles Goldman, Erjen Khamaganova, Tatiana Strijhova, and Rachel Sigman, *Lake Baikal Watershed: Lake Basin Management Experience Brief* (South Lake Tahoe, Calif., and Irkutsk: Tahoe-Baikal Institute, 2004), p. 4.

PAGE 24

Galazy, *Baikal in Questions and Answers*, "Who was the first to tell about the nature of the lake?".

CHAPTER 3

PAGE 28

Galazy, *Baikal in Questions and Answers*, "Who was the first to tell about the nature of the lake?".

Gurulev, S.A., "The face of Baikal—water: A description of Baikal's water and questions concerning its pollution," in Baikal Web World, [Online.] Accessed April 2, 2004. Available: http://www.bww.irk.ru/baikalwater/depth.html.

CHAPTER 4

PAGE 34

Feshbach and Friendly, *Ecocide in the USSR*, p. 44.

PAGE(s) 35-36

The Russian Primary Chronicle of 1113, quoted in Mikkel Aaland, *Sweat: The Illustrated History and Description of the Finnish Sauna, Russian Bania, Islamic Hammam, Japanese Mushi-Buro, Mexican Temescal, and American Sweat Lodge* (Santa Barbara, Calif.: Capra Press, 1978). [Online.] Accessed April 1, 2004. Available: www.cyberbohemia.com/Pages/sweat.htm.

Dragomanov, M.P., *Notes on the Slavic Religio-Ethical Legends: The Dualistic Creation of the World*. Russian and East European Series, vol. 23. (Bloomington: Indiana University Publications, 1961), cited in Billington, *The Icon and the Axe*, p. 636, n. 17.

Viinikka, Lasse, *Sauna and Health* (Finnish Sauna Society). [Online] Accessed April 1, 2004. Available: www.sauna.fi/englanti/lasse.html.

Inlander, Charles B., *12 Tips to Prevent Cold and Flu the "Natural" Way: #5 Take a Sauna* (WebMD). [Online.] Accessed April 3, 2004. Available: my.webmd.com/content/pages/5/4068_103.htm.

Kihara, T., S. Biro, M. Imamura, et al., "Repeated sauna treatment improves vascular endothelial and cardiac function in patients with chronic heart failure," *Journal of the American College of Cardiology*, vol. 39, no. 5 (March 6, 2002), pp. 754-759. [Online.] Accessed March 25, 2005. Abstract available: www.ncbi.nlm.nih.gov/entrez/query.fcgi?cmd=Retrieve&db=PubMed&list_uids=11869837&dopt=Abstract.

Finnish Sauna Society, *Introduction to Sweat Baths*. [Online.] Accessed April 1, 2004. Available: www.sauna.fi/englanti/englanti.html.

CHAPTER 5

PAGE 41

Komarov, Boris, *The Destruction of Nature in the Soviet Union* (Armonk, N.Y.: M.E. Sharpe, 1980), quoted in Matthiessen and Norton, *Sacred Sea of Siberia*, p. 26.

PAGE 43

Baikal Web World, *Ichthyofauna*. [Online.] Accessed October 12, 2005. Available: www.bww.irk.ru/fauna/ichthyofauna.html.

Fiondella, Paul, posting on *Johnson's Russia List* (Center for Defense Information, January 15, 1999). [Online.] Accessed Oct 18, 2003. Available: www.cdi.org/russia/johnson/3017.html#%233.

PAGE 47

Maksimov, Slava, Sr., interview with the author, October 2000.

Todd, Martin C., and Anson W. Mackay, "Large-scale climatic controls on Lake Baikal ice cover," *Journal of Climate*, vol. 16 (2003), p. 3186.

Hohmann, R., M. Hofer, R. Kipfer, F. Peeters, H. Baur, M. N. Shimaraev, and D. M. Imboden, "Distribution of helium, and tritium in Lake Baikal," *Journal of Geophysical Research*, vol. 103, no. C6 (1998), pp. 12823-12838. [Online.] Accessed October 21, 2005. Abstract available: http://www.eawag.ch/research_e/w+t/UI/baikal/results/helium/e_helium.html.

Ravens, Thomas M., Otti Kocsis, Alfred Wüest, and N. Granin, "Small-scale turbulence and vertical mixing in Lake Baikal," *Limnology and Oceanography*, vol. 45, no. 1 (January 2000), pp. 159-173.

Hohmann, R., R. Kipfer, F. Peeters, G. Piepke, D.M. Imboden, and M. N. Shimaraev, "Processes of deep-water renewal in Lake Baikal," *Limnology and Oceanography*, vol. 42 (1997), pp. 841-855.

PAGE 48

Wüest, Alfred, Thomas M. Ravens, Nikolai G. Granin, Otti Kocsis, Michael Schurter, and Michael Sturm, "Cold intrusions in Lake Baikal: Direct observational evidence for deep-water renewal," *Limnology and Oceanography*, vol. 50, no. 1 (2005), pp. 184-196.

PAGE 49

Galazy, *Baikal in Questions and Answers*, author's preface.

Page 52

Seal Conservation Society, *Baikal Seal (Phoca sibirica)*. [Online.] Accessed June 25, 2005. Available: www.pinnipeds.org/species/baikal.htm.

BBC News Online, *Russian "ice expedition" to save seals* (April 18, 2001). [Online.] Accessed October 13, 2005. Available: news.bbc.co.uk/1/hi/world/monitoring/media_reports/1283713.stm.

Schofield, James, "Lake Baikal's vanishing nerpa seal," *Moscow Times* (July 27, 2001).

Chapter 8

Page 77

Barduyeva, O.I., *Selenga: River Without Borders, International Conference* [presentation] (Ulan-Ude: Buryat State University, 2002), cited in Greenpeace International, *Environmental Situation*, table 4, p. 16.

Institute of Biology, *On the Strategy of Biodiversity Preserving of the Lake Baikal Ecosystem* (Irkutsk: Scientific Research Institute of Biology, Irkutsk State University, 1998), p. 17.

Page 79

Knyazev and Sergeyev, *Irkutsk*, p. 41.

Chapter 11

Page 114

U.K. Hydrographic Office, *Bering Sea and Strait Pilot*, 5th ed. (Taunton, U.K.: Admiralty Charts and Publications, 1980).

Chapter 13

Page 133

Thomas, *Trans-Siberian Handbook*, p. 264.

Chapter 14

Page 141

Fraser, John Foster, *The Real Siberia, Together with an Account of a Dash Through Manchuria* (London: Cassell and Company, 1902), cited in Thomas, *Trans-Siberian Handbook*, p. 109.

Page 149

Anton Chekhov, letter to his brother Alexander, June 5, 1890, in *Letters of Anton Chekhov to His Family and Friends, with a Biographical Sketch*, ed. and trans. by Constance Garnett, 1920 (Reprint; Adelaide: The University of Adelaide Library, eBooks@Adelaide, December 13, 2002). [Online.] Accessed October 21, 2005. Available: http://etext.library.adelaide.edu.au/c/chekhov/anton/c51lt/index.html.

PAGE 151

Sigachyov, Sergey, and Mikhail Krainov, *Circum-Baikal Railway on the Web*. [Online.] Accessed October 13, 2005. Available: kbzd.irk.ru/Eng/.

CHAPTER 15

PAGE 153

Chekhov, letter to his brother.

PAGE 154

Knyazev and Sergeyev, *Irkutsk*, p. 43.

PAGE 155

Knyazev and Sergeyev, *Irkutsk*, p. 37.

PAGE 162

Piter Schutt, quoted in Knyazev and Sergeyev, *Irkutsk*, p. 51.

CHAPTER 16

PAGE 173

Peterson, *Troubled Lands*, ch. 3, map 3.2.

Kibal'chich, O., quoted in P.I. Miroshnikov, *Ekologicheskiye problemy territory I puti ikh resheniya*, abstract of paper presented by at a scientific-practical conference, July 1989, in Irkutsk, in *O7. Geografiya 5* (1990), p. 25, cited in Feshbach and Friendly, *Ecocide in the USSR*, p. 98.

USSR Goskomstat (State Statistics Committee), *Okhrana okruzhayushchei sredy i ratsional'noe ispol'zovanie prirodnykh resursov v SSSR* (Moscow: Finansy i statistika, 1989), pp. 22-23, cited in Peterson, *Troubled Lands*, p. 84.

Greenpeace International, *Environmental Situation*, pp. 45-47.

Danilov-Danilyan et al., *Annual Report*, pp. 22-26.

Mamontov, Alexander A., Elena A. Mamontova, Evgenia N. Tarasova, and Michael S. McLachlan, "Tracing the sources of PCDD/Fs and PCBs to Lake Baikal," *Environmental Science and Technology*, vol. 34, no. 5 (2000), pp. 741-747.

Mamontova, E.A., A.A. Mamontov, N.I. Matorova, E.N. Tarasova, and U.A Chuvashev, "PCB in snow of the Baikal region," *Organohalogen Compounds*, vol. 32 (1997), cited in Mamontov et al., "Tracing the Sources," pp. 741, 744, and in Greenpeace International, *Environmental Situation*, p. 47.

Brunello et al., *Lake Baikal Watershed*, p. 10.

Belt and Leen, "The World's Great Lake," map, p. 11.

Tumenbayar, Beater, et al., "Environmental hazard in Lake Baikal watershed posed by Mercury placer in Mongolia," *World Placer Journal*,Vol. 1 (November 2000). [Online.] Accessed October 29, 2004. Available: http://www.mine.mn/WPJ1_7_mercury_placer.htm.

Greenpeace International, *Environmental Situation*, pp. 20-22.

Page 174

Greenpeace International, *Environmental Situation*, pp. 41-51.

Mackay, Anson W., "Lake Baikal," in *Encyclopedia of Global Environmental Change*, Vol. 3: *Causes and Consequences of Global Environmental Change*, Ted Munn, ed.-in-chief (Chichester: John Wiley and Sons, 2002), pp. 413-417.

Brunello et al., *Lake Baikal Watershed*, pp. 9-12.

Clarke, Renfrey, "The Killing of Lake Baikal," *Green Left Weekly*, Sydney, Australia (January 17, 1999).

Loginova, Viktoria, "World Bank Loan could end Baikal pollution, but ecologists have doubts," *Agence France Presse* (August 14, 2003).

Greenpeace International, *Environmental Situation*, p. 24.

Page 176

Merkulov, A., "Tregova o Baikale" *Pravda* (February 28, 1965), cited in Weiner, *A Little Corner of Freedom*, p. 364.

Belt and Leen, "The World's Great Lake," p. 8.

Konstantin, et al., "Collective Letter to Komsomolskaia Pravda," May 11, 1966, cited in Weiner, *A Little Corner of Freedom*, pp. 368-369.

Zenin, A. A., Director, Institute of Geochemistry, remarks to meeting of the Commission of the Siberian Division of the Academy of Sciences on the problems of Lake Baikal, September 23, 1971, Novosibirsk, cited in Stanislav Goldfarb, *The Baikalsk Syndrome* (Irkutsk, 1996), p. 74, cited in Jennie Sutton, *The Battle for Baikal*. [Online.] Accessed October 21, 2005. Available: www.baikalwave.eu.org/Oldsitebew/battle.html.

Baikalsk Pulp and Paper Mill presentation, *Sostoyanie BTsBK i prespektivy ego resvitiya, Baikalsk 2003*, cited in Greenpeace International, *Environmental Situation*, p. 104.

Sutton, Jennie, interview with the author, October 2000.

Danilov-Danilyan et al., *Annual Report*, p. 30.

Figure for total wastewater based on extrapolation of data from various sources, including Danilov-Danilyan et al., *Annual Report*, p. 7; Dinar et al., *Restoring and Protecting*, p. 62; USSR Goskomstat (State Committee on Statistics), *Narodnoe khozyaistvo SSSR v 1987 g* (Moscow: Finansy i statistika, 1988), pp. 574-575, cited in Peterson, *Troubled Lands*, p. 83.

Danilov-Danilyan et al., *Annual Report*, p. 7.

Galazy, G.I., and E.N. Tarasova, *The Impact of Anthropogenic Activity on the Chemical Composition of Lake Baikal* (Irkutsk, 1995), cited in Greenpeace International, *Environmental Situation*, pp. 29-30.

Mackay, *Encyclopedia of Environmental Change*, p. 4.

Page 177

USSR Goskompriroda (Soviet State Committee for the Protection of Nature), *Sostoyanie prirodnoi sredy v SSSR v 1988 g* [*The State of the Environment in the USSR in 1988*] (Moscow: VINITI, 1989), p. 126, cited in Peterson, *Troubled Lands*, p. 83.

Kozhova, O.M., *On the Results of Hydrobiological Monitoring of Lake Baikal in the Area of the Town Baikal'sk* (Irkutsk: Institute of Biology, Irkutsk State University, 1998), cited in Greenpeace International, *Environmental Situation*, p. 28.

Dudley et al., *Pulp Fact*, p. 22.

Galazy and Tarasova, *The Impact of Anthropogenic Activity*, cited in Greenpeace International, *Environmental Situation*, p. 66.

ICF Kaiser Consulting Group, "Rescuing one of the world's oldest natural resources," *Consult* (fall 1998), p. 3.

Danilov-Danilyan et al., *Annual Report*, pp. 34-35.

Saiko, Tatyana, *Environmental Crises: Geographical Case Studies in Post-Socialist Eurasia* (London: Prentice Hall, 2001), ch. 4, cited in Greenpeace International, *Environmental Situation*, p. 33.

Galazy, Grigory, ed., *Baikal Atlas* (Moscow: Federal Service on Geodezia and Cartography, 1993), cited in Greenpeace International, *Environmental Situation*, p. 31.

Brunello et al., *Lake Baikal Watershed*, p. 6.

Danilov-Danilyan et al., *Annual Report*, p. 35.

Grachev, M.A., and N.A. Aldokhin, *Environmental Impact of the Baikal'sk Paper and Pulp Plant and the Ways of Sustainable Development of the Economy of the Southern Coast of Lake Baikal* (Irkutsk: Limnological Institute, Russian Academy of Science, 1995), cited in Greenpeace International, *Environmental Situation*, pp. 32-33.

Dudley et al., *Pulp Fact*, p. 22.

Danilov-Danilyan et al., *Annual Report*, p. 36.

Page 180

Agency for Toxic Substances and Disease Registry *Toxicological Profile for Hydrogen Sulfide* (Washington, D.C.: U.S. Department of Health and Human Services, Public Health Service, 1999).

Page 181

Mackay, *Encyclopedia of Environmental Change*, p. 4.

Dinar et al., *Restoring and Protecting*, p. 63.

Danilov-Danilyan et al., *Annual Report*, pp. 46, 51, 52.

Baikalsk Pulp and Paper Mill, cited in Greenpeace International, *Environmental Situation*, p. 102.

Danilov-Danilyan et al., *Annual Report*, p. 7.

Dudley et al., *Pulp Fact*, p. 26.

Paper Task Force (Duke University, Environmental Defense Fund, Johnson and Johnson, McDonald's, Prudential Insurance Company of America, Time Inc.), *White Paper No. 5: Environmental Comparison of Bleached Kraft Pulp Manufacturing Technologies* (Environmental Defense Fund, December 1995), p. 47. [Online.] Accessed October 25, 2004. Available: www.environmentaldefense.org/documents/1626_WP5.pdf.

PAGE 183

Technical Assistance to Confederation of Independent States, European Union, *The Baikalsk PPM: Preliminary Analysis of Profitability of Development Options*, May 1999; *Environmental Impact Assessment of the Baikalsk PPM and Options for Its Development*, July 1999; *Assessment of Three Variants of Continued Production at the Baikalsk PPM*, November 1999; and *The Baikalsk PPM: Assessment of Short-Term Options for Chemical Pulp Production*, December 1999 (Brussels: Technical Assistance to Confederation of Independent States, European Union).

Brunello et al., *Lake Baikal Watershed*, p. 9.

CHAPTER 17

PAGE 197

Rasputin, "Your Siberia and Mine," pp. 175-176.

CHAPTER 18

PAGE 200

Galazy, G.I., cited in *Baikal Web World: Invertebrates of Lake Baikal*. [Online.] Accessed November 12, 2004. Available: http://www.bww.irk.ru/baikalfauna/baikalinvertebrates.html.

PAGE 201

Damstra et al., *Endocrine Disruptors*, p. 91.

Michael Rivlin, "Northern exposure," *OnEarth* (fall 2001). [Online.] Accessed December 4, 2004. Available: www.nrdc.org/onearth/01fal/seals.asp.

Tanabe et al., "Polychlorobiphenyl, SDDT and hexachlorohexane isomers in the western North Pacific ecosystem," *Archives of Environmental Contamination and Toxicology*, vol. 13 (1984), pp. 731-738, cited in Bruce D. Rodan, ed., *The Foundation for Global Action on Persistent Organic Pollutants: A United States Perspective*, (Washington, D.C.: U.S. Environmental Protection Agency, Office of Research and Development, 2002), p. 6-3, table 6.1.

Mamontov et al., Tracing the Sources," p. 743.

PAGE 203

Damstra et al., *Endocrine Disruptors*, p. 117, table 16.

Oceana, *Toxic Burden: PCBs in Marine Life* (Washington, D.C.: Oceana, 2003). [Online.] Accessed September 29, 2003. Available: www.oceana.org/index.php?id=701.

World Health Organization, *Executive Summary, Assessment of the health risk of dioxins: Re-evaluation of the Tolerable Daily Intake (TDI)* (Geneva: WHO European Centre for Environment and Health/International Programme on Chemical Safety, 1998), p. 7, table 1. [Online.] Accessed October 21, 2005. Available: www.who.int/ipcs/publications/en/exe-sum-final.pdf.

U.S. Environmental Protection Agency, *Information Sheet 1—Dioxin: Summary of the Dioxin Reassessment Science* [Update] (Washington, D.C.: United States Environmental Protection Agency, Office of Research and Development, May 25, 2001).

PAGE(s) 203-204

Tarasova, E.N., A.A. Mamontov, and E.A. Mamontova, "Polychlorinated dibenzo-p-dioxins (PCDDs) and dibenzofurans (PCDFs) in Baikal seal," *Chemosphere*, vol. 34, no. 11 (1997), p. 2424, table 3.

Mamontov, A.A., E.A. Mamontova, E.N. Tarasova, M.V. Pastukhov, H. Lutz, and M.S. McLachlan, "Dynamics of PCDDs and PCDFs in the pelagic food web of Lake Baikal," *Organohalogen Compounds*, vol. 32 (1997), pp. 275-276.

Tarasova, Evgeniya N., Alexander A. Mamontov, and Elena A. Mamontova, "Pollution and eutrophication in Lake Baikal," *Journal of Lake Sciences*, vol. 10 suppl. (1998), p. 177.

Bignert, A., M. Olsson, P.A Bergquist, S. Bergek, C. Rappe, C. de Witt, and B. Jansson, "Polychlorinated dibenzo-p-dioxins (PCDD) and dibenzofurans (PCDF) in seal blubber," *Chemosphere*, vol. 19 (1989), pp. 551-556, cited in Tarasova et al., "Polychlorinated dibenzo-p-dioxins."

Bergek, S., P.A. Bergquist, M. Hjelt, M. Olsson, C. Rappe, A. Roos, and D. Zook, "Concentrations of PCDDs and PCDFs in seals from Swedish waters," *Ambio*, vol. 21 (1992), pp. 553-556, cited in Tarasova et al., "Polychlorinated dibenzo-p-dioxins."

Oehme, M., M. Schlabach, and I. Boyd, "Polychlorinated dibenzo-p-dioxins, dibenzofurans and coplanar biphenyls in Antarctic fur seal blubber," *Ambio*, vol. 24 (1995), pp. 41-46, cited in Tarasova et al., "Polychlorinated dibenzo-p-dioxins."

Damstra et al., *Endocrine Disruptors*, annex I, table 10.

PAGE 204

Nerpa, 3.5-64 parts per million (ppm) PCBs: Nakata, Haruhiko, Shinsuke Tanabe, Ryo Tatsukawa, Masao Amano, Nobuyuki Miyazaki, and Evgeny A. Petrov, "Persistent organochlorine residues and their accumulation kinetics in Baikal seal (*Phoca sibirica*) from Lake Baikal, Russia," *Environmental Science and Technology*, vol. 29, no. 11 (1995), p. 2879, table 1.

Baltic seals, 20-770 ppm PCBs: Damstra et al., *Endocrine Disruptors*, p. 110, table 1; p. 111, table 2; p. 117, table 16.

Background, 0.6 ppm PCBs in ringed seals, Baffin Bay: Damstra et al., *Endocrine Disruptors*, p. 117, table 16.

Immunosuppression and depressed vitamin A found at 16.5 ppm PCBs in harbor seal blubber, and impaired reproductive success found at and 25.0 ppm PCBs in harbor seal blood: Wilson, Simon J., and Glen Packman, eds., *AMAP Assessment 2002: Persistent Organic Pollutants in the Arctic* (Oslo: Arctic Monitoring and Assessment Programme, 2002), p. 168, fig. 6-3.

50 ppm PCBs: *Basel Convention on the Control of Transboundary Movements of Hazardous Wastes and Their Disposal Adopted by the Conference of the Plenipotentiaries on 22 March 1989, Entry into Force May 1993, Annex VIII, List A.*

Nerpa, 4.9-160 ppm DDT and related compounds: Nakata et al., "Persistent organochlorine residues."

Baltic seals, 6.4-970 ppm DDTs: Damstra et al., *Endocrine Disruptors*, p. 110, table 1.

Background, 0.51 ppm DDTs in ringed seal, Baffin Bay: Damstra et al., *Endocrine Disruptors*, p. 117, table 16.

Hormonal problems, concentrations of 7.6-16.5 ppm DDE in blubber correlated with reduced testosterone in blood of Dall's porpoises: Subramanian, A.N., S. Tenabe, R. Tatsukawa, S. Saito, N. Miyazaki, "Reduction in the testosterone levels by PCBs and DDE in Dall's porpoises of northwestern North Pacific," *Marine Pollution Bulletin*, vol. 18 (1987), pp. 643-646, cited in Center for Biological Diversity et al., *Petition to List the Southern Resident Killer Whale (Orcinus orca) as an Endangered Species Under the Endangered Species Act* (Berkeley, Calif., May 1, 2001).

Tumors, concentrations of 3.36-389 ppm DDTs correlated with tumors in St. Lawrence beluga whales: Center for Biological Diversity et al., *Petition to List.*
Mamontov et al., "Tracing the Sources," p. 743.

Page 205

MacArthur Foundation: Tarasova et al., "Polychlorinated dibenzo-p-dioxins."

Germany, Ecological Chemistry and Geochemistry, University of Bayreuth: Tarasova et al., "Polychlorinated dibenzo-p-dioxins"; Mamontov et al., "Dynamics of PCDDs and PCDFs"; E.A. Mamontova, A.A. Mamontov, E.N. Tarasova, and M.S. McLachlan, "PCDD/Fs and PCBs in human adipose tissue from the Irkutsk Oblast, Russia," *Organohalogen Compounds*, vol. 38 (1998), pp. 131-134; E.A. Mamontova, A.A. Mamontov, E.N. Tarasova, and M.S. McLachlan, "PCDDs, PCDFs and PCBs in food from the Irkutsk Oblast, Russia," *Organohalogen Compounds*, vol. 38 (1998), pp. 135-138; A.A. Mamontov, E.A. Mamontova, E.N. Tarasova, M.S. McLachlan, and P.N. Anoshko, "Assessment of PCDD, PCDF and PCB pollution in Lake Baikal using two species of sculpins: *Comephorus baicalensis* and *Comephorus dybowskii*," *Organohalogen Compounds*, vol. 39 (1998), pp. 319-322; A.A. Mamontov, E.A. Mamontova, E.N. Tarasova, and M.S. McLachlan, "PCDD/Fs in soil and sediment from the Baikal region," *Organohalogen Compounds*, vol. 39 (1998), pp. 327-330; A.A. Mamontov, E.A. Mamontova, E.N. Tarasova, and M.S. McLachlan, "Levels of PCDD/Fs in omul from Lake Baikal," *Organohalogen Compounds*, vol. 39 (1998), pp. 323-326; Mamontov et al., "Tracing the Sources."

Baltic Sea Research Institute Warnemunde: E.A. Mamontova, A.A. Mamontov, E.N. Tarasova, S.I. Kolesnøkov, P. Fürst, O. Päpke, J.J. Ryan, and M.S. McLachlan, "PCDD/Fs in human milk and blood samples from a contaminated region near Lake Baikal," *Organohalogen Compounds*, vol. 44 (1999), pp. 37-40.

Chemical and Veterinary State Laboratory, ERGO Forschunggesellschaft mbH, and Health Canada: Mamontova et al., "PCDD/Fs in human milk and blood samples."

Peer-reviewed journals: *Organohalogen Compounds* (U.S.), *Chemosphere* (U.K.), *Environmental Science and Technology* (U.S.).

Kucklick, John R., Roger Harvey, Peggy Ostrom, Nathaniel E. Ostrom, and Joel Baker, "Organochlorine dynamics in the pelagic food web of Lake Baikal," *Environmental Toxicology and Chemistry*, vol. 15, no. 8 (1996), pp. 1388-1400. (Research institutions and funding: University of Maryland, Michigan State University, National Oceanic and Atmospheric Administration, University of Connecticut, National Science Foundation.)

Nakata et al., "Persistent organochlorine residues." (Funding: International Scientific Research Programmes of the Ministry of Education, Science and Culture, Japan; Nissan Science Foundation.)

Kucklick et al., "Organochlorine dynamics," pp. 1391-1392, tables 2 and 3.

PAGE 206

Rodan, pp. 6-9–6-11.

Allsopp, Michelle, Bea Erry, David Santillo, and Paul Johnston, *POPS in the Baltic: A Review of Persistent Organic Pollutants (POPs) in the Baltic Sea* (Exeter, U.K.: Greenpeace Research Laboratories, University of Exeter Department of Biological Sciences, 2001), p. 64.

de Swart, R.L., P.S. Ross, L.J. Vedder, H.H. Timmerman, S.H. Heisterkamp, H. Van Loveren, J.G. Vos, P.J.H. Reijnders, and A.D.M.E. Osterhaus, "Impairment of immune function in harbor seals (*Phoca vitulina*) feeding on fish from polluted waters," *Ambio*, vol. 23 (1994), pp. 155-159, p. 155.

de Swart, Rik L., Peter S. Ross, Joseph G. Vos, and Albert D.M.E. Osterhaus, "Impaired immunity in harbour seals (*Phoca vitulina*) exposed to bioaccumulated environmental contaminants: Review of a long-term feeding study," *Environmental Health Perspectives*, vol. 104 Suppl., no. S4 (August 1996). [Online.] Available: ehp.niehs.nih.gov/members/1996/Suppl-4/deswart.html; see also Center for Biological Diversity, *Petition to List*, p. 39.

Damstra et al., *Endocrine Disruptors*, pp. 2, 35, 36, 90, 95.

PAGE 208

1994 estimate, 1 cancer per 10,000 people: U.S. Environmental Protection Agency, *Information Sheet 1*.

U.S. Environmental Protection Agency, *Information Sheet 2—Dioxin: Scientific Highlights from Draft Reassessment (2000)* (Washington, D.C.: U.S. Environmental Protection Agency Office of Research and Development, May 2001).

PAGE 209

Iwata, H., et al., "Persistent organochlorine residues in air, water, sediments, and soils from the Lake Baikal region, Russia," *Environmental Science and Technology*, vol. 29, no. 3 (1995), pp. 792-801, cited in Mamontov et al., "PCDD/Fs in soil and sediment," p. 741.

Page(s) 217-218

Danilov-Danilyan et al., *Annual Report*, pp. 22, 41, 30-36, 45-52 (typos corrected as necessary for understanding but other translation errors from original left in place).

Chapter 19

Page 219

Nebesky and Selby, *Russia, Ukraine and Belarus*, p. 808.

Page 225

Kapitsa, Pyotr L., quoted in Weiner, p. 372

Page 229

Shimaraev, M.N., Kuimova, L.N., Sinyukovich, V.N., Tsekhanovskii, V.V., 2002. Klimat i gidrologicheskie protsessy v basseine oz. Baikal v XX stoletii. (In Russian)

Meteorologiya i gidrologiya (ISSN 0130-2906) 2002 (No 3), 71-78, cited in Straskrábová, V., L.R. Izmest'eva, E.A. Maksimova, S. Fietz, J. Nedoma, J. Borovec, G.I. Kobanova, E.V. Shchetinina, and E.V. Pislegina, *Primary Production and Microbial Activity in the Euphotic Zone of Lake Baikal (Southern Basin) During Late Winter* (Ceské Budejovice, CZ: Hydrobiological Institute, Czech Academy of Sciences, undated), pp. 4-5. [Online.] Accessed October 16, 2005. Available: continent.gfz-potsdam.de/upload/pdf/gpc/Straskrabova.pdf.

Shimaraev, Michael Nikolaevich, *Tendencies in Changes of Some Elements in Lake Baikal Ecosystem in 20th Century*. Paper delivered at Tokyo University of Marine Science and Technology, September 22, 2004 (Irkutsk: Limnological Institute, Siberian Branch of Russian Academy of Sciences). [Online.] Accessed October 16, 2005. Available: liaison.s.kaiyodai.ac.jp/bikal.pdf.

McCarthy, James J., Osvaldo F. Canziani, Neil A. Leary, David J. Dokken, and Kasey S. White, eds., *Climate Change 2001: Impacts, Adaptation, and Vulnerability, Contribution of Working Group II to the Third Assessment Report of the Intergovernmental Panel on Climate Change* (New York: Cambridge University Press, 2001), p. 298.

Chapter 20

Page 238

Schiffman, Richard, "India cleans the Ganges River," *Living on Earth* (National Public Radio, November 1, 1996).

Page 241

Stegner, Wallace, "Wilderness letter," written to the Outdoor Recreation Resources Review Commission, December 3, 1960. In Stegner, W., *The Sound of Mountain Water*. 1969. Reprint, New York: Penguin Books, 1997, p. 147.

Epilogue

Page 270

Greenpeace International, *Environmental Situation*, pp. 4, 5, 85.

Page(s) 270-271

Brunello et al., *Lake Baikal Watershed*, pp. 9-11.

Page 271

Greenpeace Russia, *Russian Government Pledges to Save Lake Baikal* (Moscow: Greenpeace Russia, August 1, 2003).

Interfax/Asia Paper Markets.com (August 12, 2004). [Online.] Accessed December 8, 2004. Available: 203.81.45.44:8081/apm/apm/common/mktbuzz_archiveweek37.jsp.

Loginova, Viktoria, *World Bank Loan Could End Baikal Pollution, but Ecologists Have Doubts* (Agence France Presse, August 14, 2003).

Page 272

Houghton, J.T., Y. Ding, D.J. Griggs, M. Noguer, P.J. van der Linden, X. Dai, K. Maskell, and C.A. Johnson, eds., *Climate Change 2001: The Scientific Basis: Contribution of Working Group I to the Third Assessment Report of the Intergovernmental Panel on Climate Change* (New York: Cambridge University Press, 2001), cited in Todd and Mackay, "Large scale climatic controls," p. 3186.

Shimaraev, *Tendencies in changes.*

MacKinnon, Mark, "New battles loom over Russia's great lake: Plan to pipe water to a thirsty world pits entrepreneurs against ecologists," *Globe and Mail*, Toronto (August 13, 2002).

Records of meetings of Bureau of the World Heritage Committee, United Nations Educational, Scientific and Cultural Organization. [Online]. Accessed June 25, 2005. Available: whc.unesco.org/en/statutorydoc/.

Page 273

U.S. Environmental Protection Agency, "Message from President George W. Bush," July 1, 2002. [Online.] Accessed June 7, 2005. Available: www.epa.gov/air/clearskies/wh.html.

White House, *President Bush Signs Healthy Forests Restoration Act into Law*, December 3, 2003. [Online.] Accessed June 7, 2005. Available: www.whitehouse.gov/infocus/healthyforests/.

"Empty Promises" [editorial], *New York Times* (January 31, 2003).

White House, *Global Climate Change Policy Book, Executive Summary*, February 14, 2002. [Online.] Accessed October 8, 2005. Available: www.whitehouse.gov/news/releases/2002/02/climatechange.html.

Pew Center on Global Climate Change, *Analysis of President Bush's Climate Change Plan*, February 2002. [Online.] Accessed October 8, 2005. Available: www.pewclimate.org/policy_center/analyses/response_bushpolicy.cfm.

PAGE 274

MacKinnon, "New battles loom."

Tsydenova, O., T.B. Minh, N. Kajiwara, V. Batoev, and S. Tanabe, "Recent contamination by persistent organochlorines in Baikal seal (*Phoca sibirica*) from Lake Baikal, Russia," *Marine Pollution Bulletin*, vol. 48 (2004), pp. 749-758, cited by M. Moore, personal correspondence with the author.

Greenpeace International, *Environmental Situation*, p. 85.

AFTERWORD

PAGE 279

"Russia's Anti-West offensive" [editorial], *New York Times* (December 27, 2005).

Illarionov, Andrei N., quoted in C.J. Chivers, "Outspoken Putin aide quits, scolding Kremlin," *New York Times* (December 28, 2005).

PAGE(s) 279-280

Korchagina, Valeria, and Galina Stolyarova, "Putin does an about-face on Baikal pipeline," *St. Petersburg Times* (April 28, 2006).

"Far east pipeline rerouted" [Business Briefs], *Moscow Times* (May 25, 2006).

FURTHER READING AND RESOURCES

PRINT

Agence France Presse. "Russia's Siberian forests falling to illegal logging." *AFP*, May 2, 2004. [Online.] Accessed October 21, 2005. Available: www.terradaily.com/2004/040502030651.y5wzzm8d.html.

Atkinson, T.W. *Travels in the Regions of the Upper and Lower Amoor and the Russian Acquisitions on the Confines of India and China.* New York: Harper, 1860.

Baikal Watch. *Combating Dioxin and Toxic Pollution in Lake Baikal.* May 30, 2000. Accessed October 21, 2005. Online. Available: www.earthisland.org/project/reportPage.cfm?reportID=12&pageID=71&subSiteID=1.

Ball, Philip. *Life's Matrix: A Biography of Water.* New York: Farrar Straus Giroux, 2000.

Bizioukin, V.I., N.J. Bech, V.V. Bizioukin, and P. Veijola. *Sustainable Forestry in the Baikal Basin.* Brussels: Technical Assistance to Confederation of Independent States, European Union, 1999.

Bobrick, Benson. *East of the Sun: The Epic Conquest and Tragic History of Siberia.* New York: Poseidon Press, 1992.

Boym, Svetlana. *Common Places: Mythologies of Everyday Life in Russia.* Cambridge, Mass.: Harvard University Press, 1994.

Bronmark, C., and L. Hansson. *The Biology of Lakes and Ponds.* New York: Oxford University Press, 1998.

Brooke, James. "Disputes at Every Turn of Siberian Pipeline." *New York Times,* January 21, 2005.

Buccini, John. *The Global Pursuit of the Sound Management of Chemicals.* Washington, D.C.: The World Bank, 2004. [Online.] Accessed October 21, 2005. Available: lnweb18. worldbank.org/ESSD/envext.nsf/50ByDocName/PersistentOrganicPollutants.

Bukharov, A.A., and V.A. Fialkov. *Baikal in Numbers.* Irkutsk: Siberian Branch of Russian Academy of Sciences, Irkutsk Scientific Center, Baikal Museum, 2001.

Bull, Bartle, with photographs by Kerim Yalman and John Boit. *Around the Sacred Sea: Mongolia and Lake Baikal on Horseback.* Edinburgh, U.K.: Canongate Books, 2000.

Carson, Rachel. *Silent Spring.* Boston: Houghton Mifflin, 1962.

Cohen, Andrew S. *Paleolimnology: The History and Evolution of Lake Systems.* New York: Oxford University Press, 2003.

Colborn, Theo, Dianne Dumanoski, and John Peter Meyers. *Our Stolen Future: How We Are Threatening Our Fertility, Intelligence and Survival: A Scientific Detective Story.* New York: Penguin Group, 1997.

Curtin, Jeremiah. *A Journey in Southern Siberia, the Mongols, Their Religion and Their Myths.* Boston: Little, Brown, 1909.

Davis, George, and Sergei G. Shapkhaev, project director and coordinator. *The Lake Baikal Region in the Twenty-First Century: A Model of Sustainable Development or Continued Degradation?* San Francisco, Ulan-Ude, Wadhams, N.Y., and Irkutsk: Center for Citizen Initiatives-USA; Center for Socio-Ecological Problems of the Baikal Region; Davis Associates; Russian Academy of Sciences, 1993.

deVillars, Marq. *Water: The Fate of our Most Precious Resource.* Boston: Mariner Books, 2000.

Dezhina, I., and L. Graham. "Science and higher education in Russia." *Science,* vol. 286 (October–December, 1999), pp. 1303-1304.

———. "Is Russian science recovering?" *Nature,* vol. 408 (November 2, 2000), pp. 19-20.

Diment, Galya, and Yuri Slezkine, eds. *Between Heaven and Hell: The Myth of Siberia in Russian Culture.* New York: Palgrave Macmillan, 1993.

Dmytryshyn, Basil, E.A.P. Crownhart-Vaughan, and Thomas Vaughan, eds. and trans. *Russia's Conquest of Siberia: To Siberia and Russian America: Three Centuries of Russian Eastward Expansion,* 2 vols. Portland: Oregon Historical Society Press, 1986.

Dostoevsky, Fyodor. *Crime and Punishment.* Transl. by Constance Garnett. 1866. Reprint, New York: Bantam Classics, 1984.

Ely, Christopher. *This Meager Nature: Landscape and National Identity in Imperial Russia.* DeKalb: Northern Illinois University Press, 2002.

Figes, Orlando. *Natasha's Dance: A Cultural History of Russia.* New York: Picador, 2002.

Figes, Orlando, Robin Milner-Gulland, and Lindsey A. Hughes, eds. *The Russian Chronicles: A Thousand Years That Changed the World*, rev. ed. London: Quadrillion Publishing, 1998.

FitzGerald, Nora. "The soul of Russia in a fur hat." *International Herald Tribune*, November 27, 2004.

Gibbs, Lois Marie. *Dying from Dioxin*. Boston: South End Press, 1995.

Gleick, Peter. *Water in Crisis*. New York: Oxford University Press, 1993.

———. *The World's Water 2004-2005: The Biennial Report on Freshwater Resources*. Washington, D.C.: Island Press, 2004.

Graham, L.R. *Science in Russia and the Soviet Union*. New York: Cambridge University Press, 1993.

Grimes, David. "The big room." *Prairie Schooner*, vol. 74, no. 1 (spring 2000), pp. 187-203.

Guerney, Bernard Guilbert, ed. *The Portable Russian Reader*. New York: The Viking Press, 1947.

Gusev, Oleg Kirillovich. *Around Lake Baikal* [in Russian]. Moscow: Soviet Russia, 1979.

Hirschmann, Kris. *The Deepest Lake*. Extreme Places Series. Farmington Hills, Mich.: Kidhaven, 2002.

Knox, Thomas W. *Overland Through Asia: Pictures of Siberian, Chinese, and Tartar Life*. 1870. Reprint, New York: Arno Press, 1970.

Knystautas, Algirdas. *The Natural History of the USSR*. London: Century, 1987.

Komarov, Boris. *The Destruction of Nature in the Soviet Union*. Armonk, N.Y.: M.E. Sharpe, 1980.

Kozhov, M. *Lake Baikal and Its Life*. The Hague: Dr. W. Junk, 1963.

Kozhova, O.M., and L.R. Izmest'eva, eds. *Lake Baikal: Evolution and Diversity*, 2nd ed. Leiden, The Netherlands: Backhuys Publishers, 1998.

Krakauer, Jon. *Into the Wild*. New York: Villard, 1996.

Lengyel, Emil. *Siberia*. New York: Random House, 1943.

Limnological Institute of the Siberian Branch, Academy of Sciences of the USSR. *Lake Baikal Guidebook*. Moscow: Publishing Office Nauka, 1979.

Lincoln, W. Bruce. *The Conquest of a Continent: Siberia and the Russians*. New York: Random House, 1993.

McGinniss, Joe. *Going to Extremes*. New York: Knopf, 1980.

McKibben, Bill. *The End of Nature*. New York: Random House, 1989.

Meakin, Annette B. *Ribbon of Iron*. New York: E.P. Dutton and Co., 1901.

Montaigne, Fen. "Russia's iron road." *National Geographic*, vol. 193, no. 6 (June 1998).

———. "Water pressure." *National Geographic*, vol. 202, no. 3 (September 2002). [Online.] Accessed October 14, 2005. Available: magma.nationalgeographic.com/ngm/0209/feature1/index.html?fs=www7.nationalgeographic.com.

O'Neill, Catherine, and the Fish Consumption Work Group. *Fish Consumption and Environmental Justice: A Report Developed from the National Environmental Justice Advisory Council Meeting of December 3-6, 2001*. Washington, D.C.: National Environmental Justice Advisory Council, U.S. Environmental Protection

Agency, 2002. [Online.] Accessed October 14, 2005. Available: www.epa.gov/compliance/resources/publications/ej/nejac/fish_consump_report_1102.pdf.

Oxenhorn, Harvey. *Tuning the Rig: A Journey to the Arctic.* New York: Harper & Rowe, 1990.

Pallas, Peter Simon. *The State in Asiatic Russia of All the Animals in the Extent of the Russian Empire and of Those Observed in Nearby Seas (Latin).* St. Petersburg: Petropoli, 1861.

Phillips, G.D.R. *Dawn in Siberia: The Mongols of Lake Baikal.* London: F. Muller, 1943.

Radio Free Europe Online. *Russia: Old Believers Struggle to Keep the Faith amid Isolation.* December 1, 2003. [Online.] Accessed April 1, 2004. Available: www.rferl.org/features/2003/12/01122003170536.asp.

Rasputin, Valentin. *Siberia, Siberia,* trans. by Margaret Winchell and Gerald Mikkelson. DeKalb: Northern Illinois University Press, 1996.

Reid, Anna. *The Shaman's Coat: A Native History of Siberia.* New York: Walker and Company, 2003.

Remnick, David. *Lenin's Tomb: The Last Days of the Soviet Empire.* New York: Random House, 1993.

Richmond, Yale. *From Nyet to Da: Understanding the Russians (Interact Series),* 3rd ed. Yarmouth, Me.: Intercultural Press, 2003.

Robson, Roy R. *Old Believers in Modern Russia.* DeKalb: Northern Illinois University Press, 1995.

Rothenberg, David, and Marta Ulvaeus, eds. *Writing on Water.* Cambridge, Mass.: MIT Press, 2001.

Rzhevsky, Nicholas, ed. *The Cambridge Companion to Modern Russian Culture.* New York: Cambridge University Press, 1999.

Semyonov, Yuri K. *The Conquest of Siberia: An Epic of Human Passions,* trans by E.W. Dickes. 1944. Reprint, Safety Harbor, Fla.: Simon Publications, 2001.

Service, Robert. *A History of 20th Century Russia.* Cambridge, Mass.: Harvard University Press, 1998.

Shapera, Todd. "By the shores of a Siberian Galapagos." *Financial Times* (May 1-2, 2004).

Sher, G.S. "Why should we care about Russian science?" *Science,* vol. 289 (July-September 2000), p. 389.

Solzhenitsyn, Aleksandr Isaevich. *The Gulag Archipelago, 1918-1956: An Experiment in Literary Investigation I-II.* New York: Harper and Row, 1974.

Stegner, Wallace. *The Sound of Mountain Water.* 1969. Reprint, New York: Penguin Books, 1997.

Stevens, William K. "Water: Pushing the limits of an irreplaceable resource." *New York Times,* Special Section: The Natural World, December 8, 1998, p. E1.

Stewart, John Massey, *The Nature of Russia.* London: Pan Macmillan, 1992.

——. *Lake Baikal: On the Brink?* Cambridge, U.K.: International Union for the Conservation of Nature, 1991.

Stiffler, Lisa. "Toxic fish imperil tribes." *Seattle Post-Intelligencer,* July 31, 2002. [Online.] Available: seattlepi.nwsource.com/local/80720_columbia31.shtml.

Strebeigh, Fred. "Where nature reigns: Russia's underfunded yet vast ecological reserves are rich with brown bears, wild honey-and rare humanity." *Sierra*

(March/April 2002). [Online.] Accessed October 21, 2005. Available: www.sierraclub.org/sierra/200203/russia.asp.

Sutton, Jennie, and Mikhail Matkhonov. *Non-governmental and State Action and the Protection of Lake Baikal*. Newsletter and Technical Publications Freshwater Management Series No. 3, 2001. Osaka: United Nations Environment Programme, Division of Technology, Industry, and Economics. [Online.] Accessed October 21, 2005. Available: www.unep.or.jp/ietc/Publications/Freshwater/FMS3/3/baikal1.asp.

Taplin, Mark. *Open Lands: Travels Through Russia's Once Forbidden Places*. Hanover, N.H.: Steerforth Press, 1998.

Tayler, Jeffrey. *Siberian Dawn: A Journey Across the New Russia*. St. Paul, Minn.: Ruminator Books, 1999.

Thoreau, Henry David. *Walden: or, Life in the Woods*. 1854; Reprint, New York: Penguin, 1983.

Thubron, Colin. *Among the Russians*. New York: Picador, 1995.

———. *In Siberia*. New York: Harper Perennial, 2000.

Tickner, Joel, Carolyn Raffensperger, and Nancy Myers. *The Precautionary Principle in Action*. Ames, Iowa; Science and Environmental Health Network, 1999. [Online.] Accessed October 21, 2005. Available: www.sehn.org/rtfdocs/handbook-rtf.rtf.

U.S. Environmental Protection Agency. *Information Sheet 1—Dioxin: Summary of the Dioxin Reassessment Science*. Washington, D.C.: U.S. Environmental Protection Agency, Office of Research and Development, 2000. [Online.] Accessed October 21, 2005. Available: www.epa.gov/ncea/pdfs/dioxin/factsheets/dioxin_short.pdf.

———. *Information Sheet 2—Dioxin: Scientific Highlights from Draft Reassessment (2000)*. Washington, D.C.: U.S. Environmental Protection Agency, Office of Research and Development, 2000. [Online.] Accessed October 21, 2005. Available: www.epa.gov/ncea/pdfs/dioxin/factsheets/dioxin_long.pdf.

———. *Persistent Organic Pollutants: A Global Issue, A Global Response*. Washington, D.C.: U.S. Environmental Protection Agency, Office of International Affairs, 2002. [Online.] Accessed October 21, 2005. Available: www.epa.gov/international/toxics/pop.htm.

———. *The Pulp and Paper Industry, the Pulping Process, and Pollutant Releases to the Environment*. Washington, D.C.: U.S. Environmental Protection Agency, Office of Water, 1997. [Online.] Accessed October 21, 2005. Available: www.epa.gov/waterscience/pulppaper/jd/fs2.pdf.

Weiner, Douglas R. *Models of Nature: Ecology, Conservation, and Cultural Revolution in Soviet Russia*. Pittsburgh, Pa.: University of Pittsburgh Press, 2000.

———. *A Little Corner of Freedom: Russian Nature Protection from Stalin to Gorbachev*. Berkeley: University of California Press, 1999.

Williams, Laura. "Russia's global treasure: A national network of protected land needs help," *E: The Environmental Magazine*, vol. 14, no. 5 (September-October 2003).

Wilson, Edward O. *The Diversity of Life.* Cambridge, Mass.: Belknap/Harvard, 1992.

Wong, Ming H., regional coordinator. *Regionally Based Assessment of Persistent Toxic Substances, Central and North East Asia Regional Report.* Châtelaine, Switzerland: U.N. Environment Program/Global Environment Facility, 2002. [Online.] Accessed October 14, 2005. Available: www.chem.unep.ch/pts/regreports/C&NE% 20Asia%20full%20report.pdf.

World Resources Institute. *EarthTrends, the Environmental Information Portal: Water Resources and Freshwater Ecosystems.* [Online.] Accessed August 23, 2003. Available: earthtrends.wri.org/searchable_db/index.cfm?theme=2.

Zabelina, N.M., L.S. Isaeva-Petrova, and L.V. Kuleshova. *Zapovedniks and National Parks of Russia.* Moscow: Environmental Education Center "Zapovedniks"; Federal Ecological Foundation of the Russian Federation; Ministry of Agriculture, Nature Management and Fisheries, Directorate for Nature Management, of the Netherlands; World Wide Fund for Nature, 1998.

Zlobin, A. *The Baikal Meridian.* 1961. Reprint, Honolulu: University Press of the Pacific, 2005.

Zucco, Catherine, and Patricia Cameron. *WWF Briefing: Effects of Endocrine Disrupting Chemicals on Seals.* Bremen, Germany: World Wildlife Fund North-East Atlantic Programme, 1998. [Online.] Available: www.ngo.grida.no/wwfneap/Publication/pubframe.htm.

Online

Baikal Business Incubator: baikal.irtel.ru/eng/.

Baikal Environmental Wave: www.baikalwave.eu.org.

Baikal Information Center "Gran," *Baikal as a World Heritage Site*: gran.baikal.net/whs/en/index.html.

Baikal Watch: www.earthisland.org/project/viewProject.cfm?subSiteID=1.

Center of Adventure Travel, *Lake Baikal Guidebook*: www.baikal.eastsib.ru.

Center for Russian Nature Conservation: www.wild-russia.org/.

Chlorine Chemistry Council, *Dioxinfacts.org*: www.dioxinfacts.org/index.html.

Eyak Preservation Council, *About Our Home at the Copper River Delta, Alaska*: www.redzone.org/v2/about/index.shtml.

Great Baikal Trail, *Homepage*: http://www.greatbaikaltrail.org/.

Greenpeace Russia, *Baikal Campaign*: www.greenpeace.org/russia/en/campaigns/lake-baikal.

Greenpeace Russia, *Keeping Baikal Alive*: savebaikal.org/index.php?akus=46?lang=1.

LakeNet: World Lakes Network: www.worldlakes.org/.

Magic Baikal: Photographia Ozero Baikal (Russian): www.magicbaikal.ru/album/index.htm.

NASA/Lyndon Johnson Space Center, *The Gateway to Astronaut Photography*: eol.jsc.nasa.gov/sseop/clickmap/.

Pacific Environment: www.pacificenvironment.org/.

Seal Conservation Society: www.pinnipeds.org.

Tahoe-Baikal Institute: www.tahoebaikal.org.

Trans-Siberian Web Encyclopedia: www.transsib.ru/Eng/.

UNESCO World Heritage List, *Lake Baikal*: whc.unesco.org/en/list/754.

Visible Earth, *A Catalog of NASA Images and Animations of Our Home Planet*: visibleearth.nasa.gov/.

Water on the Web, *Understanding Lake Ecology Primer*: waterontheweb.org/under/lakeecology/.

Water Policy International Ltd., *The Water Page*: www.thewaterpage.com.

World Resources Institute: *EarthTrends, The Environmental Information Portal*: earthtrends.wri.org/index.cfm.

Zabaikalsky National Park, *Homepage*: ngo.burnet.ru/znp/index_e.html.

Zoological Excursions Around Lake Baikal: zooex.baikal.ru/.

Index

Acanthogammarus victorii 53

Activism, activists 81-82, 106, 168, 190-191, 195, 202, 279

Air pollution
annual report and 217, 218
Baikalsk paper mill and 177, 180, 218
government regulation and 274
locations and sources of 173, 177, 180, 208-209, 217, 271
morbidity rate and 218
Selenga watershed/Baikal and 173

Akademichesky Range 51

Alaska
Alaska Marine Highway 98-101
Amatignak Island in 114-115
Copper River in 106, 106f
Cordova 105-106 Dogpatch 102-103
Exxon Valdez disaster and 104-106, 195, 197
Fairbanks 12, 101-103 inexhaustibility myth and 197
Ketchikan 99
Prince William Sound in 103-105
Railroad 103
Skagway 98, 101
trip plans regarding 98
White Pass Railroad trip in 101-102

Aleutian Islands 114

Alexander, Tsar, III 139

Alfa Bank 160

Algae blooms 223-224

Amatignak Island 114-115

Amazon rainforest 197

American House
arrival at 157-158
finding 155-156, 157

American West 95-96, 110, 165, 197

Amtrak
Empire Builder 94-97
Lake Shore Limited 93f, 93-94
Midwest and 94
Pacific Northwest and 96-97

passenger types on 94, 95
upper Midwest and 94-95
West and 95-96

Amur region 143, 147

Amur tiger 141, 141f

Angara River and Valley 21, 61, 62, 154, 220, 234, 235, 237
Great War and 172
hydroelectric dams and 171, 172, 215
industry and pollution and 172-173, 193, 199, 209, 212, 217
Irkutsk and 152, 155, 161, 189
nerpa and 50
Shaman Rock and 171
Trans-Siberian Railway and 151

Angarsk 172-173, 217, 237

Annual Report of the Governmental Commission on Baikal Lake 1998 217-218

Antonina Nezhdanova 129-131, 131f, 136, 142

Arctic National Wildlife Refuge 103, 273

Arkhara 144

ATM. *See* Automatic Teller Machine

Automatic Teller Machine (ATM) 159-160

Avvakum (renegade priest) 23, 63

Babkha River and Trail 265-266, 273

Baikal Environmental Wave 189-196, 273-274
Baikalsk Business Incubator and 195-196
bus to 189
circuitous path to 190
Failed Promises Monument and 271
founding of 190
paper mill and 271
programs of 194-195
research funding by 205
tourism and 196

Baikal, Lake 9f, 16f, 23f, 25f, 32f, 40f, 265f.
See also Great Baikal Trail
age of 26
author's reflections on 238-241
depth of 11, 24, 28, 43-45, 240

Baikal, Lake *continued*
early residents surrounding 21-22
general facts about 10-11, 18, 26-29
geology of 26-29
name origins 22
shoreline 20, 30-31, 33, 55, 151
volume of 19, 27-28
Baikal mountains 3, 5, 19-20, 30-32, 151,
    171, 187, 191, 220-221, 225, 267
early Russian explorers and 22-24
Baikal Watch 56, 277
Baikal WATER 234, 235*f*
Baikal water 3*f*
China and 272
clarity of 20, 43-45, 239
dissolved oxygen in 44-48, 239-240
marketing of 233-234, 235*f*
purity of 20, 31, 41, 47, 199, 201
quantity of 27-28
salinity of 47-48
self-purification of 31, 199
    Baikal's slight-of-hand regarding
        199-200
    contaminated animals from 201, 204
    Epischura baicalensis and 4, 41, 200, 239,
        240
    faith and 216
    Maximov on 4, 227
    Malevsky on 211-212
    oligotrophic organisms and 4, 43
    Parfenova on 179
    Russia and 198
temperature of 44, 48-50, 272, 275
Baikalsk
Baikalsk Business Incubator in 186-187
children 180, 218
feeling of 174-175, 276
paper mill and 175, 183
previous name 179
public health and 218
sewage treatment in 213
transit train out of 187-188
Baikalsk Business Incubator 186-187,
    195-196, 273
Baikalsk Pulp and Paper Mill 77, 150,
    171*f*, 185*f*
airborne pollutants from 177, 218
annual report and 217-218
Baikalsk and 175, 183
Baikalsk Business Incubator and 186-187

Baksheeva's ideas for 272-273
dilemmas surrounding 184-185
effluent contaminants from 176-177
environment regarding 150, 174-179
fish and 180
government promises regarding 271
Law of Baikal and 183
Maksimov on 227
Malevsky and 212, 213
Miller on 179, 183-184
mollusk species and 223
nerpa die-offs near 206
original purpose of 175-176
outworn equipment and 218
Parfenova on 178-180, 182-183
PCBs and 209
pollutant reductions at 213
pollution regarding 174, 176-183
POP concentrations and 209
public opposition to 176, 181-182
regulation violations of 181
Soviet Union and 175, 176, 185*f*
Starostenko and 273
structures of 177-178
Sutton and 191-192
waste treatment system at 179-181, 183
Baikalsky Nature Reserve 267-269
Baksheeva, Olga 167-168, 233, 237, 272-273,
    274
information imparted by 4, 180, 236
Baltic Sea 50, 203-204, 206
Baltic seals. *See* Seals, Baltic
Baltica beer 164
Banya (Russian sauna)
experience of 36-38
history/legend surrounding 35-36
lake immersion and 37
science and 36
sleeping in 38-39
at Snake Bay 32-33, 35-39
tourism and 32-33
Barguzin 85*f*
arrowheads and 88
Jews of 89
museum in 88-89
school in 87-88
trail above 79, 83-84
Barguzin Mountains 30, 32, 76, 77
Barguzin River 76*f* 76-77, 85
Barguzin sable 22*f* 22-23, 34, 172

Barguzinsky Nature Reserve 34, 172
Barrikadnaia metro station 246
Belogorsk 146-147
Bering, Vitus 154
Berlin, Germany 254-255, 260
Biomagnification 200-201, 204
Blagopoluchnoe 4-5, 227, 229, 232
Bligh Reef 105, 106
Bliny (rolled pancakes) 141, 144
Bolshie Koty 221-222, 225-226,
    231-232, 271
Boston Red Sox 13, 89, 93, 109, 120, 159,
    258, 276, 277, 279
Bratsk 218
Brower, David 56
Buddhism 59-61
Bukhta Zmeevaia (Snake Bay) 31, 35*f*
Bureia 145
Buryat 19-20
    Buddhism and 59-60
    health clinic of 58-59
    origins of 21
    public health and 218
    religion and 22
    Ulan-Ude and 58
    visas regarding 126-127
Buryatia 59, 62, 80, 87
    regional government of 213-214

Cafe Nostalgia 135-136
Café Tête-à-Tête 163-165
Cancer 177, 208, 218
Cargo ship passage 108-117
Carson, Rachel 201
Caspian Sea 10, 29
Cemeteries 222, 255
Chauvinism, Russian 133, 250
Chekhov, Anton 149, 153, 155*f*, 242
Cheremkhovo 172-173, 217
Children 87, 99, 180, 218
    on Amtrak 94-95
    Alaska Marine Highway, on 99
    Fairbanks, in 102
China 23, 215, 272
    Border with Russia 141, 143, 144
    Lake Baikal and 22
    Potential water pipeline to 272
    Russian tensions with 139
Chita 149
Chita region 143

Chivyrkuysky Gulf 30*f*, 32, 68, 68*f*
Chlorinated hydrocarbons. *See also* DDT;
    Dioxins; Organochlorines; PCBs;
    Persistent organic pollutants (POPs)
    178, 201-203, 223
Chlorine bleaching 178-179, 213
Circum-Baikal Railway 151
Cold 4-5, 15, 227, 229
    Banyas and 36
    water 37, 41, 46-48, 50, 51, 229, 240
Cold Place. *See* Kuitun
Cook, Gary
    Lake Baikal activism and 56, 191, 277
    health clinic and 58
    Suknev and 56, 277
    Baksheeva and 167
    on travel in Russia 251
    visas and 124, 125-126, 127
Cordova, Alaska 105-106
Crater Lake 46-47
Cuyahoga River 182

Darasun 149
Darwin, Charles 49
DDT 204
Denali National Park 103
Detergents 181
Diatoms 41
Dickey, Lisa 142
Dioxins. *See also* Chlorinated hydrocarbons;
    Organochlorines; Persistent organic
    pollutants (POPs) 178, 199*f*
    annual report and 217
    day rate of 208
    fish and 207
    Maksimov on 228
    in people 207-208
    in seals 203-206
    toxicity of 203
Dublin, Ireland 257
Dzhugashvili, Iosif (Stalin) 154

E. coli 177
Earthquakes 191-192, 218
Ecosystem
    annual report and 217-218
    Baikal's surrounding 32, 54-55
    biomagnification and 201
    deep water 43-45
    delicate balance of 224-225

Ecosystem *continued*
  fish and 42-43
  global warming and 229, 272
  oligotrophic conditions and 43
  phytoplankton and 41-42
  temperatures, water, and 44, 49-50
  zooplankton and 41
Ecotourism. *See* Tourism, low-impact
Eisenhower, Dwight 219-220
Embassy of the Russian Federation in
    Tokyo 125-127
Entrepreneurship 32-33
Environment
  activism and 195
  air pollution and 173, 177, 217, 218
  algae blooms and 223-224
  annual report and 217-218
  bad news regarding 14-15
  Baikal and 15, 32, 192
  Baikalsk Business Incubator and 186-187
  biomagnification and 201
  chlorine bleaching and 178-179
  delicate balance of 224-225
  faith and 216
  free enterprise vs. 215-216
  general principles and 193-194
  global warming and 229, 272
  government protection of 33-35
  Great Lakes and 182
  Greenpeace International report and 270
  inexhaustibility myth and 196-98
  oil pipeline and 271-272
  outside investment and 214-215
  paper mill and 150, 174-179
  political atmosphere and 194
  POPs and 202-203, 208-209
  Putin and 194-195
  reporting on 14, 184
  scientific debate on 193-194
  Senenga River and 173-174
  Severobaikalsk and 174
  Tahoe-Baikal Institute Policy Brief
    270-271
  tourism and 78
  Ulan-Ude sewage and 150
  uncertainty surrounding 193
  World Heritage Committee Report and
    269-270
Environmental Protection Agency (EPA)
    203
EPA. *See* Environmental Protection Agency

Epischura baicalensis 41f
  algae blooms and 223-224
  background on 40-41
  decline of 192, 223-224
  filter feeders, as 4, 32, 41, 200-201, 204,
    223-224
  invasive species and 228-229
  phytoplankton and 41-42
  as unique to Baikal 4, 41
  zooplankton and 41
Erie Lake. *See* Lake Erie
Evenki 21, 22
Evolution 48-49, 50
Evreiskaia Avtonomnaia Oblast 143-144
Exxon Valdez disaster 104-106, 195, 197

Fairbanks, Alaska 102
Faith 120-22, 216
Filippoy, Sergei 89f, 273
  dinner with 89-90
  English and 85
  opportunities for 86-87
  world of 85-86
Filippoy, Tania 89f, 273
  background on 87
  conversation with 90
  dinner with 89-90
  school/museum tour by 87-89
Filter feeders 32, 41, 200-201, 204, 223-224
Finland 252-253
Finland Station 251
Fish 180
  algae and 224
  biomagnification and 201
  dioxins and 207
  golomyankas 42-43, 45, 201, 231
  migratory/nonmigratory 208-209
  omul 172, 201, 207, 224
  POPs in 208-209
  sturgeon 53, 172
Flatworms 45
Food chain 201, 202-203, 208-209, 224
Fraser, John Foster 141
Fukuoka train station 118-119
Fur trade 22-23, 57
Fushiki, Japan 128-130

Gagarin, Yuri 160, 160f
Galazy, Grigory 49, 200, 233
Gamerova, Olga 187, 196, 273
Gammarid shrimp 43, 45, 53

Ganges River 238
Geology 26-27
  depth and 28, 44-45
  future regarding 28-29
  lake types and 27
  water quantity and 27-28
Georgia Strait, British Columbia 98-99
Global warming 15, 68, 102, 229, 272, 275
Golden Gate Bridge 110
Golomyankas 42*f*, 42-43, 45, 201, 231
Gorbachev, Mikhail 34, 132, 183, 245
Government, Russian. *See* Russian/Soviet
  Government
Graben lakes 27
Great Baikal Chain 269
Great Baikal Trail
  Baikalsk Business Incubator and 273
  connections and 269
  origins of 266-268
  Reida and 277
  success of 280
  supporters of 268
Great Circle Route 114
Great Lakes 27, 182
Great Slave Lake 45, 46-47
Great War 172
Greenpeace International 270
Greenpeace Russia 181-182, 271
Gusev, Oleg Kirillovich 268

Hawsehole 111
Health clinic, Buryat 58-59
Heavy metals 177. *See also* mercury
Hiking trails. *See* Babkha Trail; Barguzin;
  Great Baikal Trail; Osinovka Trail;
  Suknev, Andrei
Holyhead, Wales 255-256
Hunter, Celia 102-103
Hydrobiology Laboratory 219*f*, 222

Inexhaustibility myth 196-198
Inside Passage
  Georgia Strait and 98-99
  Ketchikan, Alaska, and 99-100
  North of Juneau and 100-101
Internet cafe 159
  Ireland 256-257 cliffs in 252*f*, 256-257
Irkut River 152
Irkutsk 10, 17
  air pollution and 173
  American House in 155-158

appearance of 152, 154
arrival in 152, 155
ATM in 159-160
author's reflections in 165-167
background/history of 153-154
bus ride in 189
Café Tête-à-Tête in 163-165
as city of logs 153*f*, 161, 163*f*
dam 151
exchanging money in 160
factory contamination and 172-173
Internet cafe in 159
paper mill and 182
past/future of 160-163
POP concentrations and 209
road to Baikal from 219-220
Shelgunov on 154-155
trams in 158-159
transit train to 187-188
tsars and 153
as unique 162-163
visa problem and 236
Ivanov, Kurbat 22
Ivolginsk Datsan (Buddhist temple) 59-61,
  60*f*
Izmesteva, Liubov 222-223

Japan
  experiences in 123
  exploring new places and 123-124
  ferries from 128
  Fukuoka train station in 118-119
  Fushiki in 128, 129, 130
  temples of 60
  train rides in 122-123, 129
  Thomson, David and 114
Jewish Autonomous Region 143-144
Jewish cemetery, Berlin 255
Jews, of Barguzin 89
Jokkmokk, Sweden 253-254
Journalism, ix 100, 184

Karelia region 250
Karymskaia 149
Katun 19, 20
Ketchikan, Alaska 99-100
Khabarovsk 143
Khamar-Daban Mountains 16, 30, 266
Khan, Genghis 21
Khrushchev, Nikita 176
Kilmihil, Ireland 256

Kirov, Sergei 154
Klepikova, Mila 248-249
Klondike Gold Rush 101
Komsomolskaia metro station 246
Korea 115-117, 119, 120
Kozhov, Mikhail 222-223
Kozhova, Olga 222-223
Kremlin 245, 246
Kuitun (Cold Place) 64
Kurbulik 20
Kurikani 21

Lake Erie 182
Lakes
  Baikal compared to 26, 27
  Caspian Sea vs. 29
  formation/types of 26
  graben 27
Law of Baikal 33-35, 215
  government inaction regarding 35
  paper mill and 183
  science and 210
  UNESCO and 33
  violation of 225
Law on nature protection of the Russian
    Federation 225
Lenin, Vladimir 34, 133, 244f, 251
  head, largest 56
  memorabilia 244
  statues 128f, 135, 146-147, 237, 253
Lignin 181
Limnological Institute 220, 233-234
Limnology 233
Listvianka
  leaving 235-236
  Limnological Institute and 220, 233-234
  museum in 234
  stay in 233
Living on Earth 13-14, 238
London, England 258
  Irkutsk, compared to 154

Maksimov, Slava, Sr. 229f
  anti-evolutionary device of 230-231
  author's perspective on 229-230,
    231-232
  background on 3-4
  blagopoluchnoe and 4-5, 227, 232
  on dioxins 228
  on environmentalists 228

  follow-up with 275
  global warming and 229
  invasive species and 228-229
  museum of 231
  oligotrophic organisms and 4
  optimistic nature of 226
  on paper mill 227
  Pavlov and 226, 228
  skepticism of 227-228
Maksimov, Slava Jr. 225
Malawi, Lake 45, 46
Malevsky, Anatoly 215f
  annual report and 217
  author's perspective on 216-217
  concerns of 213-214
  contradictory statement by 211-212
  credibility of 212-213
  demeanor of 212
  Globe and Mail article and 274
  interview with 211-217
  outside investment and 214-215
  paper mill and 212, 213
  position of 211
  on purification 211-212
  Putin and 214, 273
Mamontova, Elena 207-208
Market stops 141
Marx, Karl
  memorabilia 244
Matanuska, M. V. 98, 99f, 101. See also Alaska
    Marine Highway
  Georgia Strait and 98
  passengers on 99-100
Matoso, Gary 142
Measure, systems of x
Melnikov, Vladimir 35
Mercury 173, 177
Microbiology Laboratory 226
Microorganisms, See also Epischura baicalensis,
    phytoplankton, zooplankton 4, 227
Miller, Natalia 179, 183-184
Ministry of Natural Resources 214
Mogocha 148
Mogzon 150
Mollusk species 53, 223, 229
Molotov, Viacheslav 154
Monakhovo 20
Money, exchanging 160
Mongolia 212
Mongols 21, 22

Monkey Mind, reflections of 72-75
Moscow
    arrival/accommodations in 243-244
    bronze disk in 244
    metros/museums in 246, 246f
    Red Square in 244-246, 247f
    things to do in 246-247
    time 137-138, 244
    train to St. Petersburg from 247-248
Museum(s)
    in Barguzin 87-89
    Kremlin 246
    in Listvianka 234
    Maksimov's 231
    in St. Petersburg 249-250
Mutation 48-49

National Geographic 12, 13, 33, 77
Natural gas 213-214, 225
Natural selection 48-49
Nerpa. See Seals, freshwater
New Russians 163, 278
New York Harbor 261, 262f
NGOs. See Nongovernmental organizations
Nongovernmental organizations (NGOs) 279
Novosibirsk 242

Obluche 143-144
Oceans, Baikal's similarity to 29
Oil pipeline 271-272, 279-280
Old Believers 54f, 65f
    color and 62-63
    Russian Orthodox Church and 63
    singing of 63, 64, 65, 66
    visit with 63-67
Oligotrophic conditions 41, 43
Oligotrophic organisms 4, 43
Omsk 242
Omul 41f, 42, 77, 172
    algae blooms and 224
    biomagnification and 201
    dioxins and 207
    eaten by author 32, 85, 207
    food chain and 201, 224
Orekhi (pine nuts) 16-17
Organic compounds 176
Organochlorines 177, 180, 181, 192. See also
    Chlorinated hydrocarbons; DDT;
    Dioxins; PCBs; Persistent organic
    pollutants (POPs)

local concentrations of 208-209
nerpa and 204, 206-207
origin of 203
paper mill reductions in 213
reduction in animals of 274
seal die-offs and 206-207
Osinovka Trail 267-269
Overgrazing 213
Oxygen
    biologically unavailable 45-46
    dissolved/free 32, 45-47, 224
    oceans and 46
    salinity and 47-48
    temperature/density and 46-47, 48

Pacific Champion 107f, 111f, 113f, 114f
    Amatignak Island seen from 114-115
    appearance of 107-108
    bow/side rails/wings of 111-112
    cargo/route of 112
    crew of 112, 113-114, 116
    Great Circle Route and 114
    leaving Bay Area on 109-111
    mundanity on 112-113
    Queen Elizabeth 2 compared to 258
    ship passage and 108
    Typhoon Samoai and 115, 117
Pacific Ocean, ix 96, 111, 112
    crossing by ship 108, 110
    Marianas Trench in 28
    Russia and 10, 21, 23, 78, 132-133, 140
    Top Ten Best Places and 260
Panzeka, Captain 113, 115
Paper mill. See Baikalsk Pulp and Paper Mill
Parfenova, Natalia
    on closing mill 183
    Great Lakes and 182
    paper mill and 178-180, 182-183
    waste treatment system and 179-181
Paris
    Irkutsk, compared to 154
Pavlov, Boris 223f, 222-225, 274-275
    algae blooms and 223-224
    background on 222
    follow-up with 274-275
    Maksimov and 226, 228
    mollusk species and 223
    research emphasis of 222-223
    Russian government and 225
PCBs 173, 192, 204-206, 208, 209

Pearmain family. *See* Thomson/Pearmain
    family
Perestroika 66, 86-87
Perm 242
Persistent organic pollutants (POPs). *See also*
    Chlorinated hydrocarbons; DDT;
    Dioxins; Organochlorines; PCBs
  in food chain/environment 202-203,
    208-209
  local concentrations of 208-209
  Mongolia and 208, 212
  origin of 202-205, 208-210
  in people 207-208
  seals and 201-204, 206-207, 212, 217,
    274
Pesticides 15, 173, 204, 212
Phenols 176-177
Phytoplankton 41-42, 217, 223, 227
Pirozhki (filled dumplings) 141, 148
Ploshchad Revoliutsii metro station 246
Pollution. *See also* Air pollution; Chlorinated
    hydrocarbons; Dioxins;
    Organochlorines; Persistent organic
    pollutants; PCBs
  Angara Valley contamination and
    172-173, 199, 209, 212, 217
  in Barguzin River 77
  paper mill and 174, 176-183, 213
  in Selenga River 173-174, 212
  from Severobaikalsk 174
  from Ulan-Ude 173
POPs. *See* Persistent organic pollutants
Powers, Gary Francis 220
Pribaikalsky National Park 33
Primorsky Mountains 23, 30
Prince William Sound 103-105
Professor Kozhov (ferry) 220-221
Provodnitsa (train conductors/attendants)
    136-137, 144, 150, 151
Pusan 120
Pusan Harbor 116
Putin, Vladimir 35, 66, 183
  environmental protection and 194-195
  Malevsky's agency and 214, 273
  NGO law and 279
  oil pipeline and 279-280
  Suknev's hope for 84

Queen Elizabeth 2
  crossing on 258-262
  gusting winds and 258-259
  New York arrival on 261-262
  Pacific Champion compared to 258
  Secret desire to sail on 73
  time zones and 259

Railroads. *See* Amtrak; Train(s); Trans-
    Siberian railway
Ramirez, Manny 258
Raskolniki. See Old Believers
Rasputin, Valentin 191, 197
The Real Siberia (Fraser) 141
Red Square 244-246
Reida, Ariadna 277-278
Rickey, Branch 122
Rubles, acquiring 160
Russia
  activism in 195
  chauvinism of 133, 250
  Cook on 251
  through customs in 133-134
  exchanging money in 160
  ferry to 129
  Finland compared with 252-253
  high school teacher and 132
  inexhaustibility myth and 197-198
  trains in 136
  Vladivostok and 132-136
Russian culture
  cultural superiority and 198
  greatness obsession of 150
  inexhaustibility myth and 197-198
  Samovar as window into 148
  recurrent theme in 159
Russian/Soviet Government 33-35
  Baikal protections and 33-35, 183, 194,
    210, 213-215, 270, 275
  Baikalsk Pulp and Paper Mill and 183,
    271
  environmental and pollution standards
    176, 194, 210-211
  cultural power and 138
  Malevsky and 211-218, 274
  nerpas and 52
  pollution studies and 173, 177, 181,
    217-218, 225
  resources of 82
  Siberian oil pipeline and 271, 279-280
  St. Petersburg palaces and 250
  Vladivostok ferry and 128, 131

Russian Orthodox Church 63, 198
Russian State Zoological Museum 249
Russians
    Fushiki and 129-130
    Lake Baikal and 10-11, 22-24, 198, 238-239
    New 163, 278
The Russian Chronicles (Matoso & Dickey)
    142, 143

Sakhalin Island 153
Salt water 24, 29, 47-48
Samovar 148
San Francisco
    City Lights Bookstore in 132
    Golden Gate Bridge in 110
    Pacific Champion and 107-108, 109-111
    Pier 80 and 107-109
    sailing out of 109-111
    Top Ten Best Places and 260
    waterfront of 107
San Juan Islands 97-98
Science 36, 210-211, 211
Sculpin 42f, 42-43, 45
Seals, Antarctic 203
Seals, Baltic 203, 204, 206-207
Seals, freshwater (nerpas) 11, 18, 49f, 192
    annual report and 217
    appearance/lifespan of 50-51
    Baltic seals and 203, 206-207
    biomagnification and 201
    challenges facing 52-53
    contamination effects on 206
    die-offs of 206-207
    dioxin study regarding 203-206
    evolution of 50
    golomyankas and 43
    Malevsky on 212
    numbers of 52
    POPs and 202, 203
Sediment 28
Selenga River 62f
    natural gas drilling and 213-214, 225
    oil and 225
    path of 61-62
    pollution carried by 173-174, 212
    sewage and 150
Sergeyev, Mark 154
Severobaikalsk 174, 269
Sewage treatment. *See* Wastewater
    treatment

Shaman Rock 171
Shelekhov 172-173, 217-218
Shelgunov, Nikolai 154-155
Shelikhov, Grigory 154
Shilka 149
Shinkansen bullet trains 122, 129
Shrimp. *See Epischura baicalensis*; Gammarid
    shrimp
Siberia. *See also* Irkutsk; Trans-Siberian
    railway
    Alexander and 139
    Arkhara in 144
    Baikalsk in 174-75
    Belogorsk in 146-47
    books on 141
    boundaries regarding 143
    Bureia in 145
    Chekhov on 149
    Chita/Darasun/Karymskaia/Shilka
        in 149
    empire building and 139-140
    exchanging money in 160
    flora of 25
    Great War and 172
    inexhaustibility myth and 197
    Jewish Autonomous Region in 143-144
    Mogocha/Zilovo in 148
    Rasputin and 197
    Russian conquest of 22-23, 139-140
    Sleeping Land and 148-149
    Sliudianka in 151, 151f
    traveling through 9-10
    Ulan-Ude/Mogzon and 150
    western cities encountered in 242
    western stretch of 237
    Zeisko-Bureinskaia Plain in 147
Sibirtsevo 141
Silent Spring (Carson) 201
Skagway 101
Sleeping Land 148-149
Sliudianka 151, 151f, 213
Snake Bay. *See* Bukhta Zmeevaia
Soft class 137, 247
Song lyrics x-xi
Soviet Academy of Sciences 176
Soviet Government. *See* Russian/Soviet
    government
Soviet Union. *See also* Russia
    author's background and 132
    city names and 242

Soviet Union *continued*
 cliché about 248
 Ivolginsk Datsan and 59
 Lenin and 146-147
 paper mill and 175, 176, 185*f*
 Red Square and 244-246
 Vladivostok 133-134, 140
Spafary, Nikolai 23-24, 29
Spelling x
St. Basil's Cathedral 245
St. Petersburg
 accommodations in 248-249
 as big museum 249-250
 palaces in 250
 return to 265
 train from Moscow to 247-248
 Zoological Museum in 249
Stalin 59, 64, 146, 154
Starostenko, Evgeny 185-186, 196, 273
Starovery. See Old Believers
State Committee on Environmental
    Protection 194, 212, 214
Streetcars. *See* Trams
Sturgeon, Baikal 53, 53*f* 172
Subjectivity ix
Suknev, Andrei 16
 background on 80
 Berkeley reunion with 266
 democratic processes and 82-83
 on entrepreneurship 32-33
 on government controls 34, 35
 hiking trails and 83-84, 266, 267-269
 local activism and 81-82
 low-impact tourism and 80-83
 natural gas drilling and 213-214
 nature of 56-57, 80
 on Osinovka Trail with 267-269
Sulfates 176, 179-180, 181, 213
Suspended particles 176, 181
Sutton, Jennie
 actions taken by 194-195
 background on 190-191
 Baikalsk Business Incubator and 195-196
 concerns, list of, by 192, 273-274
 earthquakes and 191-192
 on *Epischura baicalensis,* 200
 follow-up with 273-274
 Limnological Institute and 233
 Maksimov on 228
 paper mill and 191-192
 realism of 196

research funding and 205
 on Russian politics 194
 as visionary *v.* crank 192-193
Svyatoi Nos (Holy Nose) 20, 51
Sweden 253-254

Tahoe, Lake 46-47
Tahoe-Baikal Institute Policy Brief 270-271
Tanganyika, Lake 27, 45, 46
Tarasova, Evgeniia 274
 appearance of 201
 meeting with 201-210
 nerpas/Baltic seals and 206-207
 plea of 210
 POPs and 202-204, 207-208
 research and 201-204, 205
 stationary environmental media study
    and 208-209
Thermal vents 44
Thomas, Bryn 141
Thomson, David 114
Thomson, James 112*f*
 author compared with 71-72
 author's relationship with 68-72
 Baikal trip plan and 14
 early years of 69-70
 on Fairbanks 102
 jobs after trip 275
 as New Englander 17
 qualities of 17, 68, 70-72
 travel with 70, 72, 142
 voice of 69
 as wanderer 71
Thomson, John 102, 103
Thomson, Peter 113*f,* 223*f*
Thomson, R. H. 96
Thomson, William Orville 96
Thomson/Pearmain family
 complexities of 69, 73
 as explorers 12
 Pacific Northwest and 96
 qualities of 17
Thomson's Manual of Pacific Northwest Finance
    (Thomson, William Orville) 96
Todaiji 118*f*
 Ivolginsk Datsan and 60
 Ten Best Places and 260Tokmokov,
    Alexander 273
Tokyo
 train ride to 122-123
 visa problem in 124-127

Top Ten Best Places 260
Tourism
    bad roads and 79
    Baikal Environmental Wave and 196
    Baikalsk Business Incubator and
        185-186, 273
    banya and 32-33
    environmentalism and 78
    impact of 20-21, 33, 221-222
    low-impact 80-83, 185-186, 196, 268,
        273Moscow and 244-247
    political development and 82-83, 215
    prospects/challenges of 78-79
    rumors regarding 271
    Starostenko and 185-186
    Suknev and 80-83
Train(s). See also Amtrak; Trans-Siberian
    railway
    Alaska 101-102, 103
    Baikalsk/Irkutsk transit 187-188
    Japanese 118-119, 122-123, 129
    Moscow/St. Petersburg 247-248
Trams 135, 155, 158-159
Transit train 187-188
Trans-Siberian Handbook (Thomas) 141, 147,
    148, 150
Trans-Siberian railway
    Alexander III and 139
    Arkhara station 144
    Baikal and 150-151, 172
    Belogorsk station 146-147
    books read on 142
    cars of 136, 139f
    Chita/Darasun/Karymskaia/Shilka along
        149
    classes/windows/cabins on 137
    companions on 145-146, 147, 147f
    construction of 140
    dirty windows of 10, 137, 189f
    empire building and 139-140
    Irkutsk and 152
    as lifeline 148-149
    market stops and 141, 144, 146-147,
        242-243
    Mogocha/Zilovo along 148
    Moscow time and 137-138
    precision of 138, 144, 152
    provodnitsa on 136-137
    reflections while on 237-241
    Severobaikalsk and 174
    Sliudianka station on 151, 151f

Train Number One and 136-138
Train Number Two and 237, 242-243
    traveling on 9-10, 140-152
    Ulan-Ude and 150
    Ussuri region and 141
    in Vladivostok 133, 135, 136-138, 140
    Zeisko-Bureinskaia Plain and 147
Typhoon Samoai 115-117, 119

Ulan-Ude 10
    history of 57-58, 150
    pollution from 62, 150, 173
    stay in 56-59
    train station at 57, 150
Ulitsa Aleutskaia, 135
UNESCO. See United Nations
    Educational, Scientific, and Cultural
    Organization
United Nations Educational, Scientific, and
    Cultural Organization (UNESCO) 33,
    269-270, 272
Usole-Sibirskoe 172-173, 209, 217
Ussuri region 141Ussuri River 141, 143
Ust-Barguzin 35, 76-79

Victoria, Lake 27
Visas, Russian
    American embassy and 247
    Buryat special status and 127
    Cook and 124, 125-126, 127
    female embassy official and 126-127
    International Security Office and 74
    Irkutsk and 236
    male embassy official and 125-126
    problem with 72, 74, 116, 125-127, 236
    process of getting 124
    registration of 72, 74, 251, 236,
        247, 251
    Tokyo and 124-127
Vladivostok
    Cafe Nostalgia in 135-136
    climate of 134
    through customs in 133-134
    decrepitude of 133, 140
    first glimpse of 132
    history of 132-133
    outskirts of 140
    people of 134-135
    Soviet Union and 133-134, 140
    Trans-Siberian railway and 133, 135,
        136-138, 140

Vladivostok *continued*
  Trans-Siberian Railway terminal 136*f*
  Ulitsa Aleutskaia in 135
Voluntary inspectorate 195
Vyborg 251

Wastewater treatment 150, 176-177, 178,
  179-181, 183
Water
  as basic necessity 18-19
  salt vs. fresh 29
Water Code of the Russian Federation 225
WHO. *See* World Health Organization
Wood, Ginny 103
World Health Organization (WHO) 203, 204

World Heritage Committee 272, 270
  Bureau of, Report 269-270
World Heritage Site, U.N. 33, 182, 211,
  214-215

Yakuts 21, 22
Yekaterinburg 242
Yeltsin, Boris 34, 183
"Your Siberia and Mine" (Rasputin) 197

Zabaikalsky National Park 20, 33,
  35, 77
Zeisko-Bureinskaia Plain 147
Zilovo 148
Zooplankton 41, 223